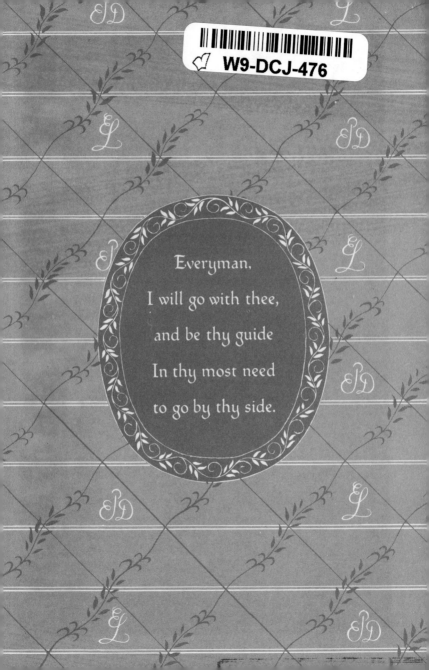

Everyman,
I will go with thee,
and be thy guide
In thy most need
to go by thy side.

THE TIMES OF
MELVILLE AND WHITMAN

THE WORLD'S MOST COMPREHENSIVE
LIBRARY OF GREAT BOOKS

There are nearly 1000 titles in Everyman's Library. This world's largest series of great books was founded 1906 by J. M. Dent and Sons, Ltd., London and E. P. Dutton & Co., Inc., New York. The number of the series followed by A, thus 953A, designates the American editions of Everyman's Library in a large format and uniform typography. A catalogue of all the volumes in print in Everyman's Library is available from the publishers, E. P. Dutton & Co., Inc., 300 Fourth Avenue, New York 10, N. Y.

ESSAYS AND BELLES-LETTRES
648A

THE TIMES OF
MELVILLE AND WHITMAN

by

VAN WYCK BROOKS

NEW YORK: E. P. DUTTON AND COMPANY, INC.
LONDON: J. M. DENT AND SONS, LIMITED
1953

Completely reset and electrotyped

American Editions Uniform with this Format:

AQUINAS—Selected Writings (953A)

ARISTOTLE—Nichomachean Ethics (547A)

Aucassin and Nicolette (497A)

AUSTEN—Pride and Prejudice (22A)

BROOKS—The Flowering of New England (645A)

BROOKS—New England: Indian Summer (641A)

BROOKS—The World of Washington Irving (642A)

BROOKS—The Times of Melville and Whitman (648A)

BROWNE—Religio Medici (92A)

COOPER—The Last of the Mohicans (79A)

DESCARTES—A Discourse on Method (570A)

DICKENS—Great Expectations (234A)

GOLDSMITH—The Vicar of Wakefield (295A)

HARDY—Far from the Madding Crowd (644A)

HOBBES—Leviathan (691A)

HOWELLS—A Hazard of New Fortunes (646A)

HOWELLS—Indian Summer (643A)

JAMES, HENRY—Selected Fiction of (649A)

LUCRETIUS—Of the Nature of Things (750A)

MARLOWE—Plays and Poems (383A)

MELVILLE—Moby Dick (179A)

MILL—Utilitarianism (182A)

PAINE—The Rights of Man (718A)

PIRANDELLO—Five Selected Plays (647A)

PLATO—The Republic (64A)

ROUSSEAU—The Social Contract (660A)

ST. AUGUSTINE—Confessions (200A)

ST. FRANCIS, The Little Flowers of (485A)

THUCYDIDES—Peloponnesian War (455A)

ZOLA—Germinal (897A)

The new American Editions of Everyman's Library are for sale only in the United States of America, the Philippine Islands, Cuba and Mexico.

Printed and bound by The Colonial Press Inc., Clinton, Mass.

Library of Congress Catalog Card Number: 53-6065

VAN WYCK BROOKS, born in New Jersey in 1886, graduated at Harvard in 1908. After teaching in California and in England, he was for several years connected with New York publishing houses and magazines. He was associate editor of *The Seven Arts* and *The Freeman*. His best known earlier books were *America's Coming-of-Age*, *Letters and Leadership* and *The Ordeal of Mark Twain*. He began in 1932 the series *Makers and Finders: a History of the Writer in America, 1800-1915*. This is one of the five volumes.

CONTENTS

CONTENTS

THE TIMES OF
MELVILLE AND WHITMAN

CHAPTER I

WASHINGTON IRVING'S NEW YORK

WHEN the Brook Farmers disbanded, in the autumn of
1847, a number of the brightest spirits settled in New
York, where *The Tribune,* Horace Greeley's paper, welcomed their ideas and gladly made room on its staff for
George Ripley, their founder. New York in the middle
of the nineteenth century, almost as much perhaps as
Boston, bubbled with movements of reform, with the
notions of the spiritualists, the phrenologists, the mesmerists and what not, and the Fourierists especially had
found a forum there for discussions of "attractional harmony" and "passional hygiene." It was the New Yorker
Albert Brisbane who had met the master himself
in Paris, where Fourier was working as a clerk with an
American firm, and paid him for expounding his system
in regular lessons. Then Brisbane in turn converted
Greeley and the new ideas had reached Brook Farm,
where the members transformed the society into a Fou-
rierist phalanx. *The Tribune* had played a decisive part
in this as in other intellectual matters, for Greeley was
unique among editors in his literary flair. Some years
before, Margaret Fuller had come to New York to write
for him, and among the Brook Farmers on his staff,
along with "Archon" Ripley, were George William
Curtis and Dana, the founder of *The Sun.*

One could scarcely recognize the old town of the
Knickerbockers in this turmoil of movements and
groups and exotic ideas, the water-cure and Graham

1

bread as well as associationism and the drab unmusical
oracles of the "Poughkeepsie seer." This was the cobbler's apprentice Andrew Jackson Davis, who was able
to read quite clearly through the back of his head, while
he spouted Swedenborg by the hour in his hypnotic
trances and spent his nights wandering in graveyards
conversing with ghosts. The "harmonial" A. J. Davis[1]
was a lion of the town whom Poe had met in 1846 and
who had suggested his hoax *The Facts in the Case of M.
Waldemar* and another tale, *Mesmeric Revelation.* But
there were numbers of other prophets and reformers,
among them William Henry Channing and Henry
James. The socialistic Channing was a nephew of the
great Boston divine who had also preached and lectured
in New York, while Henry James, a Swedenborgian,
agreed with the Fourierists too and regarded all passions and attractions as a species of duty. As for the still
youthful Brisbane, who had toured Europe with his
tutor, studying not only with Fourier but with Hegel in
Berlin, he had mastered animal magnetism to the point
where he could strike a light merely by rubbing his fin-
gers over the gas-jet. The son of a magnate of upper
New York, he had gone abroad at nineteen, with the
sense of a certain injustice in his unearned wealth, and
he had been everywhere received like a bright young
travelling prince in Paris, Berlin, Vienna and Constantinople. He had studied philosophy, music and art and
learned to speak in Turkish,—the language of Fourier's
capital of the future world,—driving over Italy with
S. F. B. Morse and Horatio Greenough and sitting at
the feet of Victor Cousin also. He met and talked with
Goethe, Heine, Balzac, Lamennais and Victor Hugo,
reading Fourier for many weeks with Rahel Varnhagen

[1] "Are you a god or a doggone clod? If the Second Advent came to
Coney Island are we ready? . . . Joking apart and getting down to
bedrock, A. J. Christ Dowie and the harmonial philosophy have you
got that?"—Elijah, in James Joyce's *Ulysses.*

von Ense, whom he had inspired with a passion for the "wonderful plan." He had a strong feeling for craftsmanship, for he had watched the village blacksmith along with the carpenter and the saddler when he was a boy, so that he was prepared for these notions of attractive labour, while he had been struck by the chief Red Jacket, who had visited the village, surrounded by white admirers and remnants of his tribe. In this so-called barbarian he had witnessed aptitudes that impressed him with the powers and capacities of the natural man, and he had long since set out to preach the gospel of social reorganization that Fourier had explained to him in Paris.

At Robert Owen's "World's Convention," held in New York in 1845, many of the reformers' programmes had found expression, and, since then, currents of affinity had spread from the Unitary Home to the Oneida Community and the Phalanx at Red Bank. The Unitary Home, a group of houses on East 14th Street, with communal parlours and kitchens, was an urban Brook Farm, where temperance reform and woman's rights were leading themes of conversation and John Humphrey Noyes of Oneida was a frequent guest. There, with his family, for a while, Edmund Clarence Stedman lived,—the young New England poet,—towards the end of the fifties. There was a Phrenological Cabinet,— Fowler and Wells's,—in Nassau Street, where one could have one's "chart of bumps" made out, and perfectionists, itinerant healers and advocates of all manners of cults addressed the excitable New Yorkers from a dozen platforms. American science, coming of age with Joseph Henry and Asa Gray, evoked illimitable visions of the powers of the mind,—though the spurious and the real were confused in this dusk of morning,—and the sense of interior possibilities harmonized with the outward mood of a moment of "Manifest Destiny" and national expansion. The Mexican War had been fought and won, Texas and California were states, while the vast region of Oregon had entered the Union, and the pioneers were swarming to the gold-fields of the Western slope, to the valleys of the Columbia river, to the Rio Grande. The republic had all but absorbed the continent and the temper of the American people was exuberant and more than ever uncritically sanguine. They felt that anything might happen in the nation, in the mind.

New York, once so bland and simple, had become a metropolis overnight, a city, with circles and circles, that nothing surprised, and the sprightly figure of Washington Irving, on a pleasant afternoon, tripping with elastic step along Broadway, suggested an age as remote as Rip van Winkle's. For Irving often came to town on a brief jaunt from Sunnyside, his chubby frame enveloped in a talma,—with the low shoes that he wore where others wore boots,—smoothly shaven, twinkling, chirping, somehow quaint with his old-school air, followed by respectful bows as passers-by observed him. His cheery, shrewd and kindly face, equally plump and vivacious, recalled the more comfortable days of the vrouws and the burghers and the charm of a loitering life in woods and fields, although Gotham, which owed him this nickname, abounded in tributes to his fancy, Knickerbocker steamboats and companies, omnibuses, hotels. The one universally famous New Yorker,—with Fenimore Cooper in the west of the state,—he stood for a cosmopolitan past, for the *piccolo mondo antico* of a time before the dollar became almighty. But he had kept up with the new writers and acclaimed the songs of Stephen Foster, as he had been the first to recognize Cooper and Bryant; and only the other day in London, —in 1846, on his homeward journey from Madrid as ex-minister to Spain,—he had delighted in Herman

Melville's *Typee*. Melville's brother Gansevoort had read him portions of the manuscript, which he had found exquisite at moments and graphic in style, and, lifelong lover of voyages that he was, he had prophesied the success of a book that had made the author a man of mark already. Irving was always young for style, as Channing said he was young for liberty, and the new writers were loyal to the old story-teller, the "father,"— more properly, the uncle,—"of American letters." New York was still Washington Irving's town, remote as he was from the new ideas that seemed especially alien when they came from New England.

It was the other older worthies who marked the change in the spirit of the age, Cooper, for instance, and Audubon and Fitz-Greene Halleck, the poet who had left New York and retired to his native Connecticut, bewildered in a world that admired Longfellow and Lowell. He preferred the thin clear music of Campbell and Moore, which had none of the overtones of these younger poets, and the brisk little dandified Halleck, now poor and pathetic, was doubly an exile, in time as well as in place. Cooper, a less familiar presence,—for he despised all trading towns,—and Audubon, living at Minnie's Land at the top of Manhattan, were further from the commercial present than even Halleck, Astor's clerk, and both were to die in 1851. Audubon, the romantic frontiersman, seemed half a creature of myth in New York, and Cooper brought back the heroic past with which his spirit was in tune as it never could be with a day of reformers or traders. He had felt at home in Jefferson's world, even in the world of Andrew Jackson, but the "hoi polloi of the later presidents," as he called them in *Jack Tier*,—and the people who elected these presidents,—could not stir him. In fact, they aroused only his distaste and scorn. With the America of 1850, Cooper was wholly out of key, and even William

Cullen Bryant, the editor of the *Evening Post,* had begun to seem old-fashioned as a poet, cold and bald and all too simple beside the later New England poets who were so much richer in their diction and warmer in their tone. Everyone respected this first of the living American bards, with his slight hardy figure and rustic air, grave, severe, frugal, plain, a breathing symbol of the early republic and already almost a Nestor in latter-day New York. Bryant was travelling widely now and in 1852 he returned from the Holy Land with the palmer-like beard that was to make him look like Father Time, though he still had many years to live and work of importance to do as an editor, as a leader of opinion, as a patriot and sage. Bryant, a reformer too, was a simple Jacksonian democrat who had little in common with the prophets of the new dispensations. He was far removed from the isms and plans for turning the world upside down that flourished among the Brook Farmers and their friends in New York.

There was no sharp break in feeling, however, between the younger writers and the veteran triumvirate Bryant, Cooper and Irving, coevals of that other trio, Webster, Clay, Calhoun, who played an analogous role in the political sphere. Irving especially had scores of followers and the *Knickerbocker Magazine* perpetuated his atmosphere and manner, while new young men of greater power, with tendencies wholly unlike his, were affected, as Hawthorne had been, by his style. Herman Melville, for example, whose *Typee* had been a great success and who had just bought a farm at Pittsfield in the Berkshires, had imitated Irving's *Salmagundi* in earlier crude compositions, and even Walt Whitman had done so in his *Sun-Down Papers.* Whitman, who had edited the Brooklyn *Eagle* and who wrote for the New York magazines, had also imitated Poe in a fantastic sketch, and he had published an Indian tale suggesting

Cooper whom he admired and who would survive, he thought, into the furthest future. Cooper, for Melville, was a "great robust-souled man," while for Whitman he was "as strong and sweet as sunlight"; [2] and Whitman loved and reverenced Bryant, who often crossed the Brooklyn ferry and spent an afternoon rambling with him. Walt Whitman and Herman Melville, two young men of the same age, were in and about New York in the later forties, and, although they never perhaps encountered one another, they shared many of the tastes of the time in common. Irving struck Whitman as pleasant but weak, suckled on Addisonian milk, and for Melville he was a "grasshopper" beside Hawthorne. But Melville recalled him as

> happiest Irving
> Never from genial verity swerving

in a charming sketch that he wrote at the end of his career. *Rip van Winkle's Lilac* related a final episode in the life of the tattered old vagabond who returned to the village to find his abandoned dwelling a tenantless ruin. Too lazy even to have finished the house, he had planted a lilac to please his bride, a poor little slip that stood beside the door, and this lilac, grown gigantic, had spread its roots all round the yard and the neighbours had transplanted hundreds of bushes from it. The region roundabout was a paradise of lilacs, all thanks to the sorry good-for-nothing Rip, and Melville inscribed his tale to Irving as one of those "mellowing Immor-

[2] Whitman never lost his love of Cooper, who had stirred him, as he said, "clarionlike . . . Cooper was a master-man in many very significant ways . . . There was a healthy vigour in everything Cooper did—even to the libel suits he had so many of . . . I always liked the make-up of the man . . . Essentially fresh, robust, noble: one of the original characters, the tonic natures . . . He was never gloomy—was always as strong and sweet as sunlight."—Quoted in Horace Traubel's *With Walt Whitman in Camden.*

tals" who were "excellent in their works" and "pleasant and love-worthy in their lives." [3] For the rest, Whitman and Melville alike were keenly aware of the new reformers, the invaders from New England as well as the native brand. When Melville's Pierre came to New York, he lived at the "Apostles',"—which might have been suggested by the Unitary Home,—the former church, turned into chambers, where the "Teleological Theorists" unfolded their "Flesh-Brush Philosophy" and their "Apple-Parings Dialectics." Melville had no doubt observed a Plotinus Plinlimmon in New York and these others with their Graham crumbs and Adam's ale. Walt Whitman was more intimately connected with them. He was not merely an "expansionist" editor who had preached Manifest Destiny, he was taking part in many of the movements of the time, and, attending meetings of the Swedenborgians and Owen's World's Convention, he had reprinted writings of Margaret Fuller. He had written on temperance and abolition, and, if not now, then certainly later he met and talked with the socialist Albert Brisbane. It was Charles Dana, the late Brook Farmer, who advised him to publish the letter that Emerson presently sent him, acclaiming his poems.

Of the many living links between New England and New York the most active were Greeley and Barnum and Henry Ward Beecher, all Yankee authors in a sense and the most conspicuous men by far, the most representative figures, of Manhattan and Brooklyn. As late as 1870, when Joaquin Miller arrived from the West, his first acts were to call upon Horace Greeley and pluck a leaf from a tree by the door of Beecher's Plymouth Church to send it back to Oregon for his mother. Already twenty years before, Greeley and Beecher, with

[3] *Rip van Winkle's Lilac* was left unpublished at Melville's death. The manuscript was dated 1890.

P. T. Barnum, had very largely ruled the New York mind, which remained predominantly rural in tone, as the characters of these three men showed, in spite of its reformers, its frivolities and its hard-driving traders. Most of the New York merchants and bankers had grown up as farm-boys and retained their "country wisdom" and "country knowledge," as well as their country manners in many a case, and often, like the rich Mr. Bennett, in R. B. Kimball's *Was He Successful?*, they did not care a fig for a "city-bred boy." They kept an eye out for junior clerks who had been trained in village stores and acquired a practical knowledge of barter and trade selling a shilling's worth of calico or a cent's worth of snuff, or accepting a dozen eggs, across the counter. The acutest sharpest-witted men kept their greenness in certain respects, their rustic tastes and a piety that savoured of the country, and something in them responded to Greeley's abhorrence of over-crowded streets and his constant advice to young men to flee from the city. "Return to first principles," he said. "Cultivate the soil."

At heart a farmer, Greeley himself, dressing the part of a rustic sage, with his white hat and always rumpled duster, had captivated the national mind because his passion for the land expressed an America that was still overwhelmingly rural. Beecher too was a country minister on the scale of the metropolis who looked and dressed like a prosperous Western farmer, in his loose coat, low collar and broad-brimmed hat, and his methods never essentially changed from those he had developed in Indiana as a youthful preacher at forest camp-meetings and revivals. He had farmed between whiles and written for agricultural papers, as later he prided himself on the cattle and swine that he bred on his great farm Boscobel, although he delighted in roaming the city, even as Walt Whitman did, observing the shops, the museums, the factories and the wharves. He loved to

feel the people surging about him and he was not unhappy that they came to hear him preach in the spirit
in which they went to Barnum's Museum. This was a
rural spectacle too,—its note was that of a county fair
spread out for all to see in the heart of the city, patron-
ized by country folk very largely, as Barnum said, "with
a worthy curiosity to see the novelties of the town." It
was one of the landmarks of New York, like Castle Garden and Tammany Hall, and its object might well have
been described as astonishing the natives, while Barnum's hoaxes often suggested the tall tales of the frontier, the stories of David Crockett and even of Poe. Barnum symbolized a time when the masses, still rustic in
their mentality, were meeting all manner of phenomena,
as the towns grew larger, which they were unable to
judge, types of foreign lands, for instance, customs they
knew nothing of and oddities of natural history brought
from afar. Curious, good-natured and gullible, they delighted in wonders, while, belonging to a nation of
practical jokers, they enjoyed the sheer artistry of the
situation when the joke they might have played recoiled
on them. The *dramatis personae* of Barnum's half-fic-
titious world impressed the imagination like the characters of Dickens,—Tom Thumb and the Aztec children, the Feejee Mermaid, George Washington's nurse
and the Woolly Horse captured by Frémont in the passes
of the Rockies. They were more or less lasting figures of
American folklore. Barnum himself had been bred at
the plough-tail, and he, too, exalted the life of the
farmer with his own prize cattle and poultry and broad
acres on the shore.

Thus the three leading New Yorkers of the moment
were a wandering village showman, a backwoods reviv-
alist minister and a rural printer,—transformed in scale
alone, unchanged in nature,—all of them New Englanders and all reflecting the rustic tone that still prevailed

in the metropolis as throughout the country. They
seemed to prove that "in this republic the people of the
country are a little less country, and the people of the
towns a good deal less town, than is apt to be the case in
great nations." [4] Of the new generation, meanwhile, the
most popular writer of the fifties was another transplanted New Englander, George William Curtis, a
highly ornamental young man who might have been a
hero of N. P. Willis if he had not happened to sit at
Emerson's feet. Born in Providence, he had gone to
school in the suburbs of Boston and moved to New
York with his family when he was fifteen,—his father
had become the president of a well-known bank there;
and his later association with the Concord Transcendentalists set the key of his career as an orator and writer.
He had spent two years at Brook Farm, where his special task was to trim the lamps, while he studied the
chemistry of agriculture, music and German, and many
later accounts of the farm and the Transcendental Club
as well were based on the essays that Curtis wrote about
them. He was at home in New York for a while in 1844,
after he left the farm, reading Goethe; then, boarding in
Concord with his brother Burrill at the house of one of
the village worthies, he had passed his mornings working
as a farm-hand. The brothers sold their own vegetables
too, while they read in the afternoons in their rowboat
on the river. Curtis was one of the little party who, on
a summer's day, helped to raise Thoreau's hut at
Walden. As for the Transcendental Club, it lacked the
fluent social note, and Curtis was amused when the erect
philosophers serenely ate their russet apples and sol-
emnly disappeared into the night. But Emerson had
touched his spirit for good and all. He had seen the
sage not only in Concord but lecturing in country meeting-houses when the neighbourhood stamped in on win-

4 Cooper, *Miles Wallingford.*

ter nights, chattering to the door in hood and muffler or buried under buffalo-robes in wagons and sleighs. In the dim light of the lamps the boys clumped round the stove in cowhide boots until they were enthralled into silence by the musical spell. The incessant spray of Emerson's fancies, glittering like a night of stars, expanded and exalted the susceptible Curtis's mind.

As a literary publicist later, as a mentor of the young, who reminded them constantly of the "duty of the American scholar," Curtis was perhaps the foremost of Emerson's apostles, while he shared some of the tastes of Willis,—for he liked to "dance with the graces" at Newport,—and was also in certain ways a follower of Irving. Meanwhile, returning to New York in 1845, he spent his days reading Italian and German, and then he went abroad for winters in Rome, Berlin and Paris and a fourth winter on the Nile and in Palestine. He was writing for the New York papers, for *The Tribune* especially on politics in Europe; and his first book, *Nile Notes of a Howadji,* was published in 1851,—it was followed by *The Howadji in Syria,*—on his return. His picturesque and amusing impressions of Karnak and Luxor and the Valley of the Kings were written with much grace of style and sensuous feeling, but they were singularly empty of thought beside the travels of John Lloyd Stephens, with his vigour and gravity and power of observation. Curtis had followed the trail of Stephens, as Bayard Taylor was soon to do, on the Nile and over the desert to the Holy Land, on camel-back to Lebanon and Damascus, lingering among the remains of Thebes with their population of merchant-ghouls, trafficking in the legs, feet, arms and heads of mummies. The Egyptian ruins stood bare in the sun, free from green mosses and flowering vines, and his feeling shared the freshness of the sculptured forms.

Curtis, returning to New York for good, was active on

The Tribune as a critic of art and music and a para-
grapher, and somewhat later he was connected with
Harper's Magazine, the monthly that was established in
1850. He was a reporter of events in the theatre, Fanny
Kemble's readings, the annual shows of the Academy,
Jenny Lind, and he began to lecture too, following Willis to the watering-places which he described in *Lotus-
Eating.* Could there be greater extremes of experience
than to step on a Hudson river boat, after a morning in
Wall Street, and sail to West Point and read *The Cul-
prit Fay* by moonlight on the piazza of the hotel, looking up the river to the craggy steep of Cro' Nest? The
sloops moved as if in a dream, beautiful to behold from
the banks, bending and dipping under the gusts from
the hills, and Curtis spent days with Downing at New-
burgh and visited Bryant's Catskill Falls, driving over
gorges and bridges to the Mountain House. The flashing water, the June clouds, fleecily hanging or sweeping
so close that they might have been formed by the spray
of the cascade itself, were veritable pictures by Thomas
Cole or Bryant's friend Durand, while Curtis's companion sometimes announced "a Kensett." Perhaps it was a
bit of mossy rock or a shapely stretch of trees with the
outline of a mountain beyond, recalling this artist, an
intimate friend of Curtis who travelled with him now
and then and drew the illustrations for *Lotus-Eating.*
With other connoisseurs of landscape, Curtis discussed
the Hudson and the Rhine and the way in which Darley
had caught the spirit of the river, or the poet of the
Hudson, Joseph Rodman Drake; then he went on to
Saratoga and to Lake George and Niagara Falls, to
Trenton Falls, to Newport, to Nahant. The mists and
fogs of Newport were the delight of artists, and Curtis
had known this old town as a Southern resort, so many
of the frequenters came from Savannah and Charleston.
It was becoming rapidly the greatest of all the resorts of

fashion, while Saratoga was still an oasis of repose, where business seemed merely an amusement, in the American desert. There one met arctic Bostonians, with a touch of scorn in their stately fairness, crisp New Yorkers and Southerners cordial and careless, and when the lights at last went out, with the dying strains of "Lucia" or "Ernani," one could listen to the midnight gossip on the great piazzas.

Now Curtis was a moralist. He was not merely amused, like Willis, in this little world of gaiety and fashion, and he grieved over "our best society" and presently wrote *The Potiphar Papers* to show how "unspeakably barren," as he said, it was. Suggested by Irving's *Salmagundi,* though very much more by *Vanity Fair,* it satirized the parvenus of a time of rapid money-making whose only idea of behaviour was extravagance and display. Unlimited supplies of terrapin and champagne were their sole test of hospitality, and they had pushed into the background the more distinguished older circles that could not compete with them in wealth. They talked about liveries and coats of arms, which they bought as they bought other coats, about muslins, imported millinery and footmen, while they despised their republican government, dreamed of the court of Napoleon III and collected the pictures that "Mr. Düsseldorf" painted. For Curtis "good society" was a mystic communion that ought to consist of the worthy, not of the rich; and where, in these circles in New York, were the eminent men and women that one found in the London or Paris of which they talked?

Cooper had asked a similar question in his *Hundred Dollar Handkerchief,* and so in a way had Fitz-Greene Halleck in *Fanny,* while other voices were raised in the fifties regarding this dominant theme of a time when society in America was becoming fully conscious. Howells later used this phrase in connection with the author of *Nothing to Wear,* the well-known lawyer William Allen Butler, the son of the attorney-general in the cabinet of President Jackson who was briefly connected with literature in the later fifties. Acting as a *locum tenens* when Curtis was occupied elsewhere, he was a writer of clever parodies of Halleck, Longfellow, Holmes and others whose only rival at the moment was John Godfrey Saxe. Miss Flora M'Flimsey, who had "nothing to wear," although she took ten trunks to Newport, with bonnets, mantillas, capes, shawls and dresses in them, belonged to a set, with the Stuckups and the Flashers, that might have been Mrs. Potiphar's too, or the circle of John Godfrey Saxe's "Proud Miss MacBride." Fanny Kemble observed these young ladies, one prettier than the other, as she said, who looked like fairies, dressed like duchesses, behaved like housemaids and screamed like peacocks. Their showy prodigality, together with their insolent pride of place, so often followed by a fall "from an Avenue to an Alley," attracted other moralists, including Edmund Clarence Stedman, the young poet who arrived in New York in 1855. One of Stedman's first compositions was a travesty in verse, *The Diamond Wedding,* suggested by the vulgar parade of a parvenu marriage, while Donald G. Mitchell, "Ik Marvel," another disciple of Irving, reproached this society also in *The Lorgnette.* He hoped to dismantle the scaffoldings of the social architects who were seeking to restore the fabrics of the feudal past.

Not all the writers on the fashionable world dwelt on these elements in it, of course. There were others, following Willis, Charles Astor Bristed, for example, who described its more durable qualities in *The Upper Ten Thousand* (a phrase that had recently been coined by Willis himself). This grandson of John Jacob Astor, a graduate of the English Cambridge, wished to show his friends abroad that the life which his friends lived at home was not altogether savage, wild and frightful. Bristed's pictures of the real "exclusives" with their odd blending of Puritan ways and acquired continental habits dimly foreshadowed Edith Wharton's; and there were bits for the social historian in his descriptions of a fashionable wedding and the life of an ancestral West-chester country-house. This was called "Devilshoof" after Cooper's "Satanstoe." Some of Bristed's scenes of skating and sleighing recalled the prints of Currier and Ives and their lightning-foot pacers and young ladies in furs. Most of the other books about the social world were satires, thanks largely to Thackeray's influence, no doubt, and they had appeared in growing numbers since 1844, when Anna Mowatt published *The Fortune Hunter*. This "glamour girl" of the middle of the century, whose merchant-father had financed Miranda when he tried unsuccessfully to liberate the South American states, had scandalized her family by appearing on the stage, for which she wrote the satirical comedy *Fashion*. The fraudulent count of so many tales[5] appeared in pursuit of the young girl in this play which also made fun of the newly rich.

All these works were unimportant, although two or three were remembered later, but they signalized a tendency that was pronounced by 1850 in the life of New York and the consciousness of the New York writ-ers. Nor was Curtis himself an author of any great moment, for all the high prestige that he and his books enjoyed. If, aside from his popularity, he ranked with the best for a generation, it was partly because of his moral

[5] And poems also,—*The Finishing School* of Fitz-James O'Brien, for instance. In this satirical tale in verse, suggesting *Fanny* and *Nothing to Wear*, the wicked Count Cherami makes off with an heiress, spends all her money in seven years breeding race-horses and building yachts, and the hapless couple starve in a comfortless attic. This was all the fault of Madame Cancan's Frenchified teach-ing in her finishing-school where Miss Mary Degai was the victim of low dresses and unreason.

force, which expressed itself in other ways, and partly because of his friendship with the New England authors. He was associated with Lowell and Norton, his literary executor, who invested his fame with an aureole forty years later, and meanwhile, as a Yankee born, he shared the repute of the New England circle in the years when this was at its peak. His writing was far too soft and much too sweet,—Correggio, as it happened, was his favourite painter,—and this was true especially of the book that he was most widely known for, the series of story-essays, *Prue and I*. This "I" was an elderly bookkeeper, with a prim cravat and a well-brushed coat, who lived in a neat little house with his faithful Prue and who had a better time, he thought, with his limited means and his plain black clothes, than the rich and the fashionable who fancied they owned the world. He watched the steamers sailing off to legendary isles and sometimes he sallied forth to observe the gay world of youth and beauty hurrying to some congress of fashion in Washington Square. He enjoyed the entertainment that nature provided for those whom she meant to keep at home, and he ate all the delightful dinners in his imagination while his actual palate rejoiced in mush and stew. The sunset was his "Western property,"—he owned its pinnacles and towers,—and he saw more of Italy by staying in his room than most of the short-sighted people who really went there, people whose bodies had liver-complaints and whose minds were asleep while his was awake and therefore possessed whatever it looked upon. One orange was enough to take him to Sorrento, and while the rich owned only the fences and the soil he owned the beauty that properly made the landscape.

Here in a New York setting was the plain living and high thinking that Emerson had touched with poetry in many of his essays, and Thoreau too had "owned" the fields which the Concord farmers thought were theirs in just the same fashion as Prue and her humble spouse. This doctrine was the pure milk of Concord, but with Curtis's treatment it suffered the change which the shell underwent that Emerson took from the beach: it lost its sheen with the place and the air and what was intense became sentimental when it passed through Curtis's tamer and shallower mind. It was one thing to say that the joy of living consorted with these mundane deprivations when the speaker lived whole-heartedly in the world of the spirit,—and lived moreover with the ardour of the poet and the sage,—but it was quite another thing when the speaker was one whose tastes were mundane and who only wished to live in the world of the spirit. Curtis valued too many of the things that "Prue and I" went without, or he would never have written *Lotus-Eating,* and this had the effect of spoiling a book that remained, however, a popular classic during all the years that Melville was left unread. It rivalled the *Reveries of a Bachelor,* "Ik Marvel's" similar book, as a theme for the black-and-white artists for forty years; but Curtis's literary gift was mimetic and he soon ceased to publish books,—he was an author of the eighteen-fifties, mainly. He came in on the wave of the Transcendental writers, of Thackeray's vogue and the fame of Washington Irving, and he continued to write indeed as a literary journalist, the "Easy Chair" of *Harper's Magazine.* He was known for many years as a whimsical censor of manners, facile and rather inclined to the namby-pamby,[6] but he was more important as a publicist and

[6] On the margin of one of his books, Herman Melville wrote "G. W. C." beside the following sentence of Matthew Arnold: "It is comparatively a small matter to express oneself well, if one will be content with not expressing much, with expressing only trite ideas."

In a letter of 1884, John Burroughs thus described Curtis, who was introducing Matthew Arnold at a lecture in New York: "A pity he is not a little more robust and manly. He fairly leans and languishes on the bosom of the graces."

reformer. In fact, he played a large role in the movement of civil-service reform in the turbulent years that
followed the Civil War. As an orator he was Emerson's
understudy, the only rival of Wendell Phillips in arous-
ing young men of college age to a sense of their political duties as citizens of the republic. He addressed the
rural colleges, in the vein of William James later, on
the need of educated men to lead the country, men who
were willing to pursue the truth where others pursued
the expedient and who would serve as a sort of public
conscience. He pointed out that republics were possible
only among thinking men. For Curtis men were always
young, as they had been for Emerson, and the golden
age was not yesterday or tomorrow but today.

Thus, for three or four decades to come, Curtis maintained in New York the note of the New England springtime and the old Brook Farmers, and young men continued to be young for him in the days when Henry
Adams and others were actually old and sceptical and
prematurely wise. His hero was Sir Philip Sidney, the
type of manly honour and of ardent and generous
scholarship and chivalrous action, and for all his naivety and sentimentality there was something large
about Curtis too, as the young Walt Whitman felt and
later averred.[7] He was the most conspicuous of all the
younger New York writers in the years when Whitman
himself was appearing on the scene, although most of
Melville's work preceded his; while another transplanted
New Englander was Richard Henry Stoddard, who had
been brought to New York as a boy of ten. This was in
1835, when Stoddard sold matches in the street,—he
remembered a Broadway swarming with scavenger hogs,
—for his father, a Hingham shipmaster, had been lost

[7] "Curtis always had the big manner,—yes, big without being offish:
his personality has a large swing, as if it had plenty of time and
space in which to live."—Quoted in Horace Traubel's *With Walt
Whitman in Camden.*

at sea, like Hawthorne's father, and his mother had been left penniless with three small children. He worked in an iron-foundry, where he had been placed to learn the trade, though in after years, like Melville, he earned his living in the custom-house, thanks largely to the aid of Hawthorne who had preceded him at Salem. Stoddard wrote at night the poems that began to appear in the later forties, while he haunted the second-hand bookshops, where rarities were still to be found, feeling that he might have been a scholar. He was drawn to the lonely unhappy poets whose childhood had been like his own, the poorest of the poor, humble and embarrassed, Bloomfield, George Darley, John Clare, or those who had been worsted by misfortune, and he wrote essays on some of them, with Peacock, Blake and Hartley Coleridge, in a later book called *Under the Evening Lamp*. For all their rather low vitality, these essays had a certain interest precisely because of their somewhat bitter tone, in a day when a shallow optimism was all too common, while Stoddard's many poems were sometimes good. Unlike the Yankees who stayed at home, he was purely aesthetic in his point of view, with a fierce contempt for politics as a concern of poets. Keats was Stoddard's idol, and his poems were full of the deities of Greece and the mediæval images beloved by Tennyson also. He produced hymns to the beautiful and odes to autumn and classical story-poems in the manner of the day, with numbers of musical songs suggested by Persian, Arab and Chinese poets, the work of a conscientious craftsman and a man of taste. But there was nothing to distinguish him from a hundred nineteenth-century poets who were equally accomplished, prolific, laborious and adroit. Perhaps the too-long *On the Town*, singled out by Whitman, was the best piece that Stoddard wrote in verse.

There was little cohesion among the writers of New

York,[8] which differed in this respect widely from Boston, while the New York writers were far less scholarly as well. Literature in the metropolis was never a learned profession as it was in eastern Massachusetts, where almost all the important writers, from Thoreau and Dana to Motley and Parkman, had passed through the Harvard mill of Edward Tyrrel Channing. Even the New Englanders who lived in New York were seldom college-bred, whether Fitz-Greene Halleck or Curtis or Richard Henry Stoddard, while Bryant himself was scarcely so and Cooper had been removed from Yale and Irving had little formal education. Whitman and Melville[9] had still less, the two great writers of the coming age. This fact meant something when one considered certain defects of Whitman's style that all his genius could not wholly atone for,[10] as the lack of a certain philosophical training was more than a little responsible for some of the anomalies and flounderings of Melville's thought. For the rest, there were various circles in New York that had small connection with one another, from the circle of *The Tribune* to the circle of the "Knickerbocker school," which maintained the note of Washington Irving with odds and ends of the quainter sort and a touch that was light and generally Epicurean.[11] The

[8] Nothing seemed stranger in the twentieth century than that Herman Melville and Walt Whitman should scarcely have become aware of each other's existence. There is no record of any meeting between these two contemporaries who were also the greatest New York writers of their day. Nor was Melville mentioned in the *Retrospect* of William Allen Butler, although both had been the children of prominent families of Albany at almost the same time.

[9] "A whale-ship was my Yale College and my Harvard."—Melville.

[10] "How plenteous! how spiritual! how resumé!"—Whitman, *Night on the Prairies*.

[11] "There was never anything like the Knickerbocker, and there never will be again. It required a sunny genial social atmosphere, such as we had before the war, and never after; an easy writing of gay and cultivated men for one another . . . It sparkled through its summertime, and oh! how its readers loved it! I sometimes think that I would like to hunt up the old title-page with Diedrich Knickerbocker and his pipe."—Charles Godfrey Leland, *Memoirs*.

"school" gathered loosely round the *Knickerbocker Magazine,* and, with its air of the festive and gay, it was composed of authors mainly whom—a later critic said— "we all remember as forgotten." The most scholarly circle was that of the brothers Duyckinck, old New Yorkers, Episcopalians, like the veteran Gulian C. Verplanck, who also stood for the dying Dutch element of the town. The sons of a publisher of earlier days, with a certain hereditary interest in books, Evert and George Duyckinck edited *The Literary World,* a weekly journal of literature and art. A little later, in the middle fifties, they were to compile the *Cyclopædia of American Literature,* a rival of Rufus Griswold's anthologies, which had recently proclaimed that America had a literature of its own. Somewhat staid, with a clerical air and with little of the gusto that marked a few of the Boston and Cambridge bookmen, they were rather antiquarians than critics in the proper sense, for all their hospitality to the younger men. Their cyclopædia especially dwelt on the early obscure American authors whom they rescued from oblivion for a time, while Evert Duyckinck's well-known library all but overflowed a house that was a rendezvous of men of letters. There authors, artists, editors and actors met and discussed the events of the day, the revolutions of '48, the gold rush on the Western coast, the slavery question, Manifest Destiny, Frémont. The talk in the parlour of the Duyckinck house was reflected in Herman Melville's *Mardi,* which had appeared in 1849; for Melville, a family friend of the Duyckincks who had settled in New York in 1847, had spent many evenings in their circle. For *The Literary World* he also reviewed Cooper's *The Sea Lions* and *The Red Rover, The Scarlet Letter* and Parkman's *The Oregon Trail.*

Of literary "evenings" in New York the most successful were Miss Anna Lynch's, at one of which Poe had

given his first reading of *The Raven*. Miss Lynch, a Ver-
monter born, who had once been the secretary of Henry
Clay and who later married Professor Vincenzo Botta,
was herself a minor poet of sorts who had lived in New
York since 1846 and was famous for her conversazioni.
There Emerson and Margaret Fuller mingled with the
New York writers, Bryant, Fitz-Greene Halleck, N. P.
Willis, with various ladies who had known Poe, George
P. Morris, the writer of songs, and the artists Asher
Durand and Henry Inman. Seba Smith was often there,
the author of the "Jack Downing" letters, and Elizabeth
Oakes-Smith, his formidable wife, a lecturer on the rights
of women who had written a poem that Poe had praised
and was soon to produce a novel called *The Newsboy*.
This might have been the story of one of Horatio Alger's
heroes, and it gave one vivid glimpses of the New York
of the fifties, the ferry-boats and the pilot-boats, a
Broadway jammed with drays and stages and the grand
bazaar of the merchant-prince A. T. Stewart. There was
a rival New York salon, Mrs. Lewis's,—Poe's "Estelle,"
—in an old brick house on East Fourth Street, with evil-
smelling ailanthus trees in the yard,—a "bower of the
muses" that bloomed on Friday evenings when the hos-
tess appeared in a garland of forget-me-nots. According
to one of the visitors there,[12] "Estelle's" inspiration
came regularly at about three in the afternoon, when the
wind blew from the South and the poetess donned a
long white gown and let her hair ripple down her back.
But hers was an affair of small fry compared with Miss
Anna Lynch's evenings, the resort of Horace Greeley
and Rufus Griswold, who had returned to New York
after his ill-fated marriage in Charleston, where he
had met the South Carolina writers. He had spent a
week at The Woodlands, the plantation of William Gil-

---

[12] Bayard Taylor. In his novel *John Godfrey's Fortunes*, Mrs.
Lewis appeared as "Adeliza Choate."

more Simms, who was constantly in New York during
these years. Richard Henry Stoddard was another member of Miss Lynch's circle, with Bayard Taylor, who had
met him in 1848, when Taylor was already connected
with *The Tribune* and Stoddard was working in the
iron-foundry and they always spent their Saturday evenings together. Taylor loved Shelley as much as Stoddard loved Keats, and they read their poems aloud to
one another. One evening at Miss Lynch's the guests
arrived in fancy dress as Ivanhoe, an Italian cavalier
and what not,—types that appeared in the stories and
paintings of the moment,—the poet Thomas Buchanan
Read as a Tyrolese minstrel and Bayard Taylor in the
character of Goethe's Faust. On another occasion Taylor
wrote the valentine for Herman Melville, who came to
a valentine party with one of his sisters. Taylor was already known as a traveller and poet, and, young as he
was, he could remember the literary tone of 1840,[13]
which seemed like ancient history a decade later; for
already American literature was beginning to count in
the world, even aside from the writings of the more famous authors.[14] He had come from the region of Phil-

[13] "I remember that in 1840 there were many well-known and
tolerably popular names, which are never heard now. Bryon and
Mrs. Hemans then gave the tone to poetry, and Scott, Bulwer
and Cooper to fiction. Willis was, by all odds, the most popular
American author; Longfellow was not known by the multitude,
Emerson was only 'that Transcendentalist,' and Whittier 'that Aboli-
tionist.' We young men used to talk of Rufus Dawes and Charles
Fenno Hoffman, and Grenville Mellon, and Brainard, and Sands.
Why, we even had a hope that something wonderful would come
out of Chivers!"—Bayard Taylor, *Diversions of the Echo Club.*

Grenville Mellon was admired for an oft-quoted line, "High over
all the lonely bugle grieves."

[14] "With reference to your literature, it may interest your patriotism to be told that Moses Stuart and Dr. Robinson taught me my
little Hebrew, that Abbott helped my early Christian course, that I
found Anthon a vast improvement on the old classical Lempriere,
and that 'Peter Parley' now instructs my children."—Letter of Mar-
tin F. Tupper to the publisher George Palmer Putnam, 1845.

adelphia, once the centre of American letters, which
had given place to Boston and New York. It was "merely
an immense provincial town," he had written in a letter
of 1846, while New York was "the metropolis of a continent."

New York, the commercial metropolis, was at least a
lively literary centre, if Boston decidedly excelled it as a
focus of minds, with dozens of more or less promising
writers whom Poe had described in his *Literati* and who
had small expectations in the matter of wages.[15] There
were numbers that suffered from the "Willis affection,"
as "Ik Marvel" called it, with pencillings, inklings,
glimpses, hurry-graphs and dashes, and reputations
could still be made on the score of a sonnet like *The
Tropical Summer* of Herman Melville's hero Pierre
Glendinning. Pierre, well known at nineteen, had written, like others of the literati, "brief meditative poems
and moral essays," along with the sonnets he contributed to the "Gazelle Magazine"; but, as for criticism,
he found the reviews all "prudently indecisive . . . pan-
egyrics, without anything analytical about them." So
did Bayard Taylor's John Godfrey, whose "fortunes"
were his own, as he looked over the reviews of his first
book, all of them vague and mechanical;[16] and Taylor

"I stopped at a bookstore [in Edinburgh, 1844] . . . and to my
surprise nearly half the works were by American authors. There
were Bryant, Longfellow, Channing, Emerson, Dana, Ware and
many others. The bookseller told me he had sold more of Ware's
Letters than any other book in his shop, 'and also,' to use his own
words, 'an immense number of the great Dr. Channing.' "—Bayard
Taylor, *Views Afoot*.

[15] "Washington Irving, one of the most brilliantly successful of our
authors, received just two hundred and four thousand dollars for
more than fifty years of arduous literary labour,—four thousand
dollars a year, the wages of a chief clerk."—Bayard Taylor, *Critical
Essays and Literary Notes*.

[16] "I was struck with the vague, mechanical stamp by which they
were all characterized. I sought in vain for a single line which
showed the discrimination of an enlightened critic. The fact is, we
had no criticism, worthy of the name, at that time. Our literature

regretted Poe, the "tomahawk man," who had left no followers behind him. The reviewers might all have been Henry T. Tuckerman, another member of Miss Lynch's circle who figured, somewhat dubiously, in Poe's *An Enigma,* a writer, still young, shallow and diffuse as a critic but a well-read literary essayist with an attractive style. He expressed the intelligent common-place on a high level, and moreover he had something resembling a passion for letters. As a boy he had ob-served Washington Allston, he had watched John How-ard Payne and he had followed Judge Hopkinson through the streets of Philadelphia with the tune of *Hail Columbia* humming in his ears. During two long visits in Italy, largely passed in Turin and Florence and re-corded in his *Italian Sketch Book* and other collections, he had met Alfieri and the pensive Silvio Pellico, whose energy had been virtually crushed by his life in prison. Tuckerman's biographical essays were perhaps the best he wrote, and his *Book of the Artists* remained as a re-cord of early American painters that continued Dun-lap's *History of the Arts of Design.* It was Tuckerman who assembled the essays of Horatio Greenough and wrote the memoir of this American sculptor.

As for the literary scene, on the whole, it was more trivial in New York,—much more trivial, no doubt,—than it was in Boston. It was there that Pierre Glendin-ning found the world had "only fire and sword for all contemporary grandeur." But Poe had lived there off and on, with Cooper and Bryant and Washington Ir-

---

was tenderly petted, and its diffuse, superficial sentiment was per-haps even more admired than its first attempts at a profounder study of its own more appropriate themes and a noble assertion of its autonomy . . . All our gentle, languishing echoes found spell-bound listeners whom no one,—with, perhaps, the single exception of Poe,—had the will to disenchant."—Bayard Taylor, *John God-frey's Fortunes.*

ving, and one might have guessed that the day of small things was passing. Two writers at least who were rising in the town were among the greatest of their age, in America and one might say perhaps the world.

CHAPTER II

PHILADELPHIA

THE white-headed boy of the new generation, a favourite with editors and readers alike, was the youthful Pennsylvanian Bayard Taylor, an assistant on the New York *Tribune* since 1848 and a rather special protégé of Horace Greeley. Taylor, at that time twenty-three, was already well known as a traveller, the author of the popular *Views Afoot,* who had wandered with a knapsack for two years in Europe, plodding through Germany, Italy, Switzerland and France. With somewhat vague commissions from Greeley and *The Saturday Evening Post,* he had written his letters by the wayside, on the tops of mountains, in the stillness of deserted ruins and in peasant inns. In the middle forties, simple accounts of foreign cities and details of travel still interested a multitude of readers, and this young man found himself famous when he came home. He was the envy of other young men from the country, for he had seen Europe on less than a dollar a day,—a touch that appealed to the thrifty and the self-reliant,—while he had an unusual gift of enjoyment and wonder. He was invited to dinner at once with George Bancroft and Fenimore Cooper, he dined the following night with Herman Melville, and N. P. Willis wrote an introduction for the book of which he had already suggested the title. Five editors offered Taylor posts and Greeley was lucky to capture him, so energetic he was, so competent and willing and moreover so skilful and ready as a literary craftsman.

A poor boy of Quaker stock, who was partly "Pennsylvania Dutch,"—his grandmother spoke German in the household,—Taylor had grown up in Chester County, where his father was sheriff for a while and where he lived later at Kennett Square, his birthplace. His forbears had all been farmers for many generations, Mennonites or English Quakers who had come over with Penn, as deeply attached to the soil, he said, as the serfs of Russia ever were and primitive and simple in their habits. Few of them had ever travelled further than Philadelphia, or the Wilmington market, to sell their poultry and pigs, and they clung to their rich rolling fields and the bountiful orchards and old stone dwellings that were set in the park-like landscapes of the winding valleys. In the novels that he was soon to write, Taylor described their pastoral world, their massive chimneys and heavy projecting eaves and the diamond-shaped panes brought over in the days of Penn, the walled gardens, the flag-stone paths, the well-trimmed hedges of hawthorn and blackthorn, the box and the holly that flourished in the mild misty air. This was the region where Benjamin West and Robert Fulton had grown up in the heartier days before the Revolution, when ancient English pastimes survived in the country. The Quaker dress and plain speech still prevailed when Taylor wrote, and farming and religion were the principal interests of the people, though the younger women were reading Carlyle, Margaret Fuller and George Sand in the manner of their contemporaries in Massachusetts. There was a station of the underground railroad not far from Kennett Square, and temperance, peace and women's rights were much discussed by the stronger-minded, while oddities of type and character abounded among them. One heard of a spinster, for instance, who ordered her coffin and used it meanwhile as a trough for mixing her bread. There were obstinate sectarians of many kinds and earnest free Quak-

ers. The frame of mind and the way of life suggested
New England in various ways, as Mrs. Stowe described
it in her rural novels,—which the novels of Bayard Taylor in turn resembled,—though the people were less
keen and their interests were narrower and simpler, as
Taylor's novels were dimmer than Mrs. Stowe's.

This had been still more the case when Taylor was a
boy, when the air of the great world scarcely reached
these valleys, and Quaker sermons, John Woolman's
Journal and Penn's *No Cross, No Crown* had virtually
bounded the mental horizon of the people. His one wish
was to get away and possibly in later years the weakness
and paleness of his novels were results of this, as if he
had never felt his surroundings deeply. He dreamed of
travel in the Mediterranean as he tended the cattle and
hoed the corn, for at ten he had read in a country paper Willis's *Pencillings by the Way;* then he happened
on Irving and Longfellow's *Outre-Mer.* The village
schoolmaster told him tales of an earlier American traveller, John Ledyard, who had found a grave beside the
Nile at the outset of a journey undertaken to discover its
sources, and Taylor, apprenticed to a printer, felt that
he was born to travel, as he longed to be a linguist, a
scholar and a poet as well. He often walked to Philadelphia, thirty miles away, while he developed an inherited
knowledge of German that prompted his later studies
of Goethe and *Faust;* and, saving money as a printer's
boy, he made his first journey with a knapsack to the
Catskills and the Highlands of the Hudson. Presently
walking to Washington too, where he talked with John
Quincy Adams and the Secretary of State, Calhoun, who
gave him a passport, he called upon Greeley and Willis
in New York and set out on his European travels. He
interviewed Freiligrath, Longfellow's translator, and
found that Mendelssohn was eager to hear about the
American Negro melodies; and he was wandering along

the Danube in the summer of 1845 at the time when Thoreau was building his hut at Walden. Everyone helped him and passed him along, and Mrs. Trollope, who had settled in Florence and who read the poems that he was writing, gave him letters to her publishers in London. At Lockhart's he met Bernard Barton, the friend of Lamb and a Quaker poet, like Whittier whom Taylor went to see when he returned to America and who described him at length in *The Tent on the Beach.* The circle of Boston and Cambridge poets received him "like a swarm of brothers," as James T. Fields, the publisher, remarked, while he was deeply drawn to them and grateful to them for creating a large and eager audience for American poets. He had dedicated his own first book to Griswold, the anthologist, and Poe had reviewed and praised his *Rhymes of Travel,* his "glowing imagination," his terseness and vigour, his admirable rhetorical gift and perfection of skill.

Thus began the resounding career of a many-sided man of letters who ranked in his time with the first in both poetry and prose, a writer who accomplished all that energy, talent and will could do and who certainly excelled in many of the literary virtues. His animal spirits were exceptionally high, he was variously learned, he was competent or more than competent in several fields, in poetry, the drama, fiction, translation, reviewing,[1] and his books of travel were lastingly readable, while his contemporaries were impressed by Taylor's prodigious memory and gift of tongues. He was taken for a native in more than one land where he learned the language as he went along,—he spoke the

---

[1] Taylor was capable of extraordinary feats as a reviewer. He received the two volumes of Victor Hugo's *La Légende des Siècles,* read them and despatched within twenty-four hours a full-length critical essay that was admirably written and that included translations of six lyrical poems, all carefully rendered and as if composed in English.

obscurest dialects of Norwegian and German,—and before the fifties were well advanced he was known as the
"great American traveller" who was roving the planet
virtually from pole to pole. Washington Irving had
urged him to see the Oriental world, and he visited
China, India, Russia, Palestine, Arabia and Turkey and
travelled over Lapland in winter in a sledge with reindeer. He was one of the first to enter Nubia beyond the
Second Cataract,—with a boat that he named the "John
Ledyard,"—and one of the first white visitors to the city
of Nanking. He had been with Commodore Perry when
he "opened" Japan, and roaming the forests of Phrygia
or crossing the hills of Loo-Choo he had felt at times the
passion of the explorer. Again and again he returned to
Germany, on which his mind dwelt more and more, the
sphere of many of his future studies and essays, constantly visiting Weimar, preparing for a book on Goethe
and Schiller that he hoped to make the great work of
his life. There later, when he was well-known himself, he
was invited to lecture before the assembled grandchild-
ren of Goethe and Schiller, of Wieland, Herder, Karl
August and Frau von Stein, and, speaking on American
literature, he read passages from Emerson, Longfellow
and Bryant and the younger writers Bret Harte, Stedman and Stoddard. He had seen in 1852 the sole survivor
of the minor gods who had once inhabited the slopes of
the Weimar Olympus, the old poet Friedrich Rückert,
deep in Sanskrit studies and glad to see Taylor, who
had just returned from the East. They met in the garden
at Coburg, among the late-blossoming roses, and Rückert's conversation was a monologue on Arabian poetry, which Taylor was keen about and had learned
to read. Then twice he called on Humboldt, the most
renowned of living men,[2] and the greatest of travel-

---

[2] Even in the heart of the Sierra Nevada, in the mining-camp
where "Dame Shirley" lived in 1852, the hotel, a large rag shanty

writers in his descriptive power, who was writing his *Cosmos* at eight-seven with a brain that suggested to Taylor the still, deep, tranquil fountain of Vaucluse. For, although there was not a ripple on its surface, it was creating a river by its overflow. Humboldt in 1804 had visited Philadelphia, where a great dinner was given for him at Peale's Museum, and he had heard of George Washington's death while he was travelling in South America, whence he had returned to Paris with an unheard-of collection. Universal in his tastes, he had assembled specimens that revealed the whole natural history of a continent, its botany, geology, mineralogy, zoology and what not. Mexico had remained the country that interested him most outside of Europe, and he had been pleased by a visit from John Lloyd Stephens, whose writings on the Central American ruins he knew, while, speaking of *The Conquest of Mexico*, he said there was no historian of the age either in Germany or in England who was Prescott's equal. He had also read some of Taylor's books, which had spread through the European countries, and said he had done a real service in picturing the world, as scientists could not do it, observing for them.

For a quarter of a century Bayard Taylor filled a large space in the American scene as a rival or rather a companion of the New England authors, as a poet but especially as a writer of travels, of a long series of books in which he surveyed the world from China to Peru. Everyone knew his visage of bronze and the Asiatic costume in which he appeared for the multitude in the portrait by Hicks, in burnoose and turban, smoking a Syrian pipe, as he sat cross-legged on a Damascus roof-top. Even in the woolliest corner of the West everyone heard his trav-

with a barroom floor for the miners to dance on, was called the Hotel Humboldt. The New York poet Richard Henry Stoddard, Taylor's friend, wrote a life of Humboldt.

elogues. The pioneers crowded in from all over the prairie when the buoyant Bayard Taylor was to speak, for they were familiar with the New York *Tribune,* where his letters from abroad were printed first, and he shared much of the prestige of Horace Greeley. His eye for landscape, his curiosity and the happy spirit behind his writing accounted for his popular success, though his method, as he said, was pictorial only and he deliberately eschewed affairs of religion, statistics, politics and science. He was fresh, accurate and entertaining. For many a decade to come the guide-books of Africa, Asia and even Europe contained passages from Taylor's descriptions as still the best, though more and more he lamented the fate of the literary globe-trotter whose deepest desire was always to excel as a poet. His poetry was good, as Tennyson observed, in its conscientious finish and the richness of imagery especially of his Oriental pieces, while in range it included the themes and modes that were generally shared by poets of the time, sonnets, odes, idyls, love-lyrics and narratives in verse. Most of it was quite as good as the mass of Lowell's and Whittier's verse, but it lacked the few characteristic poems that carried both Lowell and Whittier, for instance, out of the ruck of mere skilful and commonplace talents. There was in Taylor nothing like *Snow-Bound* or *The Biglow Papers* that gave their authors a place in the history of the country, if not for all time in the history of poetry itself. Taylor's poems were deficient, in short, in the strong individual note that might have kept them alive for another generation, and one welcomed the local subjects and touches that gave them now and then a flavour at least that belonged to this poet alone. In *The Quaker Widow, The Holly Tree, The Old Pennsylvania Farmer* and other rhymed soliloquies and ballads,—no better perhaps as poems than some of the rest,—one felt a certain actuality as

Taylor recalled his native scene, the old houses, the plodding neighbours, the cattle in the meadows. With a little more intensity he might have made rural Pennsylvania what others made New England, a country of the mind.

Already at the opening of the eighteen-fifties Taylor was a young man of mark, and one might have foreseen his coming fame as a sort of poet laureate who was constantly asked to write odes for national occasions. He was known as a student of German already whose future translation of *Faust* was by far the most brilliant achievement of a crowded career, and in this he stood for the time-spirit, for more than any other country the Americans admired Germany for two generations. The Transcendentalists of New England had popularized German literature, while Germany was the model for America in education, and typical Americans like Mark Twain were to idolize Germany and the Germans as Americans of an earlier day had idolized France.[3] In the forties and fifties they thought of Germany as the most enlightened country, in the sixties and seventies they thought of it as the most efficient, and when Bayard Taylor at last became the American minister to Germany he had long been a symbol and spokesman of this national taste. He had written and lectured much on the minnesingers and the German epics as on Lessing, Klopstock, Wieland, Herder and Goethe, while his translations from German authors were only rivalled in his time by those of his fellow-Pennsylvanian Charles Godfrey Leland.

Meanwhile, in 1853, he returned to Pennsylvania and lived off and on at Kennett Square, where he built a

---

[3] "What a paradise this is! what clean clothes, what good faces, what tranquil contentment, what prosperity, what genuine freedom, what superb government."—Mark Twain, Letter to Howells from Germany, 1878.

great house, Cedarcroft, in the pastoral region that he loved and delighted for a while in horticulture and farming. There he raised exotic plants, tobacco he had brought from Egypt, figs, pomegranates and Oriental melons, and there he kept the relics that included Schiller's court-sword, which had fallen into the hands of Thackeray, who gave it to him. It never seemed to occur to him to live in Philadelphia, which remained the centre of the world of magazines, with *Graham's* and *Sartain's, Godey's Lady's Book, The Saturday Evening Post* and various others. He accepted the direction of *Graham's Magazine* himself, on condition that he could continue to live in New York, for Philadelphia had wholly lost its magnetism of earlier times and men of letters no longer felt at home there. They averred that all the Philadelphians had the same ideas and that few were enthusiastic about the city,[4] that it was tame and uniform, dull and indifferent and even disparaged and depreciated the writers who were born there.[5] Many of them were bitter about it and left the city for New York, while George H. Boker, who remained, felt in after years that he had been "choked" and "slain" by neglect

---

[4] Philadelphia, "of which city, at that time, there was not one in the world of which so little evil could be said, or so much good, yet of which so few ever spoke with enthusiasm. Its inhabitants were all well-bathed, well-clad, well-behaved; all with exactly the same ideas and the same ideals . . . When a Philadelphian gave a dinner or supper, his first care was to see that everything *on the table* was as good or perfect as possible. I had been accustomed to first considering what should be placed *around* it on the chairs as the main item."—Charles Godfrey Leland, *Memoirs.*

[5] "When Philadelphia ceased to be a literary centre . . . the tone of society there seemed to change. Instead of the open satisfaction of Boston in her brilliant circle of authors, or the passive indifference of our New York, there is almost a positive depreciation of home talent in Philadelphia. Boker is most disparaged in his native city, and most appreciated in New England. There is always less of petty envy where the range of culture is highest."—Bayard Taylor, *Diversions of the Echo Club.*

and silence.[6] "No Philadelphian ever yet was a genius in Philadelphia," a later writer[7] remarked with a show of reason. Yet this old capital had given birth to the first American daily paper, the first circulating library, the first magazine, as the first American flag had been unfolded there and the first medical college had risen and flourished. Writers had even continued to come there from Boston and New York, as Lowell came for a while in 1845, writing for the *Pennsylvania Freeman,* a fortnightly anti-slavery journal of which Whittier had been the editor in 1838. There Robert Montgomery Bird lived, the author of *Nick of the Woods,* and Edgar Allan Poe had spent some years there, while Griswold was also an editor of *Graham's Magazine.* But more and more the interests of science, always predominant in Franklin's town, where the Franklin Institute was founded in 1824, had prevailed over the interests of literature. It was symptomatic that the great house of Mathew Carey, the foremost general publishers in the United States, which had published works of Cooper, Poe, Irving and Simms, had gradually become a minor company in this wider sphere as it specialized more and more in medical books.

In science as in scholarship the town was still predominant, with the old Philosophical Society as a centre

[6] "In four successive years, from 1822 to 1825, were born, in or near the city, Thomas Buchanan Read, Boker, Leland and Bayard Taylor. That all four of them found the gates of recognition closed to them at home is significant. Three of them spent the bulk of their lives in other places and gained their reputation outside their city; Boker alone remained a part of his life, breaking his heart upon her indifference."—Edward S. Bradley, *George Henry Boker.*
"This man, with encouragement, might possibly have developed into something; the world must add: But we choked him into silence, we gave him no welcome . . . We slew him with neglect." —Letter of Boker to Taylor, 1874, referring to himself and recalling their common ambitions and Taylor's success.
[7] Elizabeth Robins Pennell, *Charles Godfrey Leland.*

of attraction, and aside from Boston its libraries were the best in the country. Charles Godfrey Leland as a young man found all manner of treasures there, Chaucer and Gower in black letter, Cornelius Agrippa and Paracelsus, together with the earliest and rarest editions of authors who were dear to him, the old German mystics and François Villon. The Anglo-American writer Frank Forester,—Henry William Herbert,—who was planning an ambitious work on ancient Rome had had to give up the task in New York because he could not find there the necessary books for consultation. The only adequate library was closed to the public, while he found all his materials at once in Philadelphia, to which he felt he owed the book's existence. It was in Philadelphia that Austin Allibone soon produced his *Dictionary of English Literature and British and American Authors,* while two of the greatest scholars of the English-speaking world were already reconnoitring the fields of their future studies. Henry Charles Lea, the author of the *History of the Inquisition,* a grandson of the publisher Mathew Carey, was one of a family of men of science three of whom were eminent and whose own first publications were scientific. He was a nephew of Henry C. Carey, the widely known economist, and his father was a notable collector of Italian art. Lea made original contributions to botany and conchology before he became absorbed in his historical work. As a boy, at school in Paris, he had made a journey down the Rhine with his father and Fenimore Cooper, whom the Careys had published; then he had translated Anacreon's odes and written on Greek epigrams in a paper for the *Knickerbocker Magazine.* He had begun meanwhile the study of the Middle Ages that was to lead him far in later life. One of Lea's lifelong friends, Horace Howard Furness, who was to spend fifty years on his variorum Shakes-

peare[8] had been stirred by Fanny Kemble's Shakespearean readings, which began in Philadelphia in 1849. No
doubt he owed much to Fanny Kemble, who married
a Philadelphian and was besides a parishioner of his
minister-father, the Unitarian Dr. Furness, an early
friend of Emerson whose house for years was a haven for
fugitive slaves. Emerson and Channing and Garrison
were often there. The younger Furness studied at Munich after leaving Harvard, and Shakespeare was never
out of his mind, though he did not begin to prepare his
first volume, *Romeo and Juliet,* until after the war. Furness was an artist among scholars, like Francis J. Child
and Charles Eliot Norton, as one saw once more when
his beautiful letters were published. The prodigy Horace Binney Wallace, also a Philadelphian, had gone
abroad in 1849, a young man of large means who died
in Paris in 1852 after making a serious study of positiv-
ism. He was the leading American disciple of Auguste
Comte, who referred to him, comparing him to Thomas
Jefferson, in a later preface, for Wallace's interests were
exceptionally wide and he wrote with great intelligence
on painting, acting, philosophy and architecture.[9] Two
younger Philadelphians who were growing up in 1850
were Henry George and the novelist Frank R. Stockton,

[8] "Here is a feast of reading enough to fill a lifetime—the accumu-
lated essays and interpretations and controversies of hundreds of
past critics . . . I find of the utmost fascination these ponderous
volumes, where a few lines of the text hardly raise their heads above
the mad seas of comment at their base; and where often a single
phrase is followed by page after page in which critics fly at each
other's throats. Dr. Furness accumulates these records of wild absurdity; and then raising his head like Neptune, with his own calm
wisdom, rebukes these surges."—Logan Pearsall Smith, *On Reading
Shakespeare.*

[9] Rufus Griswold dedicated his *Prose Writers of America* to
Wallace as the most promising of all the younger men. He had
made a special study of mediæval architecture, and perhaps the
most interesting essays in his two posthumous collections were those
on the churches of Italy, Germany and France.

a wood-engraver there through the eighteen-fifties. Henry George, a publisher's son, who worked for a while in his father's store, a restless energetic boy, was often present at the popular lectures on scientific subjects at the Franklin Institute.

There was one Philadelphian book of the fifties that lay on countless parlour tables, acclaimed by Irving, Bancroft, Prescott and Bryant, the *Arctic Explorations* of Dr. Elisha Kent Kane, who had reached the highest latitude, the furthest north. A surgeon in the navy in Oriental waters, he had previously explored the Philippines in 1844 more extensively than any traveller before him; then he led one of the expeditions in search of the British explorer Franklin, who had vanished with his ship and crew in the northern ice-fields. He spent two winters in the arctic zone, encountering with his comrades the utmost of hardship and danger that men can endure, beset by darkness, cold, scurvy and rats and the perils of lockjaw and floating ice, subsisting on blubber and the beef of walrus and bear. Obliged at last to abandon their brig, the party escaped on sledges, having found what they thought was an open polar sea, and Dr. Kane's record of these adventures, describing their daily arctic life, revealed a world that was all but unknown and new. It abounded in pictures of Eskimo customs, seal-stalking and walrus-hunts, and Dr. Kane sketched landscapes that Dante might have conjured up, so mysterious, so inorganic and so desolate they were. They appeared to have been left unfinished when the earth was formed. The moonlight painted on the snow-fields fantastic profiles of crags and spires, and the firmament seemed to be close overhead with the stars magnified in glory in the awful frozen silence of the arctic night. One felt amid these night-scenes as if the life of the planet were suspended, its companionships and its colours, its movements and sounds.

Readers who still delighted in Byron were entranced by Dr. Kane's descriptions of these "icy halls of cold sublimity." Two of them were young men, Samuel Clemens and Bret Harte, who were both in California when the book was published.[10] Meanwhile, three friends of Bayard Taylor, born like him in the early twenties, were known already as writers in 1850, George Henry Boker, the poet and playwright, Charles Godfrey Leland and the painter-poet Thomas Buchanan Read. Boker's poetic play *Calaynos,* performed in London in 1849, had run with applause for more than a hundred nights, while Read's first poems, published in 1847, were highly praised by Rossetti and some of his friends. Rossetti subscribed to the newspaper in which Read's poems appeared at home and cut out and pasted up a large album full of them, though a generation later they seemed sufficiently pallid and tame and were lost

---

[10] Thoreau remarked, when he returned *Arctic Explorations* to a friend, that "most of the phenomena therein recorded are to be observed about Concord."

One of the Fox sisters, the "spiritualists,"—Margaret,—was the heroine of a curious story related in *The Love-Life of Dr. Kane* (1856). When, at the age of thirteen, she was appearing in Philadelphia a few years after the "Rochester knockings," Elisha Kent Kane fell in love with her and resolved to reëducate her first and marry her later. Piqued by the "strange mixture in her of child and woman, simplicity and cunning, of passionate impulse and extreme self-control,"—while he shrank from her associates and her "obscure and ambiguous profession,"—he detached her from her family and placed her in care of his aunt with a governess, a library and a piano in a house in the country. As his family violently opposed his marriage with this humble inferior, as they thought her, and he himself feared the ridicule of the fashionable world, he maintained the utmost secrecy about the relation, although he constantly sent her presents of laces, jewels, bracelets and books and carried on his polar wanderings her portrait by Fagnani. For his sake Margaret abjured the "spirits," though she slipped back again and again into the heady excitement of the seances. The claim was made on her behalf that before his early death Dr. Kane formed a common-law marriage with her. The story suggested in certain ways Henry James's *Watch and Ward* and the relation in *The Bostonians* between Verena Tarrant and her lover.

in the enormous ocean of Victorian verse. Read never lingered in Philadelphia, where he spent an occasional year or so, after walking to Cincinnati at seventeen, roaming Ohio as a portrait-painter, painting his way East again and living for many years in Rome and Florence. In England he painted portraits of Thackeray and Browning, but if he was remembered later it was mainly for the poem *Sheridan's Ride,* the record of a stirring incident of the Civil War. He was a major on the staff of General Lew Wallace. Boker, a young man of wealth and Leland's inseparable friend,—their fathers, old Philadelphia merchants, were partners,—the "handsomest man in America," as N. P. Willis called him, was the "best reader," Edwin Forrest said. For Boker, an admirer of Fanny Kemble, sometimes gave public readings of plays. He had been the best boxer and fencer at Princeton, where he and Leland studied together, as they had learned the fables of Æsop from the Queen Anne tiles of the parlour mantel in the "Dolly Madison house" where Leland was born. A "natural exquisite and arbiter elegantiarum," as Leland remarked, Boker was a serious writer, a poet of a higher type than Read and one whose plays were the earliest in America with a value as literature, as poetry, as well as of the stage. They were performed at intervals through the fifties and sixties, and *Francesca da Rimini,* for one, had a long life. Produced in 1855, it was revived with great success in 1882 by Lawrence Barrett and again by Otis Skinner in 1901.[11]

But Bayard Taylor prophesied that the nineteenth century would prove to be an "immense graveyard of poems," and writers of agile informative prose were sometimes much more salvable than even eminent poets

---

[11] Boker is "pretty genuine, after all," Walt Whitman said. He added, referring to *Francesca da Rimini,* "Yes, it is excellent: I have seen it, enjoyed it."—*With Walt Whitman in Camden.*

when their vogue had passed. For many readers in the
twentieth century Charles Godfrey Leland's books on
the Gypsies were better than all but the best Victorian
verse, and so were Leland's *Memoirs* and even three
or four other books by this most engaging of minor
men of letters. "The rye," well known in the Gypsy
world, who was famous for two generations as a lover of
the marvellous, the forbidden, the droll and the wild,
was one of those people to whom queer things happen,
as Dr. Johnson said, not once a year but every day. He
was drawn naturally to sorcerers and fakirs, wizards,
tinkers, tramps and those who dwell in tents and caravans, and even as a boy in Philadelphia he knew two
Negro witches who practised voodoo among the Eboe
men. Born in 1824, in a circle that remembered Washington's court, he had grown up amid anecdotes of
Priestley, Franklin, Cobbett and Rush and the days
when the city was the second of the British empire.
Bronson Alcott at the Germantown school had encouraged Leland's passion for books, and, happening on
Urquhart's translation of Rabelais, he knew he was
"gifted to understand" this mixture of ribaldry and
learning, wisdom and fun. Later the suggester, father
and founder of the Rabelais Club in London, he delighted in Casanova also, in Joaquim du Bellay, in the
Rosicrucians, the Neo-Platonists and scores of writers on
the occult from Agrippa, as he said, to Zadkiel. By the
time he went to Princeton, where he was a pet of Joseph
Henry, he was deep in *Sartor Resartus* and all things
German, for he shared the new interest in Germany
that was spreading from New England in the forties,
like his fellow-Pennsylvanian Bayard Taylor. Deeper
than ever in German writers at Heidelberg, where he
knew Captain Medwin, who told him many stories
of Shelley and Byron, he studied aesthetics at Munich,
revelling in the life of a German student, youth on the

prow and pleasure at the helm. He felt an incredible enchantment in gazing on a Gothic ruin, walking with his
knapsack down the Rhine, where he knew every village
and old town on the banks, the green mounts and grey
rocks with castles on their crests, the merrymakings of
the peasants harvesting their hay. Wandering over Europe, he fell in with Spanish smugglers, pirates at Marseilles, Gypsies and brigands; then he entered the Sor-
bonne in Paris in 1848 at the moment when the revolution was about to begin. Finding himself in a lodging-
house with students who were plotting it, he was aware
of the date a month in advance when the chief of police
had only three hours' warning, and later he found that
he had known an astonishing number of the chief republicans and had somehow stumbled into their inner
circle. With long hair and student's cap, pistol, dirk,
monocle and sash, he was chosen as a leader in the fighting at the barricades.

At home again in Philadelphia, restless after these
years abroad, unable to forget the past or accept a future in the "pleasant sunny Philistia" where he studied
law, Leland edited a newspaper while he resumed the
writing that he had already begun as a student at
Princeton. He had written a romance in French, which
the publishers in Paris refused, they said, because of its
too great freedom from the moral conventions,—an
event that seldom befell Americans there; but his parents had passed on his letters to the editor of *Godey's
Lady's Book* and he was soon writing for all the magazines. His *Meister Karl's Sketch Book* was a serial in
the *Knickerbocker* in the manner of Washington Irving,
who enjoyed and praised it, while it also recalled the
Reisebilder with which Leland began the translation
of Heine that delighted countless readers in decades to
come. He was popularly known by 1856, when the *Hans
Breitmann Ballads* began to appear. These German-

American dialect poems, mostly written to amuse a friend, the New York writer Charles Astor Bristed, related the adventures of a battered survivor of '48 who had come like so many others to the United States. They pleased a far-off generation that liked Teutonic sentiment and revelled in German philosophy, music and beer. Leland wrote serious poems too, many of which were stories in verse that later appeared in *The Music Lesson of Confucius,* based in several cases on mediæval legends, that suggested Longfellow in their melody and their curious learning.

Leland was a prolific writer. His career continued for two generations in America and in Italy and England, for having inherited ample means he was one of many who preferred to live in Europe after the war. It was in England that he undertook the study of the Gypsies that made him something more than a second Borrow, as later still in Italy, where he knew all the witches in Florence, he became an authority on Tuscan legends and folklore. Detesting aesthetic prigs, he cultivated showmen and acrobats, cheap-jacks, thimbleriggers, knife-throwers and exhibitors of giants, who were seldom without a dash of gypsiness, while he was an all but intimate friend of Joshua Cooper, White George and the "old Windsor Froggie," the English Gypsies. It was the latter, Matty Cooper, who taught him the language of the roads in his camp at the Devil's Dyke, near Brighton, and many and many an hour he spent in Plato Buckland's van or sitting beside Bill Bowers while he made baskets. He knew Mat Woods the Fiddler and Old Moll of the Roads, who pretended to be a Methodist washerwoman but, throwing off her mask, admitted, when he challenged her, that she was a "reg'lar shrewd old female thief." For in their fierce spirit of social exile from the world in which they sojourned, rejoicing in their secret language and private superstitions, the dwellers in tents and caravans, who lived among the gorse and fern, concealed their true nature and life from the hostile gorgios. But in his long rambles on hedge-lined roads, Leland was familiar with their hidden ways, and he told them their stories and sang them their songs,— and even told fortunes to the Gypsies,—for he knew more than they of the affairs of Egypt. Often, when their elders were away, he made up to the Gypsy children, who were like young foxes in their artful artlessness. Well he knew the field-lairs and the lonely woodpaths where they camped,—and the deep ravines recalling Salvator Rosa,—with their wagons, asses and smouldering fires, the small dark forms of the Gypsy brood, the young men fishing in the streams, the basket-makers. He traced them by the curling blue smoke rising in the distance. It was a charming experience to be asked to buy a terrier in words one found in the Ramayana and the Mahabharata, a full-blown Hindu dialect still spoken in the heart of the Western world, the spray of the primitive Aryan-Indian ocean. Leland was especially drawn to the Gypsies, living as they did like the birds and the hares, under old chestnut trees, in grassy nooks, because they were human links, he felt, that bound one to the natural world and awakened a thousand sympathies with its inner life.

In his pursuit of the lore of the Gypsies, Leland followed them to Belgium and France. He found traces of them even in Egypt. He visited St. Petersburg and Moscow to see the musical Gypsies there, reading the hands of the pantherine girls, who had never seen a rye like him, and singing them songs of their kindred in distant lands. In England they were vanishing as rapidly as the Indians in North America. There was no spot left for the dwellers in tents in many a day's journey where they could boil their kettles undisturbed, and a real old-fashioned Gypsy would soon be as rare a sight in England as a Sioux or Pawnee warrior in the streets of New York. They were coming to America, their true Canaan, —a "fair land for timber," as one of them said,—where they could roam forever from sunrise to sunset and pick up a living easily in the woods, on the roads. Studying the Gypsies there too, Leland observed the Algonquin Indians, the Micmacs and Penobscots in New Brunswick and Maine, who pitched their tents in summer under the pines along the coast and from whom he gathered a mass of myths and legends. Theirs was the grand mythology that had given heroes, fairies and elves to every rock, river and hill in New England, and Leland, like Schoolcraft before him in the wigwams at Mackinaw, took the tales down directly from the Indians themselves. Living later for years in Florence, where he collected the local legends of the fountains, towers, bridges and palaces of the city,—old wives' tales that were told by the people still,—he assembled quantities of unrecorded lore of the Tuscan countryside round about. He learned the rude form of the Bolognese dialect that was spoken in the Tuscan Romagna, where the old Etruscan gods were still remembered, together with the rural deities of the most ancient Romans, like Heine's gods in exile, for whom rites were still performed, with all manner of secret prayers and invocations.[12] For the peasants clung to the "old religion," which had survived from the earliest times, jealously guarded from the priests and from people of culture, to whom it was as little known as the voodoo sorcerers who were Leland's friends were known to the respectable people of his native town. Retaining their old heathen faith, they still believed in the red-caps and goblins

---

[12] See Hawthorne's *The Marble Faun* and Henry James's story *The Last of the Valerii* in the volume called *A Passionate Pilgrim*.

that haunted rocks, ruined towers, firesides and kitchens, and witchcraft throve among them, with magical remedies, charms and spells, an art preserved in families of witches and wizards. Leland collected the dying coals and the last sparks of this ancient fire, the sorcery and the occult rites that were disappearing.

But this was in the future when Leland was a grand old man to whom Gypsies and generals[13] alike told their stories and the veteran author of thirty books produced the charming *Memoirs* that abounded above all in the sense of his own picturesqueness. Those were the days when Leland owned the conjuring-stone of the voodoos that entitled its owner to the rank of a master of witchcraft, and the towering old man in his velveteen coat, with his wide-brimmed hat and flowing white beard, had become one of the living sights of Florence. His pockets were always full of amulets and charms and fetishes in little red bags, and Negroes had been known to travel a thousand miles or more merely to hold the conjuring-stone in their hands. Leland, who had grown to look like Borrow, fresh at eighty and hearty still, full of Gypsy craft and merry tricks, busied himself restoring madonnas, carving panels, binding books and working in gesso, mosaic, leather and brass. He kept up his study not only of Romany but of Pidgin-English, Icelandic, Provençal, and made some headway even with Illyrian and Serb. As a writer on the Gypsies, on the Negroes, on peasants, so much of whose lore he collected, he was sometimes condemned as inaccurate, with truth perhaps. For how could one always be accurate, working with primitive people, feeling one's way as it were through a

[13] "One of the greatest generals of modern times, Lord Napier of Magdala, told me that he believed I was the only person to whom he had ever fully narrated his experiences of the Siege of Lucknow. He seemed to be surprised at having so forgotten himself."—Leland, *Memoirs*.

jungle or a cane-brake, groping blindly in the dark from one conjecture to another, stumbling into mares' nests, dealing with evasive minds? He had the rarest feeling for whatever was odd in letters and life and a gusto that was all but unique among collectors of folklore.[14]

[14] See Leland's books, *The Gypsies, The English Gypsies, The Algonquin Legends, Legends of Florence, Etruscan Roman Remains in Popular Tradition.*

CHAPTER III

THE SOUTH

IT WAS in Philadelphia that Leland first studied the lore of the Negroes. The town abounded in Southern traits, in the so-called Southern atmosphere and in family ties and other connections with the South. The medical schools had been thronged with students from Georgia, Virginia and the Carolinas, while some of the writers maintained relations of a special warmth and sympathy with the novelists and poets of the South. George Boker was a constant correspondent of Simms and Paul Hamilton Hayne, and Bayard Taylor, a friend of them all, introduced Sidney Lanier, after the Civil War, to the world of letters. Besides, Philadelphia was the port whence the great stream of Scotch-Irish settlers had spread through Pennsylvania to the West and the South, flowing down the Valley of Virginia and covering the clefts and mountain slopes with red-brick dwellings, hamlets, spires and manses. Most of the new Southern leaders were of Scotch-Irish descent, Calhoun, Toombs, Alexander Stephens, Jefferson Davis, and theirs was the stock of "Stonewall" Jackson, who was living and teaching at Lexington, where the blue limestone streets looked hard and grim. So, at least, thought John S. Wise when he rode over from Richmond to call on the Presbyterian girls who lived there. He never forgot their vault-like parlours, the horsehair sofas, the drawn curtains, the engravings of Oliver Cromwell and the Rock of Ages. It was all as chilly as a dog's nose, formal, dark and stiff and very unlike the Virginia in which he was at home.

There was much else, to be sure, in the valley, where
the novelist John Esten Cooke was born,—he still returned to spend his summers there,—much that was
warm and expansive too, Virginians of the convivial
sort, sportsmen, lovers of scenery, lovers of horses. This
was the region that Governor Spotswood explored in
the days of the first King George when he founded his
well-known order of the Golden Horse Shoe, and Cooke
had gathered in his boyhood there from the country
people and village folk many of the stories that appeared in his romances. The valley, with its green floor,
teemed with historical memories, as thick as the blossoming locusts and the blue-grass verdure, the oaks and the
climbing red roses in the quiet gardens, but the suggestion of coldness and grimness that John Wise found in
Lexington was also a part of the atmosphere, especially
at the moment. While, generally, the Southern way of
living was genial, elastic and hearty still, an icy wind
blew over the mind of the South, which had grown singularly narrow and bleak in many a notable case as compared with its warmth and breadth in earlier times. It
had lost its universality and the spaciousness of feeling
that characterized so many of the older statesmen, the
sympathetic amplitude that went with Jeffersonianism,
which the new Southern thinkers derided or ignored.
The day had long since passed when Stephen Girard of
Philadelphia named his ships after Voltaire and other
free-thinkers, and especially in the Southern states people spoke of deists now as they spoke of thieves and murderers. For the evangelical sects were in power,[1] and

---

[1] The South became, so to speak, officially Calvinistic just at the
moment when New England ceased to be so.

The English deist, Jefferson's friend, Dr. Thomas Cooper, the
president of the College of South Carolina, was tried for his
"shameful atheism" and forced to resign in 1833. Similarly President
Horace Holley was deposed at the university (Transylvania at
Lexington, Kentucky) which owed its importance so largely to him.

political heresy-hunters were active in a land where people were constrained in their opinions. The liberal old
Virginians had yielded to the "cotton snobs," the new-
rich cotton planters who reigned over the region and
who were determined to spread their empire through
Cuba, Mexico and Central America, controlling the
government at Washington by acting as a group. With
none of the scruples of the older gentry, they bred slaves
for the market and presently reopened the long-aban-
doned slave trade, directing the policy of editors and
colleges and churches that had formerly opposed the
system, like Calhoun himself. The ministers supported
slavery, citing Scripture for it, professors acclaimed and
extolled it, citing the classics, and more and more boldly
the leaders of thought in the South defended the principle of caste and the law of force.[2] They vindicated the
order of nature in which animals preyed on one another
and the natural propensity of men to grovel or to rule,
and this new Carlylean point of view,—for the vogue of
Carlyle was widespread in the South,[3]—was peremptorily
enforced by law or controlled opinion.[4]

It was true that the older type of mind, spacious and
humane, survived and even flourished here and there, in
the most intolerant regions, moreover, or those where

[2] E.g., Thomas R. Dew, William Harper and George Fitzhugh,
whose writings suggested at many points the later apologetics of
Nazism and Fascism in Europe.

[3] The Carlyle admired by these Southern thinkers was the author
of *Cromwell* and *Frederick the Great*. It was mainly the author of
Sartor Resartus who was admired in New England.

[4] Among hundreds of instances that might be cited, there was a
Maryland law against the publishing of any book with a tendency
to excite discontent among people of colour. This made it impossible for H. R. Helper to publish in Baltimore *The Impending
Crisis of the South*. The somewhat intemperate Helper exclaimed:
"What wonder is it that there is no native literature in the South?
. . . Slaveholders are too lazy and ignorant to write it, and the non-
slaveholders—even the few whose minds are cultivated at all—are
not permitted to make the attempt."

the new thought most prevailed, Calhoun's South Carolina and Mississippi. There was no living American who
was more truly a citizen of the world, in the old Jeffersonian way, than Joel R. Poinsett, the Charleston friend
of Petigru and William J. Grayson, the poet, who were
also opposed to the sectionalism of the adored Calhoun.[5]
This first American minister to Mexico, whence he had
brought back the Christmas flower and plant that bore
his name, retained the universal mind, with the courtier's manner and the versatile charm, of the days before
cotton filled the horizon of the South. In years of travel
in his youth he had visited Madame de Staël, studied at
Edinburgh, lived for a while in Russia, and in 1811 President Madison had sent him to Chile and Argentina to
cultivate friendly relations with these embryo republics.
As one of the Americans, like Madison and Clay, for
whom their country was ordained to establish an order
superior to that of the old world, he encouraged the
liberals in these insurgent colonies of Spain on this first
of the inter-American "good will" missions. Then Poinsett, as secretary of war, furthered the exploration of the
West, enabling the Charlestonian Frémont to show what
he was made of, while he appointed Charles Wilkes to
command the South Sea expedition[6] and tried to secure
George Catlin's pictures for the nation. A naturalist and
an antiquarian, always a patron of learning and art, he
had helped Prescott in his work on the Mexican conquest, preserved examples of the Indian crafts, rescued
Peruvian manuscripts and made a collection of ancient
Mexican sculpture. Still later, on the Pedee river, he had

[5] Both Calhoun and Poinsett were pupils of Timothy Dwight in
Connecticut, Poinsett at the Greenfield Hill Academy, Calhoun at
Yale.

[6] Mark Twain said in his *Autobiography* that when he was a boy
on the Mississippi the name of Charles Wilkes the explorer was as
famous as Theodore Roosevelt's later. He was regarded as another
Columbus who had discovered another world. See Wilkes's *Narrative* of his expedition, 6 vols., 1845.

experimented with grapes and rice, assembling countless specimens of trees and shrubs from all over the
world in the park that surrounded his plantation-house.
Benjamin L. C. Wailes of Natchez, the Mississippi
planter, showed some of this Jeffersonian breadth of
mind, although Wailes's interests were those of a naturalist mainly whose father had been one of Audubon's
hosts and friends. He studied the aboriginal mounds,[7]
collected fish for Agassiz and reptiles, eggs and shells
for the Smithsonian Institution, assisted Joseph Leidy
in his work on prehistoric life and arranged and conducted an important museum of his own.

No doubt there were many Southerners still of this
old and delightful classic type like Wailes of Mississippi
and Poinsett of South Carolina, the states that were
leading the others in the movement for secession, but
certainly the new public men had none of their universality and even Calhoun seemed bigoted and insular beside them. The leaders of the "cotton kingdom" knew
little of the world outside, and they looked towards Europe chiefly for aid, towards the West merely to extend
their power, towards Latin America only as a field of
conquest. Too self-absorbed for curiosity, narrow, legal-
istic, with scarcely a trace of the older disinterested mind,
they studied antiquity in the main for the purpose of
bolstering their own regime and looked to the future
for an endless repetition of the present. They took John
Randolph as their model, the enemy of Jefferson, who
resented the democratic changes that his kinsman had
wrought and who wished to revive primogeniture and
entail, while he clung to the past, contemned the West

[7] *Ancient Monuments of the Mississippi Valley*, 1848, by E. G.
Squier, was the first publication of the Smithsonian Institution. It
was a full and accurate account of the work of the mound-builders
with many admirable illustrations. Later Squier became the leading American authority on the ethnology and archæology of Central
America.

and reverted to an out-worn colonialism in matters of culture.

Survivors of the old school were apt to look down on the new politicians, regarding them as partisans rather than statesmen, yet they represented the mind of the region, as the cotton-power had formed it, better perhaps than the novelists and men of letters. Where the mails were closed to dissentient books and agents were punished for selling them, the writers were "tonguetied by authority," at least in a measure,[8] and they very seldom rose above the conventional grooves of thought and feeling, while the statesmen, who shared none of their doubts, were bold and frank. The writers, moreover, were not highly esteemed; in fact, they were scarcely respected at all; they were commonly treated with "contumely and a thinly veiled contempt," as Paul Hamilton Hayne observed in a letter. This attitude had never changed since the days when Ralph Izard of South Carolina had been sent as minister to Tuscany in the seventeen-nineties. Finding himself in Paris one evening at Benjamin Franklin's house, in the company of Buffon, Turgot, Condorcet and D'Alembert, he asked, "Why couldn't we have some of the *gentlemen* of France?" Three quarters of a century later, Mrs. Chesnut in her *Diary from Dixie* referred to writers generally as "literary fellows," and the scorn and neglect they had to endure, their "discouragements," [9] their "embarrass-

---

[8] "The Southern Thackeray of the future will doubtless be surprised to learn that if he had put in an appearance half a century sooner he would probably have been escorted beyond the limits and boundaries of our Southern clime astraddle of a rail. Thackeray satirized the society in which he moved and held up to ridicule the hollow hypocrisy of his neighbours. He took liberties with the people of his own blood and time that would have led him hurriedly in the direction of bodily discomfort if he had lived in the South." —Joel Chandler Harris, editorial in the Atlanta *Constitution*, 1879.

[9] Paul Hamilton Hayne. "But ah! sir, to a young literary aspirant, it is very hard to know that his *very profession* is looked upon with

ments," [10] were a constant burden of comment in their
essays and their letters. They were driven to complain
of their isolation, the uncongeniality of the atmosphere,
the limited audience at best which the South afforded,
conditions that obliged them to publish their work in
the North or abroad if they wished it to receive the least
attention. The thinkers of the "cotton kingdom" con-
templated a great society where art, philosophy and literature were to rise and thrive, while actually the system they sustained still further blighted a literary mind
that had scarcely as yet begun to develop in the South.
They did not correct the disesteem in which writers had
always been held in a region where Hugh Legaré lamented that the literary fame of his earlier days had
hampered his professional advancement and local recognition. It mortified Henry Timrod, the poet, to compare
the standing of the Northern writers with the stolid indifference of the Southerners towards their own, while
Hayne expressed to Lowell the sadness that he felt when
he thought of the literary society of his friends in Boston.[11]

---

contempt, or, at best, a sort of half-pitying patronage by those he
would fain delight and satisfy."—Letter to James Russell Lowell.
"These Southern communities, intelligent in other respects, actually
look down upon the *Litterateur*, with a species of scorn, as a half
crazed enthusiast, having no firm, wholesome root in the soil of
social existence."—To Moses Coit Tyler.

[10] Henry Timrod. "In no country in which literature has ever
flourished has an author obtained so limited an audience . . . It
would scarcely be too extravagant to entitle the Southern author
the Pariah of modern literature . . . Not once, but a hundred
times, we have heard the works of the first of Southern authors
(Simms) alluded to with contempt by individuals who had never
read anything beyond the title-pages of his books."—*Literature in
the South.*

[11] "It is *too* true that to any earnest literary mind the society of
the South *is* uncongenial.

"You will not deem me unpatriotic, or false to my people and
section, in making *such* a confession. But often,—how often!—I
think of the dear friends I have in Boston, and contrasting the
society *there*, and the society in Charleston (I mean of the literary

Few and depressed as the writers were,—at least, as they were apt to be whenever they cherished serious aspirations,—they shared John Randolph's tendencies in retiring from national to sectional concerns, in clinging to the past, in reclaiming the heritage of England. At the moment when literature in the North was making its independence good in the name of an autonomous America with a genius of its own, the Southern writers, disconnected from this larger movement of the national mind, resumed their ancestral feeling for the mother-country. They remembered that Shakespeare was inspired to write *The Tempest* by a romantic event in the history of the Dominion, and it pleased the "first families" to give their places English names like Stonehenge and to think of the English pimpernel growing in their soil. More than ever the writers dwelt on the cavaliers of colonial times, who appeared in John Esten Cooke's novels, in the train of Caruthers, and they delighted in recalling that the Old Dominion was the oldest community of Englishmen outside England. In their dream of "Southern books written by Southern gentlemen," they repudiated the potent influence of the New England writers, seizing on Poe's remarks discrediting them, although Simms broke only at the last his lifelong friendship with Bryant's circle and Hayne was devoted to Emerson, Whittier and Lowell. The Northern writers were too often tainted with a dangerous anti-slavery feeling. Just so Southerners more and more withdrew from the Northern colleges and schools, to the vast numerical advantage of the colleges of the South, and they travelled at home rather than abroad, rambling through western Virginia, summering in the mountains, visiting the caverns and the springs. They felt a sort of obligation to show the world outside the graces and

---

kind), it is impossible for me to feel otherwise than sad."—Letter to Lowell.

beauties of the Southland and its picturesqueness, a motive that General Strother shared in his charming *Virginia Illustrated,* the book for which he assumed the name Porte Crayon. He related in this the engaging story of the belle of Cacapon valley, the true Virginia girl Sally Jones, who refused to follow her father west when he sold his fertile ancestral farm and set out for the Rockies, the Pacific, the Columbia river. She offered herself to any young man who had the spunk to ask her to stay, and Porte Crayon did not fail to remark that if all the girls were like Sally Jones the prosperity of the Old Dominion would be permanent and solid. Meanwhile, the new plantation literature, as it was called in later days, became a political instrument of the cotton regime, an apology for it that was also a glorification, and the critical attitude itself was felt to be disloyal after *Uncle Tom's Cabin* appeared in 1852.[12] Many writers rose at once to give the lie to Mrs. Stowe and to prove that the Southern system was both lovable and just, and scores of "domestic romances" appeared, creating a picture of the South that lingered on for decades and became a legend. They were tales of palatial planta-tion-houses where all the men were cavaliers and the women were all exquisite heroines, tender and true, where the slaves were invariably devoted and happy and visiting Yankees were abashed and amazed by a culture that had never been heard of in benighted New Eng-land.

[12] The editor of the *Southern Literary Messenger* wrote as follows to the reviewer of this book: "I would have the review as hot as hell-fire, blasting and searing the reputation of the vile wretch in petticoats who could write such a volume."
The obsession of slavery completely dominated the critical mind. For another instance, Webster's Dictionary was ostracized in Ten-nessee because of its definition of a slave as "a person subject to the will of another, a drudge."—See F. G. Davenport, *Cultural Life in Nashville, 1825-1860.*

This rapturous vision of the Southern romancers was destined to survive the Civil War,—in which flags were commonly described as oriflammes,—and it sprang partly from the need of defending the South in the face of a world that was hostile to Southern institutions. It was true too that the new-rich planters wished the writers to create a noble Southern past that enhanced their prestige. Yet this was only half the story,—there were other elements behind the vision,—it conventionalized much that was actual, authentic, true. The convention was largely shaped by Scott, whom Southerners especially idolized,[13] and other historians and romancers of the feudal world,—Froissart, for one, a favourite of the Southern writers,[14]—and it gained its power not merely because it expressed an ideal of the South but because it corresponded in a fashion with the realities of life there. Ancient ways survived there, vestigial remains of earlier times, and in many respects the region was still

[13] "I have heard from my father, a pioneer of Kentucky, that in the early days of this century men would saddle their horses and ride from all the neighbouring counties to the principal post-town of the region when a new novel by the author of 'Waverley' was expected."—John Hay, Address, 1897, at the unveiling of the bust of Scott in Westminster Abbey.

Sidney Lanier's grandfather named four of his five sons after characters in the novels of Sir Walter Scott.

Frederick Douglass adopted this surname at the suggestion of a friend who had been reading The Lady of the Lake and thought Douglas was a name of great romantic meaning.

The presence of the English novelist G. P. R. James, a disciple of Scott, as consul at Richmond and Norfolk, is sometimes supposed to have strengthened the cult of the romancer.

In the late seventies, Ellen Glasgow learned to read, she later said, by "picking the letters out of Scott's novels."

[14] John Esten Cooke's earlier work was largely suggested by Froissart, before his mind was focussed on Virginian subjects. The only published book of his brother, Philip Pendleton Cooke, partly based on Froissart, was called Froissart Ballads.

Sidney Lanier later wrote a Boys' Froissart and Paul Hamilton Hayne also wrote a simplified Froissart for children.

genuinely feudal, while, as Thackeray observed when he
visited Richmond in 1856,[15] the Virginians were more
like the English than Americans elsewhere. They had remained more like the English because their life had
changed less and because their American nationality had
never been very real to them as compared with their
allegiance and devotion to the region, to the state. The
Revolution, for the South, had been much more political than social and had left the old order largely as it
was before, while the Industrial Revolution that severed the link with the feudal past had touched the South
even less, far less, than England. The gentry in the older
states had carried on without a break immemorial customs that had long since vanished elsewhere, and tournaments were held as annual events in Maryland, Virginia and South Carolina in spite of the disapprobation
of the killjoy preachers.[16] Young men tilted on dec-
orated steeds and the Queen of Love and Beauty, surrounded by her maids of honour, crowned the victor,
a relic of the antique fairs that vanished [17] as the rising
puritanism more and more steadily blighted the gaieties
of old. Fox-hunting remained a pastime not of the fashionable few alone but of many a simple old country

[15] When John Esten Cooke interviewed him. Thackeray was at
that time planning to write *The Virginians* and made some studies
for the background of this novel.

[16] Similar survivals in Brazil are described in *Rebellion in the
Backlands (Os Sertões)* by Euclides da Cunha. Festivals and caval-
cades, wholly forgotten in Portugal, were preserved for three centuries in all their details in the backland settlements. One of these
was the Camisado, adhering to the most remote traditions, representing nocturnal assaults and ancient sallies against Moorish
castles. They were staged by the light of lanterns and grass torches
with long processions of men on foot clad in white. Others wore
Musselman garb, while still others were on horseback dressed in
weird animal disguises. Their skirmishes and mock encounters were
the greatest delight of the backwoods people.

[17] From the foreground of society. In the most primitive rustic
form, tournaments were still to be seen as late as 1936 in Maryland,
at least.

doctor also, who was passionately fond of the chase and kept his own hounds, while men of spirit followed the *code duello,* in perfect good faith, well into the seventies and beyond. Certain of these customs were revived artificially in later days and much of the mediævalism was factitious in the fifties, worked up to lend an air to the new regime, as the so-called domestic romances showed only the amenities of Southern life, dissembling or glossing whatever was unjust or unpleasant. But the feudal note in these romances existed here and there in fact, and Scott was really closer to this old plantation world than writers who spoke for the nineteenth century elsewhere. When the Southern ruling class called itself "the chivalry," it challenged the wit of others who were less self-immersed, though Southerners were generally cavaliers in the most primitive sense, at least,—they spent much of their lives on horseback, always armed. And as for their dream of chivalrous times, one saw how genuine it could be when Sidney Lanier set out for the Civil War, a Georgian who had been brought up on Scott and Froissart in his father's house and thought of himself as a knight who was also a minstrel. He saw in himself, in all sincerity, a troubadour wandering about the world, with a lute and the ribbon of his lady-love slung on his back. The fact that the lute was a flute did not alter the vision.

These actual Southern states of mind and these customs and modes of behaviour, together with the singular characters who expressed and upheld them, appeared occasionally in the books of the time, enough to excite one's regret that literature so failed to do justice to life in the South. What would not readers in later days have given for a genius of the fifties, a Virginian Turgenev, a Gogol of South Carolina, who could have amplified the glimpses that actual writers conveyed of the picturesque, noble or fantastic people of the South. What made many of these characters so striking was that they lived in a timeless world, a society that was little touched by modern conditions, so that they embodied traits of the eighteenth, seventeenth, sixteenth centuries, either wholly unaltered or so altered as to be still more striking. There was William Walker, for one example, the filibuster from Tennessee, a well-trained surgeon who had studied medicine in Paris, in whom all the accretions of the modern man merely threw into bolder relief a character that properly belonged in Elizabethan times. Half-consciously an agent of the cotton kingdom that aspired to be an empire, this latter-day Cortes had much of the original in him, and Sam Houston had still more of the ancient swashbuckler in a composition that savoured, like so many others, of the militant South. Knight-errantry and quixotism throve on every hand there, ideals of the moment were mingled with ideals of the past, and men could be taken for practical leaders who ignored in their dream of romance the most essential elements in the situation. Robert Barnwell Rhett, for instance, was wholly oblivious of economics when he strove to make South Carolina an independent nation: he proposed to liberate it as Perseus freed Andromeda, and he thought of this purely in terms of knightly prowess. The romantic type of the soldier of fortune existed in the North, of course, in stirring figures like Samuel Gridley Howe, the champion of the Greek revolution and later of the Poles, but it seemed more congruous with the South when James J. Pettigrew, the Charleston lawyer, fought for the "sacred liberty" of the Italians. For the Southerners were generally less given to counting costs. It was part of their code to think of life as something to be "put in risk," as Shaler[18] said,

[18] Nathaniel Southgate Shaler. For two generations of Harvard men the geologist Shaler was a living example of all that was most admirable and winning in the older South. William James said in a letter that of all the minds he had known Shaler's had left upon him the "largest impression." It was characteristic of his point of

"in the pursuit of manly ideals," and this explained the violence of the South, and some of its courtliness too, survivals of the seventeenth century or the Middle Ages. By no means defending this violence,[19] the Kentuckian Shaler pointed out how much that was obviously admirable lay behind it, how much could be said for a view of life as something to be recklessly cast away for honour, for a generous impulse or the merest whim. This careless irresponsible indifference to life had characterized the greatest ages, which had given more nobility and ability to history than others, and one might have said that the burden of proof lay rather on the modern concern for continued mundane existence at any price. Sometimes blackguardly, often rowdy, especially along the frontier,[20] where it merged with the border ruffianism of the unsettled regions, this headiness and touchiness was a genuine survival of the chivalrous life that appeared in a variety of types all over the South. Many different points

---

view that towards the end of his life he wrote a poem in five volumes called *Elizabeth of England*. This celebrated a world and time in which, like others in the South, Shaler felt that he would have been at home.

[19] It is recorded that five editors of the Vicksburg *Journal* were killed in duels within thirteen years. The editor of the Lynchburg *Virginian* was killed in an impromptu duel in front of the market-house in 1851. When Dr. George Bagby alluded to this in his satire *The Virginia Editor* he was challenged at once to a duel by a reader who thought the satire was directed at him.

In his *Autobiography*, Shaler, discussing the "fighting propensities" of his native Kentucky, observed that more than thirty of his kindred and friends were killed in "street-fights" after the regulated practice of duelling was abolished.

Colonel E. M. House, in his *Intimate Papers* (I, 25), relating his childhood in Texas, connected the Southern courtesy with the violence of the South: "In Texas . . . no words were wasted. Frequently the first symptom of mild disapproval would be a blow or a revolver shot. People praised us Southerners for our courteous demeanor. We learned it in the school of necessity."

[20] Where Mark Twain found "Tennessee journalism . . . too stirring" for him. This was when he, or the narrator of the sketch, had been so "freckled with bullet-holes" that his skin would not hold his "principles" any longer.

of view had chivalrous defenders there, and the deadliest of all the foes of slavery was also a Southerner born and bred, the first candidate of the new Republican party. Frémont in 1856 brought to the abolitionist cause the ardour with which others championed the Southern system. He fought for the freedom of the Negroes as he would have fought for Jerusalem if he had lived in the days of the Crusaders.

Bizarre or noble, these provocative types[21] seldom appeared on the printed page, not merely because there was no one with the genius to describe them. It did not interest Southerners to read about themselves or people they knew and encountered in their ordinary living, and this alone was enough to discourage the writers. There were many readers like Mrs. Lightfoot in Ellen Glasgow's *The Battle-Ground* who detested Dickens's common chimney-sweeps,[22] while, weeping as they did over *Thaddeus of Warsaw,* they would scarcely have preferred realistic pictures of people they admired and respected. Indifferent as they generally were to psychological observation, they were not given to analysis or the discussion of motives, and nothing could have bored them more than to read about the life they were living

[21] One of the noble was Leonidas Polk, the general who was bishop of Louisiana and who "buckled the sword over the gown," as he said. One of the bizarre was John Wilkes Booth, who assassinated Lincoln and for whom nothing was real but the unreal, the theatrical and romantic. Apparently for Booth the world was a stage on which men were acting, not living, their parts, and he was, as Joel Chandler Harris said, "as much a creature of fiction as you find in books."

[22] "None of your new-fangled writers for me, my dear. Why, they haven't enough sentiment to give their hero a title,—and an untitled hero! I declare, I'd as lief have a plain heroine, and, before you know it, they'll be writing their Sukey Sues, with pug noses, who eloped with their Bill Bates, from the nearest butcher shop! I opened one of Mr. Dickens's stories the other day and it was actually about a chimney-sweep,—a common chimney-sweep from a workhouse! Why, I really felt as if I had been keeping low society."—Mrs. Lightfoot, in *The Battle-Ground.*

with such cheerful insouciance every day. In books they looked for something else, for something far away from home that left the placid flow of their minds unruffled, something that savoured of the past, of England, of a stable unchanging social scene that was undisturbed by new ideas or "progress."

It was related that John M. Daniel, the best-known Richmond editor, had a "sovereign contempt for the so-called 'literature of the day,'" and in this he reflected the general feeling of a world in which letters to the press were still universally signed "Vox Populi" and "Scrutator." The Charleston Library, piled to the ceiling with venerable works in morocco and calf, contained, as the librarian said, "but few new books," and the quaint little "neighbourhood libraries" in the country, established for the families of the planters, were seldom invaded by nineteenth-century authors. Only a few old French books were mingled with the dust that covered the fine editions of the English classics; and this was true also in private houses where men who still wore ruffles and wigs read Addison aloud in the evening while the ladies embroidered. They discussed the question whether Fanny Burney, undoubtedly the greatest, was not also the last female novelist who would probably appear,—for who was there since her day worthy to hold a descriptive pen and what had been written since that was worth one's reading? Old gentlemen recited Swift with the zest of a schoolboy, or perhaps two hundred lines from *The Rape of the Lock,* quoting Spence's anecdotes, the maxims of La Rochefoucauld and the letters of Madame de Sévigné and the witty Walpole. They questioned their nephews and grandsons, who had returned from the grand tour, about Westminster Abbey, St. Paul's and the London streets. Had they remembered to look up the haunts of Steele and Goldsmith? Was Dr. Johnson's coffee-house still open for guests? Anything more modern than *Bracebridge Hall* or *Swallow Barn* was likely to have too much "nature" in it, which had nothing to do with literature that one called "polite," and men who were faithful to the classic muse continued to model their own lucubrations on the writings of Matthew Prior, Shenstone or Johnson. When the Charleston poet Grayson was asked to mend a lady's quill, he returned it as a matter of course with a copy of verses, and *The Bee* was in Mr. Turner's mind when he established *The Countryman* as late as 1860 on his Georgia plantation. This was the weekly on which Joel Chandler Harris, who was twelve years old that year, learned to set type. In the most enlightened Southern circles Wordsworth was a bone of contention still when that question had been settled in New England for thirty years, and Grayson attacked the "hypocrites" who dared to disparage the poet Pope in the book that he wrote on Petigru in 1863. Timrod was one of these hypocrites, the brightest of the younger Charleston minds, who constantly lamented the "backwardness" of the literary South.[23]

Despite these many handicaps, more books than ever were appearing in the South, for the abolition movement roused its literary consciousness and put the Southern authors on their mettle. Of these books many were merely defensive: others teased the imagination,—unhappily, they could not satisfy it,—with flashes that il-

[23] "The opinions and theories of the last century are still held in reverence. Here Pope is still regarded by many as the most *correct* of English poets, and here Kames, after having been everywhere else removed to the top shelves of libraries, is still thumbed by learned professors and declamatory sophomores . . . Here no one is surprised when some fossil theory of criticism, long buried under the ruins of an exploded school, is dug up, and discussed with infinite gravity by gentlemen who know Pope and Horace by heart, but who have never read a word of Wordsworth or Tennyson, or who have read them with suspicion, and rejected them with superciliousness."—Timrod, *Literature in the South*.

lumined the scene and the people at moments. In
Miss Wormeley's novel *Our Cousin Veronica* one caught
delightful glimpses of certain of the "visiting Virginians" and their drawing-rooms and houses, Clairmont
and the seat of Governor Tyrell, the courtly old survivor, in his feelings, tastes and habits, of Jefferson's
times. Who could forget the dinner-party, with the governor himself as the Lord of Misrule, that so surprised
the decorous English cousin, at which there were twenty-
eight chairs for thirty-five guests, for the host was "too
genuine a Virginian" to count them in advance. What
most amused the alien observer was the total change
from foreign ways, the absence of city airs and modern
conventions, the jokes, the merriment unconfined, the
guests that foraged for themselves while a crowd of
Negroes scrambled round the table. Everything was at
sixes and sevens, with the small darkies dodging about,
while over all the gaiety and humour that recalled a
mediæval feast the distinguished old governor presided
with stately grace. The drawing-room at Clairmont was
littered with oboes and flageolets, flutes, fiddles and
guitars that all the cousins played, too busy and happy
with picnics and cards, horses, dogs, hunting and talk to
bother their heads with books or the writing of letters.[24]
There was always a place at the breakfast-table for the

[24] " 'Cousin Tyrell,' said I, 'doesn't anybody read books in Virginia?
I have seen nothing since I came newer than Johnson's Lives of
the Poets, and a torn copy of Rienzi. As to correspondence, I asked
Mr. Morrison for a pen, and he went out into the yard and pulled
me one of a goose's tail feathers, which did not profit me, as it
turned out, for Phil had been blacking his boots with the ink, and
had not left a drop in the bottle.'
"Tyrell laughed. 'I was once in a valley about sixty miles from
here, high up in the mountains, with a friend who wanted to write
a letter to his wife in Baltimore. He put a Negro on a horse and
sent him round the country to borrow a sheet of writing paper.
The man was gone all day and returned at nightfall with no better
'raise' than the fly-leaf from the Bible of a Methodist farmer.' "—
Mary Wormeley, *Our Cousin Veronica*.

kindly old tailor Mr. Felix, who passed from house to house in summer and winter cutting out clothes for the Negroes and who was admitted without apology to any circle at any time in this world where so few existed between the nobles and the serfs.

What would Aksakov not have done with these patriarchal scenes that were so much the same in Russia as they were in the South, true survivals of a feudal world that appeared in *The Two Country Houses,* Philip Pendleton Cooke's skeleton of a novel.[25] This tale of the Hunters of Winisfalen and the Cars of Cotsworth owed something,—the banshee perhaps,—to the author's reading, but the wild young heir, the stable-boys, the generous old magnifico were authentic reflections of the place, the people and the time. So was the splendid hospitality and the mean little family attorney who might have stepped straight out of Hogarth or Sterne. But Cooke, who wrote on scraps of paper that he carried on his hunting trips, stowed in his hat, for gun-wadding, was too casual and careless, too much the spendthrift Southerner to develop the sketch, and most of the books remained unwritten that might have given after times an adequate and veritable picture of the ways of the South. Most memorable of all perhaps, *Memorials of a Southern Planter,* the life of Colonel Dabney of Mississippi, a Virginian who had moved southwestward in 1835, published after the Civil War, remained the classic story of the model country gentleman of the old regime. The narrative was interspersed with letters relating the daily life at Burleigh, the great plantation near Vicksburg where the children grew up with governesses and music-teachers, Belgian and German, and with Negro "aunts" and "uncles" who were cherished as if they were nearest of kin, while the colonel with fatherly care watched over all. The archetypal "good master," stricter

[25] In the *Southern Literary Messenger,* 1848.

with his children than he was with his servants, a passionate lover of music, affectionate and kind, he was always ready to sign notes for friends who were sometimes
untrustworthy or present a sick pedlar with a horse to
help him on his way. This was the nobly courteous
Dabney, ruined by the war, all too confiding as he was
and as generous as proud, who after he was seventy performed the household laundry-work, for he could not
permit his five daughters to do manual labour.

Meanwhile, a number of Virginia writers, Bagby,
Strother, John Esten Cooke, Philip Pendleton Cooke's
younger brother who continued the Southern tradition
of the historical novel, stirred no doubt in a measure
at least by Northern attacks on Southern pride, wrote
much on the life and scenery of the Old Dominion.
Cooke, a Richmond lawyer,—what Southern writer was
not a lawyer? [26]—produced a long series of Virginian
historical romances, representing first and last a stretch
of more than a hundred years from colonial times to
the Civil War and after. Voluminous and facile,—he
could write in a day a hundred pages,—he turned out
three long novels in a year, and one of these, the best of
all, *The Virginia Comedians,* was a very good book indeed of the romantic type. Another, *Leather-stocking
and Silk,* published somewhat earlier, was a tale of the
Virginia border, suggested by Cooper, and the contrast
of the old forest life in the valley where Cooke had lived
as a child with the new civilization from the East that
pressed upon it. Cooke's father had known old Hunter
John, another Natty Bumppo, who had seen the pines
cut down to make streets for towns, and Cooke had studied the history of his state as William Gilmore Simms
had previously studied the history of South Carolina.
Like Simms, he was interested in all the social classes

[26] "Of course John Sterling studied law—what young man in our
part of the country did not?"—Sidney Lanier, *Tiger Lilies.*

and the conflict of the old world and the new, the clash
of the American and the European, of the fashionable
world and the backwoods, the planters and the homespun folk, the past and the future. But he was charmed
especially by the elegance and colour, the costumes and
manners of the gentry of the old regime before the
harsh winds of the Revolution blew upon it, and he
liked to introduce historical figures, Washington, Fair-
fax, Jefferson, Patrick Henry. The scene of *The Virginia Comedians* was Williamsburg in 1765 when the
first stirrings of revolt were beginning to appear and
men already suspected of treason openly spoke of free
schools, much to the annoyance of the Effinghams of
Effingham Hall. At the Raleigh Tavern, the actor family, the Hallams, lived, comedians playing at the theatre in Gloucester Street, and the tale turned on the ri-
valry for the charming young actress Beatrice Hallam of
two young men who spoke for the old order and the
new. One was a friend of Patrick Henry, the mysterious
"man in the red cloak," the other, Champ Effingham,
had just returned from London, where his tastes had
been shaped in the world of gallantry and wit. All this
offered an excuse for a vivid picture of colonial manners, the fox-hunt, the cock-fight, the races, the state
banquet and ball, the roaring fires and flaming candles
at Christmas in a river-mansion, the meeting of the bur-
gesses, the pageantry of the governor's court.

In later romances of the Civil War and the years before and after it, Cooke followed the history of Virginia
through his own generation, while he edited the *Southern Literary Messenger,* the magazine published at Richmond of which Poe and "Deep-Sea" Maury had been
editors before him. He was known throughout the country,—as Simms of Charleston also was,—unlike "Porte
Crayon" Strother and George W. Bagby, who remarked

that Cooke's eyes were in the back of his head and that he wore rose-coloured glasses and indulged too much in romantic idealization. As for Bagby's own writing, its charm lay in its localism, for this Lynchburg doctor was another Dr. Holmes who said he could never live in a country that had no sumac or brier-patches or under a sky without a buzzard in it. He averred that he was one of the people who would leave paradise any day for another glimpse of Orange Court-house, and his great ambition was to write a record that might endure of all that was distinctive in Virginia character and life. As one who had gone to an "old field" school, he knew the country inside and out, the ancient Virginia types and dwellings and taverns, the sights and sounds of highway and lane, the people one passed on the stage-coach, the Negro on the boot, the leathery smell within. There were farmers on plantation-mares trotting on to court, pedlars with packs, doctors with saddle-bags and leggings, lawyers in stick-gigs, occasionally in single-chairs, the old-fashioned tobacco-wagon with its melancholy horn. Now and again a florid old gentleman cantered by, with a servant guarding his portmanteau jogging behind, and turned off and disappeared on one of the vague little roads through the woods that led to Bellefield, perhaps, or Oaklands or Mount Airy. Dr. Bagby's essays were all compact of these notes and touches, evoking the old Virginia rural scene, the tilted and swaying tobacco-houses, the planter's abode embosomed in trees, the sycamore, resort and dormitory of the "tukky-buzzard," and, best of all, the Kanawha canal on voyages between Lynchburg and Richmond, following the winding valley of the river James. With what excitement, as a boy, he had seen the capital, with the glow of evening on its spires, appearing round a bend, and what perfection of cultivation the great plantations seemed to have when the packet-boat faced the other way. As he bobbed up from the depths of the cabin into which he dived at intervals to devour a few more pages of the alluring Dickens, they rose with ducal splendour from the banks of the canal; but how mournful were the notes of the boat-horn as one drew nigh the locks, so different from the joyous ring of the horn of the stage. The scenery grew more and more captivating as one ascended, lock after lock, into the rock-bound eminences of the western regions. Round about were the laurel brakes, the forests of hemlock and pine, the mountain streams that murmured of deer and trout and the "fine romantic dangerous roads" Porte Crayon followed with his three girl-cousins when they set out in search of the picturesque. These four passed monstrous herds of cattle straggling eastward through the glens, and lonely teamsters advancing at a snail-like pace, while everywhere they found cheerful inns with fires that crackled in parlour and bedroom and incomparable corn-dodgers, venison, bacon and greens. This was the merry autumn tour, with "Little Mice," the coachman, and the roan and the sorrel harnessed to the revarnished carriage, during which Porte Crayon sketched the Springs, the Natural Bridge and Monticello, where woodwork and stucco and brick had fallen to decay. Jefferson's house, like his fame, was tumbling into ruins.

For all these Virginia writers, Charleston remained the centre of the South, a focus of activity and thought, in literary matters, another proof, like Baltimore, that, where cities existed, the Southern mind responded to the stimulus of life there. Among the planters public opinion was hostile to the growth of towns, which Jefferson had called the sinks and sewers of the state, but Charleston had long been a shining exception to the rule of an agricultural world that suffered their existence as unclean necessities merely. It was larger than

any of the Virginia towns[27] and the principal market
for six states, its waterfront bristled with the ships of all
the nations, and just as the political leader of the South,
Calhoun, had kept his town house there, so Charleston
was also the home of the literary leader. For what
Southerner compared with Simms as an ardent professional man of letters, immensely productive, experienced, versatile and able? An all-round writer, novelist,
poet, historian, biographer and playwright, he carried
on the humorous realism of Longstreet and Baldwin,
and many of his pages were still to seem alive and fresh
in later years when other historical romancers were extinguished and forgotten. The principal figure in literary Charleston since Hugh Swinton Legaré died,—in
Boston, at George Ticknor's house, in 1843,—this am-
plest of all the authors of the South was also a planter,
the master of The Woodlands, though the scholarly
older gentry slighted or decried him. With the need that
all great natures feel to be loyal to their own, Simms
clung the more closely to Charleston the more he was
ignored there, and the young men revered him for it,
generous and bold as he was and the friend and helper
of every aspiring writer. They loved him for his "Vi-
king's mien," his leonine bearing and liberal air, his
depth of feeling and flashes of sudden fire, his voice,
"jocund as Falstaff's own," his angers and indignant

[27] "North Carolina's largest city, Wilmington, had a population
in 1850 of 7,264 people, of whom 3,683 were Negroes, Richmond
contained 15,274 whites, but the whole great state of Virginia had
only seven towns with a population above five thousand. Montgomery boasted a population of 6,511 whites, Charleston 20,012
whites and 22,973 blacks. The two largest towns in Mississippi,
Natchez and Vicksburg, had populations of less than three thousand
white people . . . Most of the villages of the South were merely
political and trading centres, the rendezvous for the country people who would flock to town on court-days, talk politics and swap
horses. These meetings of the squires and yeomen farmers at the
court-house took the place of the New England lyceum."—Clement
Eaton, *Freedom of Thought in the Old South.*

pride, his lordly-natured magnanimities.[28] Whether at his plantation-house or at his "Wigwam" in town, they flocked about him for advice and reassurance, and he heartened the desponding and the self-distrustful like Henry Timrod, the shy young poet whose bookbinder-father had been a poet before him. Timrod, a good craftsman, was a more than competent classical scholar who made a complete translation of Catullus in verse. He earned his living as a tutor on various plantations.

It was at one of Simms's suppers that *Russell's Magazine,* the Charleston review of the fifties, was first conceived, with Paul Hamilton Hayne as editor, a nephew of the Senator Hayne to whom Daniel Webster "replied" on a famous occasion. Hayne had grown up in his uncle's house, a schoolmate of Timrod and of Basil L. Gildersleeve, later renowned as a scholar, who had just returned from Göttingen with a German degree. As for the magazine, it bore the name of the bookseller Russell whose sanctum was a resort of the illuminati. There students, professors and writers met, on the chairs and sofas at the rear of the shop, James L. Petigru among them, the Rabelaisian lawyer,[29] in whose office the youthful Timrod had studied for a while, and the older poet Grayson, the defender of Pope; and there they engaged in lively discussions, which the magazine reflected, of the old school of poetry and the new. For Grayson the essence of poetry lay in the metrical and rhythmical arrangement of the words, for Timrod it lay in the character of the words one used,—the poet should be sensuous and concrete, avoiding abstractions,—a view he developed in one of the essays in *Russell's Magazine*

[28] See Paul Hamilton Hayne's ode to Simms, 1877.
[29] It was Petigru whose epitaph, written by his daughter, commemorated his intransigent Unionism in the Civil War: "In the great Civil War he withstood his People for his country, but his People did homage to the man who held his conscience higher than their praise."

that revealed a vigorous and penetrating critical mind. Timrod disagreed with Poe, whose theories were too narrow for him, not only in regard to the possible length of poems: he pointed out that Poe admired only the mysterious and the beautiful in verse and had small feeling for the terrible and the sublime. Then, while he felt there was a need for a special Southern literature to express peculiarly Southern ideas and feelings, he said it should never be confined to local themes. It was not enough to make all one's trees palmettoes and all one's fields white with cotton, to derive one's thought and imagery from the Southern scene, though certainly, as Timrod proved in his fine ode *The Cotton Boll,* a poet gained much by drawing from local sources.

Timrod hoped to establish in the South a generous and catholic criticism. Meanwhile, he was an abler poet, as Hayne said later, than all his coevals in the South taken as one: all, that is, but Hayne himself, who gathered Timrod's poems together and wrote a memoir of him after the war. The most distinguished Southern poets between Poe's day and Sidney Lanier, both spoke in different ways for the older South, Hayne, more copious and less intense, reflecting its grace and its courtesy, Timrod its martial spirit and latent fire. It was this that made Timrod the "Trumpet of the Confederacy" later.

CHAPTER IV

THE MIDDLE WEST

THERE was no one in all the Western regions with a livelier eye for the shows of things, together with their insides and undersides, than Samuel Clemens, aged fifteen in 1850 and already setting most of the type on his brother's paper at Hannibal, Missouri. He had watched a mesmerist perform and must have seen "world-renowned tragedians" like the "Duke" in *Huckleberry Finn,* and there was little that he missed in the frontier life of a river-town on the densely forested banks of the Mississippi. He had been the leader of a band of boys whose fantasies suggested the Murrell gang of outlaws and the pirate Lafitte and who staked out claims in their island cave and played at digging for gold there when the forty-niners passed through Hannibal on their way to the coast. He witnessed the violence of the frontier and had seen an old man shot in the street and a youthful emigrant stabbed with a bowie-knife, and he had rejoiced in the pleasant fare on the frontier table at his uncle's farm, the wild turkeys and venison, prairie-hens, squirrels and rabbits. He was charmed by the lordly packet-boats that passed Hannibal every day when the Negro draymen shouted "Steamboat a-comin'!" and the village drunkard stirred on the steps, the clerks woke up and the streets came alive with a clatter of trucks and men hurrying to the wharf. He dreamed of being a pilot on one of these boats, the permanent ambition of all the village boys.

In later years Mark Twain made the Mississippi what

Irving had made the Hudson and a great deal more, as much more, in point of fact, as the river of Audubon and Catlin exceeded in grandeur the stream that flowed to New York. Already the Father of Waters had been signalized on a panorama,—"the largest picture ever executed by man,"—a stretch of canvas three miles long, wound on revolving upright cylinders, that had been shown through the country and in England as well. Queen Victoria had seen it and praised it, as she had seen Catlin's show and Barnum's, and in Boston in 1847 special trains were run to accommodate the curious crowds from the rural districts. It was one of those grandiose projects that American painters entertained in the days of "manifest destiny" and the spreading eagle when they longed to live up to the natural wonders of the land,—like Albert Bierstadt's pictures of the Rocky Mountains,—a lifetime's dream of the artist John Banvard, born in New York, brought up in Kentucky, who had first conceived it as a boy sailing on the river. He had spent more than a year in a skiff sketching along the mighty stream, making preliminary drawings of the towns and the bluffs, attacked on one occasion by some of the members of Murrell's gang, the pirates who infested the river as far up as Memphis. Earlier still in 1840 he had turned a flatboat into a gallery and floated down the Wabash exhibiting his pictures, and he finally painted the Mississippi from St. Louis to New Orleans, villages, banks, woods, islands and all. He showed the aborigines harvesting their crops, the shipping, the village activities, the Indian mounds that were scattered in thousands all over the Western regions in the forms of animals and serpents, circles and squares. The river was a multitudinous world and all sorts and conditions of men were found already on the Mississippi steamboats, with their sunny balconies, domed saloons, galleries, passages, bridal chambers and smokestacks cut to look like clusters of plumes. There Mark Twain said in one of his books that he had encountered first or last all the types of human nature one met in biography, history, or fiction.[1] The river was a school for novelists, and Herman Melville, in *The Confidence-Man*, describing the population of one of these steamboats, called it "a piebald parliament, an Anacharsis Cloots congress of all kinds of that multiform pilgrim species, man."[2] On the "Fidèle," as he styled this boat,—it might have been the "Walter Scott" or the "Waverley" or the "Lalla Rookh," which were actual names,—he placed a pedlar, hawking pamphlets, among them a life of the pirate Murrell, and one of the herb-doctors Mark Twain was also to describe.

For the books that Mark Twain was to write were full of the frontier life of this time, fuller perhaps than

[1] "In that brief, sharp schooling [as a pilot], I got personally and familiarly acquainted with about all the different types of human nature that are to be found in fiction, biography and history . . . When I find a well-drawn character in fiction or biography I generally take a warm personal interest in him, for the reason that I have known him before,—met him on the river."—Mark Twain, *Life on the Mississippi.*

[2] "As among Chaucer's Canterbury pilgrims, or those Oriental ones crossing the Red Sea towards Mecca in the festival month, there was no lack of variety. Natives of all sorts, and foreigners; men of business and men of pleasure; parlour men and backwoodsmen; farm-hunters and fame-hunters; heiress-hunters, gold-hunters, buffalo-hunters, bee-hunters, happiness-hunters, truth-hunters, and still keener hunters after all these hunters. Fine ladies in slippers, and moccasined squaws; Northern speculators and Eastern philosophers; English, Irish, German, Scotch, Danes; Santa Fé traders in striped blankets, and Broadway bucks in cravats of cloth of gold; fine-looking Kentucky boatmen, and Japanese-looking Mississippi cotton-planters; Quakers in full drab, and United States soldiers in full regimentals; slaves, black, mulatto, quadroon; modish young Spanish Creoles, and old-fashioned French Jews; Mormons and Papists; Dives and Lazarus; jesters and mourners, teetotallers and convivialists, deacons and blacklegs; hard-shell Baptists and clay-eaters; grinning Negroes, and Sioux chiefs solemn as high priests. In short, a piebald parliament, an Anacharsis Cloots congress of all kinds of that multiform pilgrim species, man."—Herman Melville, *The Confidence-Man.*

any others, and he too described the Indian doctors,
versed in the mysteries of herbs, whose powers were seldom questioned by the backwoodsmen. Many of his
longer stories reflected the Hannibal of the years before
the Mexican War and the trek of the Mormons,—1840,
say, to 1845,—even *The Mysterious Stranger* with its
Austrian setting; and they were unrivalled as authentic
pictures of the Mississippi valley life, its violence and its
poetry, its indolence and kindness. This was the wild
Missouri world in which in 1844 a magistrate killed a
senator in a fight on the street, and judges, delighting
in impromptu duels, adjourned their courts to witness
one and travelled with an arsenal of carving-knives and
pistols. It was the land of the "Pikes," so called,—from
the two Pike counties that faced each other, in Illinois
and Missouri, across the river,—celebrated by many
writers in poetry and in prose, a byword for all that was
ruffianly in the frontier life. [3] Many of the Pikes moved

[3] "A 'Pike,' in the California dialect, is a native of Missouri,
Arkansas, Northern Texas or Southern Illinois. The first emigrants
that came over the plains were from Pike County, Missouri; but
as the phrase, 'a Pike County man,' was altogether too long for
this short life of ours, it was soon abbreviated into 'a Pike.' Besides, the emigrants from the aforementioned localities belonged
evidently to the same genus, and the epithet 'Western' was by no
means sufficiently descriptive. The New England type is reproduced
in Michigan and Wisconsin; the New York, in northern Illinois;
the Pennsylvania, in Ohio; the Virginian, in Kentucky; but the
Pike is a creature different from all these. He is the Anglo-Saxon
relapsed into semi-barbarism. He is long, lathy and sallow; he ex-
pectorates vehemently; he takes naturally to whiskey . . . he has
little respect for the rights of others; he distrusts men in 'store-
clothes,' but venerates the memory of Andrew Jackson; finally, he
has an implacable dislike to trees."—Bayard Taylor, *At Home and
Abroad*, second series.

"America is manufacturing several new types of man. The Pike is
one of the newest. He is a bastard pioneer. With one hand he
clutches the pioneer vices; with the other he beckons forward the
vices of civilization . . . He is hung together, not put together. He
inserts his lank fathom of a man into a suit of molasses-coloured
homespun. Frowsy and husky is the hair nature crowns him with;
frowsy and stubbly the beard. He shambles in his walk. He drawls

westward to California over the plains, with wagon-
loads of pork and pork-fed children, while others appeared in Mark Twain's tales along with many another
type that flourished throughout the woollier Western
regions. One found the "village atheist" there, the spec-
ulator in Western lands, the hawker of patent medicines
and the fortune-teller, who sometimes "worked" camp-
meetings, as the versatile Murrell had often done, like
the horse-thief Simon Suggs in the well-known story. It
was at one of these camp-meetings where teams of
preachers for days on end exhorted a swarming multitude in the depths of the forest that the "King" in *Huckleberry Finn* collected money for his noble plan of working his way back to the Indian Ocean. He knew all the
pirate crews in that ocean and meant to put in the rest
of his life trying to bring back these pirates to the true
path. There were the untidy villages, with yards full of
jimson weeds, and the towns where the immigrant from
Europe was a stranger still. For most of the Western folk
as yet were Americans of British-island stock who had
seldom seen Germans[4] or Italians,[5] and Mark Twain

in his talk. He drinks whiskey by the tank . . . I have seen Mal-
tese beggars, Arab camel-drivers, Dominican friars, New York alder-
men, Digger Indians; the foulest, frowsiest creatures I have ever
seen are thorough-bred Pikes."—Theodore Winthrop, *John Brent.*

It was the paradoxical point of John Hay's *Pike County Ballads*
that a soul of goodness might exist inside the Pike.

[4] See Edward Eggleston's *The End of the World*, a story of an
Indiana village in 1843: "The few Germans who had penetrated to
the West at that time were looked upon with hardly more favour
than the Californians feel for the almond-eyed Chinamen. They
were foreigners who would talk gibberish instead of the plain
English which everybody could understand."

[5] Observe the excitement of the people in Mark Twain's *Those
Extraordinary Twins* when the two Italians appeared. There had
"never been one in this town." The time of the story was 1830-1850,
and the village in reality was Hannibal again. No doubt Barnum's
plate-spinner Signor Vivella had been a mild sensation in regions
where an Italian was as rare as a dodo.

Of British stock mainly, the settlers had no use for the Yankees,
or so Mark Twain remembered, in the Mississippi Valley. "When I

at his village school, encountering two or three Jewish children, had felt that he was in the presence of characters from the Bible.[6] He remembered later that, for all the violence and the freedom of manners among the young, no girl was ever seduced or gossiped about,[7] and that "there was nothing resembling a worship of money, or of its possessor, in our region." For the rest, the frontier was generally stagnant in its formal culture, and the practice of Galen was "the only practice known to Missouri doctors,"—Galen was the only authority they recognized. Mark Twain recalled the books one found on parlour tables in the river mansions, Ossian, Tupper, *Ivanhoe, Alonzo and Melissa.* Perhaps there were two or three albums and keepsakes and a volume of the speeches of Henry Clay, together with the *Columbian Orator,* the repository of schoolboy pieces from Joel Barlow, Red Jacket and Patrick Henry. William Wirt's "Who is Blennerhasset?" from his speech at the trial of Aaron Burr, appeared with Fitz-Greene Halleck's *Marco Bozzaris.* These books were all piled and disposed with cast-iron exactness, in strict accordance with an inherited and unchangeable plan.

---

was a boy, in the back settlements of the Mississippi Valley . . . the Yankee (citizen of the New England states) was hated with a splendid energy. But religion had nothing to do with it. In a trade, the Yankee was held to be about five times the match of the Westerner. His shrewdness, his insight, his judgment, his knowledge, his enterprise and his formidable cleverness in applying these forces were frankly confessed, and most competently cursed."— Mark Twain, *Literary Essays.*

[6] "In that school were the first Jews I had ever seen. It took me a good while to get over the awe of it. To my fancy they were clothed invisibly in the damp and cobwebby mould of antiquity. They carried me back to Egypt, and in imagination I moved among the Pharaohs and all the shadowy celebrities of that remote age." —Mark Twain, *Autobiography.*

[7] "There was the utmost liberty among young people—but no young girl was ever insulted, or seduced, or even scandalously gossiped about. Such things were not even dreamed of in that society, much less spoken of and referred to as possibilities."—Mark Twain, quoted in Bernard De Voto's *Mark Twain at Work.*

There was "as yet no room in the West for a genius," another young writer observed who was growing up there, although there were numbers of John Hays in the Mississippi valley states, or eastward in Indiana, or northward in Wisconsin. Lew Wallace had already begun to write as early as 1843, before he set out as an officer for the Mexican War, after living as a boy in Indianapolis when his father was governor of the state and the village was scarcely more than a clearing in the forest. He had fallen in with Irving's *Astoria* and Cooper's Leather-Stocking tales in the library at the Indiana statehouse, and carried them off to read in the haymow and the woods, at a time when Henry Ward Beecher was preaching in the infant capital and living in a cabin with his wife in a muddy lane there. John Hay, born in Indiana, had been taken to Warsaw, Illinois,—a name suggested by the novel *Thaddeus of Warsaw*,—while Joaquin Miller and Edward Eggleston were also children of Indiana, where Eggleston was a Methodist circuit-rider later. Miller's family, living for a while by making maple-sugar and selling an occasional coonskin, was constantly moving, shifting from clearing to clearing with sheep and a cow. Ambrose Bierce was a smaller boy whose family drifted through Indiana, although he was born on a camp-meeting site in Ohio, where William Dean Howells also had been born in 1837, the same year as Eggleston and Miller and a year before Hay. Joseph Kirkland spent his childhood in the backwoods of Michigan and in Illinois, and John Muir, born in Scotland in 1838, had emigrated with his family to Wisconsin in 1849. Contemporaries more or less, maturing through the fifties and often indebted to the region for their atmosphere and subjects, these writers in several cases lived elsewhere later, though few were as bitter about their world as the young John Hay, whose father was a frontier doctor on the Mississippi. Returning home from an Eastern college, he wrote that he found only a "dreary waste of heartless materialism" there, where "great and heroic qualities" might "bully their way up into the glare, but the flowers of existence inevitably droop and wither." The "great unshorn of the prairies" were not for Hay. The West for him was "barbarous," though later he returned to live in Ohio, unlike Howells, who was filled with a "morbid horror of going back," and Mark Twain, who settled early in the East for good. In those days, after the Civil War, Howells confirmed the "grim truth" of E. W. Howe's *Story of a Country Town,* while Mark Twain said this picture of the "arid village life" was true,—"I know, for I have seen it all and lived it all." He corroborated John Hay's remark that there was "no room in the West for a genius" in his story of the poet Edward J. Billings, whom "Homer and Shakespeare couldn't begin to come up to" and who was ridden on a rail out of the village. This genius was obliged to wait for Captain Stormfield's heaven, where, for his reward, he became a grandee.

Many of the pictures of Western life that appeared a few years later, when some of these writers grew up, were sufficiently grim, those, for example, of Joseph Kirkland, the son of the author Caroline Kirkland, who had written *A New Home—Who'll Follow?* His *Zury,* the story of a pioneer settlement in central Illinois, was full of the "truth" about this life, so largely hard and loveless, that Kirkland himself urged Hamlin Garland to tell. Ambrose Bierce, who never forgot, could never forgive the "unwashed savages,"—of his own flesh and blood,—whom he left behind him, types that appeared among others in Eggleston's novels, with their scenes of Indiana, Minnesota and Illinois. In these raw mushroom villages, the desperado was ever-present, and there were horse-thieves, border ruffians, grafting politicians and land-sharks speculating in imaginary titles to claims. It was thought sinful in these bubble-towns to take a bath on Sunday or shave or brush one's boots or walk in the woods, and the best fare in the sod-built taverns consisted of salt pork floating in lard, bread that was only half-baked and waterlogged potatoes. In decades to come "novels of protest" appeared in ever-increasing numbers revealing the inevitable flaws of this pioneer world, novels that Eunice Beecher foreshadowed, Henry Ward Beecher's wife, when she published her Indiana story *From Dawn to Daylight*. This "simple Western home history" was a tale of the Beechers' own life, mainly in Indianapolis, in the thirties and forties, and the callous indifference of their niggardly neighbours, who were always down with chills and fever, tired, unfeeling, overworked or lazy. An occasional circus or minstrel-show was the only relief from the mud and the pigs, and there were odd do-nothing characters, misfits haunting the river and the stores, who suggested Sherwood Anderson's people later. It was they whom Beecher attacked in his *Lectures to Young Men*. One would scarcely have looked for "idees" there, any more than in Eggleston's Minnesota,[8]—for ideas "paid no interest" in this widespread country of "corner lots," in these opening phases of a rapidly developing world.

But there were a dozen Wests, there were countless types of Western folk and virtually, at one point or another, all levels of culture. In Eunice Beecher's Indianapolis one also found Lew Wallace's father, a cultivated Pennsylvanian who had taught at West Point, and Wallace himself recalled later the admirable Indiana school where he had been drilled in Latin and Lindley Mur-

---

[8] "Wouldn't fetch no sich notions into this ked'ntry. Can't afford tew. 'Tain't no land of idees. It's the ked'ntry of corner lots. Idees is in the way—don't pay no interest. Hain't had time to build a 'sylum for people with idees yet, in this territory."—Whisky Jim, the stage-driver, in Edward Eggleston's *The Mystery of Metropolisville*.

ray. John Hay, whose family were people of culture, had learned his Greek in Illinois, and there were households like that of the Kirklands in the loneliest hamlets on the frontier as well as in the spacious brick dwellings on the Ohio river. One might have encountered on any road an exiled Virginian like Eggleston's father, a planter's son, a graduate of William and Mary, who had pushed West for his fortune, like the masterful Senator Thomas Hart Benton of Missouri whose daughter had married the explorer John C. Frémont. It was Benton, the "greatest man in the world," who so disillusioned Tom Sawyer because he turned out to be less than twenty-five feet tall, but he had read his Greek Testament at eight, as the younger Brackenridge had also done and many another frontier doctor and lawyer. One also encountered backwoods philosophers like Eggleston's Andrew Anderson, who built a castle in the forest where he lived with his books and whose eccentricity was a natural outgrowth of a literary culture that was not balanced by any knowledge of the world. He fell to living the romance that others would have written, for in this out-of-the-way community he had never been led to distinguish the world of ideas from the world of practical life.

The New England schoolmistress was abroad in the land, and even in little Hannibal there were no less than three bookstores in 1854. As for Cincinnati, the liveliest centre of culture in the West, it had its own magazines and publishers and a hundred thousand people, many of whom were transplanted New Englanders like the Cary sisters, Alice and Phœbe, who had lived as children in a farmhouse in a valley near by. The family had settled there in 1802, when the state of Ohio was a wilderness still, maintaining in their poverty the literary tastes and the love of learning that characterized so many of the New England farmers. The daughters had grown up on

Josephus and Pope, Lewis and Clark and *Charlotte Temple,* reading by saucers of lard with a rag for a wick, writing ballads and verses for children, hymns and poems of the flowers and birds that first appeared in the Cincinnati papers. Their artless tales of the pastoral neighbours and the vine-covered cottages and grassy lanes suggested that Ohio was really an extension of New England, and Whittier had written to encourage them, as Horace Greeley had visited their farm before, in the early fifties, they went to New York. They soon had their evenings there that rivalled Anna Lynch's and attracted Barnum and Robert Dale Owen, George Ripley and Bayard Taylor. There too Greeley often appeared, the oracle of the Ohio valley, though *The Tribune* was read indeed all over the West.[9] Greeley, with his passion for the land and his understanding of rural problems, was especially aware of the hardships of the pioneers. Their struggles seemed to weigh on him as if he had experienced them, and in fact he had tasted pioneer life as a boy in his family's log-cabin when they moved to Pennsylvania, which was then the frontier. This enabled him all the better to spread the culture of his native New England, and the literary news, the reviews, the poems that appeared in *The Tribune* with extracts from essays very largely formed the frontier mind. Greeley travelled through the West and visited northern Michigan twice before he crossed the continent to San Francisco.

The hunger for knowledge throve on lonely farms throughout the region, in the "oak openings," for instance, where John Muir lived, the immigrant boy, growing up in Wisconsin, who knew three-quarters of the Bible by heart and who had been put to the plough when he could reach the handles. At school in Scotland,

[9] "Oberlin is a grate place. The college opens with a prayer and then the New York Tribune is read."—Artemus Ward.

eight or nine years old, he had read Audubon's story of
the passenger pigeon and, struck by Alexander Wilson's
description of the bald eagle and the fish-hawk, he had
dreamed of exploring the depths of the American forests. Swapping books with other farm-boys, he longed to
be a Humboldt, as he walked barefoot in the furrows
and fed the stock, rejoicing in the glorious Wisconsin
woods where there was no gamekeeper to stop him in all
the wild happy land, a paradise for songbirds. The trees
there stood wide apart so that one could readily study
the birds, mating, building their nests, feeding their
young, the bobolinks, brown thrashers, nuthatches,
chickadees and bluebirds, and Muir, already a naturalist, observed the habits of the dragonflies too, the wild
bees, butterflies and wasps. On winter nights in this
northern region the whole sky at times was draped in
graceful folds of crimson and purple. Fanning the wheat,
splitting rails, sometimes as many as a hundred a day,
Muir was impressed by the knowledge of the Indian
hunters, their understanding of animals and their for-
est-wisdom, interested as he also was in the minds and
intelligence of the animals themselves which he was to
defend against the behaviourists later. Years before, in
the Sangamon country, Abraham Lincoln as a boy had
shared Muir's sense of the mystery of the life of the
woods, the hunger for learning that impelled him to master the whole of Euclid on his solitary drives, the compassion Muir felt for animals and his interest in them.
A natural story-teller himself, Lincoln had known Æsop's
fables of the talking beasts and birds, and countless
stories were told of him, how he befriended the poor
dog "Honey" and how he prevented the sow from devouring her pig. He had pursued a snake through thickets
to keep it from swallowing a frog, he had saved a fawn's
life by scaring it away from a rifle. Lincoln, for the rest,
with his faith in dreams, in presentiments that took

possession of him, shared also the forest-religion of the old frontier, "unbeliever" that he was, a reader of Volney[10] and Thomas Paine, who had run against Peter Cartwright as a candidate for Congress. Cartwright, the Methodist son of thunder, who preached in the Sangamon country, shaking his "brimstone wallet" over the people, had made a great point of his opponent's unbelief; but Lincoln was a mystic too in a world that believed in signs and tokens and came to see him as the Moses of a new dispensation. For many the rise of the Republican party was an "inspiration," another revival, and they felt as if the prophet had come once more in person to lead the people into a promised land.[11]

Meanwhile, like Pittsburgh, Cincinnati was an early home of the blackface minstrels, and it may have been there that Daddy Rice, the father of American minstrelsy, first sang and "jumped" Jim Crow. It was in one of the river towns that he had encountered the rheumatic old Negro whose shuffling and crooning he copied in his well-known performance, between 1828 and 1831, and he had sung and danced his way through most of the frontier settlements of Ohio, Tennessee and Kentucky. So had Dan Emmett's[12] Virginia minstrels,

[10] The French author of *The Ruins*, which Joel Barlow translated into English, continued to be read on the frontier for decades to come. In one of Bret Harte's stories, the gambler Jack Hamlin was represented as reading Volney's *Ruins*.

[11] For this aspect of the frontier see *The Valley of Shadows*, by Francis Grierson, describing his childhood on the Illinois prairie and at Alton on the Mississippi, where he heard a debate of Lincoln with the "Little Giant." Later as a page of General Frémont, in command at St. Louis in the Civil War, Grierson met various old scouts and pioneers who had accompanied Frémont on his Western explorations.

[12] D. D. Emmett, born in Ohio, where he wrote *Old Dan Tucker*, was the author of the best-known version of *Dixie*.

" 'I wish I was in Dixie.' The origin of this song is rather curious. Although now thoroughly adopted as a Southern song and 'Dixey's Land' understood to mean the Southern States of America, it was, some seventy-five years ago, the estate of one Dixie on Man-

Christy's minstrels and various others that were well established by 1850 all over the West and the South,—although in several cases they began in New York,—and Christy's minstrels introduced the songs of Stephen Foster, a young man born in Pittsburgh, to the American public. E. P. Christy was one of the first to sing *My Old Kentucky Home, Massa's in de Cold, Cold Ground* and *Old Black Joe,* songs that won the praise of Washington Irving, and the vogue of Negro minstrelsy was at its peak for about two decades, the years before and after the Civil War. The minstrel shows, prefigured by the singing and dancing of the slaves in the South, soon evolved a conventional form with a central interlocutor and two end-men with tambourines and bones. Beside the stage Irishman with his shillalah the stage Negro thus appeared, usually strumming a banjo and ready for a break-down, with a mouth as big as the words that he used, gaudy clothes and a broad grin suggesting that Negroes were invariably lazy and shiftless. Jim Crow with his dilapidated coat and worn-out shoes and hat was a broken-down variation of the universal type.

It was generally thought in later years that the minstrel shows had begun in the forties, although there were blackface performers in previous decades, but instances were known of regularly-appointed minstrel troupes at least as early as 1835,[13] and some of the songs they spread through the country, Emmett's *Old Dan Tucker,* for one, *O Susanna* and Farrell's *Old Zip Coon,*

---

hattan island, who treated his slaves well; and it was their lament, on being deported South, that is now known as 'I wish I was in Dixie.' "—Charles Godfrey Leland, note in *Hans Breitmann's Ballads* (collected edition).

[13] "It is very commonly asserted that the first regular Negro minstrel troupe appeared in 1842. This is quite an error. While I was at Mr. Green's [school] in 1835 there came to Dedham a circus with as regularly-appointed a Negro minstrel troupe of a dozen as I ever saw . . . Nor do I think that this was any novelty even then."—Charles Godfrey Leland, *Memoirs.*

were heard before long even in the remotest regions. When J. Ross Browne was in Syria in 1853 he sang *Zip Coon* to his flute among the ruins of Baalbek, where it was taken up at once by the Arabs and their damsels who sang it themselves henceforth as "Ezepa Kouna." At about the same time Bayard Taylor heard an old wandering Hindu minstrel sing *O Susanna* and *Old Dan Tucker* at Delhi, though he did not understand the words which he had picked up at Madras from a group of young English officers who knew them. Taylor heard Arabs at Alexandria singing songs by Stephen Foster. The "Ethiopian melodists," as they were called in Sacramento at the time of his visit there in 1849, had attracted crowds that jostled the players at the monte-tables, for the miners were fascinated by these "national airs." There were versions of *O Susanna* in Chinese and Greek. This was the song of the forty-niners that Foster had written in Cincinnati, where the seekers of gold streamed through the town in tens of thousands during these years either in boats on the river or in covered wagons. Foster had been a bookkeeper in his father's steamboat-agency there, with an office on the river among the wharves. He knew little of the South that appeared in his songs till he visited New Orleans in 1852, though he had seen Bardstown perhaps and Louisville surely, where Keats's brother George lived, as Bayard Taylor wrote, in a Grecian house with antique statues in the garden. It happened that Harriet Beecher Stowe, who was in Cincinnati when Foster was there, visited one of the plantations across the river,[14] and it was probably her description of this in *Uncle Tom's*

---

[14] This was perhaps the plantation on which Nathaniel Southgate Shaler, later the Harvard geologist, spent his boyhood. His family believed that Mrs. Stowe drew St. Clare from Shaler's grandfather. According to Shaler in his *Autobiography*, Legree was exactly like one of their neighbours and the story of Eliza's flight over the ice was a well-known tradition in their household.

Cabin that suggested Foster's *Old Kentucky Home*.[15]
But he had long been familiar with the songs of the
Negroes. He knew the Negro boatmen at Pittsburgh,
at the head of the Ohio, as he also knew the stevedores
on the Cincinnati wharves, and he had heard Daddy
Rice sing *Jim Crow* when he was a boy and had written
his own earliest songs for the Pittsburgh minstrels. Foster was a flute-player, like virtually all the writers of the
time, Irving, Longfellow, Cooper, Audubon, Poe, and
he wrote the music for most of his songs, indeed he
wrote the music first and later composed the lines that
fitted the tune. The longing for a lost home was the
constant note of the mind of a man who was to be
picked up dying in the slums of New York.

Music was ubiquitous in the lonely cabins of the frontier as well as in the pioneer settlements and the rising
towns. There were flutes and fiddles everywhere, even
pianos, while troupes of singers and other performers
straggled along the muddy roads and made their way in
showboats up the rivers. The long-haired bediamonded
medicine-showman, with his Indian elixirs and wizard
oils, often travelled with a troupe in a covered wagon,
and exhibitors of waxworks, giants, monkeys or camels
accompanied wandering circuses on all the roads. Barnum, who had settled in New York, had toured the
country as a travelling showman, ranging through the
Carolinas, Alabama and Tennessee, having previously
learned his art as an auctioneer. He exhibited the plate-
spinner Signor Vivella and a group of blackface dancers
and singers; then, buying a showboat on the Mississippi,
he hired the captain and crew and stopped with his
show at every town between Natchez and New Orleans.
There were showboats on many of the Western rivers,

[15] See Mornaweck, *Chronicles of Stephen Foster's Family*. The
"Old Kentucky Home" was a slave-cabin, not a "mansion." The
name "Uncle Tom" occurred in the first draught of the poem.

sometimes equipped with a small museum, wax figures and a stuffed giraffe, a puppet-show and a minstrel-troupe. Ralph Keeler, who had started life as a cabin-boy on a Great Lakes steamer and who later told his story in *Vagabond Adventures,* ran two showboats of his own, one on the Ohio, one on the Missouri, stopping at all the landings on the stream. He remembered the settlers coming on board with pistols sticking from their pockets and bowie-knives protruding from the legs of their boots. As an end-man in the minstrel-show, with corked face and woolly wig, his specialty was plantation jigs and banjo solos.[16]

As Keeler recalled them, the older showmen constantly dreamed of rural pursuits and planned to retire to farms in the evening of their days, and this was the type that Charles Farrar Browne conceived in his character of Artemus Ward, the old showman-farmer of Baldwinsville, Indiana. Browne, who adopted the name of this character, wandered West from Boston and Maine, working his way as a printer, in the middle fifties, through western Massachusetts and New York to Ohio, setting type in Cincinnati, Dayton, Toledo and Cleveland, where John D. Rockefeller was working as a bookkeeper already. Tall, gawky, lean and green, a caricature of Uncle Sam, a lover of circuses, clowns and minstrel shows, Browne was soon known for his writings in the Cleveland *Plain Dealer,* where another compositor and reporter was David R. Locke. This was the humorist whose pen-name later was Petroleum V. Nasby, another of Lincoln's favourites in the Civil War years and later still a comic lecturer who toured the East with Mark Twain and a third follower of Artemus Ward, Josh Billings. For Browne, the first of these comic

---

[16] For a few years after the Civil War, Keeler lived in Cambridge near Howells, who drew him in the character of Fulkerson in *A Hazard of New Fortunes.*

lecturers,[17] had evolved a new form out of the end-man of the minstrels and the clown of the circus, while most of the humorists of his type, several of whom were Eastern men, first found themselves as wanderers in the Western regions. They haunted the newspaper offices, and often, like Nasby and Artemus Ward, they were the tramping "jour printers" Mark Twain remembered,— from the days when he was an itinerant printer himself,—who flitted by with a shirt in a wallet and were ready to give a temperance lecture if they did not succeed in getting type to set. Mark Twain drew the "Duke" in *Huckleberry Finn* from one of these printers he met in Virginia City. Nasby, or Locke, came from New York, while Josh Billings of Massachusetts, the Poughkeepsie auctioneer, had spent ten years in his youth roaming the West. Their humour was generally known as Western,—it throve on the frontier,—and they looked the part of the showman-farmer that found its most famous embodiment in the Hoosier Yankee of the backwoods, Artemus Ward. No doubt the watchword of Artemus Ward "Come the moral on 'em strong" along with his "moral bears" were suggested by Barnum, whose equally moral "lecture-room" in the museum at New York reassured thousands for whom ordinary theatres were immoral. There, thanks to the name of the auditorium, they could enjoy in repose the scandalously edifying story of Charlotte Temple. Perhaps the character of Artemus Ward owed something to Barnum in other respects, though he seemed an authentic product of the land of the Hoosiers, a land that was supposed to abound in the odd and the quaint, and one might have encountered his travelling show on any of the Western roads,—the wax-works and the snakes and

---

[17] While without question Josh Billings followed and imitated Artemus Ward, it appears that as early as 1835 he delivered a comic lecture at Napoleon, Indiana, on Mesmerism.

the kangaroo. Browne may well have conceived the
show,—his manager Kingston believed he did,—on his
first visit to the museum at Cincinnati, where the birds
that Audubon had stuffed were jumbled with wax fig
ures and Indian relics and Hiram Powers's clockwork
chamber of horrors. One found fragments there too of
the temples of Sodom and Gomorrah, worthy of the
biblical museum of the Mormons at Nauvoo, where Jo
seph Smith's mother, who had charge of them, showed Jo
siah Quincy autograph manuscripts of Abraham, Moses
and Aaron. This museum also contained a leg of Phar
aoh's daughter, the one that rescued the infant Moses in
the Nile. The will to believe was active on the frontier,
where the persons and places of the Bible were vividly
real.

As for the Mormons, they thought of themselves as
Old Testament people, and the atmosphere of Western
New York when Joseph Smith was a boy there was all
compact of biblical fancies and daydreams. His parents
and his grandfather had practised faith-healing, they be
lieved in miraculous cures, they had visions of angels
and when Joseph was visited by John the Baptist and
presently received the gift of tongues he was following
the lines of a fantasy that was general in the region. For
the Millerites began there too,—some of their preachers
"talked with Daniel,"—and the well-known Sibyl of
Crooked Lake and the Fox girls, the Rochester spirit-
rappers, flourished, like the Shakers, in the lonely forests
of New York.[18] Hallucinations, demoniac possessions,
hysteria, witchcraft, occultism were accompanied by re-

[18] The "spiritualism" of the Fox sisters flourished further West as
well. Artemus Ward described the new-fangled ideas about spirits
in Baldwinsville, Indiana, where four or five long-haired fellows had
settled. An attempt was made to get Mrs. Ward into the spirit-
business, but she was proof against this as against the woman's
rights advocate who said that every woman should have a "spear."
Artemus and Betsy Ward were invariably conservative in temper.

vivals and schisms in the existing sects, new religions rising from the old and new ideas like communism and the
patriarchal polygamy that was practised at Oneida. No
doubt the monotonies of pioneer life added a zest to the
new sensations which the Millerites carried, like the
Mormons, to the further frontier, their vision of an im-
minent end of the world and their imagery of trumpets
and thunders and vials, the ten-horned beast and the
other apocalyptic wonders. Joseph Smith may have had
in mind Captain Kidd's buried treasure, and he may
have drawn from the *Arabian Nights* a mental picture
of the magic cave where the golden plates lay on the
table and the sword hung on the wall. He had certainly
been stirred by the strange aboriginal monuments, the
Indian mounds near Lake Ontario, the broken pots
and bones and spear-heads that were dug up on the
farms near by and the crude archæological notions that
were prevalent at the moment. This country was the
scene of Cooper's tales, where many people still believed that the Indians were the lost tribes of Israel, and
this was a natural time and place to elaborate an American mythology, with fragments of Methodism and communism floating through it.

The Mormons had wandered through various regions,
driven to and fro, before they built the City of the
Saints, in the land of the honey-bee Deseret, which blossomed as the rose on Great Salt Lake. It was in Ohio
that Brigham Young met Joseph Smith,—he found the
prophet in the forest chopping wood,—and the saints
had gathered for a while in Missouri before they settled
in Illinois and erected their temple at Nauvoo on the
prairie. Then Brigham Young had led them out of
bondage, and they had set out for the wilderness and the
solitary place, for the promised land that would never
attract the gentile fortune-seekers, where they could go
from strength to strength alone. They had been wan-

derers but only of necessity, unlike the families of "movers," so common in the West, who were constantly shifting from spot to spot with no apparent object, as if their covered wagon were always at the door. The cattle of the movers seemed to be always yoked and the plough tied on behind, and they roamed from Tennessee to Kentucky and over the border to Illinois, or perhaps to Indiana or Missouri. The family of Abraham Lincoln, for instance, originally Virginians, had drifted over Kentucky and Indiana, thriftless, unstable, roving mountain folk, and Mark Twain's family drifted and shifted from hamlet to hamlet in Tennessee before they settled in Hannibal, Missouri. Just so Hamlin Garland's family, two or three decades later still, moved on from village to village and from state to state, always a little further westward, while the father and mother of Joaquin Miller moved four times in Indiana before they decided to follow the Oregon trail. What worked in the minds of all these movers?—for they usually preferred this name, regarding the word "pioneers" as too high-flown. Hopes that could scarcely be imagined later, mortifications, despairs, chagrins and visions that were always credible in the unknown West. Most of the movers took root at last in the Mississippi valley, but more and more were heading now for the lands of promise beyond the Rockies, the Pacific slope to which Frémont had opened the way. All day the covered-wagon trains crawled along the winding trails where campfires sparkled at night in the villages of tents.

While Frémont, more than anyone else, had spread the germs of the "Oregon fever" and the roads were alive with settlers bound for the coast, the vast intermediate regions beyond the Missouri were known as the "great American desert" still. The Indian and the buffalo freely ranged over Kansas, Nebraska, the Dakotas until they were opened for settlement in 1854, though the eastern ends of Nebraska and Kansas were fairly filled by 1860 with cities of three log-cabins, as Greeley called them. A stick of timber and a blazed tree that bore perhaps the name "Vienna" was often the site, within two or three years, of a hall that resounded with debates and plays and lectures by Bayard Taylor or Greeley himself. For civilization followed the plough as rapidly as the prairie-fire and the blizzard and the flood that ravaged the outlying cabins, where over their milk-pails or knitting their stockings one sometimes heard the frontiersman's daughters discussing Longfellow and Cooper, Dickens and Scott. The towns first rose on the Missouri and the Platte, then slowly spread on the over-land trails, and, where hunters and trappers alone had roamed, Leavenworth, Lawrence and Omaha soon passed beyond the stage of the sod-house and the dug-out. The name of Kansas City had been heard as early as 1848 as the starting-point for emigrants on the Ore-gon trail, and thence the traders who had come from St. Louis also started for Santa Fé on the trail that was still at the mercy of the terrible Comanches. When, in 1851, Willa Cather's Father Latour[19] set out to assume his see in the New Mexican desert, no one in Cincinnati could tell him how to get there, and it took him the greater part of a year to reach Santa Fé by way of New Orleans and the valley of the Rio Grande. Caravans had been following the trail at least since 1831, when Josiah Gregg joined one at Independence, but the country it traversed was all unsettled, wild as the region one had to cross to reach the Mormon outpost, established in 1847, at Great Salt Lake. Brigham Young's oasis became at once the resting-station for emigrants who would otherwise have perished on their way to the coast. There

[19] In *Death Comes for the Archbishop.*

they replaced their exhausted teams and procured fresh milk and garden-truck. The wilderness and the desert had always been the cradle of religions.

Voyageurs, fur-traders, trappers and scouts had ranged all over this open country, discovering the natural highways and passes of the mountains, but they had kept no journals and made no maps and their information had never been pieced together. It was of little value to the multitudes in the Eastern states who were eager to emigrate westward but needed directions, and before the Frémont expeditions of 1842-1845 the regions beyond the Missouri were scarcely known. They were sterile in parts, they were still forbidding, but Frémont's eloquent reports had not merely dispelled the terrors of the Oregon trail; they had proved that large areas of the further West, far from being arid, were admirable for pasturage and farming. While all the trails had been vaguely known, Frémont surveyed and related them, describing their flora and fauna and geology as well, providing full and precise information and detailed maps for the emigrant trains, showing them where to cross the rivers and the mountains. He suggested lines of military posts, each one the germ of a town, for the relief of settlers, to afford them protection from the Indians and supply them with grain, situated in fertile valleys with wagon-roads between them, posts that would command the mountain passes. Frémont's reports were magnetic, full of life and poetry, and they were discussed and read on thousands of farms, in country stores, in bars and in clubs east of the Missisippi. Brigham Young read about Great Salt Lake in one of these reports, which he followed, using the maps, on his westward trek, for he had not known, when he set out, whither he was leading his band of saints and had California and Oregon vaguely in mind. Joaquin Miller's father and mother painfully studied Frémont's directions all the way on their trail to the Willamette.[20] On the table at night in Indiana they had pored over Frémont's maps till the tallow-dips burned to the socket, and the father had read the book aloud until every scene and circumstance was printed on the mind of the boy for the rest of a lifetime. Joaquin Miller saw Frémont's men hauling the cannon up the Rockies, with Frémont at their head waving his sword, his horse neighing wildly in the mountain wind; and he was thrilled when the great man related how a little weary brown bee rested on his knee for a moment. The bee was trying to make its way from a valley of flowers far below over the snow to the flowery fields beyond, and it perched to recover strength as he too was resting. Miller felt he was no longer a boy: he longed for adventure and glory along the trail in the path of the setting sun. Years later on his Oakland heights he built a monument on the spot where Frémont was supposed to have named the Golden Gate.

The Millers were one of countless families whom Frémont's reports drew to the coast, and he was still more the hero of boys than the mountain men whom he had met and whose names were soon to be legendary in the settled regions. Frémont had written of some of these. He had fallen in with James P. Beckwourth, the long-haired mulatto who had left St. Louis as a boy and had since lived with the Crows and become a chief, and he also happened on Jim Bridger, the discoverer of Great Salt Lake who was conducting a party of trappers and traders. Beckwourth was looking for a band of runaway

[20] Francis Parkman, who left St. Louis in 1846 on the westward tour recorded in *The Oregon Trail*, treated Frémont's book with less respect. He used some of its leaves to astonish the natives. He made small fireworks with them, squibs and serpents, by rolling them and packing the cylinders with gunpowder and charcoal. It gave him great repute as a medicine-man when, sitting in a camp of Indians, he lighted them and tossed them, over the heads of the company, sputtering in the air.

horses, while Bridger, with whom Frémont camped for a night, had had a skirmish with the Sioux and told his adventures after supper. Bridger had known Marcus Whitman and the famous Narcissa, the first white woman ever to cross the Rockies, the missionaries who had spread their news of the fortunate land of Oregon earlier even than Frémont wrote about it. Whitman, a doctor and surgeon too, had removed an arrowhead from Bridger's neck, and Narcissa had brought up his half-breed daughter.

In after times these characters were all folk-heroes in their way, and more than any of the others perhaps the man who was Frémont's chief scout, Kit Carson, later the "Nestor of the Rocky Mountains." A small man, bandy-legged, matter-of-fact, modest, shy, with nothing of the showman about him, temperate and peaceful, Carson, a Kentuckian by birth had grown up in Missouri, where he had been apprenticed to a saddler. He had learned to make fringed gun-covers, sheaths for knives and the buckskin shirts and leggings that he wore,—while he rode his charger Apache without a saddle,—but, hearing tales of adventures in the Rockies and running away to the Santa Fé trail, he never slept under a roof for fifteen years. He had roved on foot or horseback over a region as large as Russia, setting his traps in all the mountain streams, learning Spanish at the trading-posts, an honoured guest in the Indian lodges, reserved and retiring himself as Natty Bumppo. He was regarded as wise in council at the great rendezvous of the trappers, when they assembled in scores for the disposal of their furs. Frémont, who thought the world of him, named a river and a lake for him in the Great Basin which they explored together, and perhaps it was the largest of all the feathers in Frémont's cap that Carson heartily returned his respect and liking.

CHAPTER V

THE FAR WEST

In 1849, at the time of the gold-rush in California, Bayard Taylor had been busy on the New York *Tribune,* and naturally Greeley turned to him as a skilful and experienced writer of travels for a full report of the land of marvels in the West. Taylor set out by way of Panama and reached San Francisco in August for a stay of four and a half months during which the little town of tents became a city of thirty thousand people.

At New Orleans his ship had taken on an ominous number of gamblers, all bound for California, Southerners mostly,—for gamblers inevitably followed a trail of gold,—some of whom he met again at the monte-tables spread under the trees when he rode up to the diggings round Sacramento. There in a hamlet of lean-tos and canvas, the forest-trees stood in the streets, near Captain Sutter's fort on a rise of ground, with its square bastions and thick adobe walls, and Taylor, tempted to try his own luck for a day or two with pick and pan, talked with the other miners in their gulches and cabins. Among them were lawyers, editors, doctors, educated men from all the states, such as the eccentric "Buckshot," for example, who drank a bottle of champagne every night in his solitary tent and had made and spent more than thirty thousand dollars. In the groves of live oak, Taylor shared their wildwood fare, sleeping on the ground with his saddle for a pillow, always in the open, travelling on horseback; then, returning to San Francisco, he walked down to Monterey by the Santa Clara

valley and Salinas. In the tranquil little old Spanish
town, with its tiled roofs and adobe houses, where Dana
had stopped on his voyage before the mast, he found
Captain Sutter, hale, ruddy and good-natured, and Frémont, grown suddenly rich from his land in the gold-
fields. A state convention had assembled there to frame
a constitution. Taylor explored the pine forest behind
the town of Monterey, where the mild air was fragrant
with bay and laurel and the grey sea-mist crept up the
hill, and he rode four miles to the ruined Carmel mission that stood at the mouth of the beautiful empty valley.

Many writers in later years were to celebrate these
themes and scenes, which Taylor described in *El Do-
rado,* and the *California Ballads* that followed in *The
Tribune:* poems that were full of the poppy and the
lupin, the drifting sea-fog and the pines, the barking
seals, the white foam of Point Lobos. There too were the
California types that soon appeared in scores of tales,
the bearded miners, the gamblers, the Chinamen, the
Pikes, the Mexican rancheros and vaqueros with sombrero and lasso, some of whom J. Ross Browne encountered on his ride to San Luis Obispo at about the time
when Taylor was in this region. For Browne also
passed through Salinas in 1849, with a commission from
Washington to establish a line of post-offices on the land-
route to Los Angeles from San Francisco. An Irish boy,
brought up in Kentucky, Browne was a soldier of fortune with an admirable gift for describing his travels
through the world who had reported debates in the
Senate before he sailed on the New Bedford whaler and
wrote his well-known *Etchings of a Whaling Cruise.*
Herman Melville, reviewing this book, a detailed account of the business of whaling that in certain ways
anticipated *Moby-Dick,*—as Browne's later *Yusef* antic-

ipated *The Innocents Abroad*,—said that as a picture of the whaleman's life it achieved what Dana had previously done in describing the vicissitudes of the life of the merchant-sailor. Browne, leaving his ship at Zanzibar in the same way and for much the same reasons that Melville had left the "Acushnet" at Nukahiva, had finally turned up in California, where he settled in later years, sailing round the Horn by way of Juan Fernandez. Dana had stopped in 1835 at this island of Robinson Crusoe, an isle of romance that Defoe had half in mind, with weird red peaks towering over tropical valleys, where Alexander Selkirk at least had lived, and Browne, visiting Crusoe's cave, found fragments of an earthen pot with Selkirk's name and date lying in the rubbish. Riding on his mule from San Francisco, he was enchanted by the live-oak groves, the wild oats and the flowers strewn down the valleys, the park-like pastures where mustangs and antelopes browsed, with their ruinous old ranchos and thriftless Indians sleeping in the sun or ragged Sonoranians with ponchos playing cards. There were no settlers as yet in the Salinas valley, where the coyote and the wildcat stealthily crossed the trail, and Browne, after witnessing a battle to the death between a bull and a grizzly bear, stumbled into a camp of American outlaws. He was robbed of his money and his pistol and, escaping, found himself penned for the night in a cabin with the murdered bodies of an emigrant household. He fell in with Texans, whose bowie-knives swung from their belts, with travelling gamblers, wary, glossy and suave,—such as Bayard Taylor had encountered and Bret Harte described,—and caballeros in velvet jackets, red sashes and embroidered pantaloons with strings of bells jingling down the seams. Finally, at a wild fandango, where all the rancheros of the region appeared and danced with their seno-

ritas to fiddles and guitars, Browne saw a bandit who
had befriended him stabbed to death. Later he described this ride as a "dangerous journey."

For the state was infested with desperados, especially
after the gold-rush began, frontier ruffians, robbers, Sydney convicts, and the only law that prevailed as yet, till
the vigilance-committees rose to power, was the loose
law of a handful of Mexican alcaldes. Joaquin Murieta,
whom Frémont had rescued when he was a boy and
who had lived for some years with the Bentons in St.
Louis,—the Robin Hood of the mining regions,—was
one of a number of outlaws who espoused the lost cause
of the Mexicans and preyed on the gringos. Everywhere
violence naturally throve in a time of transition between regimes on this wildest of all the frontiers with
its clash of races. The Mexicans were unruly enough, and
the author of the *Shirley Letters* described the sangui-
nary turbulence of the mining camps, the murders, the
fatal duels, the suicide, the hanging that occurred in
one of these camps in twenty-four days. For the rest, an
air of old Spain hung over the little towns and ranches
and the missions of the Franciscan fathers that dotted
the Camino Real, one day's march apart from San
Diego. Bull-fights were held in San José in a small rude
white-washed stadium, and the feudal system lingered
at the haciendas, with their low rambling adobe dwellings full of cool shadowy halls and chambers that
opened on balconies whitened by the wind and the sun.
Flowers grew on the tiled roofs and jessamine crept up
the columns, festooned with passion-vines and Castilian
roses, and gnarled old pear-trees blossomed in the pa-
tios, throwing their branches over the walls, with tree-
like fuchsias, olives, oranges and lemons. Now and then
along the road one met an antique Spanish carriage,
drawn by four white gayly caparisoned mules, the picturesque holiday equipage of some local grandee whose

herds of cattle ranged the surrounding hills. For the day of manorial estates persisted in this half-wild land that was innocent of newspapers, post-offices, libraries and schools. Already the Spaniards were forming alliances with the newly arrived Americans, who sometimes adopted the "true caballero style" and even took Spanish names and titles, but oftener the older Californians observed with dismay or amazement the bustling swaggering invaders of their somnolent land. The Americans were always on the go, pushing to the gold-mines or hurrying away to look for other mines elsewhere.

Whenever they pushed, wherever they went, they always returned to San Francisco, already a vertiginous town in 1852, when Kit Carson, who had conducted a flock of sheep to California, hearing of its rapid growth, came to see it. Remembering little Yerba Buena, the old Spanish hamlet, he felt like David Crockett visiting New York, but he did not like the glitter and the crowds, though the San Franciscans made much of him and gave him free passes to concerts, shows and steamboats. He shrank from notoriety, for he had none of the vanity of Crockett, and turned his back on offers to make him rich, while, preferring the timeless world of the plains, the modest Kit was not impressed by the sudden transformation that had startled Bayard Taylor. One saw vaqueros swinging their lariats and capturing wild bulls in vacant fields where houses rose overnight with families in them, and a visitor in 1851 counted six hundred ships in the bay, almost as many as one saw at the port of London. It was generally supposed in San Francisco that traders and farmers of the plodding sort had stopped on their westward march to people the prairie, while only the adventurous and reckless pressed on to the coast, and the cosmopolitan crowd brimmed over with soldiers of fortune from every land, prepared for any turn of the wheel of fate. One of these was Heinrich Schliemann, a German pastor's son, the discoverer of Troy and the treasure of Priam later, a naturalized American who spoke eighteen languages and opened a bank in the city for the purchase of gold-dust. There were ex-doctors sweeping the streets, ex-ministers who were gamblers, bankers and Sicilian bandits who were waiters in cafés, lawyers washing the decks of ships and penniless counts and marquises who were lightermen or fishermen or porters. The spirit of chance prevailed in the town, where the topsy-turvy was almost the rule, though the golden stream from the mines flowed over all. The streets swarmed with spendthrift miners who came down the rivers from their gulches and bars, hungry for any amusement and ready for a fling.

Thus, while the towns of the Middle West were relatively poor and provincial, San Francisco was rich and savoured of the world, and the large French population added another urban touch, with the Russians from the north and the women from Peru and Chile. For the flesh and the devil throve there as well as the world. The French, who were sometimes prodigal sons, opened hotels and kept cafés, where the songs of the boulevards mingled with the ballads of the miners, and they were croupiers in gambling-houses that had an air of Paris with their plush and their diamonds and velvet and chandeliers and mirrors. Saloons and parlours, both public and private, blossomed with Second Empire furniture, which the pioneers imported from France in the flush of their wealth, a note of gilded opulence that flourished in the Chinese restaurants too and the shops that recalled the bazaars of Canton and Peking. There were theatres and fandango-houses, pantomimes and minstrels, for the town was full of actors, musicians and dancers, who had crossed the plains or sailed round the Horn from New Orleans or New York or had come perhaps from showboats on the Mississippi. Two daily

papers were printed in French and others in half a
dozen tongues, and some of the San Francisco editors
were adventurers from the South who had much in
common with the gamblers and the errant young
Frenchmen. For many French royalists and Southerners
alike were stirred by the dreams of an earlier age, the
days of the wandering knight and the buccaneer, and
San Francisco was a natural centre for Raousset-Boul-
bon, the Marquis de Pindray and the editor William
Walker from Tennessee. It was easy to recruit there restless fortune-seekers who were ready for adventure, for
exploits, for conquest, for excitement, to establish
French colonies in Mexico or new republics, to emulate
Houston's deeds in Texas and Frémont's in the further
West and win still more of the hemisphere for the Stars
and Stripes. Or, rather for the slave-holding South, since
the grey-eyed little fanatic Walker believed in slavery as
a blessing for the Negroes too.

Already the resplendent river-boats ran up to Sacramento, with their hanging galleries and fragile colonnades, those airy structures, frescoed and gilded, on
which the miners who had spent their pile returned to
the camps and diggings in the Sierra foothills. For the
sprawling town of Sacramento was one of the gateways
of the mines,—like busy little Marysville and Stockton
to the north and the south,—where the talk was all of
ledges and lodes, croppings, claims and lucky strikes in
flats, bars, pot-holes, gravel-beds and tunnels. There the
good-hearted Sutter lived, the stout blond blue-eyed
Swiss pioneer, the first to establish a foothold on the
Western slope, a trader for a while on the Santa Fé trail
who had settled in California in 1839. He had established at New Helvetia a little kingdom of his own that
was larger than the whole Swiss canton where he was
born, and, tactful with the Indians, whom he employed,
he had imported Kanakas too and his settlement had

the air of a South Sea village. The garrison of his great
fort was uniformed on a Russian model in blue and
green cloth with red trimmings and armed with ancient
flintlocks he had bought in Russia, left behind by Napoleon's retreating troops. For several years he had
sent out hides, flour, cheese and grain to Vancouver,
Sitka, Mexico and the Sandwich Islands. This Thomas
Jefferson of the West experimented with cotton, indigo
and rice, while he raised apples, peaches, figs and pears,
and he had been the first to raise wheat in the interior
of the state. But Sutter, who had rescued the Donner
party, had been ruined when the gold was discovered at
his mill and the troops were themselves demoralized in
the first stampede and marauders burned his buildings
and plundered his stock.

At Sacramento within a few years Henry George was
to live as a printer and Edward Rowland Sill as a post-
office clerk. There now the "Big Four" of the future
worked, behind the counters of pioneer stores, as gro-
cers, drygoods merchants and dealers in hardware, Stan-
ford, Crocker, Huntington and Hopkins, the builders
of the Central Pacific, who were busy providing the
miners with their clothes and equipment. Sacramento
was the headquarters of John Oakhurst and Jack Hamlin, gamblers in fiction who might have been gamblers
in fact and who practised their art with the Argonauts
in the camps in the neighbouring counties in the "dry
diggings" of the hillsides and the "wet diggings" of the
streams. For beyond lay the enchanted ground of a thousand later stories, Angel's, Rough and Ready, Sandy
Bar, Tuolumne, Hangtown, Poker Flat, Sonora, names
that were soon to be famous on the map or in legend,
towns on the forks of the Sacramento or southward on
the Stanislaus or somewhere in the mountainous country
that lay between. Most of them were scarcely more than
clustering nests of tents and cabins with a groggery and

a rickety hotel in a clearing full of stumps, a gambling-joint, a dance-hall and a grim little zinc or wooden chapel where a Methodist exhorter "ladelled out hell-fire free." For the old religion of the frontier followed the gold-seekers westward and revivalists and Presbyterian preachers abounded even in San Francisco, upholding the strictest rigours of Puritanism there. Immigrant wagons and prairie schooners stood on the slopes and arid flats or beside red holes by the crumbling mountain roads, and glade and canyon were fissured and broken while miners thronged the water-courses with long-handled shovels, picks, trowels, rockers and pans. Often up to their waists in the stream, they washed the sand for gold or searched the gravel, the banks and the roots of the trees. The fragrance of balsam, spruce and fir filled the air about them, with the sounds of the rushing river and the wind in the pines.

Among the miners there were countless types, educated men, blackguards, galoots who swaggered through the camps and painted them red,—like Prentice Mulford's Barney McBriar, the "shootist,"—and men who had crossed the plains on foot perhaps with a pack on their backs or trundled a wheelbarrow from Illinois to Salt Lake City. There were quiet men in clean cabins, covered with flowering vines, with books on a swinging shelf and woodcuts on the walls, and pedlars who tramped through camp and stream with rolls of silk and broadcloth coats, trinkets and yellow-backed novels, Shakespeare and Dickens. There were storekeepers and farmers too, like the father and mother of Josiah Royce, who was born in Grass Valley in 1855 and spent a good part of his childhood in this richest of the camps where the miners found gold clinging to the roots of the grass. The first home of the Royces was a tent on the edge of the diggings. They had toiled over the desert in a wagon drawn by cows and oxen, floundering through

floods and storms with broken wheels, beset by roving
Pawnees and Sioux, guided by the light of Frémont's
travels and the Bible and the Milton they carried in a
writing-desk. They felt they were alone with God in the
waste, among the withered sagebrush, and Mrs. Royce,
with her mind full of Hagar in the wilderness, felt she
was Hagar herself plodding through the sand.[1] Grass
Valley was also the home of the Crabtrees, where Lotta
Crabtree lived as a child and her mother was the keeper
of a boarding-house near the Royces' farm; and there in
1853 Lola Montez arrived one day, in a coach from
Marysville, with a new miner-husband. She had appeared in New York two years before, in the guise of a
Spanish dancer on a tour of the country, still "merci-
less in her man-eating propensities," as one of her admirers said, the mistress of Liszt who was looking for
new worlds to conquer. As the protégée of the king of
Bavaria, this beautiful wild Irish girl had virtually run
the kingdom until she was banished, and she bought a
cottage in Grass Valley and trained two bear-cubs there
while she taught Lotta to sing ballads and dance High-
land flings. For a year before she left for Australia she
played herself in the mining-camps, where Lotta was
famous soon as a dancer and singer, one of a number of
the child-performers, "fairy minstrels" and "fairy stars,"
who were so much in vogue in the avid mining-towns.
For children were rare in this mountain region and the
miners came in crowds to see a little girl who appeared
at one of the camps. In almost all the growing
towns there were theatres of cloth and paper at
least, and stages were erected in bar-rooms and village stores among the smoked hams and the shovels
that were stacked in the corner. Sometimes two or three

[1] Mrs. Royce wrote her story down to help Josiah Royce at the
time when he was writing his book on California. The narrative
was published as *A Frontier Lady*.

billiard-tables were pushed together, with blankets for curtains, or planks were laid over saw-horses for the pantomimes and ballets. Before the middle fifties the best actors were touring the camps. There Junius Brutus Booth had left his son Edwin Booth, who rode from camp to camp with a wagon-show. At times he appeared merely as a banjo-player, and he posted his own bills and beat his own drum. His father, telling him he looked like Hamlet, had urged him to play the part that was later the chief means of his development, fortune and fame.

There were songs and ballads from the first recounting the adventures of the forty-niners, reciting "miners' laments" and "miners' dreams," and the stories followed the song-books, soon to be followed in turn by the "Westerns" for which they afforded the models and many of the types. Meanwhile, "Old Block" was writing in the mines, describing the Pikes and the gamblers, the idle and industrious miners and Sunday in camp, the author of *Chips from the Old Block* and various other collections, with a realism and humour that were relished by the miners themselves. This writer, whose name was Alonzo Delano, had crossed the Rockies with an ox-team, when he was reduced to eating crows, hawks and rats, and, reaching Sacramento, he had bought a stock of goods and presently set out to sell it with a pack-train in the gold-fields. He also drew portraits of the miners at an ounce a head. His papers were printed in *The Golden Era,* known at once as the miners' favourite, a weekly that first appeared in 1852, with stories and poems, news, jokes and gossip, preceding the monthly *The Pioneer,* which was also published in San Francisco and modelled after the *Knickerbocker Magazine.* For magazines and publishing-houses had sprung up at once in San Francisco. *The Pioneer* published "John Phœnix,"—George H. Derby,—the first of the Far Western humorists, a West Point man, an army engineer and a member of the topographical corps who was sent to California in 1849. Active in tours of reconnaissance to find sites for army-posts, he also built a dam at San Diego, writing humorous descriptive letters from Benicia, Sonora and other towns and employing in comic drawings his talent as a draughtsman. But the humour of his *Phœnixiana* was irrecoverable in later times and in general the gold-rush had little attraction for writers, although the Virginian John Esten Cooke, seriously tempted to join it, was wholly obsessed by the thought in 1849. Poe said it was not for "poor-devil authors," [2] while Thoreau in Concord regarded this digging for gold as a disgrace to mankind, and Herman Melville, who agreed with them, expressed his opinion of the matter in *Mardi,* in the words of Babbalanja, skirting the shores of Kolumbo.[3] But there were numbers of the writers of the future in the gold-fields of the fifties before Mark Twain arrived and staked his claim, before Joaquin Miller set out for the mines in the North. H. H. Bancroft, who later wrote the histories, mined with his father near

[2] "Talking of gold and temptations at present held out to 'poor-devil authors,' did it ever strike you that all that is really valuable to a man of letters—to a poet in especial—is absolutely unpurchasable? Love, fame, the dominion of intellect, the consciousness of power, the thrilling sense of beauty, the free air of heaven, exercise of body and mind, with the physical and moral health which result—and such as these are really all that a poet cares for: —then answer me this—*why* should he go to California?"—Letter of Poe to F. W. Thomas, February 14, 1849.

The poem of Poe called *Eldorado,* written in 1849, also suggests the futility of the rush for gold.

[3] " 'No Yillah there,' says Babbalanja. 'Vain . . . to snatch at happiness. Of that we may not pluck and eat. It is the fruit of our own toilsome planting; slow it grows, nourished by many tears, and all our earnest tendings . . . Deep, Yoomy, deep, true treasure lies; deeper than all Mardi's gold, rooted to Mardi's axis. But unlike gold, it lurks in every soil, all Mardi over . . . Gold is the only poverty; of all glittering ills the direst . . . But man still will mine for it; and, mining, dig his doom.—Yoomy, Yoomy!—she we seek lurks not in the golden hills.' "—Melville, *Mardi.*

Marysville in 1852, and if Henry George was not actually a miner he was a victim of the gold-fever twice and joined the stampede to Fraser river. Then he started for Placerville, hoping for a lucky strike there, walking, sleeping in barns, working his way. Bret Harte had previously set out for the Mother Lode country. He had arrived in California, aged seventeen, in 1854, and taught for a while in one of the mining towns. He too tried his luck in the mines and had to borrow twenty dollars, after a three-weeks' adventure, to return to Oakland.

Several of these writers in times to come were to picture the miners in prose or in verse. Another of them was Prentice Mulford, who sailed round the Horn in a clipper-ship and arrived in San Francisco in 1856, the first of sixteen years that he spent in California, partly on the Tuolumne river at Hawkins' Bar. As a seacook on a whaling-schooner, before he went up to the gold-fields, he had stopped in Lower California at Magdalena Bay, the nursery for cow-whales where the mothers brought forth and nursed their young in the warm quiet waters of the long lagoons. He had learned to make plum-duff and sea-mince pie with salt beef, and he peddled meat in the mining-camps, scouring the gulches and the flats with beef-steaks in the panniers of his horse. He was a barkeeper too and an errand-boy in a saloon before he set up his own cabin on a rocky ledge, washing gold with a pan at first, then trying the rocker and trying the pocket, finally working a placer-claim with partners. Then he taught for a while, like Bret Harte, in a school-house in a camp for which gamblers had contributed much of the money. He had brought with him a trunk from "the States" with one good suit of ancient cut, a Bible, two or three shirts and a bundle of letters, and he added to these a tarantula's nest, a rattlesnake's tail and other treasures of the sort which the miners gathered in their solitary cabins. He made friends with the Chinese, the Kanakas and the Negro singers,—one of whom, known as "old Harry," performed on the bugle,—sharing the miners' "rainy day," which they spent in baking pies and bread, writing letters home and chopping their fuel. "Going to camp" meant on Sundays setting out in a white shirt for the nearest centre of billiards, news and faro.

The vivid *Prentice Mulford's Story* was a prototype from real life of Bret Harte's imaginary tales. Another was *Dame Shirley's Letter,* a record of 1851-'52, the work of a clever young woman who had lived in the gold-fields. Known as Shirley to her family and friends, though her real name was Louise Smith, she was the wife of a Dr. Clappe, with whom she had arrived in 1849 and presently settled for a while in the Sierras. She lived at Rich Bar on the Feather river and, shortly after, at Indian Bar, in a cabin surrounded by shanties of calico and pine-boughs, her only fare consisting for weeks of ham as hard as mahogany, dried-out mackerel and barrels of rusty pork. The camp hotel, known as the "Humboldt," was largely constructed of cotton sheets, though it had a wooden floor for the miners to dance on: one side was fitted up as a store, the other side with bunks, hung with red calico draperies, for the lodgers. A ranch near by was conducted by a minister who had become a jockey and a monte-dealer. More than half a dozen tongues were spoken in the little camp, among them Chinese and Hindustani. Shirley wrote good letters. She had gone to school at Amherst, where she had known Emily Dickinson, and writing on her rough plank table she sketched this violent little world with a gaiety and veracity that few could have equalled at the moment. It was she who related the incident of the new-born baby and the mother's death that probably suggested *The Luck of Roaring Camp,*—

the cover of a monte-table was used as a pall,—together with shooting and stabbing affrays, dances in the bar-room, picnics in the woods, the arrival of the mules with baskets of champagne and brandy. She described the river with its flumes and dams and the wing-dam that gave its name to the later fanciful capital of Bret Harte's country,—it divided the river lengthways instead of across,—and better than anyone else in the fifties she conveyed the spirit of the restless miners, swept as they were blindly from camp to camp.

Later, as a teacher in San Francisco, Shirley befriended Charles Warren Stoddard, the shy young poet who appeared there in 1855, while numbers of writers made use of her letters,—Bret Harte was undoubtedly stirred by them as he was by Charles Nahl's admirable drawings of the miners. Meanwhile, near Shirley's camp, James P. Beckwourth also lived, the trapper and squaw-man who had acted as a scout for Frémont and who chilled the marrow of the green young miners by the cold-blooded stories of Indian fights that soon appeared in his ghost-written *Life and Adventures*. For Beckwourth was a natural story-teller and the book, though composed by another hand, remained the best story perhaps of a mountain man. This former adopted chief of the Crows had discovered a pass in the Sierras and built a hotel and a trading-post for emigrants there, the first they reached in California, the first in fact beyond Great Salt Lake, and he piloted parties of emigrants across the mountains. Shirley saw him in the very year when Ina Coolbrith, ten years old, rode on the saddle before him as he guided the train. The centre of a circle of writers later, Ina Coolbrith was a daughter of the brother of the Mormon prophet, Don Carlos Smith,[4] the president of

---

[4] "In those old days, the average man called his children after his most revered literary and historical idols; consequently there was hardly a family, at least in the West, but had a Washington in it

the Quorum of High Priests who had died at Nauvoo a few months after she was born there. Her mother had met him when the Mormons were at Kirtland and had mended clothes for the men who were working on the temple, but she left the church when her husband died, married again and set out for the West, where the family stopped to try their luck in the mines. This was in 1851, but they soon pushed on to Los Angeles, the lawless pueblo-capital of the great cow-counties.

The wild Sierras, beyond Beckwourth's pass, were a no-man's-land for years to come, the haunt of outlaws, Diggers and grizzly bears, where the Sons of Dan, the "destroying angels," were supposed to have committed holy murders and apostates of the Mormons mysteriously disappeared. There James Capen Adams lived, with his wild beasts for companions, the Yankee forty-niner who had vanished in the woods, where he trained Ben Franklin, the favourite grizzly, captured near the Merced river, that carried his pack at times and was always his pet. Together with two young Indian friends, Tuolumne and Stanislaus, they roamed as far as Oregon and the Klamath lakes, encountering all manner of adventures with the wolves and the panthers, the snakes and the bears that Adams exhibited later in his Mountaineer Museum. He averred he had seen a strange great beast, a hedgehog with a bear's head, and fabulous beings undoubtedly existed in the mountains, or men at least who bred fables in the minds of ordinary pioneers and romantic young poets who were all too ready to receive them.

Hundreds of miners were lost there, and Joaquin

---

and also a Lafayette, a Franklin and six or eight sounding names from Byron, Scott and the Bible, if the offspring held out. To visit such a family was to find oneself confronted by a congress made up of representatives of the imperial myths and the majestic dead of all the ages. There was something thrilling about it, to a stranger."
—Mark Twain, *The Gilded Age*.

Murieta was one of the bandits who lurked in these alpine recesses, where Joaquin Miller, further north,—the writer who adopted this sinister name,—professed to have encountered other Byronic heroes. One was the splendid apparition, with the costly cloak and the rich red sash, whom he met, in his gay attire, in the morning sun, the noble and generous ex-gambler, the "Prince," who presently adopted the helpless boy and the Indian children, one of them the girl Paquita. Another was the Swiss de Bloney who had crossed the plains with an impulse like Brigham Young's and William Walker's to found a new state, an Indian "Mount Shasta Republic." There were three tribes that lived round the base of the mountain, and his plan was to unite them in a sort of Utopian national park where the Indians would continue to follow their natural existence. A third character was Indian Joe, who had also been one of Frémont's scouts and who carried a rough gold bullet in his pocket that he had cut from the neck of his horse after some earlier battle with the Apaches. Indian Joe was Miller's partner for a while when they kept a mountain roadhouse in the northern gold-fields. The Millers had reached Oregon in 1852, and Joaquin, tired of splitting rails and clearing land on his father's farm, ran away with hopes of adventure and a fortune. Crossing the California line, he worked as a cook in the camps, preparing the miners' "eternal beans, bacon and coffee," falling in with the Mexicans and trappers who mingled with the gold-seekers and who soon appeared in his poems, stories and plays. He dreamed of riding as a vaquero with a party of Mexicans to the Rio Grande, ranging through Colorado and Arizona, and he liked to imagine that he had gone with William Walker to Nicaragua and later wrote a poem that seemed to say so. His real life was adventurous enough, for he lived with the Indians round Mount Shasta, the solitary peak that

rose out of the great black forests, hunting elk and bears
with them, dressed like them in buckskins, virtually
adopted as an Indian in a village on a stream. It may
have been true that he could ride as only Murieta rode,
the outlaw whose legend he liked to connect with
his own,[5] and he shared his tent with the Indian girl
who appeared in *My Life Among the Modocs,* the fanciful autobiography that he wrote in England. He fought
on the side of the persecuted Indians, though in other
engagements he fought against them, and he was undoubtedly wounded by one of their arrows.

Soon after the Millers had settled in Oregon, Theodore Winthrop, fresh from Yale, arrived there in the
spring of 1853, stopping on the way in San Francisco,
where he found the young men speculating in steamboats, politics, beef, land-titles and lumber. The first
steam sawmills on Puget Sound were set in motion that
year, when Washington was declared a separate territory, and Captain McClellan, later the general, and his
army engineers were surveying for a railroad over the
Cascade mountains. Seattle was only a name and a mill,
and to travel from point to point on the sound one
hired the sort of boat and crew that Winthrop presently
described in *The Canoe and the Saddle.* His own canoe-
trip over Whulge, the Chinook name for Puget Sound,
with the bibulous "Duke of York" and his frowsy crone,
was the passage that one remembered longest from this
classic of the "last frontier," a most engaging tale of the
forests and the mountains.

Winthrop, a New Haven boy, descended from Jonathan Edwards as well as the colonial governors who had

[5] "I don't know why I always encouraged this idea of having been
an outlaw, but I recall that when Trelawny told me that Byron
was more ambitious to be thought the hero of his wildest poems
than even to be king of Greece I could not help saying to myself,
as Napoleon said to the thunders preceding Waterloo, 'We are of
accord.' "—Joaquin Miller, note for *The Tale of the Tall Alcalde.*

borne his name, had been living abroad for a year and a
half, especially in Paris, where he and William Morris
Hunt were inseparable friends. He had been stirred by
Hunt's ideas, as William and Henry James were later,
when Hunt returned to America and lived at Newport,
and he thought for a while of writing a book on art;
then, at home in New York again, he had studied Spanish and gone to Panama in 1852. He was connected with
a steamship company that was engaged at the time in
carrying fortune-hunters to the Western coast, for this
and the Nicaraguan route were thronged with belated
seekers of gold who wished to avoid the journey over
the plains. While many crossed the plains, of course, and
others sailed around Cape Horn, the voyage described
by Dana and in *Prentice Mulford's Story,* the Isthmian
and Nicaraguan routes were better known than either
because so many of the writers followed one or the
other. Bayard Taylor and "John Phœnix" in 1849
sailed up to San Francisco by way of Panama. So did
Artemus Ward and John Muir soon, while Bret Harte
and Charles Warren Stoddard, Eastern boys going West,
travelled by way of Nicaragua. Mark Twain returned
that way in 1866, at the time when he met the original
of Captain Stormfield, the old seadog who fancied that
he alone of all men living knew the real secret of the
miracles in the Bible. Several of these men wrote vivid
accounts of their days or weeks on the "deadly Isthmus"
when they passed through the heart of the Central
American forest, whether by Lake Nicaragua and the
saffron-coloured San Juan river or by the chocolate-
coloured Chagres. Either on muleback or on boats they
penetrated jungles of canes and lilies, gorgeous tropical
growths and gigantic vines that clambered over the path
and bridged the bayous, where clouds of flamingos flew
overhead and scarlet parrots and splendid macaws
flashed through the leafy caverns like jewels and flames.

Chattering monkeys hung from the boughs and skir-
mished in the creepers that sometimes shot halfway
across the stream, and John Muir said he had cried for
joy in this most glorious of forests, glowing with purple, red and yellow flowers. But the beautiful Isthmus
was ridden with fever and the railroad was being built
at a fearful sacrifice of life. One of the victims in 1852
was the president, "Central American" Stephens,—the
great travel-writer John Lloyd Stephens,—whom the
Frémonts had met in Washington when the Panama
railroad was being discussed and he was appointed super-
intendent of it. Mrs. Frémont later recalled the quick
boyish manner in which he said they must be good to
him because he was being sent to the Isthmus "to die."
When he was really dying and the Frémonts were there
and had caught the fever he came in every afternoon
"to take my chill with you," he said. He sent his best
Indian bearers with a palanquin to carry Mrs. Frémont
across the Isthmus. Travellers were shown for many
years the cottage where Stephens had lived and the tall
"Stephens tree" beside the railroad, draped with garlands and wreaths of trailing vines.[6]

A few months after his own first visit, Winthrop returned to the Isthmus with an expedition exploring for
a ship's canal, and he wrote a fine sketch *Isthmiana* describing Panama, the ruinous old Spanish town with
huts like ant-hills. The roof and spire of the cathedral
were inlaid with mother-of-pearl and the wharves were
heaped high with coffee and boxes of gold-dust. He had
canoed a hundred miles up the coast, past undulating
green savannahs and mangrove swamps, with conical
peaks in the distance, and he found nothing in the
Northwest, when he sailed there by way of San Francisco, more difficult and dangerous than the mule-path

---

[6] When, in 1855, Charles Warren Stoddard sailed up the Western
coast from Panama, his ship was called the "John L. Stephens."

over the Isthmus. It was infested with plundering natives and poisonous mosquitoes, though the trails in
Oregon and Washington were perilous enough. Sometimes one could find them only when a root had been
scraped by a hoof or a tuft of moss perhaps had been
kicked away or the brown pine-leaves had been trodden
to a yellower tint: then, as Winthrop said, they declared
themselves distinctly like pleasant associations reawak-
ening in the mind. By April, 1853, he had reached the
mouth of the Columbia river and the few poor remains
of Astoria standing on the bank,—all but engulfed in
mud in their rude clearing,—ready for adventures in the
Cascade mountains and along this grandest of the Western streams, rushing through forests as thick as the jungles of the tropics. Not long afterwards, at Vancouver,
he stayed in the house of Colonel Bonneville, the com-
mandant of the American army-post, the hero of Washington Irving's book and the same Bonneville who, as
a boy, had been brought to America in the care of
Thomas Paine. But Winthrop spent most of the summer camping with Indians or alone in the wild dells of
the mountains or in chasms of the river. The elevations
he knew at home were hillocks beside the Cascades,—
Katahdin, the knolls of New Hampshire, the Alleghenies, mere knobs of earth or excrescences more or
less rough. There was never a summit among them all
that was brilliant forever with snow, golden in the sunshine, silver when the sunshine vanished.

Winthrop, who loved luxury, liked also to dispense
with it, and as ever he found this savage life alluring,
with heather or hemlock for a bed and bracken for a
curtain and feasts of game cooked under the greenwood
tree. He had learned in Maine that the shade of pines
made those who were subjected to it tough, wiry, tireless and keen, and, waking in a mountain meadow, or
by a torrent in a gorge, or beside some arrowy river clear

and cold, he felt fresh vigorous influences in the air about him. The flowers opened boldly, there was no languid droop in the stems, and the grass-blades stood upright and alert, each having lightly tossed off its burden of a dewdrop. He felt that he rose himself from sleep taller by fractions of an inch, with a brain that was leagues above all doubt and depression, and he liked living with frontiersmen to whom no man was anything unless he could saddle, lasso, cook, sing and chop. These were the "Bostons" or the "Boston men," as the Indians had called the American whites since their first ships appeared, commonly from Boston, and Captain Gray discovered the Columbia river.[7] Winthrop encountered a few of them, but he was thrown more with the Indians, and he had for a while an Indian guide who knew every lane and alley green as well as Comus ever knew his wild wood. He studied the Indian ways and speech and made up a word-list of Chinook, the lingua franca of the Indians and the whites on the coast, a jargon of English, French, Spanish, Chinook and other native tongues that had risen since the Chinook tribe first met the traders. He learned how to gutteralize, sputter and swallow in Chinook. He fell in with a Yakimah chief and with Flatheads and Klalams, exuding salmon-juices and varnished with fish-oil, and he might have met the "travelling squaw," the aging Sacajawea, who had once been the Indian guide of Lewis and Clark. This was the girl who had saved their instruments and records when the dugout canoe was upset on a famous occasion, and Sacajawea still had many years to live, until 1884, when she was a century old. She was to live long enough to ride with free passes through the Western country, mediating again and again between the Indians and the

[7] Nearly half a century later, as he recorded in his *Travels in Alaska*, John Muir found that English-speaking people were still called "Boston men" in the Chinook Northwest. The Indians also spoke of "Boston food."

whites. Winthrop was not entirely fair to the "Dooker-yawk," the Chinook chief whose wives were named Queen Victoria and Jenny Lind, the mendacious unsavoury Duke who had been loyal to the whites in various Indian uprisings along the sound. But he had decided to remain himself an American of the nineteenth century and not subside into a Klalam brave.

After these weeks in the mountains, he launched out across the plains on a two-months' homeward gallop through the Mormon country. He had bought a superb black stallion with a lope as elastic as the bounding of a wind-sped cloud, and he stopped at trading-posts where the Indians exchanged their furs for blankets, beads and 'baccy, the three B's of their desire. The forts in these bleak sere regions, Laramie and Bridger, recalled the blockhouses and refuges of early New England. Winthrop halted at Salt Lake City, where he talked with Brigham Young, and he passed throngs of emigrants with flocks and herds, patriarchal trains of saints, struggling with handcarts and wheelbarrows and urging their ox-teams along to the faraway Canaan. Many suggested the Israelites or Ishmael Bush and his clan in *The Prairie,* while others were poor English factory-folk and withered little tradesmen hastening to their promised free acres and their thrones in the sky. Still other caravans with white-roofed wagons, strewn over the plains like sails on a populous sea, were moving away from the tame levels of the middle of the country to the more dramatic scenes of the Western slope.

All these appeared in *The Canoe and the Saddle* or in Winthrop's novel *John Brent,*—a story of adventure on the plains and an early "Western" with a freshness that later tales seldom possessed,—two books that opened the eyes of readers to the splendours of the Far Western scene and attracted the landscape-painters and the naturalists thither. They anticipated in many passages Clarence King and John Muir, in the picture of the battered crags of the Dalles, for example, the rough waste paved with dreary sheets of black basaltic rock where the mighty chain of the Cascade peaks began. It had taken Americans two hundred years to find their own Alps in the West. Hitherto, for the exaltation aroused by the presence of solemn heights, they had always been obliged to return to Europe. Convinced that civilized mankind had never had a chance to develop amid influences as stirring as one found here, Winthrop thought much of the possible effect in the future of these vast and lonely grandeurs and depths of ether. In a climate where every breath one drew was a vivid draught of life, where all the conditions of existence were calm and large, might not civilization, no longer suffering from the too close example of Europe, achieve some finer system of thinking and living? In the presence of these signal facts, Winthrop felt in the Northwest what William James felt in California fifty years later, the promise of "the new society at last, proportionate to nature" that Whitman expressed in his *Song of the Redwood-Tree*:—

Fresh come, to a new world indeed, yet long prepared,
I see the genius of the modern, child of the real and ideal,
Clearing the ground for broad humanity, the true America,
  heir of the past so grand,
To build a grander future.

CHAPTER VI

WALT WHITMAN'S YOUTH

FOR a dozen years before 1850, when Walt Whitman was thirty-one, he had sauntered about New York with a curious eye, charmed by the living panorama of the myriad-headed city, the crowds, the shops, the stages, the theatres, the wharves. A farm-boy from Long Island who had become a Brooklyn editor, Whitman had written for many of the magazines, but he was scarcely known in literary circles, though his figure was familiar enough on the ferry-boats and streets. Tall and rather heavily built, with a fresh pink skin and a lounging air, —his beard was already touched with grey,—he had, as he said, an unusual capacity for standing still, rooted on a spot, at rest, for a long spell, to ruminate. He had written a facetious paper on loafing, in praise of the "genuine inbred loafer" and the calm steady "son of indolence," and this appeared to be his role, though in truth he was living intensely: at moments he felt like a god walking the earth. Merely to move at these times was a pleasure to him; it made him happy just to breathe and see. For his physical health was superb, he was strong and buoyant. He felt as if no other mortal could enjoy this show as he did, as if it had been especially arranged for him to observe. He loved the name Manhattan, which Irving and Cooper had loved before him, as much as he loved the meaning of this Indian word, "The place encircled by swift and sparkling waters."

His forbears had been half Dutch, half English, the typical mixture of the New York breed, and the traits of both these stocks were evident in him, for he was earth-

ier than most of the Yankees, with whom he had so
much in common, and the sense of the flesh was much
more active in him. He was open to currents of thought
from New England as very few others were in New
York, and he shared some of the tastes of his Quaker
forefathers. There were times when he wondered if he
was not by spiritual bent a Quaker, for he wholly believed in the notion of the "inner light," and his father
and his grandfather had both known Elias Hicks, whom
Whitman too had heard as a boy of ten. Later he wrote
a memoir of Hicks, but as for himself he once remarked
that he could not "live inside a fence," and, while he
dressed in Quaker grey and used Quaker phrases, he
preferred the "healthy this-worldliness" of his Dutch
mother. In after years Whitman often suggested a
Quaker patriarch and as often a merry old Dutchman
whom Frans Hals might have painted.[1] His family, all
of them farmer-folk, had lived for five generations or
more on the north shore of Long Island, thirty miles
from New York, and Whitman's later memories were all
of green cornfields, flourishing orchards, sailing-parties
and clambakes on the shore of the Sound. Well he knew
the flat plains and the prairie-like vistas where the cattle and sheep browsed on the grassy patches in summer
and fall, the salt meadows, the sedgy smells, the inlets
and watery hummocks that swarmed with all manner of
fish and aquatic fowl. He could never forget the soothing rustle of the waves, or the hayboats, or the chowder
and fishing excursions. He roamed the island in all
directions from Brooklyn to Montauk, where one looked
out over the Atlantic from the bluff by the lighthouse,
passing Elias Hicks's farm at Jericho perhaps or the
rock where George Fox preached in 1692. This was at
Oyster Bay, and two white oaks still stood at Flushing

[1] It was thus that Thomas Eakins saw him in the portrait that
Whitman liked best.

where Fox had addressed the multitude as in apostolic times, expounding the doctrine of secret ecstasy without regard for formal creeds that Hicks had carried on at a later day. Whitman went sailing with parties of young farmers and girls, and he set out with gun or clam-rake, spearing eels through the ice in winter and gathering seagulls' eggs in the summer sand. He fraternized with fishermen and farmers, bay-men and pilots, and with dancing Negroes and boys with flutes like those of William Sidney Mount, who was painting his Long Island scenes at just this time. Mount, who, as a friend said, "made Long Island his Italy," had returned to his native Setauket in 1827 and pictured on canvases, distinctly American, that recalled the old Dutch painters, the world that surrounded Whitman's childhood. His farmers nooning and husking corn, boys caught napping in a field, saltbox farmhouses, mowers' and haymakers' dances might have been illustrations indeed, in treatment, theme and feeling alike, of Whitman's early memories in *Specimen Days*.

Thus Whitman was a country boy before he became a young man of the streets, and he returned to this open-air life, in the days of his invalidism, after the Civil War, at Timber Creek. He loved the old agricultural order of the world that he was bred in,—he was never as deeply at home in the industrial world,— and he hoped to see farming increase in America, as he wrote in one of his prose pieces: "Its gains are the only ones on which God seems to smile." No doubt this was the reason he was drawn to Millet more than to any other painter.[2] Meanwhile, until he was forty or more

[2] Whitman once remarked, "The man who knows his Millet needs no creed." According to Traubel, he also said, "Millet excites all the religion in me—excites me to a greater self-respect . . . The Leaves are really only Millet in another form—they are the Millet that Walt Whitman has succeeded in putting into words."—*With Walt Whitman in Camden*.

he rambled occasionally over Long Island, where he had once edited a newspaper and taught country schools, at Babylon, Jamaica, Whitestone, Woodbury and Flushing, boarding round at neighbouring farms and always more impressed by the self-reliance and native good sense of the people. In the old-fashioned schoolhouses, fastened with a padlock, with a small chimney rising through the eaves, where he taught the three R's, with a little geography and "speaking," Whitman picked up incidents that he used in some of his early stories, intended to inculcate temperance, fidelity or thrift. He liked to read the great poets in the open air within sound of the sea, and at Coney Island, in mild seasons, on the long bare unfrequented beach, he raced up and down the sand, after a swim, declaiming Homer and Shakespeare to the surf and the gulls. He first read the Iliad thoroughly in a sheltered hollow of the rocks, in the full presence of nature, under the sun, with the far-spreading landscape and vistas and the sea rolling in, as he read Dante in an old wood near the shore, and the sight of a ship that was passing under full sail had aroused his first impulse to write in early boyhood. He had longed to describe this ship exactly. The shore, where the water married the land, symbolized for him the blending of the real and the ideal, for each became part of the other on this wavering line, and he remembered feeling once that he must write a book expressing what he called "this liquid mystic theme." Then it came to him that the seashore should rather be a general influence with him, a pervading gauge or tally in his composition. Whitman's poems later abounded in sea-images, "leaves of salt lettuce" and "scales from shining rocks" and waves "reproachfully rolling sands and drift," while the rhythms of the sea were in his blood. The poetic form that he gradually evolved was oceanic, as he sometimes said, with verses that recalled the waves, rising and falling, often sunny, now and then wild with storm, scarcely two alike in length or measure. These verses suggested constant motion, and he wished them to leave an impression not of anything fixed and finished but of something "beyond."

The poet in Whitman developed late and slowly, while his early writings came only from the surface of his mind. But when he was scarcely in his teens he was publishing bits in Brooklyn papers and presently in George P. Morris's *New York Mirror*. At twelve he became an apprentice-printer, the first occupation of a dozen writers who were more or less of Whitman's time, —Bayard Taylor, William Dean Howells, Mark Twain, Bret Harte and Joel Chandler Harris among the rest. Artemus Ward was a printer in Ohio, Edward Eggleston and Ambrose Bierce and the younger poets Stedman and Gilder were printers for a while, and Henry George set part of the type of *Progress and Poverty* in San Francisco as Whitman was to set his *Leaves of Grass*. Then, as Mark Twain, among all his ventures, cared most for the Paige type-setting machine, in which he sank fortune after fortune, so Whitman retained the interest in printing that he had acquired as a little boy standing on type-cases to reach the boxes. In old age he always knew "the easiest way out of printers' puzzles," as his disciple Horace Traubel said, and he watched his proofs with anxious eye, ready to add or omit a line in cases where a page struck him as too loose or crowded. He did not love his lines "enough to let them spoil the page," he said, and he once sacrificed nine for a blank space. He would send silver dollars with thanks to the proof-takers for giving him clean dark proofs on paper that he liked. But while, in his boyhood, Whitman was a printer who was also beginning to write, his real occupation was absorbing impressions, historical impressions, among the rest, that attached him deeply from the first to the past and evolution of the country. The old printer and editor who taught him his trade, in the basement of a Brooklyn shop,—a shabby Revolutionary building in Fulton Street, with brick walls and narrow doors and windows,—described to him often the appearance and manner of Washington and Jefferson, whom he had encountered in New York in his early days. As an errand boy, Whitman had crossed the river with messages for Aaron Burr, whom he recalled as considerate, courteous and gentle and who sometimes gave him an apple or a pear, and he often saw the widow of Alexander Hamilton, who was active in various charitable societies in town.[3] Lafayette had kissed him when he was a very little boy and the old soldier was laying a cornerstone in Brooklyn, in the presence of other worthies of the Revolution, and Whitman had observed Andrew Jackson, who had driven on another occasion through the Brooklyn streets. He vividly recalled this hero of democracy with his big-brimmed white beaver hat, the white hair that was brushed stiffly up from his forehead and the spectacles with the piercing eyes behind them. Moreover, he had heard much of Thomas Paine. His carpenter-father had met Paine and he himself had known Colonel Fellows, the special crony of Paine's later years, a hearty old man, a minor official in the New York law-courts, where the young lawyers called him Aristides. For, holding his tall staff erect, with his superb white head, he seemed to them an image of absolute rectitude and justice, and, liking young men himself, he was a favourite with them all. He gave Whitman minute accounts of the last illness and death of Paine, a noble personality, as he had known him, who had lived a good life and died philosophically and calmly. Whitman had learned from Colonel Fellows

[3] Of Hamilton himself Whitman said (*The Gathering of the Forces*) that he "sowed the seeds of some good and much evil."

how literally nothing was true of the foul slanders and fictions that were told about Paine, and he made up his mind from that moment to do what he could to set Paine's memory right.[4]

This was about 1840, in the old back parlour of Tammany Hall, when Whitman was already active in the Democratic party, living in New York, meanwhile, almost as much as in Brooklyn,—he was a compositor at times and an editor there. In politics he was a radical democrat, following his father, who subscribed to a magazine published by Robert Dale Owen and who had named two of his other sons Thomas Jefferson and Andrew Jackson and brought the boys up on Paine and Volney's *Ruins*. Whitman, who had spoken at a Tammany meeting in City Hall Park in 1841, had plunged with zeal into most of the movements of reform, for restrictions of the slave-system, the abolition of capital punishment, the humaner treatment of animals and especially free trade. Jefferson for him was the "greatest of the great," and the doctrines of the rights of man, the evils of privilege, the absurdity of rank were bred as it were in his bones. They seemed natural particularly on Long Island, the most democratic of regions and the most untouched by aristocratic ideas, the aristocratic theology of the neighbouring Connecticut counties or the social aristocracy of the mainland of New York. Whitman was a Quaker equalitarian who disliked "imported feudal manners," and he wished to "encourage in the young men the spirit that does not know what it is to feel that it stands in the presence of superiors," he said. But, while he was all for the "average," for the masses, he was all for "grand individuals" too and wished to "build up the masses" by building them up, and no one was keener in his own way for "superior men," for

[4] Of Paine he once remarked, "The tree with the best apples gets the worst clubbing."—*With Walt Whitman in Camden.*

"higher men," as he did not hesitate to call them in conversation. They were the "models for democracy" that
Whitman praised in Shakespeare's plays. He was happy
that he had met a few, still living in his youth, who had
given him some of the fire of the Revolution, and his
later memories abounded with great men of every kind
whom he had met or observed with a devouring eye. In
boxes at the old Bowery theatre or promenading Broadway he had seen John Quincy Adams and Henry Clay,
and he had heard Daniel Webster often, delivering
some of his greatest speeches with a grandeur, he felt,
rather of manner than of sense. Once he had listened to
Fenimore Cooper, in the court-room in Chambers Street,
conducting one of his own libel-cases, while he had been
deeply impressed by Channing, also in New York, with
his slight frail figure wrapped in a black silk gown. The
apostle of mental independence had radiated candour
and a spiritual grace that glimmered about his person
like white flame. Then there was Bryant of the *Evening
Post,* another Jacksonian editor, who sometimes joined
Whitman in Brooklyn for an afternoon ramble. Later,
when *Leaves of Grass* appeared, Bryant lost interest in
the hardy Walt, to whom he had related his travels as
they strolled towards Flatbush.

It was not without meaning that Whitman delighted
in Carlyle, much as he disliked the "great man theory,"
the "concentration of historical meaning in single eminent persons," as he called it, together with Carlyle's re-
actionary doubts and fears. He felt that nations, like
individuals, learned most from a sincere opponent, from
the light thrown even scornfully on their dangerous
spots, and that more perhaps than other voices America
needed the warnings and threats of this candid and
heroic enemy of the democratic programme. Whitman,
who deeply admired Carlyle, had his own kind of hero-
worship and scrutinized powerful personalities wherever

he met them, the "democratic despots" whose purpose was not to enslave and who served as a leaven and a measure for the humanity of the future. He observed Kossuth and Garibaldi, when they were in New York, and orators perhaps especially, with actors and preachers, the tempestuous Junius Brutus Booth, Edwin Forrest at the Bowery theatre and religious speakers, beginning with Elias Hicks. He was more than commonly drawn to Beecher, who was a friend of the *Leaves* from the first and whose sermons were rhapsodies in praise of liberty and brotherhood, affirming that the life of the people was the life of God. On visits to Boston in his middle fifties, Whitman alternated, he said, between Theodore Parker and Father Taylor, the "perfect orator" of the Seamen's Chapel whom he described as "a first-class genius in the rarest and most profound of humanity's arts." He had trained himself in oratory, speaking in the woods and along the shore, and he made a special study of it when he thought seriously of lecturing later, expounding the gospel he expressed in *Leaves of Grass*. He noted the "sweeping movements" of actors, the "strong yet flexible face," the "expanding chest at times," the "open breast" and the art of bending and rising to the height of the figure,[5] and much of this oratorical tendency appeared in his poetic style, with occasional touches of Tammany speechifying. Many of his poems were written declamations. For the rest, he saw in great men and women merely an extension of the common man, who often shared their emotional amplitude, and he deplored all emphasis on "personalism,"—he preferred to think of men in the "average," in the mass. By choice he consorted with artisans and workmen like himself and he was on the best of terms with his father's household, congenial with all of his brothers and sisters and with his mother espe-

[5] Clifton J. Furness, *Walt Whitman's Workshop*.

cially, to whom he owed more, he felt, than to anyone else. She was the "mother of many children" who embodied maternal nature for him, and he never ceased to bask in her happiness and goodness, while he shared her country ways and rejoiced in her "splendid buckwheat cakes," for Whitman's tastes and needs were always of the simplest. He was abstemious in youth as in age, he never smoked or drank, he was never in any manner "dissipated," as one of his brothers remarked, and, indifferent to money, he liked "cheap fare," currants and raspberries mixed for breakfast or blackberries with a cup of tea and good rye bread. He relished the coffee of the stands in the market and a supper of oysters fresh from the beds at a table crowded with workingmen and sailors.

When later, in his poems and his prose alike, he dwelt on the soundness of the common people, Whitman spoke from an intimate knowledge of them, for his real occupation for years was to mingle with crowds, especially of the young, developing his gifts of sympathy and observation. Almost every day he crossed the East River on the Fulton ferry, where he made himself at home in the pilot-house, sometimes staying there half the day, enchanted by the hurrying splashing tides and the throngs that poured on and off the boat. He got a full sweep there of the bay and river scenery, the changing panorama of the passing steamers, the white-sailed schooners and the sloops and skiffs and the majestic Sound boats that rounded the Battery in the evening sailing eastward. The ferry-boats gave him, as he said, inimitable, streaming, living poems, and the pilots permitted him to steer the boats at times, though he usually preferred to watch them, marvelling, as Mark Twain marvelled on the Mississippi, over their skill at the wheel. They were sensitive to motions that he had no suspicion of and the "special water influences," as he

called them. Even their feet were sensitive, Whitman
said in later years,—they had the quality of "all men
made acute by long training in some special branch of
labour." Whitman was fascinated by their dexterity as
by the skill of the carpenters that he was soon to celebrate in *Leaves of Grass,* and he watched masons and
shipwrights in action, carriage-makers and foundrymen,
admiring their craft and their pride in the "strong day's
work." He was drawn to the Broadway stage-drivers, a
quick-eyed wondrous race over whom he felt sure that
Cervantes and Rabelais would have gloated, Patsy Dee,
Balky Bill, Big Frank and Pop Rice, mimics and spin-
ners of yarns, comradely and jovial. They were as full
of human nature as Bret Harte's Yuba Bill. Whitman
rode on the box beside them on afternoons or summer
nights, sometimes the whole length of Broadway, listening to their waggery or shouting stormy bits from Shakespeare over the unheeding heads of the passers-by. For
the loudest roars were drowned by the clattering of the
wheels on the cobble-stones and the uninterrupted bass
of the streets of the city. Whitman watched over some
of these drivers when they were in hospitals, as he
watched over the wounded soldiers later, and he drove
a stage all winter himself in order that one disabled
friend might continue to support his family while he
rested. He delighted in other New York types that had
not yet found their Hogarth or Dickens, young men,
shipbuilders, cartmen, firemen, butchers whose looks
and movements were free and picturesque, as he visited prisoners in the Tombs, poor-houses, factories and
wharves, auctions, fairs, police-courts, theatres, races.
Whitman was as pleased as a child by the great shop-
windows, the crowds of women and foreigners swarming
through the streets, bubbling and whirling like the
water that surrounded the city, the thronged excursion-
steamers, the streams of omnibuses, carriages, drays, the

perpetual movement of humanity in all its phases. Returning after a long absence, later in life, he still
rejoiced in the "prodigality," as he called it, "of locomo-
tion, dry goods, glitter, magnetism and happiness of the
city." What he loved especially in the seething American
population was its freedom, its alertness, its freshness
and turbulent good nature, the clear eye that looked
straight at you, both reticent and self-possessed, the decency, the independence, the affection and the pride.
For him, as for others in later years, the tumult even of
the political scenes was good to behold and reassuring, for
this tempestuousness showed that the people acted. How
much better than the despairing apathy of the people
of European states,—the "well-ordered" governments of
Germany and czarist Russia, of the French of the
Bourbons and the Bonapartes, Italy, Spain,—who en-
dured in silence the rapacity and selfishness of their
rulers.

Whitman never ceased to be shocked by the indifference of previous writers,—virtually all the writers of the
world, in fact,—to the "bulk of the average," the nobility of ordinary people. He was by no means dazzled by
them, and when somebody quoted Victor Hugo, who
remarked of the populace of Paris, "these are not the
people,—these are only the mournful beginnings of the
people," Whitman replied that he agreed with this. He
saw their crude defective streaks, their ignorance in
countless cases, the vast collections of the credulous, the
uncouth, the unfit, but he saw too what he described as
their measureless wealth of latent capacity, their entire
reliability in emergencies, in America at least. In politics the important point was not that the masses were
good, necessarily,—it was not even a question of the
rights of the masses,—but that, rights or no rights, good
or bad, the democratic formula was the only safe and
preservative one for the future. It was the only effective

method for slowly training people to rule and manage themselves of their own will,—far better than merely finding good rulers for them,—and in any case a main object of government should be to encourage the possibilities of all beneficent and manly outcroppings in them. They were in no position yet to do justice to themselves, and literature had never done justice to them, but Whitman was sure that their instincts were right in the main and that they made, in the long run, steady advances. He liked to think of obscure heroes, the farmer on the Hudson, for instance, who rescued the shipwrecked passengers on a winter night, as later it pleased him to remember that Grant was a common tanner of Illinois and that Lincoln, the railsplitter, worked as a hand on a flatboat. His imagination constantly dwelt on ferrymen, drovers, mechanics, on policemen, railroad employees, farmers, sailors, and their quick readiness in times of stress, their practicality and unwitting devotion, their cheerfulness, Ulyssean capacity and derring-do.

He was twenty-nine years old, meanwhile, before he saw America beyond the small corner of New York and its neighbouring island. Then in 1848 he visited the South and the West. As a Free-soil Democrat who had lost his position on the Brooklyn *Eagle,* he was invited to join a New Orleans paper, and, setting out with a younger brother by way of Baltimore, he crossed the Alleghenies in a coach to Wheeling. Travelling by boat to Cincinnati and down the Ohio and the Mississippi, he spent three months in New Orleans before returning up the river,—where Mark Twain lived at Hannibal, a boy of thirteen,—stopping at St. Louis, the gateway of the old Far West, and passing through Chicago, La Salle, Milwaukee and Cleveland. He skirted the rich northwestern region that Abraham Lincoln knew so well and visited Mackinaw island and the agency and fort there, crossed Lake Michigan and Lake Huron, passed Buffalo and Niagara Falls and came back to New York by way of the Hudson river. Writing for his New Orleans paper, he sketched types that were new to him: flower-girls in the old French market, a dandy, a drayman, an oyster-vendor and two or three characters whom he personified in their names as Mr. Daggerdraw Bowieknife and Miss Dusky Grisette. In the vast bar-rooms of the Southern hotels, where all classes met for talk, he saw men addressing a hundred persons or more, and he studied the boatmen on the bustling levees, where the river-craft were wedged in, and Negroes and mules swarmed amid the piles of cotton. The Mexican War was just over, the streets were alive with returning soldiers, and Whitman talked with General Zachary Taylor, while he made friends with the old mulatto woman from whose kettle in the market he drank his morning coffee. He probably picked up in New Orleans many of the odd French words and phrases that he was fond of using later, and he heard while he was there of Bryant's enthusiasm in New York for the new and second French republic. Whitman's use of French words, like his admiration for George Sand, reflected a lifelong feeling for France and the French, whom he liked beyond all other foreign peoples.[6] He made the acquaintance during his journey of seventeen states of the Union, with many of the varieties of character in the mountains, in the towns, Southerners and pioneers

[6] "She has my sympathy first of all," he wrote to Peter Doyle at the time when he composed *O Star of France*.

Almost all the foreign words that Whitman used were French. In one of his early magazine articles, *America's Mightiest Inheritance* (the English language), he gave a list of these foreign words running to four or five pages. These he called "tip-top words, much needed in English," though he offered some advice to working-people on their use: "Understand the meaning of the word exactly before you use it. Do not use it at all if there be an English word that fully expresses your meaning. Also, do not use any new word when the person or persons you address will probably not understand it."

of the Western prairies, absorbing with the landscapes a feeling of the prospects of the country and the spiritual wealth behind its material resources.

The long journey through "these States" quickened Whitman's consciousness and gave him an extraordinary sense of the nation as a whole, of American places, names, words, Mississippi, Monongahela, which rolled, he said, "with venison richness" on the palate. Meanwhile, he was absorbing the ideas and discoveries of the time as much as he absorbed the appearance and the ways of the people, reading and reviewing the new books, reporting concerts, operas and plays and following the progress of science and mechanical invention. He saw and heard the great actors, actresses and singers, the younger Kean, Alboni, Fanny Kemble, preparing himself for a Shakespeare play by reading it beforehand and sometimes writing in the gallery, stirred by the music. The airs of Rossini and Verdi always moved him, and later he felt that *Leaves of Grass* owed much of their style and form to the arias and recitatives of the Italian composers. He saw the early Negro minstrels, with "Daddy" Rice as Jim Crow, and the Indian Gallery of George Catlin, whom he admired and later recalled as "wise, informed, devoted." Catlin gave Whitman one of his prints of Osceola, the Seminole chief, which hung in the old man's room in Camden later. Whitman went often to Fowler and Wells's Phrenological Cabinet, where he had his own head carefully examined and charted and where the first edition of *Leaves of Grass* was later sold when the booksellers refused to handle it.[7] Familiar with the American writers Longfellow, Whittier, Bryant, Poe, some of whose work he reprinted in the Brooklyn *Eagle,* he reviewed new

---

[7] Fowler and Wells themselves published the second edition of *Leaves of Grass.* Whitman adopted several words from the lingo of phrenology,—amativeness, adhesiveness, etc.

books or new editions of Coleridge, Goethe, Lamartine, of Ruskin, Carlyle, George Sand and scores of others. While much of his reading was superficial, he read with passion here and there, and he had a tenacious affection for certain authors, among them Scott, whose minstrelsy he studied for fifty years and whose novels were a special pleasure of his old age. Describing Cooper's Natty Bumppo as "from everlasting to everlasting," he said that both Scott and Cooper "take life forward."

Some of his early tastes and interests were to leave plain traces in his poems and prose, while in other cases the effect was not apparent, Whitman's affection for Scott, for example, who was "active at the roots" of the *Leaves,* he said, and who had permeated him "through and through." The reason was that while Scott, like Tennyson, expressed the principle of caste which he felt that Americans had come on earth to destroy, he also stood for the personal qualities in which the feudal world excelled and offered examples for Americans to enlarge and spread. Certain other influences that Whitman absorbed during these years were obvious in all his later work, and when he spoke of the "day-rise of science" he recalled the zest with which he watched the progress of astronomy, physiology, chemistry, mechanics. He had in all probability heard, at the Brooklyn Institute, lectures by Agassiz and others,—it was there he listened to the "learn'd astronomer," perhaps, with the proofs and the figures ranged in columns before him, —and he planned a series of poems of science, the "poem of chemistry," of astronomy, of geology, and often referred to the poetry of mechanical inventions. He praised the new reapers and threshers and the "fierce-throated" beauty, the locomotive, and he was "an evolutionist," he said, "from A to Izzard." Like Poe, he drew from the newspapers and from popular reports in

the magazines most of his knowledge of science, philosophy and invention, though he owned and read Fred-
eric Hedge's *Prose Writers of Germany* and had some
direct acquaintance with German thought. He became
aware, in one way or another, of all the ideas that
stirred Brook Farm and formed the New England
Transcendentalism, derived from Rousseau, from Kant,
from Goethe, from Hegel, so that he was prepared for
Emerson in the early fifties, and he had followed in *The
Tribune* Margaret Fuller's writings, which he had also
reprinted in part in *The Eagle.* He shared her love of
George Sand, whose novels were appearing in the forties, and, deeply impressed by some of these novels,
which she reviewed one after another, he also reviewed
them, in two or three cases, in translations. *Consuelo*
and its sequel *The Countess of Rudolstadt,* translated
by the father-in-law of George William Curtis, had been
published as serials in *The Harbinger,* the organ of
Brook Farm, and Whitman once said he had read them
a dozen times. In these and two others of George Sand's
novels, *The Mosaic-Workers* and *The Gentleman-
Joiner,* which Whitman reviewed in *The Eagle,* he
found undoubtedly certain conceptions that helped to
form the figure already rising in his mind of the poet
and his mission. The hero of one was a mosaic-worker,
with an air of "naive nonchalance" and an idealistic
love for his companions, who kept his health robust by
walking about the streets of Venice and taking boat-
excursions on the bay. The hero of another was a handsome Christ-like carpenter, a proletarian philosopher in
labourer's garb, who, with a deep affection for his comrades, worked at carpentry with his father, as Whitman
himself was to work for a while in the fifties. Finally,
there were Albert and Consuelo, inspired musicians
both, members of a brotherhood striving for the re-
demption of the world, Albert ending as a wanderer-

poet through whom the "whole of humanity" speaks
and who also wears the dress of a workingman. Declaring that his name is Man, he proclaims a message that
is supposed to embrace both space and time, the unity of
life in humanity, human nature in every phase, the past,
the present, the future and the discoveries of science.

No doubt these novels had their effect in forming
Whitman's point of view and even, perhaps, his personal
appearance and ways, when, after wearing for a while
a frock coat and a silk hat, with a walking-stick and a
flower in his buttonhole, he dressed as a workman and
had himself portrayed so. He so appeared in the frontispiece of the first edition of *Leaves of Grass*. Whitman
dramatized himself and often romanced about himself,
even to the extent of lying to the top of his bent, as
when he announced that his first edition had "readily
sold" a thousand copies when actually it sold scarcely
five or six. As for his changes of costume, expressing
those mimetic phases through which young writers are
apt to pass, the heroes of George Sand may well have
served him as a model, while he must have been seriously impressed by her prophecy of a literature with the
manners of the people, a muse that would recover her
strength in the bosom of the masses. When he spoke of
the "ouvrier class" of America of which he proposed to
write the poem, he may have been prompted again by a
memory of her novels.

As early as 1848, Whitman worked over a passage of
verse that later appeared in *Leaves of Grass*, and perhaps he dimly foresaw already his role of the American
poet-prophet, the "new man" of the nation that was to
be. But this grew slowly in his mind; his writings were
weak and conventional still, and even as late as 1860,
long after the first *Leaves* were published, he sometimes
wrote in the commonplace manner of his youth, although in the *Democratic Review,* when he had scarcely

come of age, he had appeared with Longfellow, Thoreau and Hawthorne. Contributing to Bryant's *Evening Post* and Horace Greeley's *Tribune*, he had also met N. P. Willis and Edgar Allan Poe, whom he interviewed in the office of the *Broadway Journal* about a piece of his that Poe had published. He found Poe cordial, kindly and human but, as he recalled the meeting, subdued and "perhaps a little jaded." In *The Angel of Tears* he imitated Poe, as elsewhere he followed Cooper and Hawthorne, and a few of his stories, *The Half-Breed, Shirval* and especially *Richard Parker's Widow,* were competent, readable and vivid. Many of them were crude and trite, homely melodramatic tales that he had gathered in his wanderings over Long Island or heard as a schoolmaster there, characters and incidents that he had recorded, sometimes with cautionary intent, in the interest of temperance, patience, forbearance and mercy. Whitman, who detested flogging as much as Richard Henry Dana, had spared the rod, as a teacher, like Bronson Alcott, and his *Death in the Schoolroom* was a warning to brutal masters, while other stories were of prodigal sons, remorse and murder, young drunkards in bars and mothers who beseech their wild boys not to drink. They abounded in every known cliché of the moral-mongers. *Franklin Evans, or the Inebriate,* a short novel that Whitman wrote, recalled his own early impressions as a farm-boy in the city; he had driven in from West Hills with his grandfather Van Velsor, like this other boy, in a country market-wagon. The tale was one of many warnings against the dangers of the city, the "vortex of dissipation," as the author called it, at a time when modern urban life was just beginning in the United States and all the towns were full of young men from the country. Another, written a few years later, in 1854, was the popular novel and play *Ten Nights in a Bar-room,* by T. S. Arthur, a friend of Poe's in Baltimore, the editor of several magazines for women or children.

While in all this early prose and verse there was scarcely a line or a thought that suggested in any way an original mind, many of Whitman's editorials, especially perhaps in the Brooklyn *Eagle,* foreshadowed the point of view of the poet that was coming. He criticized the dollar-worship that went with poverty of soul, he deprecated "all unwholesome foreign sway," he begged for help for the unemployed, complained of unfair wages and advocated public baths for the use of the poor. He urged that young men should interest themselves in outdoor recreations, leave close rooms, engage in manly sports, and he insisted that girls should be taught the principles of medical science to counteract the prudery that shrouded the realities of life. He wished to encourage the "open mention" of prostitution as against the pseudo-modesty that cloaked it in darkness, counselling candour and courage on the subject of sexuality and a sane and realistic approach to the question of vice. Then he wished to cultivate a friendly spirit between the races and banish the very word "foreigner" from the press of the country. As an "expansionist" editor who was rather inclined to spread the eagle and had no qualms about the Mexican War, he also expressed the loftiest views of the destiny and scope of the republic, the continent that was becoming a nation under his eyes. All this contributed to form the immense exuberance of *Leaves of Grass* when, in good time, the poet found himself.

CHAPTER VII

MELVILLE THE TRAVELLER

When Whitman, scarcely known as yet, roamed New York in 1850, the "man who lived among the cannibals" was already famous. Herman Melville, home from the sea, had settled for a while in his native town, where he was a familiar figure in literary circles. With "his cigar and his Spanish eyes," he talked Typee and Omoo delightfully, as N. P. Willis observed in a "hurry-graph," and, often present as he was at Miss Anna Lynch's evenings, he was especially intimate with the Duyckinck set. Donald G. Mitchell, in *The Lorgnette*, spoke of the "Typee disorder" as more virulent than the "Jane Eyre malady" or the "Tupper fever," attacking adventurous schoolboys and romantic young ladies, for *Typee* had produced a great sensation with its cannibal banquets and heathenish rites of which the publishers naturally made the most. Hawthorne and Whitman reviewed the book, Longfellow read it aloud at home as Irving had had the manuscript read to him, while Thoreau and Emerson referred to it in their journals. *Typee* was in everybody's hands,[1] although people scarcely believed it was true until Toby Greene turned up and confirmed the story. Melville's companion in the Marquesas had reappeared in Buffalo, where he became a lawyer and editor later. The fame of the author had spread to England and he had published four more books, *Omoo*,

[1] Melville was read in the remotest corners of the country,—in the high Sierras, in 1851, for instance, by "Dame Shirley," who spoke in her letters of his "beautiful romance" and his "palm-girdled isles of the Pacific."

Mardi, Redburn and *White-Jacket.* One of these, *Mardi,*
puzzled and disturbed his readers, who thought of Melville as a writer of adventure-stories.

While Melville's connection with these circles was
brief,—it lasted only a few years, for he moved with his
family to the Berkshires in 1850,—it affected his mind
and his writings in various ways, and, soon forgotten as
he was, and even seemed to wish to be, he was one of
the most popular authors in the country for a decade. In
Mardi, under a thin disguise of Polynesian colours, he
reflected the ideas he had gathered in the Duyckinck
house, offering his own satirical comments on matters
he had heard discussed over bowls of what he described
as the "fine Duyckinck punch." Among the writers, artists and actors to whom the Duyckincks introduced him
were Irving and the poet Bryant, Charles Fenno Hoffman, Bayard Taylor and William Sidney Mount, intelligent men whose conversation touched on the leading
themes of the day, the topics that were presently resumed by the comrades of Taji. Slavery was one of
these, with the Abolition movement, the Mexican War,
expansionism, the chance of a war between the states,
the forty-niners, the social revolution in Europe. Melville borrowed various books from the ample Duyckinck
library that also left their stamp on his mind and his
style, among them Rabelais, whose voyage of Pantagruel
and Panurge suggested, at least in part, the voyage in
Mardi. Another was Sir Thomas Browne, whose interest
in antiquarian lore and feeling for the mystery of time
stirred Melville profoundly.

Melville's literary reputation during these years of
early promise was mirrored in George William Curtis's
widely read books. In his *Nile Notes of a Howadji,* Curtis told how, on the Nile, he had found Mardi on the
shelves of his dahabiah and drifted far into its dreamy
depths, feeling all around him the radiant rustling

of Yillah's hair, though the Polynesian peace was no deeper than his own Nubian silence. He found *Mardi* unrhymed poetry, rhythmical and measured, with a cadence like the dip of the sun-stilled Pacific waves. Again, as he said in *Lotus-Eating*, recalling a night on Lake George, he had felt on the wooded isle like Melville in *Typee*, catching a glimpse of Fayaway in the moonlit boat, while yet again, in *Prue and I*, Melville's Bartleby the Scrivener appeared on the street with Titbottom, the other clerk. "They rather clubbed their loneliness than made society for each other." As for Walt Whitman, who reviewed *Omoo* as well as *Typee*, he and Melville had more than a few tastes in common, although they may indeed never have met. They were exact contemporaries, born in 1819, of the same typical Dutch-British New York stock, big, vigorous, ruddy men with spacious views of life who had lived in close communion with the sea and the earth. While Melville's family was aristocratic and Whitman's the plainest of the plain, both were profoundly democratic in their outlook and feelings and both were essentially genial in temper despite Melville's deep reserve and the vulnerability of his nervous organization. Melville had an abundant share of Anglo-Saxon heartiness that made him like good flip and "beef done rare," [2] and his only dissatisfaction with Hawthorne, whom otherwise he admired so much, was that he did not sufficiently "patronize the butcher." He also said of Emerson, a "great man," one of the "men who dive," that his brains descended down into his neck and offered an obstacle thereby to a draught of ale. It was this "plump sphericity" he missed in the Yankees

---

[2] See, among various references to his liking for old cheese and wine, his praise of the "noble, solid, Saxon hospitality" of the passing English ship in *Moby-Dick*. With what pleasure he notes the provisions of the old Dutch whaler, the beef, pork, biscuit, cheese and beer,—"whole pipes, barrels, quarts and gills of good gin and good cheer."

that defined his own nature, like Whitman's, as a man of New York. For the rest, the "great power of blackness" in him, the trait he found in Hawthorne, distinguished his note from Whitman's sunniness or whiteness. He was a proud moody man, increasingly unapproachable, with something in the lines of his face that said "hands off."

This, like Melville's meditative humour and his growing introversion, was the fruit of a certain development, rapid enough, but scarcely visible at first in the lively, agreeable, adventurous young man who returned from the South Seas in 1844. Melville, twenty-five then, had lived for more than three years on ships, the "Acushnet" and the "Leviathan," whalers, and a frigate of the navy, spending the several months in Tahiti, Hawaii, the Marquesas, that formed the background or the subject of a number of his books. Earlier still, at seventeen, he had shipped on the voyage he described in *Redburn* which gave him his first foretaste of the evils of the world. In those days American boys had taken to the sea as in later years they looked for adventure to the West, and Melville, like Redburn, the "son of a gentleman" whose death had left his family in straits, had served as an ordinary sailor to Liverpool and back. With a youthful "itch for things remote," he had listened to his father's tales of travel, for Allan Melville had constantly crossed the Atlantic: he was an importer of fabrics, gloves, stockings and perfumes from France with a wide and largely patrician family connection. Herman Melville as a little boy who dreamed of distant voyages had delighted in the wharves and the warehouses and the shipping of New York, the yo-heave-ho of the seamen, the old anchors in the streets, but, descending the Hudson from Albany, with a dollar in his pocket, to sail himself, he had felt already somewhat defiant and embittered. The family had moved to Albany, where Melville was

put to work in a store after going to school in the town,
like Cooper before him, for he was a poor relation now
and more or less driven to shift for himself with occasional aid from more prosperous uncles and aunts. One
of his Gansevoort uncles, like the first American William
James, was a rich and important citizen of this capital of
the state,[3] and his grandfathers on both sides had distinguished themselves in the Revolution, Major Thomas
Melville and the hero of Fort Stanwix. This was General Peter Gansevoort, whom Gilbert Stuart painted.
Major Melville had been one of the "Indians" of the
Boston Tea Party, to which Alfieri referred in one of his
odes,[4]—the incident that Goethe recalled from his German childhood,—and, wearing his knee-breeches still
and his cocked hat at the time of his death, he became
the "Last Leaf" of Dr. Holmes's poem. But the glory
had all but departed for Melville when he set out from
home, dressed in his brother's cast-off shooting jacket,
and feeling, as he said, like an infant Ishmael, he was
prepared to be shocked by the bestiality he witnessed
among the sailors. Stout as he was in muscle and bone,
with physical courage to spare, he had never imagined
a forecastle and the horrors that occurred in that gloomy
hole where they burrowed like rabbits in a warren, and
the eager, romantic, sensitive boy, friendless and alone,
confronted evils that one could hardly think of. Cooper,
still younger when he sailed for England, had seen the
ship from the quarter-deck, but Melville had lived side

[3] The life of Melville's mother's family at Gansevoort, near Saratoga, the town that was named for them, somewhat resembled that
of the Coopers at Cooperstown, as Fenimore Cooper pictured it in
The Pioneers. They still carried on their lumbering interests there.
Melville as a boy spent occasional summers in the town, which he
recalled in *Pierre* as "Saddle Meadows." Gansevoort Street in the
city of New York, where later he worked in the custom-house, was
also named after his family.

[4] Expressing scorn for tea as an effeminate Oriental brew imported
by the English to drug the heroic people of New England.

by side with the baleful Jackson, a veritable Cain afloat with eyes like vaults that were full of snakes who corrupted every heart that beat near him. He had seen the villainy of the short-voyage sailors to which Hawthorne as consul at Liverpool testified later, and he saw too the miseries of Liverpool that harrowed Hawthorne as well as himself, for there was nothing like them in Boston or New York. Here, where his father had dined with William Roscoe, Melville himself was appalled by the dock-wall beggars. He was shocked by the hovels, the wretched lanes and the mother with her children starving in the pit who were only removed when they were dead and became a nuisance.

Thus early rose in Melville's mind a tragic sense of life that was amply confirmed during his later voyages by the wickedness of the lawless crews picked up in ports of the Spanish Main and governed only by scourges, by floggings and chains. Murder, suicide and syphilis throve among these rogues of all nations and colours who were shut up together with the cockroaches and the rats, and, as Melville found, even the frigate "United States" was charged with the spirit of unrighteousness to the coamings of her hatches. He saw suffering on every hand and evil at war with the good as Emerson, both sheltered and buoyant, had never seen it, as Whitman had scarcely observed it on the sidewalks of New York,—buoyant as he also was and less vulnerable than Melville,—and all this barbarity of civilization, its vices and cruelties of every kind, had made the savages seem all the more admirable in contrast. He saw them innocent and happy in the light of the baseness of the inmates of ships, those sons of adversity and calamity, the offspring of sin, and no wonder they impressed him as amiable, delightful, humane; but the blackness that overspread his mind, the obsession of the ills of existence, grew in him later and owing to a number of causes. He was obviously in

high spirits when he sailed on the "Acushnet," the little
New Bedford whaler, in 1841, as when he described his
adventures in *Typee* and *Omoo*. Nor did all the filth
and roguery he saw obscure in his mind the ideal of man
as a "noble," a "sparkling," a "grand and glowing" creature.[5] In Jack Chase and others he was far more aware
of the heroic.

Melville had been teaching in country schools, like
Whitman, trying his hand as an essayist with small success, and he was full of the zest of adventure and "visions of outlandish things" when he left home for the
sea on this second occasion. He had lived for a year with
a cousin, a junior naval officer who had visited the Marquesas and even the valley of the Typees; and another
cousin, a lieutenant in the navy, had told him tales of
the Pacific, while an uncle whom he saw near Boston
had talked whaling with him. This uncle, too, a skipper,
was full of the Marquesas, where Matthew F. Maury had
stopped in 1826 in the sloop-of-war on which he learned
navigation, and Melville's dreams of "barbarous coasts"
must surely have included glimpses and scenes of the
groves and the sunny valleys of these little-known islands,—lovely houris, tattooed chiefs, bamboo temples,
coral reefs and carved canoes dancing on flashing blue
waters. Dana had only recently published his *Two Years
Before the Mast,* which Melville, like a multitude of
others, may well have read. Moreover, he had heard, no
doubt, of the dreadful white whale who was famous at
that moment as one of the terrors of the sea. Commonly
known as Mocha Dick, he was renowned for twenty years
before he was killed at last in 1859, after causing the

[5] "Men may seem detestable as joint-stock companies and nations; knaves, fools and murderers there may be; men may have
mean and meagre faces; but man, in the ideal, is so noble and so
sparkling, such a grand and glowing creature, that over any ignominious blemish in him all his fellows should run to throw their
costliest robes."—Melville, *Moby-Dick.*

death of more than thirty men, and a regular greeting of passing sailors was "Any news of Mocha Dick?" for the whalers of all nations were aware of him. As in the case of a certain white shark, the "white steed of the prairies" and the white buffalo of Captain Mayne Reid's tale, the "supernatural" hue that Melville discussed in later years partly explained the awe in which he was held. An article called *Mocha Dick, or the White Whale of the Pacific* was published in the *Knickerbocker Magazine* in 1839 when Melville had begun to write and was teaching near home.[6]

Meanwhile, the wonders of the sea had begun at Nantucket and New Bedford for him with the wild specimens of men one saw in the streets, for the time had passed when the whaling-ships were manned by American-born seamen alone, with a few coast-bred Negroes and Indians of the region. One still met scores of green Vermonters and New Hampshire men who had felled the forests and were eager to drop their axes and snatch the whale-lance, with Gay Head Indians like Tashtego and Negroes like Daggoo; but one also saw cannibals chatting at corners, Filipinos, Lascars and Tahitians and Hawaiians brought in with the whale-oil and the whale-bone. The Polynesian languages were familiar in New Bedford with turbaned Orientals and nondescripts from far-away isles, such creatures as home-keeping Americans saw only in their dreams, and it was easy, beginning with them, to imagine more fabulous beings still, like the polyglot crew that appeared in *Moby-Dick*. There were dark old taverns like Spouter Inn, suggesting Haw-

---

[6] At least one terrible white whale was known long before this. Emerson mentioned an "old sperm whale, a white whale, known for many years among whalemen as old Tom," in his Journal for February 19, 1834. A seaman riding with him in a coach told Emerson how old Tom "rushed upon the boats which attacked him, and crushed the boats to small chips in his jaws." A vessel was fitted out at New Bedford to capture him, and he was finally taken somewhere off Payta Head.

thorne's Salem, and Quakers like the "swearing good
man" and the "pious good man," like Bildad, Peleg and
even Captain Ahab, and a real seamen's Bethel chaplain who had only to be mixed with Father Taylor to
result in the wonderful character of Father Mapple. It
was Father Taylor, Emerson's friend, the Southern
Methodist in Boston, whose preaching Dickens described
in his *American Notes* and whose "mere words," as
Whitman said, "seemed altogether to disappear as the
live feeling advanced upon you and seized you." He had
for Whitman the same fund of volcanic power as Elias
Hicks,[7] and Melville, who had heard him, had him in
mind, along with a local New Bedford preacher, in
creating the astonishing sermon to which Ishmael listened. The biblical imagery never seemed grander than
when it was combined here with the homeliest of
Yankee sailor-talk, in this drama as it were of Jonah in
modern dress, who had left his hatbox and his carpet-
bag behind him; and did not the sermon itself suggest
the magical picture of Jonah and the whale that was
painted by Albert P. Ryder, who was born in New Bedford? One saw there too the "tormented deep," the steep
gullies, the raging flood, the rush of the mighty whale
cleaving the seas, just as the old picture in the Spouter
Inn, with its vague "masses of shades and shadows,"
besmoked and defaced, suggested another Ryder. The
"black mass of something hovering" in the centre of the
picture that appeared to be a foundering Cape-Horner
in a midnight gale, together with the "indefinite sublimity" that haunted the picture, belonged as much to
Ryder as it belonged to Melville.

In his three years and more at sea, Melville had

[7] One of Father Taylor's sermons, described by Whitman in
November Boughs, might have been Father Mapple's: "Colloquial
in a severe sense, it often lean'd to Biblical and Oriental forms.
Especially were all allusions to ships and the ocean and sailors'
lives of unrival'd power and life-likeness."

visited the Galapagos islands,—Plutonian shores that might have been conceived by Poe,—and he had stopped in Peru at least along the South American coast as well as in the South Sea isles that appeared in his books. He was to revive in *The Encantadas* a memory of the grimmest spot on earth where only lizards and tortoises and snakes could live, where the one sound of life was an occasional hiss, as he remembered in Lima the herds of panniered mules driven by mounted Indians along the Callao road. Perhaps he too, like Ahab, had caught the mild, mild wind and the air that smelled as if it blew from a far-away meadow when the mowers had been reaping under the slopes of the Andes and were sleeping now among the new-mown hay. As one who had "loved ships," he said, he was to describe them well, the plump little Julia, for instance, the whaler in *Omoo,* the Yankee-built barque of a beautiful model that was always ready for the breeze and pranced and pawed the sea and flew before the wind.[8] What a fine picture he also drew of the frigate in *White-Jacket,* as the watcher in the maintop saw it of a moonlight night, going large before the wind, her stun'-sails set on both sides, a vast spread of snow-white canvas sliding along the sea. So great was Melville's own feeling for mysteries and marvels that his ocean recalled the old maps of the days of Columbus and their portents and monsters of the deep. He had certainly seen the "spirit-spout" which he described in *Moby-Dick,* the silver jet that rose in the serenity of the moonlight when the waves rolled by like scrolls of silver, and no doubt he had seen the corposants

[8] "At [sailing], brave little Jule, plump little Jule, was a witch. Blow high, or blow low, she was always ready for the breeze; and when she dashed the waves from her prow, and pranced, and pawed the sea, you never thought of her patched sails and blistered hull. How the fleet creature would fly before the wind! rolling, now and then, to be sure, but in very playfulness. Sailing to windward, no gale could blow her over: with spars erect, she looked right up into the wind's eye."—*Omoo.*

when all the yard-arms were tipped with fire and the tall masts silently burned in the sulphurous air. The great white whale itself was no more awful as it shifted, a huge milky mass, in the blue morning sea than the devil-fish that appeared like a phantom in *Mardi*[9] or the undulating, unearthly, formless chance-like apparition of life that blindly floated in the "watery immensity of terror." [10]

No writer had ever more fully conveyed that sense of the awfulness of the sea which, as Melville said, "aboriginally belongs to it," while his account of a savage society that missionaries and traders had scarcely disturbed had struck the American mind at the psychological moment. Books of travel were especially in vogue, and hardly half a dozen years had passed since John Lloyd Stephens had written about Central America and Yucatan. Stephens, whom Melville had seen and read, presented the remains of an unknown world and his books passed through edition after edition. Melville, with still greater charm, though certainly not with the same authority, presented another society that was all but unknown. With his great power of description, he offered lovely primitive landscapes, bluffs and glens, green orchards of banana and palm, gently rolling hillsides riding to majestic heights and crags pouring over with

[9] "But look! fathoms down in the sea; wherever saw you a phantom like that? An enormous crescent with antlers like a rainbow, and a delta of mouths. Slowly it sinks, and is seen no more."—*Mardi*.

[10] "Almost forgetting for the moment all thoughts of Moby-Dick, we now gazed at the most wondrous phenomenon which the secret seas have hitherto revealed to mankind. A vast pulpy mass, furlongs in length and breadth, of a glancing cream-colour, lay floating on the water, innumerable long arms radiating from its centre; and curling and twisting like a nest of anacondas, as if blindly to clutch at any hapless object within reach. No perceptible face or front did it have; no conceivable token of either sensation or instinct; but undulated there on the billows, an unearthly, formless, chance-like apparition of life . . . With a low sucking sound it slowly disappeared again."—*Moby-Dick*.

leafy cascades and vines. There were valleys like vistas of paradise full of the enchantment of a fairy world that was all fresh and blooming from the hand of the Creator,—like virginal Kentucky as Daniel Boone first saw it,—where the palmetto-thatched huts of yellow bamboo were scattered in flowery groves of the coconut and the breadfruit. One witnessed the pagan *hevar* there and the feast of calabashes and the gatherings of the talkative elders in their club, the Ti, and there the young men were as beautiful as sculptors' models and the nymphs were always ready for a frolic. For these "old gold girls," as Clarence King called them later, sparkled with savage vivacity, with gaiety and mischief. The tone of their Polynesian world was a light-hearted joyousness, as Melville found, wandering from grove to grove with his hideous, devoted servitor Kory-Kory, whose face was tattooed while his body, covered with figures of fishes and birds, suggested a pictorial natural-history museum. As for the delightful Fayaway with her endearing young charms, she was the perfection of female grace and beauty, and she showed her pliant figure to the best advantage by clinging to the summer garb of Eden. What could have been more bewitching than Fayaway with her small hand clasping a delicate, golden-hued uncooked fish and eating it as elegantly as if it were a Naples biscuit. Sometimes she wore a floating mantle gathered loosely about her person. This was the white tappa robe she spread out for a sail as she stood with upraised arms in the prow of the canoe, the figure that appealed in after years to the painter John La Farge as it suggested at the moment the bathing-nymphs of Sully.

Along with the native Marquesans and Tahitians, Melville presented a fine assortment of the rather fantastic whites one met in these regions, the beach-combers and castaways, the back-sliders and lame ducks who found an asylum in the islands or on the whalers. There was old Mother Tot, for one, the little fright of an English crone who entertained the mariners in her hut with dice and rum, and there was Doctor Long Ghost, the surgeon who had fallen from his high estate, who had quarrelled with the captain and lived in the forecastle with the crew. He looked like a land-crane blown out to sea and consorting with petrels, for he was a tower of bones, with his twinkling grey eye, and, unscrupulous as a man could be, he was a godsend to Melville and the most entertaining of companions. Along with Virgil and the *Lusiad,* he quoted *Hudibras* by the canto, and it may have been a pleasant recollection of this that led Melville in later years to choose its unsuitable metre for his long poem *Clarel.*[11] It was one of Jack Chase's charms for him that he too knew the *Lusiad* and even recited parts of it in Portuguese. For Melville was drawn to men of learning like the two scholars on the voyage to England with whom he talked metaphysics in 1849, Professor Adler, the Duyckincks' friend, and Bayard Taylor's cousin, who rode "on the German horse" with him till two in the morning.

As for the Polynesian isles that attracted so many writers in time, Melville was the first artist to represent them, and the picture he drew in *Omoo* and *Typee* was objectively true in the main, although many of the details were invented or borrowed from others. In *Omoo* the adventures had been all but literally Melville's own, in *Typee* he resorted to fiction in larger measure, while in both he drew freely from earlier travellers, recasting their descriptions and their notes on the customs of the people. Later he was to borrow much of the whale-lore in *Moby-Dick* from histories of the whaling indus-

---

[11] A "fine old spicy duodecimo" edition of *Hudibras* for Evert Duyckinck was one of the books he bought in London in 1849. Doctor Long Ghost has been more or less identified as a son of Allan Cunningham, the Scottish poet.

try and other writings, such as J. Ross Browne's *Etchings of a Whaling Cruise,*—for he "swam through libraries" also after whales,—as he drew from Smollett in *White-Jacket* and invented some of the scenes in this book,—the "white jacket" itself could never have existed. If Melville had really fallen from the masthead, the fact would have appeared in the log of the frigate, and the "massacre of the beards" again occurred only in the author's mind like the visit of Dom Pedro and his suite to the ship at Rio. The book, in short, was a romance, and yet there was never a truer picture of the actual life of an American man-of-war, of the sailors and their way of living and sleeping, how they died and were buried at sea, their superstitions, their friendships, their tastes and their talk. Melville was right in suggesting that the book would be taken for history in time,[12] as *Typee* and *Omoo* were also essentially true, good anthropology as well as the best of travel-writing, if one allowed for occasional heightenings of effect. The representation of savage life was highly complimentary, its perpetual mirth and good humour, its humanity and kindness, governed as the Polynesians were, or seemed to be, by fraternal feeling, so that Melville never witnessed a quarrel among them. Stealing was very rare with them, murder rarer still, and he found no cross old women there, no inattentive husbands, no love-sick maidens, no bachelors, no melancholy young men. After a few weeks in the valley of Typee, Melville thought better of human nature than he had ever thought in his life before, and this was not merely because he was young or because he had been living with the riffraff of ships, although these were certainly elements in the forming of his judgment. As he said later in connection with Quee-

[12] "Who knows that, when men-of-war shall be no more, *White-Jacket* may not be quoted to show to the people in the Millennium what a man-of-war was?"—*White-Jacket.*

queg and his "simple honest heart," the savages were innately delicate and naturally polite and their patriarchal communism relieved them of many of the stresses and strains that caused such havoc with the manners and morals of the whites. They had none of that root of all evil, money, and, since everyone had what he desired, this made for integrity, gentle behaviour and grace. There was no occasion for greed or theft, for nobody was hungry, and the complicated and highly developed system of taboo was quite as effective as the law of civilization. The Polynesians already possessed the "economy of abundance" of which others were to dream in later times, with the virtues that all good observers agreed were theirs.

Melville, however, was not seriously drawn to this primitive state of felicity, charmed as he was for a while by the savage life, and, far from adopting its ways himself, he eluded attempts to tattoo him and escaped by a desperate ruse from the embrace of the Typees. Nor did he ever attack civilization as such. He saw how civilization ruined the Polynesian life precisely by destroying its integrity with its taboos, how, when the temples were torn down and the people were nominally Christian, disease, vice, premature death appeared at once. Neat villas rose, with trim gardens and shaven lawns, and the poor savage became an outsider in his country, for the intruder seized the fruits of the earth and the natives became draught-horses and beasts of burden. But civilization judged in relation to a primitive culture it thus destroyed was by no means the same as civilization judged in itself, and when Melville condemned this he did so through Larry the whaleman in *Redburn,* who had visited the coast of Madagascar.[13] This was his way

---

[13] "What's the use of bein' snivelized? . . . Snivelized chaps only learns the way to take on 'bout life, and snivel . . . Blast Ameriky, I say. In Madagasky they don't wear any togs at all. Nothing but

of condemning the condemnation. He was very far from
"blasting Ameriky" himself. What he thought of civilization,—and his thoughts were affirmative though anything but simple,—he showed in his allegorical romance
of *Mardi*.

This was after Melville, returning from the sea in
1844, had written *Typee* and *Omoo*, read and thought
and mingled for many months with the circle of the
Duyckincks, during which he reflected much on the
world of the forties. *Mardi*, opening as a simple
romance, became a complex allegory in which the
islands of the Mardian world that Taji and his comrades
explored were the nations of America and Europe thinly
disguised. The luxuriant glens and arbours and temples
were those of the Marquesas, while the conversation
suggested the talk in the Ti, and Melville, with his invented mythology, aired his views on the new plutocracy,
on monarchy, imperialism, democracy, revolution and
what not. He attacked many of the shibboleths that
filled the American mind of the moment, Manifest
Destiny, expansionism, spread-eagleism,[14] the gold-rush,
deploring the "fiery and intractable" spirit of the South
and its threats of establishing a confederacy and dissolv-
ing the Union. "These southern savannahs may yet
prove battlefields," Mohi the chronicler remarked,

---

a bowline round the midships. Dine all day off fat pigs and dogs
—don't go to bed but keeps nodding all the time—plenty of 'baccy
—get drunk—fine country. Blast Ameriky!"—*Redburn*.

[14] See the words of the boisterous throng that greet the travellers
approaching Vivenza (the United States), suggesting the braggadocio
that irritated Dickens:

"Whence came ye? Whither bound? Saw ye ever such a land as
this? Is it not a great and extensive republic? Pray, observe how tall
we are; just feel of our thighs; are we not a glorious people? Here,
feel of our beards. Look round. Look round, be not afraid; behold
those palms; swear now that this land surpasses all others. Old
Bello's [England's] mountains are mole-hills to ours; his rivers, rills;
his empires, villages; his palm-trees, shrubs," etc.—*Mardi*.

though, hating slavery as he did because the slaves were "unmanned" by it, Melville insisted that the Southerners should be judged wisely. "This thing was planted in their midst," he said, long before they became responsible for it. With all these reservations, however, Melville admired "Vivenza," [15]—America,—my "forever glorious country," as he called it in *White-Jacket,*—as he fully accepted the notion of progress, the belief that history had just begun which most of the American writers of the time shared with him. In his essay on Hawthorne he spoke in a manner that suggested both Emerson and Whitman, falling into the strain of prophecy that he had sounded in his books, the strain of a youthful America exulting in its future. The world, he said, was as young today as when it was created and this morning's dew was like Eden's dew for Adam, nor had nature been all over ransacked by our progenitors so that no new charms and mysteries remained for us to find. The trillionth part had not yet been said and all that had been said but multiplied the avenues to what remained to *be* said, and Melville affirmed that America and its writers, with their democratic spirit, took, and should take, the "practical lead in the world."

Melville had already struck this note in *White-Jacket* [16] and *Redburn* too,—books that he wrote about the same time as *Mardi,*—asserting his belief in America as the "Israel of our time," the "free Vivenza" that

[15] "In good round truth, and as if an impartialist from Arcturus spoke of it, Vivenza was a noble land. Like a young tropic tree she stood, laden down with greenness, myriad blossoms, and the ripened fruit thick-hanging from one bough. She was promising as the morning."—*Mardi.*

[16] "There are occasions when it is for America to make precedents, and not to obey them. We should, if possible, prove a teacher to posterity, instead of being the pupil of bygone generations. More shall come after us than have gone before; the world is not yet middle-aged."—*White-Jacket.*

"cheers our hearts," the "rainbow to the isles," as Yoomy the minstrel called the United States.[17] He had said that Americans were the chosen people, bearing the ark of the liberties of the world, that mankind expected great things from their race, that they were the "pioneers of the world" sent on "through the wilderness of untried things," [18] with whom the children of Adam were to find their new Eden.[19] There was much in all this that paralleled Emerson's orations and essays, the note of the Transcendentalists, the visions of Brook Farm, still more that expressed or anticipated Whitman's thoughts, for the "great things" that Melville said "we feel in our

[17] "But free Vivenza! Is she not the star that must, ere long, lead up the constellations, though now unseen? No kings are in Vivenza; yet, spite her thralls, in that land seems more of good than elsewhere. Our hopes are not wild dreams; Vivenza cheers our hearts. She is a rainbow to the isles."—*Mardi.*

[18] "We Americans are the peculiar, chosen people—the Israel of our time; we bear the ark of the liberties of the world. Seventy years ago we escaped from thrall; and, besides our first birthright embracing one continent of earth—God has given to us, for a future inheritance, the broad domains of the political pagans that shall yet come and lie down under the shade of our ark, without bloody hands being lifted. God has predestinated, mankind expects, great things from our race; and great things we feel in our souls. The rest of the nations must soon be in our rear. We are the pioneers of the world; the advance guard, sent on through the wilderness of untried things, to break a new path in the New World that is ours."—*White-Jacket.*

[19] "We are the heirs of all time, and with all nations we divide our inheritance. On this Western hemisphere all tribes and peoples are forming into one federated whole; and there is a future which shall see the estranged children of Adam restored as to the old hearthstone in Eden. The other world beyond this which was longed for by the devout before Columbus's time, was found in the new; and the deep sea-land, that first struck these soundings, brought up the soil of Earth's Paradise. Not a Paradise then, or now; but to be made so, at God's good pleasure, and in the fullness and mellowness of time. The seed is sown, and the harvest must come; and our children's children, on the world's jubilee morning, shall all go with their sickles to the reaping. Then shall the curse of Babel be revoked, a new Penticost come, and the language they shall speak shall be the language of Britain."—*Redburn.*

souls" were the things of *Leaves of Grass* and the prose of Whitman. Melville used almost the same words that Whitman was to use in *Pioneers O Pioneers* and *Democratic Vistas*. With his own "unconditional democracy in all things," he largely shared Whitman's notion of the American "idea," and he too felt, as he said in his essay on Hawthorne, that America must have powerful writers to forward this idea.[20] Like Whitman and Emerson, moreover, he loved "grand individuals," [21] espe-

[20] In matters both great and small Melville and Whitman paralleled each other. In a sketch called *The Two Temples,* Melville protested, as Whitman did, when the newly-built Grace Church was opened in New York, that only the well-dressed and the rich were welcome there. He contrasted the cold welcome he had received there with the warm welcome of the workingman's gallery in a theatre in London. Whitman's sketch was entitled *Christmas at 'Grace'* (reprinted in a volume called *New York Dissected*). Whitman had been obliged to stand for an hour in the cold vestibule until the fashionable pew-holders had been seated. During this time he meditated "on inequalities of rank and the probable expansiveness of the strait and narrow way."

Reviewing Parkman's *The Oregon Trail* and resenting this writer's contempt for the Indians, Melville observed that all men, as the sons of God, were brothers. Like Whitman again, he favoured unlimited immigration,—"the whole world," he said, "is the patrimony of the whole world,"—as he remarked in *Mardi* that the state would never prosper if the miserable many supported the prosperous few.

Melville also shared with Whitman what he called "this 'all' feeling." Writing to Hawthorne, he said, "You must often have felt it, lying on the grass on a warm summer's day. Your legs seem to send out shoots into the earth. Your hair feels like leaves upon your head. This is the *all* feeling." He added, referring to pantheism, "But what plays the mischief with the truth is that men will insist upon the universal application of a temporary feeling or opinion."

[21] Several times Melville struck a note of Emerson's,—for example, in *Mardi:* "We have had vast developments of parts of men, not of any wholes. Before a full-developed man, Mardi would fall down and worship." Again, in *Moby-Dick:* "It does seem to me, that herein we see the rare virtue of a strong individual's vitality, and the rare virtue of thick walls, and the rare virtue of interior spaciousness. Oh, man! admire and model thyself after the whale! Do thou, too, remain warm among ice. Do thou, too, live in the world without being of it. Be cool at the Equator; keep thy blood fluid at

cially those whom he called the "kingly commons." For the "august dignity" of which he was to write in *Moby-Dick* was not, he said, "the dignity of kings and robes, but that abounding dignity which had no robed investiture . . . Thou shalt see it shining in the arm that wields a pick or drives a spike, that democratic dignity which . . . radiates without end from God." This was the dignity of the cannibal Queequeg whom all hands voted a "noble trump" after he had saved the boat when the captain was helpless, as it was the dignity of the "noble Negro" Daggoo, with his barbaric majesty and lion-like tread. It was Jack Chase's perhaps above all, the frank and charming Jack, whom all the officers admired, whom the sailors loved. The passengers to Nantucket murmured over Ishmael's companionship with Queequeg, "as though a white man," as Melville said, "were anything more dignified than a whitewashed Negro"; for he believed in the "spirit of equality" which had spread, as he went on, "one royal mantle of humanity over all my kind."

It was true that Melville lost for a while this confidence in humankind, with much of his faith in America as well as in himself, for his belief in the world and in men waned with his own creative powers, though in part he recovered both as time went on. But this faith superabounded in him in the great productive years that reached their highest point in *Moby-Dick,* when he shared the general Mazzinian belief that nations have their missions and Whitman's special belief in the mission of his own.

the Pole. Like the great dome of St. Peter's, and like the great whale, retain, O man, in all seasons a temperature of thine own."

CHAPTER VIII

MELVILLE IN THE BERKSHIRES

MELVILLE, who had recently married a daughter of the Chief Justice of Massachusetts, settled with his family in the Berkshires in 1850. He had bought a farm called Arrowhead on the outskirts of Pittsfield, with a big square house and a chimney like a giant sequoia, where he planned to raise potatoes and corn as a part-time husbandman, living by the hoe and the hammer as well as the pen. He had known Pittsfield as a boy, for his uncle Thomas Melville had returned there to live after twenty-one years in France, where he had married Madame Récamier's niece, and Melville, who recalled his "faded brocade of old French breeding," had often raked with him in the hayfield. Melville had taught in a school there, and there he had lived with the half-French cousin who had visited the Marquesas and seen the valley of Typee. He used his uncle's writing-desk, which he found in the corn-loft over the carriage-house, covered with the marks of fowls that had laid their eggs there. The great piazza that gave its name to *The Piazza Tales* looked towards Greylock, twenty miles away, with its surrounding hills, like Charlemagne and his peers, and walking to and fro on this Melville was reminded of the deck of a ship as the long ground-swells rolled the slanting grain. The vastness and the lonesomeness were oceanic, and the still August noon brooding over the meadows suggested a calm on the line.

Six miles away Nathaniel Hawthorne, at work on *The*

House of the Seven Gables, was living with his family in a little red cottage at Lenox; and Melville and he were soon walking and talking together. Evert Duyckinck had sent Hawthorne a set of Melville's books, and Hawthorne, who had reviewed *Typee* in the Salem *Advertiser,* read *Mardi* and *White-Jacket* in the barn, lying in the hay. Before the two had a chance to meet, Melville had been reading Hawthorne's *Mosses,* with the hillside breeze blowing over him through the wide barn-door, soothed by the hum of the bees in the meadows round; and he had written the paper for Duyckinck, *Hawthorne and His Mosses,* supposedly the work of a Virginian summering in New England. He had found in Hawthorne the "largest brain with the largest heart" that America had produced in literature up to the present, and, going beyond the immediate subject, the "great deep intellect" of this man, he had urged Americans to recognize their meritorious writers. The greatness of these writers was increasing, he said, and the day was coming when people would ask, Who reads a book by an Englishman that is a modern? instead of asking, Who reads an American book? We should contemn all imitation, though it came to us graceful and fragrant as the morning, eschewing this leaven of literary flunkyism towards England, and foster all originality, although it were at first as crabbed and ugly as our own pine-knots. Melville, who idolized Hawthorne, felt that he might shrink a little from his own "ruthless democracy on all sides," that ardent spirit of radicalism in which he was closer to Whitman, the New Yorker whom perhaps he never met.

While Melville could not be sure that his new friend shared all his views, he was overjoyed when Hawthorne praised his work. He felt as if the crown of India had been placed on his head. This was after *Moby-Dick* appeared in 1851, the book he had written at Pittsfield and

inscribed to Hawthorne, whose influence was marked in
a number of Melville's sketches as well as in the novel
that immediately followed, *Pierre*. There was something
of Hawthorne in the essay called *I and My Chimney*, in
the story of the apple-tree table that was found in the
garret, in the study of Jimmy Rose, the old New Yorker
who had lost his money and hid in a ruinous old house
with a grim arched cellar. One caught a suggestion of
Hawthorne too in the ambiguity of *The Confidence-
Man* in which so many of the characters were veiled or
bandaged, with the curious effect of a joyless masquerade, as in the "hooded and obscure-looking figure"
with "half-averted countenance" who delivered the letter to Pierre in the darkening street. Hawthorne's
"blackness" excited Melville's imagination, like the
"dark characters" of Shakespeare, whom he had read, in
whom he had immersed himself, shortly before, and
this double influence appeared in *Pierre* as well as in
Moby-Dick, with its shredded Shakespearean drama
scattered through the pages. *Moby-Dick* indeed was half
a Shakespearean play at times in its characters, soliloquies, stage-directions and all. For the rest, Melville,
with his taste for what he called "oldness in things,"
liked Hawthorne's "flavour and body," suggesting old
wine, as he loved the antique note of Burton, Jeremy
Taylor and Sir Thomas Browne, whom he had bought
in old folios on a visit to London. Melville had read
prodigiously since his return in 1844, in seventeenth-
century authors very largely, especially the Elizabethan
playwrights, Jonson, Marlowe, Beaumont and Fletcher,
whom he had found in the library of his man-of-war. In
one of his letters he praised what he called "oldageifying youth in books" [1] as one of the two great arts that

---

[1] "Ah, this sovereign virtue of age—how can we living men attain
unto it? We may spice up our dishes with all the condiments of
the Spice Islands and Moluccas, and our dishes may be all venison

were yet to be discovered, and in writing *Redburn* he had tried to extract and reproduce on his own page the antiquated style of an obsolete Liverpool guide-book. The seventeenth-century flavour of many a page of *Moby-Dick* was the fruit of a taste as consciously cherished and developed as the taste of certain American painters from William Page to Duveneck for the so-called "brown sauce" of the Munich school. These painters also wished to achieve the amber patina of age, the sombre harmonious richness of so many old masters, attempting to reach this normal effect of the gradual oxidation of the oil by constantly using bitumen as an undertone and glaze. In cultivating the antique style of the writers whom he loved, Melville used literary bitumen in a similar fashion.

When Hawthorne left the Berkshires in the autumn of 1851, Melville was deprived of a presence that quickened and sustained him, the only salient fellowship that he was to know as a writer, in the fullness of which he arrived at the height of his powers. It was during this brief period when he was at work on *Moby-Dick* that he asked a friend to send him fifty assistants, "fifty fast-writing youths with an easy style," as if he were a Dumas who could never begin to carry out the multitude of literary projects that swarmed in his mind. In what he described as the fullness of his heart he longed for a condor's quill to write with,—"Give me," he exclaimed, "Vesuvius's crater as an inkstand!"—yet scarcely more than five years later his literary life was virtually over and he seemed to agree with Carlyle that silence was best. Melville's active writing time was a great deal shorter than the fifteen years that Sainte-Beuve allotted to the normal career, but he had foreseen at its highest

---

and wild boar—yet how the deuce can we make them a century or two old? My dear sir, the two great things yet to be discovered are these—The art of rejuvenating old age in men, and oldageifying youth in books."—Letter to Evert Duyckinck, April 5, 1849.

moment that "shortly the flower must fall to the mould," as he wrote in perhaps the finest of his letters to Hawthorne. His health no doubt had been undermined by the hardships of his life at sea; he had exhausted his nerves and his imagination; his eyes gave way and *Moby-Dick* was "broiled," as he said, in "hell-fire," like Pierre Glendinning's great book in the romance that followed. Indeed, were not Pierre's experiences very much his own when this young writer supped "at black broth with Pluto," assassinating the natural day in his lonely little closet, wishing that he could behead himself to gain one night's repose when the book, "like a vast lumbering planet," revolved in his brain? The account of Pierre at this point, so highly realistic, suggested the dreary slavery of which Melville spoke at the time when he was finishing and driving the book through the press, roaming half-blind through the streets of New York, after dark, for the sake of his eyes, a victim of over-strain and vertigo. While he had written most of the book with a superabundance of confidence and power, this must have been his condition then and later, when he was examined for his sanity after writing *Pierre,* and no wonder considering the mental excitement with which in seven years he had written the long series of books that began with *Typee.*

If Melville felt that in him too the "thews of a Titan" had been cut by fate, one scarcely had to look further for an explanation. The disastrous blow of the fire at Harper's followed in 1853, destroying the plates and most of the copies of his books, just at the moment when the public had lost all interest in a writer who had no more stories of adventure, as it seemed, to tell. Thus Melville's literary life died of inanition, for another, and a better, reason along with the rest, the excess of the subjective note or the note of speculation that all but extinguished the creative power in him. Aware as he was that the "full heart" was a writer's first necessity, he deplored this "leech" of speculation that was feeding on his blood, the metaphysical way of thinking that grew upon him steadily with its "unshored harbourless immensities" and insoluble riddles. Brought up in a Calvinistic circle, he was predisposed to "grind away at the nut of the universe," as he once put it, at the problems of predestination and original sin, of moral responsibility, evil and good, and the life at sea had encouraged his meditative humour. At a time when, as he wrote in *Redburn,* common sailors debated the question whether men would stand or sit on the Last Day, on what would a young man like Melville have been apt to brood in the immeasurable stillness and seclusion of the long night-watches? All the ponderings of the inmates of frigates were introspective, as he said, and a "morbidness of mind" was often the consequence of this, the morbidness into which Melville had fallen when Hawthorne found him "overshadowed,"—and ready to be "annihilated,"—in Liverpool in 1856. He had persisted, Hawthorne said, "in wandering to and fro" over "deserts" of theological speculation, "as dismal and monotonous as the sandhills amid which we were sitting." He had become an illustration of Goethe's saying that all theory is grey while the golden bough of life,—and art,—is green.

For, whatever Melville's thought was worth, his vein of metaphysics, all the great traits of the writer withered in him, the gifts of character, humour, style, even the art of shaping a book or maintaining the unity of mood in a composition. He was an instance of the well-known fact that when artists take to theorizing it is often because their creative power is gone, and Melville, great writer though he was, lacked the developing sense of a craft that might have sustained him in the loss of other powers. He was one of the writers, like Whitman, who

prove that the rules of an art are of small importance
when the mind and the grasp of life are large enough,
whose genius far outstrips their talent, who are neither
fish, flesh nor fowl as writers and who triumph solely by
virtue of their magnitude and depth. These anomalous
spirits, who are *sui generis,* can break with impunity
every rule, and yet, when their genius fails them, they
are all but helpless, wanting the talent of the craftsman
that might carry them on; and for Melville, an unstable
writer, always in a sense an amateur, the collapse or
the frustration of his genius was catastrophic. Uncertain
often in his execution, with a very untrustworthy feeling for structure, he had shown his weakness in the shifting of the mood in *Mardi,* in which there was no unity
between the opening chapters and the long sequel after
the meeting with Yillah. But *Pierre* was more confused than this,—its atmosphere was quite unreal,—
there were two or three dissonant styles at war in the
romance, where Melville seemed almost as much at sea
as he presently seemed in *The Confidence-Man,* the last
attempt he made to write a book. The opaqueness of
this laborious satire, which Melville half-heartedly
meant to continue, resulted from his obvious inability
to draw characters any longer that were vivid enough to
support the burden of thought; and this was another of
those aberrations into which writers do not fall when
their feeling for the craft is alert and well-developed.
He spoiled the finest of his shorter stories, the otherwise superb *Benito Cereno,* by including an eighteen-
page legal report towards the end. As the joy of an
evolving craftsmanship might have sustained his waning
powers, so also a few literary friendships might have
served him well; but Melville was indifferent to other
writers, whether in Boston or New York, with the single
exception of Hawthorne for two or three years. What he
lacked especially was an interest in society, in actual

people in all the concreteness of their lives, that objective feeling for human nature, the foundation of a novelist's life, which alone could have corrected his tendency to the abstract and the subjective. Not people but their problems touched him, because they were his own problems, and his interest in society, as in people, was feeble and dim, so that his satire was ineffective alike in *Mardi* and *The Confidence-Man,* with its clutter of faceless characters and its dubious meaning. In *Mardi* especially one felt the lack of a steady and continuous point of view as of any real edge or decision in the comments on the world, the force that one found in Swift and in Samuel Butler and that gave their satire its authority, its convincingness, its grip.

Thus Melville's flower fell to the mould, as no one saw better than Fitz-James O'Brien, who observed that he was "excessively introverted," that the "healthy productive tendencies" had been arrested in his mind,[2] the gift of shaping characters, for instance, like Fayaway or Jack Chase, like Father Mapple, Jackson or Doctor Long Ghost. One never saw the man Pierre as one saw Bildad, Peleg or Queequeg; he was almost as much a ghost as the Confidence-Man, or as Isabel, who bound Pierre by an "atmospheric spell" and who appeared to "swim in an electric fluid." Moulded as she seemed "from fire and air," Isabel was perhaps suggested by Balzac's Seraphita, whom she strikingly resembled, but she no more existed as a person for the reader than the cab-drivers, turnkeys and porters in the book who were

---

[2] "The sum and substance of our fault-finding with Herman Melville is this. He has indulged himself in a trick of metaphysical and morbid meditations until he has almost perverted his fine mind from its healthy productive tendencies. A singularly truthful person—as all his sympathies show him to be—he has succeeded in vitiating both his thought and his style with an appearance of the wildest affectation and untruth. His life, as we should judge, has been excessively introverted."—Fitz-James O'Brien, in *Putnam's Magazine,* 1857.

all vaguely stylized after Shakespeare. How different
these were from the castaway crowd of tinkers, watch-
makers, doctors and farmers who formed the crew in
White-Jacket and who sprang into life, a vivid Melvil-
lean life, at the author's summons, when he wished to
bring one or another to the front; for all the characters
in the earlier books were Melville's own and freely
drawn with his gift of lucid, lively, rapid writing. When
later he drew Billy Budd, he was really drawing Jack
Chase again, recalling the fresh jubilant spirit of his old
captain of the top, as he also revived in that final tale
much of the gusto, the actuality and the clear firm style
of his earlier stories of the sea. There were fine qualities
in Pierre, however, and the first quarter of *Mardi* was a
masterpiece of iridescent prose with its portraits of the
old Skyeman Jarl and the two South Sea grotesques,
Annatoo, the pilfering termagant, and Samoe, her
spouse. As for *Pierre* and its over-wrought style and spec-
tral melodrama, it was plainly an Elizabethan drama
without the verse, incongruously written in prose in the
shape of a novel, an instance of Melville's misapplica-
tion of literary forms, like his use of the metre of
Hudibras in the poem *Clarel*. And yet the reader found
himself carried along by the logic of the book, the im-
plication that good and evil are intertwined inseparably
and that every intransigent idealism is at odds with the
world. With the playwrights that he loved in mind, Melville, to achieve the effect of distance, avoided all realistic
touches in his picture of New York,—which appeared
merely as the "vast triangular city,"—while it was just
this note of reality that one welcomed in the rural
scenes, so false, in the absence of verse, was the effect of
the rest. The old family mansion at Saddle Meadows
and the life as Melville described it there, remembering his visits as a boy to the Gansevoort house, brought
back the manorial Dutch estates, those lordships in the

heart of the republic that had come to an end in
Stephen van Rensselaer's day. Covering whole counties
here and there, with two or three thousand farmer-
tenants, they survived like Indian mounds the Revolutionary flood, and Melville contrived to convey their
spirit, which he had known so well, with the pride of
race and family that had held them up. Isabel's story,
and the tale of her mother whom Pierre's father was
supposed to have loved, evoked the legends of the émi-
grés in Western New York, like the wild, dark, wooden
forest-house that she remembered in her dreams, vaguely
built in the manner of a French chateau.

Two of Melville's later stories, following *Pierre,* were
especially good, along with *The Encantadas* and *Benito
Cereno,* both tales of lonely men that reflected the author's mind in part and the pathos of his isolation,
obscurity and silence. For there was undoubtedly something of Melville in Bartleby the Scrivener, whose reply
to every suggestion was "I would prefer not to" and who
cut off all the bonds of fellowship until he stood alone,
clinging like Poe's Raven to the office even at night. A
"bit of wreck in the mid-Atlantic," he was no more forlorn than Israel Potter, who returned to America finally
after his exile, finding that the last known member of
his family had sold his farm years before and removed
to some untraceable region of the unsettled West. The
story, which Melville dedicated to the Bunker Hill
monument, as if he no longer had friends to interest
or please, was based on the true account of a minuteman
of the Revolution who was captured and taken to England as a prisoner of war. He had grown up as a farmer's
boy in the Berkshire region that Melville described, with
many charming touches, early in the book, the Housa-
tonic valley with its old farmhouses falling to ruin over
which the lordly eagle soared aloft. Melville was never
happier than when he sketched the early spring, the

vapour of the maple-sugar boiler curling in the woods, the rising smoke of the charcoal-burner, the vast blocks of the stone walls that could only have been built, as it seemed, by a race of Titans. The bluebirds sported in clusters on the grass like moving knots of violets and like winged jonquils the yellow-birds flitted by, as in some of Melville's later nostalgic poems, pointing the contrast between these scenes and the city of Dis,—like Pierre's New York,—the London where Israel wandered for forty years. Israel, a pet of John Paul Jones, had had interesting adventures, as a secret emissary to Franklin at his house in Paris, the "homely sage and household Plato" whom Melville pictured with exceptional skill in one of a number of portraits that appeared in the book. Another was of Ethan Allen, the hero of Ticonderoga, a Samson among the Philistines as a prisoner at Falmouth, a giant with a lion's heart and full of mountain music, handcuffed but unsubdued in his forest rags. The portrait of Cooper's "pilot" was admirable also. The most significant part of the book was the picture of the city of dreadful night that was based on Melville's impressions when he visited London, to see his publishers there, in 1849,—the vistas of streets like the galleries of coal-mines, the walls of blackened stone that carried him back to the accursed Galapagos isles.

But as for these stories, after all,—even the best, *Benito Cereno*, with its fantasy of the painted ship on the painted sea and its wondrously sinister atmosphere and perfection of style,—would they have been recalled at all if Melville had not written *Moby-Dick* and the three or four books of travel that appeared before it? Melville's metaphysical cogitations appealed to certain writers later who had small interest in the more obvious notes of his work, but were they in reality of greater moment than the thoughts of a hundred other men who were obsessed at the time with the conflict of religion and science? Melville himself must certainly have known that *Moby-Dick* was his masterpiece, the token, the final expression of his own uniqueness, the "mighty book," though a "draught of a draught,"—for he left the "cope-stone" to posterity,—that owed its greatness largely to the "mighty theme." Aside from the innermost meaning of the book,—and this seemed clear enough,[3]—with what an astonishing skill he sustained the mood from the first words of Ishmael himself, with "November" in his soul, to the last wild spin of the ship in the vortex of the sea. Even the black picture of the foundering whaler that Ishmael saw in the Spouter Inn struck the note of the Pequod's tragic voyage, like Father Mapple's version of the story of Jonah and the whale and the five dusky phantoms on the wharf at dawn. The mysterious Elijah with his vague intimations of doom was another of the portents with which the book began, the "loomings" that recurred with the rumours at sea, the news picked up from passing ships as the legend of the white whale grew in the minds of the sailors. Their forebodings were constantly fed by omens, more fearful as the voyage went on, the corposants that lighted the way to Moby-Dick, the turning of the compasses when the needles went awry, the stories of crying seals and drowning seamen. Many of the scenes were loosely connected, and sometimes, as in the "Town-Ho's Story," Melville recalled the garrulities of Washington Irving and his way of dropping at ease into a traveller's tale. Then he rang

[3] See in his letter to Mrs. Hawthorne, 1852, Melville's own remarks about *Moby-Dick* and his apparent unconsciousness of certain elements in the book in which his subconscious mind drove straight to the mark: "I had some vague idea while writing it that the whole book was susceptible of an allegorical construction, and also that parts of it were,—but the specialty of many of the particular subordinate allegories were first revealed to me after reading Mr. Hawthorne's letter, which, without citing any particular examples, yet intimated the part-and-parcel allegoricalness of the whole."

the changes on the subject of whales as Burton did
with melancholy, their heads, their tails, their food,
their ambergris. He expatiated on pictures of whales, on
whales in paint, in stone, in wood, on the whale as a
dish, on the skin or blubber of the whale, on the great
order of the "folio" leviathans, with the sperm whale
and the right whale, and the Grand Armada of the
whales near Java Head. The book abounded in other
digressions, on standers of mastheads, for one example,
from Simeon Stylites to the bronze Nelson in Trafalgar
Square and Washington on his main-mast in Baltimore,
but what Melville called his "careful disorderliness" was
governed by the "large and liberal theme" and the powerful rhythm of a style that was in harmony with it.
What variety one found, moreover, in the admirable
unity of *Moby-Dick,* what humour along with the sublimity and the tragic vision, the grotesquerie, for instance, of the portrait of Queequeg, the burly humour of
the scene in which Stubb orders old Fleece to preach to
the sharks. Then what poetry there was in Melville's
description of noon on the tropical ocean, a calm "like
a universal yellow lotus . . . unfolding its noiseless
measureless leaves upon the sea," and in Ahab's apostro-
phe to the head of the whale, severed and hanging,
hooded and black, that suggested the Sphinx's head
in the hush of the desert.

For the rest, as in Whitman's *Leaves of Grass,* all the
world was in *Moby-Dick* with the "several races" of mankind that appeared on the whaler, Lascars, Chinese,
Tahitians, Danes, Portuguese, English and Dutch, Manx-
men, Malaysians and men of Martha's Vineyard. There
were Spaniards and Icelanders, "Yarmans" and "crap-
poes," sailors from Germany and France,—mere lubbers
at the art of whaling to the Yankee Stubb,—and the
Negroes whom Melville always drew with a special
delight and tenderness, full of admiration as he was for

their "great gift of good humour." He liked to speak of
little Pip's "pleasant, genial, jolly brightness" and the
coolness, indifference and easiness of the gigantic Daggoo, who made a white man standing before him seem
like a white flag that had come to beg truce of a fortress.[4] Without abasing the strong and the proud, he
exalted the humble, as Whitman did, the cannibal Queequeg, above the rest, the "soothing savage" whose honest
heart restored Ishmael's faith in a wolfish world. For he
shared Emerson's firm belief in what he called the "law"
that "has its precepts graven on every breast," the universality of the perception of the just and the noble.[5]
Like Emerson and Whitman, he ascribed high qualities to the poor and low,—"meanest mariners and
renegades and castaways,"—weaving about them tragic

[4] Referring to a Negro in *Benito Cereno,* he spoke of "a certain
easy cheerfulness, harmonious in every glance and gesture, as though
God had set the whole Negro to some pleasant tune."
Compare this with Whitman's admiring reference to the Negro in
Leaves of Grass:
"His glance is calm and commanding, he tosses the slouch of his
   hat away from his forehead.
The sun falls on his crispy hair and moustache, falls on the black
   of his polish'd and perfect limbs.
I behold the picturesque giant and love him."
Melville was much concerned with the problem of slavery in the
eighteen-fifties. See, in *Mardi,* the hieroglyphics chiselled over the
arch in Vivenza (the United States): "In-this-re-publi-can-land-all-
men-are-born-free-and-equal." Then in small letters, "Except-the-
tribe-of-Hamo" (the Negroes).
"All honest hearts," says Yoomy the minstrel, "must cheer this
tribe of Hamo on."

[5] Speaking of the Marquesans, Melville wrote: "They seemed to
be governed by that sort of tacit common-sense law which, say
what they will of the inborn lawlessness of the human race, has its
precepts graven on every breast. The grand principles of virtue and
honour, however they may be distorted by arbitrary codes, are the
same all the world over; and where these principles are concerned,
the right or wrong of any action appears the same to the unculti-
vated as to the enlightened mind. It is to this indwelling, this universally diffused perception of what is just and noble, that the
integrity of the Marquesans in their intercourse with each other
is to be attributed."—*Typee.*

graces, as he dwelt on the honour and glory of the whaler's calling, commonly thought to be devoid of aesthetically noble associations and far below the level of the liberal professions. His ship, the Pequod, with its babel of tongues, was an emblem of the world, traversing the seven seas and all sides of earth, and the book was a planetary book, like *Leaves of Grass*. One gave the dark side of the planet, the other the bright.

CHAPTER IX

WHITMAN: *LEAVES OF GRASS*

For two or three years in the early fifties, Whitman, still living in Brooklyn, worked with his father as a carpenter, building small houses, while ever since 1848, when he returned from New Orleans, he had been trying his hand at a new kind of verse. Perhaps he had fallen in love down there, he had been deeply stirred no doubt by his travels on the Mississippi, through the South and the West, and his mind had been open to the numberless influences of that "strange, unloosen'd, wondrous time," as he called these mid-century years in *Specimen Days*. It was a time when many ideas were spreading about, especially perhaps the idea of a poet with a mission, the bardic poet whom Emerson pictured in *Saadi,* the poet of humanity who appeared in the novels of George Sand. Carlyle had spoken of the poet as hero, a world-poet for "our time . . . a new instructor and Preacher of Truth to all men," the creator of a great religious poem, and Michelet, like George Sand, and Victor Hugo presently, exalted the new democratic cult of the people. For this age of the Mormons, of Comte, of Lamennais was an age of new religions and of leaders proclaiming the rise of the masses, of the workers. The idea of a great native poet was current in America, and in her essay *American Literature* Margaret Fuller had foretold the coming of a mighty genius in the Western world. He would harrow the soil and open it to the air and the sun.

Whitman, whose ear was attuned to the time, heard these and other voices,—the voice of Mazzini, the apostle

of brotherhood and progress, with his dream that every
nation had a mission of its own,[1]—and he also absorbed
the discoveries of science and the dawning conception
of evolution, of the gradual emergence of life from the
primitive chaos. Then he was aware of the many attempts to establish the kingdom of heaven on earth: the
socialist movement of the forties, the "family" at Brook
Farm, which had followed the Owenites, the Rappites,
the Zoarites and others, with the Swedenborgians, the
Millerites who were lookng for the New Jerusalem, and
the communists who had settled at Oneida in 1848. He
may well have met John Humphrey Noyes, the founder
of the Oneida community, living himself in Brooklyn
during these years, the minister from Dartmouth college,
at the height of his messianic ambitions, who had left his
own circle for a while. Noyes, having broken with puritanism, was trying to "redeem" the sexual function and
associate the physical life with the life of the spirit, including the senses in his religion, affirming that the
pleasures of the body were sacred since the body itself
was a part of God's creation. Following the lead of
Robert Dale Owen who, in 1836, had advocated birth-
control and the discussion of sex, he had made a sacra-
ment of sexual love and intercourse in the system that
he described as "complex marriage." He was to institute
in time the plan that he called "stirpiculture," the scientific breeding that was later described as eugenics,[2] and
he was virtually a neighbour of Whitman's in Brooklyn
during the five years that immediately preceded the
writing of *Leaves of Grass*. Did he influence Whitman

[1] "I have such vast love for Mazzini."—*With Walt Whitman in
Camden*. Michelet's *Le Peuple*, published in 1846, anticipated many
of the ideas of *Leaves of Grass*.

[2] See Bernard Shaw's reference to Noyes in his *Revolutionists'
Handbook*, a supplement to *Man and Superman*: "The Perfectionists
[at Oneida] were mightily shepherded by their chief Noyes, one of
those chance attempts at the Superman which occur from time to
time, in spite of the interference of man's blundering institutions."

directly? His thoughts at least were in the air, like those of Mazzini and Michelet, George Sand, Carlyle, like those of Emerson, above all, whose essays Whitman carried in his lunch-pail and read at the noon-hour on his carpentering days. When he was "simmering," he told a friend, Emerson brought him "to a boil,"—the writer who embraced "the common, the familiar, the low," who characterized the over-soul while preaching self-reliance and said that our "day of dependence" was drawing to a close. Emerson had prophesied that poetry would lead in the new day and had uttered a prayer indeed for a poet of the modern, one who would see the same deities in the vast materialism of the time that people admired so much in Greece and Rome.

Tough-minded as he was, Whitman, the most impressionable of men, absorptive as a sponge in the fertile waters of the time, sooner or later made his own, remodelled for his peculiar ends, whatever he received from other writers. But the "child" who went forth every day, becoming the objects he looked upon, became as well the minds that he read or heard of, for he flooded himself with the immediate age, as he said the poet ought to do, its thoughts and feelings as well as its appearances and facts. Meanwhile, he found himself possessed with a special desire and conviction, a desire that had hovered on the flanks of his previous life and that steadily advanced to the front and defined itself, as he later wrote, and finally dominated everything else in his mind. This was to attempt some worthy record of the faith and entire acceptance of life that seemed to him the moral foundation of the country, meeting the challenge of democracy and science to state their case in poetry, in contradiction to the songs and myths of the past. Like George Fox, he felt a call, as clear to him as the "inner light," to abandon the conventional themes of earlier poets, with all the stock poetical touches, the

plots of love and war and the high exceptional person-
ages of old-world song. He was to embody in his verse
nothing whatever for beauty's sake, neither legend nor
myth nor romance nor euphuism nor rhyme, but only
the broadest average of humanity in the ripening nineteenth century with all its countless examples in the
America of the day.

This was the new verse, stripped as a Quaker meeting-
house, into which he had been groping his way for a
number of years, the verse that he finally put to press,
setting it up in type himself, and published in 1855 as
Leaves of Grass. At intervals throughout his life he was
to add to this first book "some eight hitches or stages of
growth," as he called them, with one or two "annexes"
(finished in 1891), adding here, omitting there, retaining his first conception of the "leaves," for he saw a symbol of democracy in the summer grass. Disliking what he
once described as "fixed up poetry and art," he had dis-
carded the conventional phrases of poets, together with
illustrations and metaphors that savoured of the classics
and ornamental similes and images referring to the past.
Seeking a perfect transparent clearness, he clung to
common modes of speech, a language that was always
homely and idiomatic, renouncing rhyme and metre too,
following, as he thought, the rhythms of nature, which
were often those of the prophets of the Bible as well. He
was convinced that great poetry would never be expressed again in the "arbitrary and rhyming" metres of
the past, for, conceiving all poetry in the image of his
own, as Poe had done before him, he assumed that the
rhythms of nature were inevitably "free." As for this,
Emerson had found these rhythms precisely in the regular metres and rhyme, which corresponded, he felt, to
the beating of the blood. But Whitman's style was a
great style, one of the great original styles, while his motive was not aesthetic, it was religious. He was to repeat

again and again that one deep purpose controlled his work and had always underlain it, the religious purpose, that the "altitude of literature and poetry" had "always been religion," that "first-class works" were to be tried by their "radiation of the ethical principles" and their "eligibility to free, arouse, dilate." His hope, as he said, was to fill the reader with "vigorous and clean manliness" and "give him good heart as a radical possession and habit."

Thus in his way Whitman too was one of those prophets of new dispensations who abounded in the middle of the century in America and France, and perhaps one might say Russia as well where the Slavophilism of Dostoievsky was not without points of resemblance to this Brooklyn evangel. They were equally examples of the idea that nations had missions, roles of their own to perform for the good of mankind, perhaps the most striking examples indeed of the fervent Mazzinian belief in a symphony of humanity presented by these various performers. Both sprang from deep roots in the histories of the nations, the ancient faith in the Russian peasant as the fountain-head of the highest spiritual traits and the old feeling of countless Americans that the world was beginning afresh with them, that they were appointed to liberate and improve mankind. For the Slavophils and Dostoievsky, the Russians were a youthful race and the new world was destined to rise from them; they were to carry on the torch from the dying old feudalistic world and exemplify equality and brotherhood before the nations. Whitman, professing a similar faith, prefigured by Paine and by Jefferson, and expressed more fully by Emerson on the literary plane, recognized and celebrated, in a letter to his Russian translator in time, the correspondence between the two great nations.[3] He was

---

[3] "You Russians and we Americans! Our countries so distant, so unlike at first glance . . . and yet in certain features, and vastest

one of many in days to come who saw the deep community between these two "young" peoples and their "deathless aspirations," and this was the faith that possessed his mind when, "solitary, singing in the West," he struck up, as he put it, "for a new world." He had observed that certain nations,—the peoples of Judea, Greece and Rome,—had possessed their own distinctive and central ideas, the "principal reason-why" of their whole existence, and he was convinced that America was one of these nations, and the greatest of them, the "custodian of the future of humanity," as he called it once. His purpose was to celebrate this idea in a "psalm of the republic." To Emerson he owed much, the "original true Captain who put to sea, intuitive, positive, rendering the first report," the discoverer of "these shores" of the "moral American continent," as he described the prophet of Concord in a preface. When Whitman called himself "one of the roughs," was he not thinking of Emerson's "Berserkers," who were coming to destroy the old and build the new? Emerson had looked to Jacksonism, the "rank rebel party," to root out the hollow dilettantism of American culture. Was not Whitman's "barbaric yawp" an expression of this hope?

Whitman, who was anything but a "rough" in fact, soon ceased to dramatize the Walt who appeared as the

---

ones, so resembling each other. The variety of stock-elements and tongues, to be resolutely fused in a common identity and union at all hazards,—the idea, perennial through the ages, that they both have their historic and divine mission,—the fervent element of manly friendship throughout the whole people, surpass'd by no other races,—the grand expanse of territorial limits and boundaries —the unform'd and nebulous state of many things, not yet permanently settled, but agreed on all hands to be the preparations of an infinitely greater future—the fact that both Peoples have their independent and leading positions to hold, keep, and if necessary, fight for, against the rest of the world—the deathless aspirations at the inmost centre of each great community, so vehement, so mysterious, so abysmic—are certainly features you Russians and we Americans possess in common."—Letter of 1881.

hero in the original *Song of Myself*. He lost much of his arrogance in the course of time, he grew less nationalistic as he looked past America to embrace the world, and the "turbulent, fleshy, sensual" Whitman was more and more lost in the spiritual man after his experiences with the wounded in the war. The child of nature, "hankering" and "gross," vanished from his later poems, with most of the sexual imagery of *Children of Adam,* although he always insisted that his whole work must stand or fall with his most outspoken lines. For what could be said for the prudery that would not accept and publicly name the things on which all existence and all health depended? He wished to reclaim sexuality from the tongues and pens of blackguards and from those who impugned creation as it were from the outset, restoring a sense of the sanity of birth,—like any good physician, —and of all that produced strong-fibred perfect men. He was in reaction, like John Humphrey Noyes, against the contempt of the body, the "narrow, filthy, degenerate, poisonous distaste" expressed by the ascetic religions for the natural man, like Henry Ward Beecher too, the most popular minister of the time, who also rebelled against puritanism in many of its phases. What Whitman preferred was something else than the "love-play" of later thought or the "merely sensual voluptuousness" of "masculine circles" he disliked so much in "erotic stories and talk," [4] which he said was like a disease that comes to the surface and was "therefore less dangerous than a concealed one." For he disliked far more the "pruriency . . . sneaking, furtive, mephitic," that pervaded modern literature, conversation and manners, the modesty that was "feeble and garrulous," the verses relating the "amours of idlers" and the "sly settee and the adulterous unwholesome couple."

No, opposed as he was to the "fashionable delusion of

[4] *A Memorandum at a Venture.*

the inherent nastiness of sex," he was far from either of these attitudes, which were both so common, and even sentiment and romantic feeling were reserved in Whitman's mind rather for those he called "comrades" than for those he called "lovers." He instinctively identified the sexual impulse with biological procreation as connected with the spiritual and creative forces of life, concerned as he was with paternity and maternity, the fathers and mothers of "many children," the maintenance of the human breed, the welfare of the race. Whitman's lovers were primarily parents and he was mainly concerned with sex as conducing to the result of a race of superior men. There was something austere, in point of fact, in Whitman's sexuality, while personally he was rather under than over-sexed, mildly bisexual and mostly unconscious of the homosexual implications in *Calamus* and other passages in his poems and prose.[5] Was not his "hearty comradeship," his "manly friendship, fond and loving, pure and sweet, strong and life-long," much the same as Melville's feeling for Jack Chase and Billy Budd, whose presence had expanded his veins like the sun or like wine? He "permitted no familiarities," Peter Doyle recalled, the Washington horse-car conductor who was Whitman's friend, and his vision of "companionship thick as trees" was as far from the vision of Proust or Wilde as Whitman's America was remote from their France or England. Homosexuality in the sense of per-

---

[5] All the evidence bears out the assertion of his brother George that Whitman was not in his youth attracted to girls. On the other hand, he was obviously shocked when John Addington Symonds suggested that there was something actively sexual in his love of comrades. He was probably sincere in saying in his old age that he did not know what *Calamus* "all means" and "perhaps never did know." Two motives may well have prompted him when he made up, as he probably did, the story about his many illegitimate children, one, to assert his sexual prowess, which was deficient, in fact, and two, to combat the charge that he was homo-, not heterosexual.

version could scarcely have thriven in the climate of his time and place or in one who so liked "manliness" and all that was bracing, hardy and sane and was drawn to the strongly marked of both the sexes. For the rest, there was much of the woman in Whitman's composition. This gave one the sense of an endless present, such as women give, in *Leaves of Grass,* a feeling of the depth and reality of the here and now.

Whitman's attitude toward sex was part of a general point of view that was deeply concerned with the continuance and perfection of the species, the feeling of "cosmic continuity" that was much in the air of the time and largely inspired the sociology of Lester F. Ward. It sprang from the faith in evolution that Whitman shared with Emerson, who had earlier been equally receptive of the discoveries of science, in chemistry, botany, physiology, geology and mechanics,—the sense of Hegel's "consistent and eternal purpose" and the moral unity and sanity of the creative scheme. The divine for him was immanent in the body and soul of humanity as in the nature of which they were both a part: it was in everything, all-pervasive, so that the notion of human equality, the notion of democracy followed the notion of science. There was nothing in nature low or base, and only mistaken laws and customs had created such ideas in the minds of people. Whitman's object was to establish a basis for faith in democracy by showing that all human qualities were latent in each individual, taking himself as representative, the "Walt" of the poems,—and indeed as a sympathetic man he was really protean. There was some foundation for John Burroughs's remark that "Walt has all types of men in him,—there is not one left out."

For the rest, he saw in literature the dominant factor in humanity's progress, the principal "medicine and

ever" of civilization, and the poet retained for him the
office he had held in primitive times, adjusted entirely
to the modern and its new combinations. This poet, or
his literatus, was like Emerson's bard, the mover, the
teacher, the pace-maker, the creator of types. As the
quality and value of any nation reflected the persons
who made it up, so these were largely a consequence of
its songs and aesthetics, of the poets who afforded these
men and women the materials and suggestions of personality and enforced them in a thousand effective ways.
It was they who had fashioned the images of heroes,
Achilles, the Cid, Don Quixote, Faust, and men became
loving, generous and proud beholding in their poems
the beauty of all these qualities in the types they created.
Filled as he was with this conception, Whitman inevitably looked askance at a poetry that over-emphasized the
"mere aesthetic" and separated this special function
from all the rest, and he was bound to regard with disdain the "male odalisques" and "genteel little creatures" who stood for American poetry in this later generation. Seeing man, as he did, in nature, properly growing in the open air, he detested their indoor aroma, their
suggestion of the parlour, of "dandies and ennuyees,"
piano songs, "rooms stifling with fashionable scent,"
the tinkling rhymes of the ballade and rondeau-makers.
With their small calibre and small aims, they were, he
felt, mere hangers-on, six times diluted imitators of the
English and the French, concerned with the fashion of
the garment mainly, verbal jewelry, aborted conceits,
thin sentiment and "dyspeptic amours with dyspeptic
women." Most of their poems were but larger or smaller
lumps of sugar and the chief part of their dish was the
glucose flavours. Not one of these poets confronted,
with a feeling akin to itself, the voiceless but erect and
active spirit of the land, its pervading will and typical

aspiration, and beside them he seemed to hear the echo, as from some mountain-top far in the West, of the scornful laugh of the genius of "these States."

For the country signified to Whitman the new age he was fighting for, the incarnation and the pledge of democracy and science. It was the great test or trial case for all the problems and speculations and all the promises of humanity in the past and the present, unquestionably designated for the leading part in the drama of the race at least for many centuries in the immediate future. It was to become not a conqueror nation but rather the grand producing land of nobler men and women, healthy and free, the friendliest nation, the nation of peace, the composite nation, formed from all, and reconciling all as children of an equal brood. It was to be illimitably proud, independent, self-possessed; it was to be generous and gentle; above all, it was to be an example, not an echo. Therein lay its chief function, not to follow but to lead the way in matters that were more important than comforts for the million, urgent as it also was to remove the stigma from the workers and labour and destroy the remnants of feudalism and the iniquity of caste. There was one field, and the grandest, left open for our cultus: to fashion for the average masses, and inclusive of all, a splendid and perfect personality, not confined to a special class but in widest commonalty spread among women and men. Races of natural and beautiful persons, physically, mentally, morally sane, were to fill the ranks of the farming and working life, true as it was that, although the country faithfully acted upon them, it was least aware of the most vital things it stood for. Moreover, while the American brain was responsive and intelligent, it followed and imitated still and Europe was the leader, for the nation was ruled even yet, in its social standards, by foreign lands and where did one find America on her own soil in any loyal, highest, proud expression? Feudalism, caste, though palpably retreating from political institutions, retained their control of the more important fields, the sub-soil of literature, for instance, and education, with the fossil theology of the superstitious, untaught, credulous, fable-loving, mythic-materialistic, primitive ages of mankind. America had originated virtually nothing artistically or morally, and it seemed strangely unaware that models appropriate for former conditions and European lands were exotics and exiles here. All the more need for American teachers, a greater order of native authors, receptive of importations but adjusted to the West, to ourselves, to our own differences and our own days, fit to cope with our occasions and evoke a religious and moral character beneath the political basis of the revitalized states.

Did not Whitman see in himself perhaps the prophet of a new religion through which America was to lead in remodelling the world, the centre of a group of comrade-apostles who were devoted to the cause of advancing and spiritualizing democracy and sowing it broadcast? His symbol of manly affection for these was the sweet-flag called the calamus, which grew in great masses of fascicles clinging together, shoulder to shoulder, as it were, and back to back, while, as for himself, he spoke of trances in which a man is divinely possessed and given up wholly to the surgings of the demon within him. He knew those states of exalted musing in which one's senses were still alert though one's feeling of the material world seemed suspended for a while and one's powers attained a pitch of freedom and vision; and, following the impulse of the spirit, for he was deeply a Quaker in grain, he felt he was acting in obedience to a divine command. He foresaw democracy proving itself by luxuriantly growing its own schools, its own theology, poems and forms of art, displacing all that had previously existed or had been anywhere produced, under opposite and hostile influences, at moments in the past. It was to pervade life and govern life on all hands, beginning in America with its limitless eligibilities and air because the old world was committed to the feudal tradition,—fibred and vitalized by regular contact with out-door life and growing things, trees, animals, farm-scenes, birds and the warmth of the sun.

Later Whitman's imagination spread from America to include the world, and his dearest dream was what he called an internationality of poets and poems, uniting the nations more closely than all the treaties. At the same time his mind extended backward, and as he gradually came to feel the value of tradition he ceased to believe that America should break wholly with the past. There had always been something conservative in him. He liked to dwell on the old farm-ways and what he described as the "mother of many children," for the human types that appealed to him were "frightfully out of line," he said, with the largely imported models of the new novels and poems. He recurred to such words as virtuous, chaste, industrious, resolute, cheerful, devout, and he wrote with pleasure of the "Peacemaker" whom his mother had once described to him as one she had known on Long Island in early days. A farm-woman of nearly eighty, she was the settler of difficulties, the shepherdess, regulator, judge, a favourite of all, a sight to draw near and look upon with her large figure and snow-white hair, her clear complexion, dark eyes and magnetic power. He sympathized with Carlyle's distaste for the "caterwauling" of the radicals, their "unceasing complaints against everything," as he put it, deploring the Abolition "fanatics," much as he hated slavery, together with the "contemptible lucubrations" of the "free love" cranks. He criticized the restless spirit that caused the destruction of landmarks, composing a series of newspaper essays that showed his love for the local scene and his deep wish to preserve the relics of the past,—the old elms in the Brooklyn streets, the Revolutionary powder-houses, the graveyards that meant much to Americans of the older stock.

Moreover, having believed from the first in cosmic continuity, he came to believe in the continuity of poetry also, feeling that America should not cut its moorings to the older world, as he had wished it to do in the beginning. He hoped it might "complete" the past and "fuse with" or "enfold" the world, recalling what Longfellow had said to him, that before the new world could be worthily original she must saturate herself with the originality of others. He came to feel that he could never have written *Leaves of Grass* if he had not stood bare-headed before Shakespeare's poems, fully aware of their colossal grandeur and beauty, and he said that he dared to claim for his verse what he claimed for America also, that it was the "result and evolutionary outcome of the past." In *Passage to India* he returned to this past and its mysteries and splendours in an effort to conceive the ideal world of the future, imagining a humanity born again in the union of all that was spiritual in the East with all the materialism of the West that was truly enlightened. America and its poetry, he felt, must merge with the past of Asia and Europe, and Americans should hospitably receive and complete the work of the older civilizations and change their small scale to the largest and proudest. They should cheerfully accept the precious legacies of Egypt, India, Greece and Rome and give them a fresh physiognomy, democratic and modern. Whitman recommended young men and women to overhaul the literatures of Italy, Spain, Germany, France and England (vastly enlarging their own sources of comparison and supply), full as these were of the elements of freedom, gay-heartedness, self-possession that were needed especially in the preparation of the American future. It was there he felt the feudal past had much to give this future since everything centred at last in "personnel," and feudalism was unrivalled there, abounding in highest-rising lessons that could all be re-presented in our own growths.[6]

He never doubted at any time that America should strike out separately and have expressions of its own in literature: he merely felt that the world of the West should blend inseparably with the East and the "ever new yet old, old human race." He had filled his early work, he said, with the "vehemence of pride and audacity of freedom" that were necessary to loosen the mind of a still-to-be-formed country from the stifling anti-democratic authorities of the past, entreating it to re-examine all it was told in church or school and dismiss whatever insulted its sense of the real. He shared Emerson's faith in self-reliance, in the latent powers of the normal soul, which required no "superstitious support" whatever,—the justification of Lincoln's government of, by and for the people, the ordinary people precisely whom Whitman knew. He was to observe them by thousands in the capital in war-time, and later in the years of corruption among the powerful and great,—earnest, honest, hard-working, attentive, anxious to do the right thing, with an endless fund of buoyancy that one could rely on. Pervaded and preserved by faith, the antiseptic of the soul, they never gave up believing and expecting

[6] "We see steadily pressing ahead and strengthening itself, even in the midst of immense tendencies toward aggregation, this image of completeness in separatism, of individual personal dignity, of a single person, either male or female, characterized in the main, not from extrinsic acquirements or position, but in pride of himself or herself alone . . . This idea of perfect individualism it is indeed that deepest tinges and gives character to the idea of the aggregate. For it is mainly or altogether to serve independent separatism that we favour a strong generalization, consolidation."—*Democratic Vistas.*

and trusting, and because of them the Union, swarming with blatherers all the time, was always, Whitman felt, impregnable and sure.

He wished to praise them and their world, exalting the present and the real,—standing, as he wrote, "in my place with my own day here,"—teaching the average man the glory of his daily walk and trade and expressing the native forms, situations and settings. From Montauk to California, from the Saguenay to the Rio Grande, he wished to present America, the country and the towns, the ploughman ploughing, the sower sowing and the factories as well as the farms, the joys of the engineer and the clean-haired girl in the mill. For, agrarian that he was at heart, he was the poet of industry too and all that was involved in the intricate whirl of the present, and his aim was to endow the common scene with the grandeur and the glow that belonged to every real thing and to real things only. From Southern plantation to Western ranch, crossing the prairies or in canebrake and swamp, in adobe houses west of the spinal river, he visited in imagination the cowboy and the planter, cele-brating the boatman, the mason, the carpenter dressing the plank, with his foreplane whistling its "wild ascend-ing lisp." He evoked the mechanic, blithe and strong, the woodcutter, the shoemaker waving his thread, the Ken-tuckian walking the vale in his deerskin leggings, the Wolverine setting his traps on the creek, the hunter in the mountains kindling the fire and broiling the fresh-killed game. In fancy the comrade of raftsmen and min-ers, builders of ships, wielders of mauls, fishermen who knew the taste of the ocean and the woods, he was at home with Indians and pilots, the immigrant and the native-born, the digger of clams on Cape Cod, the canal-boy on the tow-path. All simple employments and oper-ations in which the people were engaged perpetually re-curred to him, with the motions of the workmen, the naivety and the picturesqueness suggesting the beauty and grace of animals that so often and so naturally clung to their gestures and their words. Nor could he ever deny or exclude the beggar, the prostitute, the cleaner of privies, the cottonfield drudge, the deformed, the despised, the dull, the poor whites of the Southern barrens who had never had justice done to them,—on their right cheek he placed the "family kiss."

With much prosaic realism that reminded one of the Dutch genre-painters and was sometimes flushed with an exuberance that brought back Rubens, he seemed in his ardour and elasticity and his fathomless vigour and freshness the personification and the voice of a happy young country. His "trumpet-note ringing through the American camp,"—Thoreau's phrase for *Leaves of Grass,*—expressed the vitality of the Americans and their expanding nation, their thirst for liberty, their homogeneity, their pride and their compassion, while it offered the world good will in America's name.

CHAPTER X

THE BOHEMIANS

WITH the advance of the fifties an interest in matters of art and aesthetics grew steadily among the New Yorkers as it grew in New England, where the youthful Charles Eliot Norton at Harvard was preaching art as a new dispensation and Horatio Greenough expounded his "Artist's Creed." In Florence, another New Englander, James Jackson Jarves, was writing his intelligent books on painting and painters, the teaching of art, museums and schools of design, a neighbour there of Hiram Powers, who had gone to live in Italy, like William Wetmore Story, who had settled in Rome. Meanwhile, in 1855, a younger man from West Point, a Southerner, James McNeill Whistler, appeared in Paris, where he was drawn to a circle of "no-shirt" friends. For he had read Murger's *Scènes de la Vie de Bohème*. He was associated soon with the group of Impressionists, so called, who came to the front a decade later. How rapidly the ranks of the painters and sculptors were growing in the United States one saw in Henry T. Tuckerman's *Book of the Artists*. The writers who were interested in them were also increasing.

Especially in New York perhaps,—certainly more than in Boston,—the writers and artists were drawn sympathetically together, partly because of the Sketch Club, the germ of the Century Association, which had become at once a rendezvous. Bryant, the friend of several painters, was the founder of this club, and the liking for artists that Cooper and Irving had manifested in earlier days was continued in many of the friendships of the new generation. For instance, Henry William Herbert, who called himself Frank Forester, was an all but inseparable comrade of Henry Inman, whose daughter was supposed to have been the original of the lovely Maria d'Arcey in Herbert's novel of sport, *My Shooting Box*. Asher Durand, another friend, taught Herbert how to engrave the plates that he used for the illustrations of some of his books. As Herbert and Inman were fishing companions, so Theodore Winthrop and Frederick E. Church were constantly together in Maine on the camping excursions that Winthrop recalled in *Life in the Open Air,* while Charles Godfrey Leland, who spent much of his time in New York in the fifties, was instinctively drawn to artists of every kind. Leland, who had studied aesthetics at Munich, later established in Philadelphia a school of industrial art,—which he directed for a while,—for the teaching of wood-engraving and work in mosaic, leather and brass, the subject of one of his books, *The Minor Arts*. As for aesthetic speculation, it ranged in New York from Thomas Cole, the founder of the Hudson River School, to Herman Melville, who lectured on "Statuary in Rome" in 1857 on his return from a visit to Italy and Greece. Contemplating what he called the analogy between colour and sound, Cole thought of a possible instrument on which colour could be played, forecasting the later invention of the colour-organ.[1] As for Herman Melville's lecture, it suggested the manner of Margaret Fuller in its alternations of the literal and the transcendental. It discussed the style of

[1] "I believe that colours are capable of affecting the mind, by combination, degree and arrangement, like sound . . . It is evident that there is an analogy between colour and sound . . . An instrument might be constructed by which colour could be played, and which would give to those who had cultivated their taste in the art a pleasure like that given by music."—Quoted in Louis L. Noble's *Thomas Cole.*

Roman villas and the busts that showed Nero as a "fast young man" and Julius Caesar as a practical man of business. One point in the lecture was interesting to readers in the future. Melville anticipated Henry Adams's conception of the Virgin and the Dynamo when he compared the Laocoön and the Locomotive, regarding them as emblems of the ancient system and our own.[2]

Meanwhile, in the new generation of artists, a startling development of the school of Cole was a tendency to paint the gigantesque. The general interest in mountain scenery that Cole had awakened on the Hudson river was extended to the Rocky Mountains by Albert Bierstadt, a German who had grown up in New Bedford, like Albert Pinkham Ryder later, and who made the overland journey in 1858. Then presently Church exhibited "The Heart of the Andes." A Connecticut boy who had worked with Cole, sharing the Catskill studio with him, Church had read Humboldt's South American travels, and he had visited the Andes twice, living at Quito in Humboldt's house, drawn there by his eloquent descriptions. Many American writers were stirred by Church's melodramatic picture. Thomas Buchanan Read wrote a poem about it, while Theodore Winthrop described it at length and Samuel Clemens,—Mark Twain,—learned all its details by heart when he saw it at St. Louis. For Winthrop, who was Church's friend, the picture brought back the tropical world that he had found highly exciting at Panama, a world that was little known still to "Americans of the North." It set him dreaming of luxuriant forests of the mangrove and the cocoa-palm, festooned with purple flowers and the crimson orchis, a land where volcanoes flared at night and earthquakes shook the peaks and silver hung in tubers at

[2] According to the report of a listener, his cousin Henry Gansevoort, he also described the Coliseum and the Crystal Palace as "exponents of our respective characters."

the roots of bushes. Clemens wrote to his brother Orion about it. He had counted the leaves on the tropical trees, examining the picture through an opera-glass, for many of the little wayside ferns could scarcely be seen with the naked eye. He found his brain "gasping" to take the wonder in.[3] The picture must have recalled the visions with which four years before he had planned to make a fortune in cocoa in Brazil, for, reading Herndon's *Exploration of the Valley of the Amazon*,[4] he too had caught the South American fever. He had actually set out for the Amazon and only surrendered the dream when he fell in with Horace Bixby, who offered to teach him the craft of the Mississippi pilot. Clemens as a wandering printer had visited New York in 1853. He had worked in one of the printing-shops and lodged at a mechanics' boarding-house like the one he described in *The American Claimant* later.

Another member of Church's circle was Louis Moreau Gottschalk, the Creole composer of New Orleans who had returned from Paris and who made his headquarters in New York after 1853, though he too paid long visits to the lands that lay southward. The first

[3] See also the long passage about this picture in Augusta J. Evans's *St. Elmo*:

"Felix stood in an art gallery, and leaning on his crutches looked up at Church's 'Heart of the Andes.'

"'You are impressed by the solemnity and the holy repose of nature . . . Last week you asked me to explain to you what is meant by 'aerial perspective,' and if you will study the atmosphere in this great picture, Mr. Church will explain it much more clearly to you than I was able to do.'

"'Yes, Miss Earl, I see it now. The eye could travel up and up, and on and on, and never get out of the sky; and it seems to me those birds yonder would fly entirely away, out of sight, through that air in the picture. But, Miss Earl, do you really believe that the Chimborazo in South America is as grand as Mr. Church's?'"

[4] Like Lieutenant Charles Wilkes's report of his Antarctic explorations, this book, also published by the government in 1853-4, was peculiarly thrilling to young American readers. They were almost as excited by this pioneer "opening" of South America as by Commodore Perry's actual "opening" of Japan.

American pianist, in time as in talent,—a "consummate
pianist" Berlioz said he was,—Gottschalk evoked in his
own compositions the scene and the mood of Church's
picture, the luxuriant equatorial forests and the perfumes of the tropics. Born on the banks of the Mississippi, familiar with Lake Pontchartrain, he had also
known Pass Christian as a child, brought up as a musical prodigy who had listened to the Negroes relating
their legends while he absorbed the ballads and stories
of the Creoles. Chopin, hearing him play in Paris, pre-
dicted a great future for him, and he gave a series of concerts with Berlioz, his master, touring Europe with great
success before he came back to the United States and
roved through the Western Hemisphere as a virtuoso.
He spent six years in the Antilles, Spanish, French, English, Danish and Dutch, wandering from island to island, composing and playing,—whenever, as he said, he
happened to find a piano,—sleeping where night over-
took him on horseback on the green grass of the savannah or under the palm-leafed roof of some friendly
vaquero. Rocking in his hammock, he listened to the prat-
tle of the parrots, and once he lived for several months
on the edge of the crater of an extinct volcano, in a
cabin on a rock projecting over the abyss. Every evening
he rolled his piano out on the terrace facing a scene that
more than suggested Church's vistas of the Andes, with
the gigantic amphitheatre hewn from the mountains
at his feet and the soft air bathing an incomparable landscape. Vast virgin forests and waving plains
stretched to the horizon under the azure sky. There he
wrote some of the compositions that reminded his listeners of the Caribbean,—nocturnes, elegies, caprices,
Cuban dances. He recalled for many who were not an-
noyed by what others described as his showy bravura the
banjo, the banana-tree, the crimson camellia, the scarlet
pomegranate: they saw in his romantic airs the fiery

birds in the orange-groves, the golden haze of moon-light in the flowering magnolias. In the *Notes of a Pianist,* occasionally poetic, Gottschalk recorded his impressions of travel, especially in the Western states in the Civil War years.

Still another friend of Church was William J. Still-man, who had studied with him,—indeed, he was Church's first pupil,—a young man from Schenectady, better known as a writer later, who had begun his career as a landscape artist. From Church, at whose studio he had met Poe, Stillman learned little, for he disliked the insistence on "facts" of the Hudson River School as much as the young George Inness who was born on the river. Inness persisted in omitting the famous "fore-ground plant," the obligatory emblem as it were of the Hudson river circle, and, conscious of their weaknesses, he went abroad for two or three years and studied the work of Constable and the Barbizon men. Stillman, who had read *Modern Painters,* had gone to England to talk with Ruskin. He had been greatly impressed by Rossetti and, returning to New York, he was known as the "American Pre-Raphaelite" for a number of years. Meanwhile, the New York artist-life, or certain aspects of it, appeared in Theodore Winthrop's *Cecil Dreeme,* a melodramatic novel in which a mysterious young painter who was really a girl was pursued by an evil "apostle of disenchantment." [5] The events took place in Chrysalis College, a vast old barrack in Washington

---

[5] According to Thomas Wentworth Higginson, the character of Cecil Dreeme was drawn from the "mysterious poet" William Hurl-bert, his fellow-student at the Harvard Divinity School, "a young man so handsome in his dark beauty that he seemed like a pic-turesque Oriental." Beginning as a Unitarian divine and passing through Roman Catholicism, he ended as a defender of despotism. A great breaker of hearts in America and Europe, involved in many social scandals, Hurlbert was described as magnetic and exotically brilliant. He was the hero of Higginson's own novel *Malbone* and, Higginson said, of Charles Kingsley's *Two Years Ago.*

Square, with mullioned windows, dim corridors and
Gothic doors that recalled the first studio-buildings of
the forties and fifties, whose chambers were filled with
the plunder of Europe, armour, draperies, casts and
busts, bronze candelabra and objects in ivory and glass.
The story was one of a number of books that appeared
after Winthrop's death, as a major in the Union army in
1861, for although he was writing throughout the
fifties[6] he was known only in the magazines: Lowell, for
one, published him in the *Atlantic*. He followed Hawthorne in *Cecil Dreeme* and Thoreau in *Life in the
Open Air,* in which he celebrated Maine where he,
with Church and the painter Kensett, "discovered"
Mount Desert in 1854. His pages about the Penobscot
region, Mount Katahdin, Moosehead Lake, breakfasts
of trout and fragrant beds of spruce-boughs, recalled
The Canoe and the Saddle in their freshness and vigour;
for Winthrop always wrote well of the out-of-doors and
above all whenever he wrote of horses. He excelled in
portraits of them, as in the novel *John Brent,* for example, with the superb black thoroughbred stallion that
carried the young man over the plains, caracoling at his
first appearance, circling and curvetting, with pride in
his indignant nostrils and fire in his eye. With what
power and grace, with his silky mane and his tail flying
like a banner, he dashed through the loop of the lasso
that was meant to catch him.

Like Winthrop, Stillman was a lover of the woods,
and it was he who originated the Adirondack Club in
1858. This was the club at Follansbee's Pond, including
Lowell and Agassiz, that Emerson commemorated in
The Adirondacs. Stillman had wandered in the wilder-

[6] In spite of his own sagacious remark in the novel *John Brent:*
"Observation is the proper business of a man's third decade; the
less a spokesman has to say about his results until thirty, the better, unless he wants to eat his words, or to sustain outgrown
formulas."

ness there, exploring it for subjects in the fashion of the time, and he built his own shelter of bark on Raquette Lake where he could work in seclusion apart from the others. Growing up on the Mohawk river, in the country that Cooper had written about,—his uncle had been one of the Redskins in the anti-rent war,—he had corresponded with Thomas Cole before he appeared in New York and presently sailed for England, where he met Turner. He stayed at Denmark Hill with Ruskin, who invited him a few years later to spend a summer with him in Switzerland, where they went on sketching excursions together and Ruskin expounded the mountain-forms and showed him the scenes of some of Turner's drawings. But he wished, as it were, to hold the pencil while the young man sketched,—wished him to see through his own despotic eye. Later Stillman knew Morris and Swinburne and lived for a while with Rossetti, but in the meantime he had served as an agent of Louis Kossuth, who sent him on a wild-goose chase along the Danube. He was expected to recover the crown jewels of Hungary which Kossuth had secretly buried in 1848. As a radical republican like Charles Godfrey Leland, he also studied for a while in Paris, waiting to share in Mazzini's insurrection in Milan; and between whiles, living in New York, he was connected with the *Evening Post* as the art-critic of the paper under Bryant. He had been drawn into correspondence with the newspapers on questions of art and soon acquired a certain reputation, and, as no journal existed in the country that was wholly devoted to art, he established in 1855 a weekly, *The Crayon*. In its three years of existence this was highly successful, because Ruskin was a prophet not only for Stillman and for Norton but for hundreds of the younger intellectuals who were lovers of nature. It was to win support for *The Crayon* that Stillman was drawn to Boston and Cambridge, where

Lowell along with Norton sponsored him, and the journal attracted many writers, Appleton, Whittier, Bayard Taylor, the philosopher Henry James and the painter Durand.

Throughout the long and varied life that Stillman recounted in his *Autobiography*, he drifted back and forth between painting and writing, taking up photography, which he used in his archæological ventures and his admirable collection of plates of the ruins of Athens. One of his books, *On the Track of Ulysses*, recorded a tour that he made following the hero of the Odyssey to Ithaca from Troy. For years he lived in England, for years he was consul at Crete and in Rome, a dreamland of artists still in the sixties in its picturesque neglect and decay, where Stillman sketched on the Campagna with its scattered ruins. There were many who believed in those days that any picture painted in Rome was better than any picture painted elsewhere,—precisely as many believed in Paris later,—and the Caffé Greco, where Cooper met Coleridge in the days of Irving and Washington Allston, remained the haunt of all the foreign artists. In his later writings Stillman turned against Ruskin's "peremptoriness of opinion," dissenting from his extravagances and infirmity of judgment, while he was equally opposed to the misty speculations of some of the German critics,—for example, Grimm. Those were the days when, travelling through Italy, he searched the galleries with Timothy Cole, the wonder-working wood-engraver who so impressed Burne-Jones and Watts and who made the pictures for his *Old Italian Masters*.[7]

---

[7] Too easily overlooked were the charming unguarded "Notes of the Engraver" that Timothy Cole contributed to this fine book,—for instance, the following note written when he was engraving Giotto in the Arena Chapel at Padua: "The light is good, but it is hard to keep to work with so many fine things above one's head. I can scarcely escape the feeling that the heavens are open above me, and yet I must keep my head bent downward to the earth." Or

But these were affairs of a far-away future. Meanwhile, in the fifties, a circle of the new "Bohemians" appeared in New York, counterparts with variations of Whistler's "no-shirt" friends who had also been charmed by Murger's *Vie de Bohème.* The leaders of this circle were Henry Clapp and Ada Clare, the so-called queen of Bohemia, as Clapp was the king, a somewhat ill-assorted pair who had spent some years in Paris themselves, returning about the time when Whistler went there. Ada Clare, who had assumed this name, a well-born South Carolina girl and a cousin of the rising poet Paul Hamilton Hayne, had left Charleston for Paris and a life, as she wrote, "without guidance" there, appearing in New York with a child at twenty-one. The father of her son was supposed to have been Gottschalk, who was studying with Berlioz and who parted with her at any rate in Paris, which she described as "mirth-inclined and never-too-lugubrious" in letters that she sent, with poems, to the papers in New York. She had inherited ample means, and, calling herself the "Love-Philosopher," she hoped to establish a Latin Quarter in the town, a wish she shared with Henry Clapp, a journalist and reviewer of plays, who had been living in Paris before she arrived there. Clapp, a Nantucket man, who had been for a while a teetotaller and an abolitionist editor at Lynn, had violently turned against his past and all his New England associations and hated respectability as much as he had loved it. On his return to America

---

this, when he was engraving a Giorgione in the Uffizi: "What an air of magnanimity and true greatness breathes from this canvas! No other artist knows better than Giorgione how to captivate the mind and to hold the imagination with so few means. Here is a man holding a string of beads. I hear some Americans behind me exclaim, 'Here's a grand head!' How it puts to shame all petty worrying and narrow-mindedness! . . . Now I vow I will endeavour to aim at greater simplicity and nobleness in my living,—to think of the 'Knight of Malta,' to put away all meanness and triviality by a thought of the 'Knight of Malta.'"

from Paris, he gloried in the Bohemian name and called his newspaper articles *feuilletons,* while, as Albert Brisbane's secretary, he translated the writings of Fourier for him and helped to introduce them through *The Tribune.* It was Clapp who said of Horace Greeley that he was a "self-made man who worshipped his creator." Twenty years older than Ada, with her corn-silk hair, Clapp was known in his circle as the "oldest man," for, with his Voltaire-like look, wiry, sarcastic and keen, he was bitter and already withered in his middle forties.

There had never been a time when New York was not ready for ideas from Paris, where Cooper had lived for years, like Washington Irving, and like Gouverneur Morris earlier and Thomas Paine. There Brisbane had found Fourier, as the Philadelphia prodigy Wallace had sat at the feet of Auguste Comte, but the Bohemian way of life was a new departure on the banks of the Hudson when Mimi had long since perished on the banks of the Seine. A few of the "poor devil authors" that Poe wrote about had certainly existed there in Grub Street lodgings, and people remembered in later years when Greenwich Village was a Latin Quarter that Paine, like Charlotte Temple, had lived and died there. Poe, Paine and Charlotte Temple, however, were never Bohemians in the proper sense, and what was new was the frame of mind that Whitman well described when he heard of Ada Clare's pathetic death. He spoke of her "gay, easy, sunny, free, loose and not ungood life." This characterized the lives of many of her circle. Bohemianism as a literary cult appeared with the rise of urban life and the rapid increase of writers and artists in New York, although it was largely imitative and lacked the deep reason for existence that lay behind the Bohemian cult in France. For there had never existed here that aristocratic supporting class which had formerly identified itself with the interest of artists, the virtual destruc-

tion of which in France, together with the rise of the
bourgeoisie, had left the artists with a feeling that they
had no function. To this one could attribute the irre-
sponsibility and many a trait of the Bohemian way of
life. But if the American ruling class had only occasionally supported the arts,—as in Thomas Jefferson's case
and Aaron Burr's,—it had given American society a tone
that artists found congenial, a tone that had vanished
with the rise of the traders and trade. New York was
wholly a commercial town,—anything but literary, unlike Boston,—and writers were naturally inclined to
rebel against this, while they also rebelled against New
England and the dominance of the Boston authors,
whom they attacked as solemn Philistines. More locally
they reacted too against the Knickerbocker school,
which had grown prim, ponderous, trivial, shallow and
sluggish. To many of the rising generation America
seemed prosaic, big, prosperous, monstrously busy but
dull and tame, as the artist Cecil Dreeme felt in Theodore Winthrop's novel and similar precursors of the heroes of Henry James.[8] Amid all this deaconish respectability and monotony of comfort, they called for madder
music and for stronger wine, and even for a little poison
mingled with it. They met in beer-cellars and oyster-
cellars,—unlike the coffee-houses of old, with their humdrum Anglo-Saxon associations,—for the dishes were
foreign there and the air was exotic; and they felt the
nostalgie de la boue that so many shared in Paris later:

[8] "Going back to America!—that matter-of-fact country, where
everything is in the newspapers . . . You that have lived in Italy!
. . . where the old chalice you buy at a bargain gives a mild flavour
of poison to your wine,—to America,—no past, no yesterday, no
today worth having,—life one indefinitely adjourned tomorrow.
Life without shade, life all bald, garish. Steady sunshine may do
to swell wheat and puff cabbage-heads—but man needs something
keener than monotony of comfort, something keener than the
stolid pleasures of deaconish respectability."—Theodore Winthrop,
Cecil Dreeme.

they were often drawn to the slums and even to the gutter. One or two indulged in hasheesh; numbers of them drank deep; eight members of the circle came to untimely ends. They perished by suicide, in attics, in the streets forgotten.

Not all the calamities of authors that New York witnessed during these years sprang out of the Bohemian circle and its manner of living. Major John Richardson, the author of *Wacousta,* the best of the Canadian novelists, was outside the circle; and this follower of Cooper died in New York, a pauper, forgotten even at home, after selling his faithful dog for a morsel to live on. He was buried in an unknown grave in 1852, the year in which William North arrived from England, the journalist who had studied in Germany at one of the universities and whose style was full of German metaphysics. He had published a novel attacking Disraeli, entitled *Anti-Coningsby,* and his short stories, appearing at once in *Graham's, Harper's* and the *Knickerbocker,* preceded another novel *The Slave of the Lamp.* He pictured himself as Dudley Mondell, whom the fashionable Mrs. Yonkers took up, a literary adventurer "with a scattered and fragmentary reputation and a gloomy, discontented, desolate indifference to life." At twenty-eight he killed himself with a draught of prussic acid, and a few years later Stephen Foster, whom all the writers might have known, was picked up dying in the slums where he had been living. While Henry Clapp and Ada Clare held their Bohemian court at Pfaff's, Foster had slept in Bowery lodging-houses, or in abandoned cellars at the Five Points, eating an occasional turnip or apple, peeling it with a pocket-knife, a drunkard, irretrievable, trailing his rags. On fragments of brown wrapping-paper in the back rooms of saloons he continued to write his songs of a far-away home, and the once-respectable Foster whose sister had married the brother of President

Buchanan was rescued only to die in a charity-ward. The tender-hearted Foster, who might well have been called a Bohemian, was merely one of the casualties of all great towns, which had always abounded in contrasts of misery and splendour, such, for example, as Lola Montez also represented in the days before she too died in New York. Returning in 1858, after living in Australia as well as the West, she lectured on the heroines of history and the women of Paris. Then, falling into religious scruples, a Magdalen who had just turned forty, she spent her days in seclusion reading the Bible. She was buried in Brooklyn as "Mrs. Eliza Gilbert."

Outside the Bohemian circle perhaps, these figures were on the fringe of it and sometimes had relations over the border. John Richardson knew Frank Forester, —Henry William Herbert,—who died like one of the Bohemians though he lived unlike them; and so did his fellow-suicide North, a friend for a while of Fitz-James O'Brien, that other literary adventurer from the British isles. Charles Godfrey Leland had fallen in love with Lola Montez in the days when he too was in Munich, and she had never thrown even a plate at him. He thought he was the only friend she had whom she had never attacked with dagger, poker, dish, book or chair. Meeting him in New York again, she asked him to bolt with her to Europe.[9] Leland, the young Philadelphian who edited *Graham's* in his native town, came to New York to work for P. T. Barnum, and he was more or less thrown with the Bohemians later when he was the editor of the magazine *Vanity Fair*. He had assisted Rufus Griswold on the *Illustrated News*, a weekly that

[9] "An intimate of both of us who was present when this friendly proposal was made remarked with some astonishment, 'But, Madame, by what means can you two live?' 'Oh,' replied Lola innocently and confidingly, 'people like us can get a living anywhere.' And she rolled us each a cigarette, with one for herself."—Leland, *Memoirs*.

Barnum established in 1852, and he found in the editorial desk that Griswold turned over to him a mass of papers vilifying Poe. Griswold, who had forged letters of Poe, meant to carry his malice further, though he made no objection when Leland burned the papers. As for "Uncle Barnum," Leland found him as good as gold and a genius like Rabelais, essentially innocent and honest, a prodigious type of the practical joker whose motive was the joy of engineering unheard-of paradoxes. He loved the grotesque far more than the main chance. He plunged in and out of wealth, making and squandering fortunes, like many another American of his time and later,—Mark Twain for one, who read *Struggles and Triumphs* with the zest of a fellow-adventurer, although Barnum was presumably not the author of this book. Leland, whom he asked to write it, believed it was written by Griswold. Leland later recalled Barnum entering the office like a harvest moon, always big with some new joke. The two had conducted a humorous column together.

Of the true Bohemian circle, meanwhile, some were as ineffectual as Murger's Rodolphe and Marcel, while others were writers of real distinction and others again were passing guests at the long table of Pfaff, the German-Swiss. Pfaff's was the beer-cellar on Broadway near Bleecker Street that reminded Bayard Taylor of Auerbach's cellar in *Faust*. One of the circle was Charles Henry Webb, who had read Melville's *Moby-Dick* and presently shipped on a Martha's Vineyard whaler and who had met one of the crew that rescued the author of his favourite book at the time when he was imprisoned in the valley of the Typees. Later, as a well-known fellow-humorist, he published Mark Twain's first book. There was the "female Mazeppa," Adah Isaacs Menken, who was supposed to have inspired the *Dolores* of Swinburne and who collected her own poems in the book

called *Infelicia,* in which she expressed her dreams of
genius and power. In one of her free-verse poems she
saw herself as Judith waiting for the head of Holofernes.
She was the "daughter of the stars" who trimmed her
"white bosom with crimson roses" and whose verses were
Byronic in content and Whitmanian in form. A champion of Whitman from first to last, she was only a casual
member of the circle, and Whitman himself, who often
appeared at the table of Pfaff's, had little enough in
common with many of the others. Later, speaking of
these days, he said his greatest pleasure there was to
"look on—to see, talk little, absorb," and the novelist
Howells recalled his air of purity and dignity and his
"voice of winning and endearing quietness." He was
grateful to Clapp as a loyal ally, who was "always very
close to me," as he remarked to Traubel in later years,
while he shared the general dislike of New England
though not of the New England authors, Emerson,
Alcott and Thoreau, who had been the first to recognize
him. (Perhaps Edward Everett Hale was the first of
all.[10]) For many of the New York writers detested the
ethical note of the New England mind and resented the
authority and prestige of the name of Boston.[11] The
denunciation of all things Yankee was a principal aim
of the *Saturday Press,* the weekly that Clapp established
in 1858, a bold and lively magazine that glorified Whitman the rebel as often as not at Longfellow's expense.
William Winter was Clapp's assistant, Fitz-James O'Brien
was the critic of plays and Thomas Bailey Aldrich was
the chief reviewer. It was somewhat later in the *Saturday*

[10] Whitman's champion William Sloane Kennedy said in his *Fight
of a Book for the World* that Hale was the first living man to print
words of warm approval of the first edition of *Leaves of Grass.*
William J. Stillman also acclaimed it in *The Crayon.* He spoke of
its 'wonderful vigour of thought and intensity of purpose."

[11] "It is absolutely necessary for all poetry to be published in
Boston before the discriminating American mind can see anything
in it."—Orpheus C. Ker (Robert H. Newell), *The Walking Doll.*

Press that Whitman's disciple John Burroughs first saw *There Was a Child Went Forth*. Still later it published Mark Twain's *The Jumping Frog*.

The assistant editor William Winter was also a New Englander, though he did not share Clapp's abhorrence of Longfellow, for instance, and there was never any love lost between "little Willie" and big Walt, who regarded Winter as the "weakest of the New York lot." A youthful Boston journalist who had played on the common as a boy and written poems along the waterfront, he had often called at the Craigie house, where Longfellow had read his verse and greeted him as a literary aspirant. Finding the "American Athens" oppressive, Winter, however, escaped to New York, where he was beginning the long career as a writer on the theatre that continued for more than fifty years. Far from Bohemian himself in temper, he was intimate with Fitz-James O'Brien, whose poems were as watery and commonplace as most of his own, although some of the latter belonged perhaps to the history of the American stage, —they commemorated anniversaries and farewells to actors. Winter was full of apt quotations and anecdotes of theatre-folk,—of the old school especially, which he loved and clung to,—for whom the stage was all romance, who invested it with poetry, while they regarded their art as a learned profession. He diligently studied their methods himself, a friend of many of them, and he was inevitably the foe of the naturalistic theatre later, fond as he was of the old romantic stage. He despised the "problem play," the so-called drama of ideas that converted the theatre into a forum of debate, so that his writing became in time a journalistic elegy lamenting the virtue and grace of a day that was gone. But with his biographies of Joseph Jefferson and Edwin Booth he wrote a standard book called *Shakespeare on the Stage*, assembling from history or from observation

the records of the most important actors who had appeared in the principal plays of Shakespeare. For Winter
knew well the traditions of Shakespearean acting. He
described the manner of the various performers from
the earliest times to the present and all the great Hamlets, Ophelias, Othellos and Lears.

William Winter collected later the stories and poems
of Fitz-James O'Brien, who was killed, as an officer, like
Winthrop, in the Civil War, a spirited well-born Irishman who had gambled a sizable fortune away before he
arrived in New York in 1851. Twenty-four, a lawyer's
son, born at Cork, with extravagant tastes, an admirable
horseman, a capital swordsman and shot, he was courted
for a while by the fashionable world before he descended
to the dingy lodgings where most of the other Bohemians had lived from the first. He looked like a British
tourist in a Parisian farce, while his breezy audacity and
negligent grace, his honest smile and engaging ways
won friends for him at once in every circle. Lively, virile, frank and gay, O'Brien had read Murger too and accepted the role of the literary soldier of fortune who
writes in a garret at midnight for his bread; but, gifted
as he was in a facile way, he soon had several plays produced and his verses and stories appeared in the *Atlantic*
and *Harper's*. Perhaps his best poem was an ode on
Elisha Kent Kane, the Arctic explorer who died in 1857,
while his tales represented a fanciful New York that
sometimes suggested Poe, sometimes Hawthorne. It
abounded in whimsical "wondersmiths," mesmerists,
hunchbacks, fortune-tellers and alchemists living in
shabby tenement-houses. Prosaic Manhattan, in the vision of O'Brien, was touched with a little of Hawthorne's magic in *The Golden Ingots* and *The Pot of
Tulips*, for example, with its haunted old Dutch mansion in the heart of the city, but the best tales recalled
Poe, though they lacked Poe's concentration: O'Brien

seldom knew where to begin or stop. One was a story of buried treasure on the beach at Coney Island, the storm-blown sands where Whitman walked so often; another, the ingenious *The Diamond Lens,* reminded one of Poe's curiosity about scientific discovery and explora-tion. *What Was It?* was a masterpiece of horror, ade-quately focussed and brief, O'Brien's one composition that was wholly successful, and this tale of the monster that was invisible but that one could feel and wrestle with, and even mould in plaster, was original also.[12] As for O'Brien's hasheesh-eater, he might have been suggested by another of the Bohemian circle, FitzHugh Ludlow, a young Union College man who wrote a book in 1857 relating his experiences and dreams under the in-fluence of this drug. Excited by Bayard Taylor's experi-ments with it, he believed he was the only American hasheesh-eater, and this gave him a feeling of isolation that added to his horrors, for he had formed a habit that he could not break. The record in *The Hasheesh-Eater,* he said, was at no point exaggerated, although it was obviously coloured by Poe and De Quincey, whose marvellous gift of dream-description Ludlow now and then approached in his less impressive but far from un-beautiful prose. He had always loved the *Arabian Nights* for its energy and scope of imagination, and, truly or not, regarding hasheesh, he said that the dreams it occasioned almost invariably assumed Oriental forms. In his own fantasy, visions of China and gardens of the East commingled with American scenes of Niagara and the Hudson, and he passed through sensations of a dual existence, delirium, the power of a giant or a god, infinities of space and time, unutterable calm.[13]

---

[12] Edith Wharton, in her preface to *Ghosts,* expressed a doubt that the "crawling horror" of O'Brien's *What Was It?* had ever been surpassed.

[13] Under the influence of Ludlow's book, John Hay, as a student at Brown University, experimented several times with hasheesh.

Two other writers in New York who were more important than most of these, Artemus Ward and Henry William Herbert, were sometimes in touch with the Bohemian circle, though they were no more of it than Bayard Taylor or Richard Henry Stoddard. Taylor placed his "Echo Club" in a beer-cellar resembling Pfaff's, where authors, books and plays were talked about, but their "diversions" really occurred in his own rooms or Stoddard's, where a circle gathered for years on Saturday nights. Among them were Fitz-James O'Brien and Thomas Bailey Aldrich and sometimes Charles Godfrey Leland and the Philadelphian George H. Boker, whenever he happened to be visiting his friends in New York. They played games of parody-writing, jotting down themes on bits of paper, together with the names of poets, which they placed in a hat; then, drawing them at random, they scribbled away for dear life. In these verse-combats they sometimes wrote double acrostics, occasionally introducing invented words that anticipated Lewis Carroll's *The Jabberwock*. In his later *Diversions of the Echo Club*, Taylor, recalling these evenings, revealed his own gift as a brilliant parodist in verse, comparable as no one else in America with the prose-parodist Bret Harte, who published his own *Condensed Novels* at about the same moment. But Taylor had small sympathy with the circle at Pfaff's, while Artemus Ward encountered it merely as the editor of *Vanity Fair*, a post in which he succeeded Charles Godfrey Leland. It was Leland who had observed the Shakers with his usual interest in human oddities and described them to Artemus Ward who knew nothing about them and who made them presently the subject of a memorable sketch. For Artemus Ward had come East again after three years on the Cleveland *Plain Dealer*. Earlier still as a wandering printer he had worked for a while on *The Carpet-Bag*, a comic weekly

published in Boston by the humorist B. P. Shillaber, the
inventor of "Mrs. Partington," the Yankee Mrs. Mala-
prop[14] This weekly was widely read in the West, especially along the Mississippi, where quotations from it
filled the village papers, the Hannibal *Journal,* for one,
on which Samuel Clemens was setting type and whence
he sent off a sketch that Shillaber accepted. *The Dandy
Frightening the Squatter,* which appeared in 1852, was
the first of Mark Twain's published compositions, and
the same number of *The Carpet-Bag* contained the first
paper of Artemus Ward and the first published drawings
and text of George H. Derby. Thus the "Modern Atkins," [15] Boston, at the height of its literary Renaissance,
was in a sense the cradle of Western humour, although
none of the important writers seems to have known it.

As for Artemus Ward himself, with his melancholy
air on the platform and his great nose that resembled
the beak of the macaw, he concocted burlesques in *Vanity Fair* of the high-flown French romances that were so
popular especially in the New York of the time. In fact,
he was largely effective in changing the tone of thought
and speech in more than one respect during these decades, deflating the bombast that throve on the stage with
the "world-renowned tragedians," in Congress, in thousands of orations on the Fourth of July. He made it im-

---

[14] "For my part, I can't deceive what on airth eddication is coming to. When I was young, if a girl only understood the rules of
distraction, provision, multiplying, replenishing and the common
denunciator, and knew all about rivers and their obituaries, the
convents and dormitories, the provinces and the umpires, they had
eddication enough. But now they have to study bottomy, algeberry,
and have to demonstrate suppositions about the sycophants of
circuses, tangents and Diogenese of parallelograms, to say nothing
about the oxhides, corostics, and the abstruse triangles."—Mrs.
Partington.
[15] "The Modern Atkins,—though I scurcely know what those air."
—Artemus Ward. Artemus also remarked of Harvard College: "This
celebrated institootion of learnin' is pleasantly situated in the bar-
room of Parker's in School Street."

possible henceforth to take their pomposity seriously, for he had a sharp eye for the flatulent, the pretentious and the trite, and the change to a more natural style that followed in the press and the theatre alike was due in some measure at least to Artemus Ward. He was one of many influences that marked the end of a romantic age, foreshadowing a realistic future, for his mind was dry, conservative and matter-of-fact; surrounded by optimists, he was a pessimist, a Yankee Sancho Panza abounding in the practical wisdom of the common people, a sceptic and a counterpoise to the indiscriminate quixotism, the sometimes flighty idealism of the pre-war years. He was opposed to the "long-haired reformers" for whom the world was out of joint, while he thought it needed only a little greasing, to the agitators for women's rights, temperance, free love, the "affinity business," the spirit-rappers, John Brown, abolition. He spoke for the cautious majority, incredulous, wary, cool and shrewd, that always mingled policy with its kindness; yet his sweetness of spirit was singularly winning and his humour, never pert or smart, spontaneously expressed a nature that was friendly and genial. His mind seemed to float along a current of ideas in which the most natural of all was the topsy-turvy, a novel and delightful confusion of the true and the absurd.

"Frank Forester" Herbert was no longer living when Artemus Ward arrived in New York, and besides he had gradually withdrawn from his literary friends, for this English champion of American sport had grown more and more eccentric and seldom left his chalet on the Passaic river. Occasionally he appeared in Newark, walking in to the markets there, with a troop of dogs trailing at his heels, in a shooting jacket and hunting brogans, a Scotch plaid thrown over his shoulders, a fur cap on his head, boots and spurs. Then he returned to his odd little villa in a grove on the river near by, close to the

"Cockloft Hall" of *Salmagundi*. Turbulent, wayward and quarrelsome always, generous and warm-hearted too, he produced an astonishing number of books in his seclusion, while he still set out now and then in the spring, summer and autumn months on the fishing and shooting excursions that he loved to describe. He had shot snipe on the St. Lawrence and fished in the Lake Superior region, and sometimes in Maine, Connecticut and Maryland also,—the southernmost limit of his sporting experience, he said,—but his favourite hunting grounds were the river counties of New York and the woods, meadows and streams of northern New Jersey. These and especially the neighbourhood of Warwick were the scenes of the engaging little novels of sport, *My Shooting Box, The Deerstalkers, The Warwick Woodlands,* that accompanied his many manuals and treatises on field-sports and on horses and horsemanship in the United States. By far the best of the sporting writers who were just beginning to appear in America, Herbert was one of the literary discoverers of the country,—like Audubon, Cooper and Bryant,—for he classified and enumerated the game of the various regions when few were aware of any outside their own. He was a master of woodcraft and an admirable naturalist, as a true sportsman, he said, was bound to be, observant and familiar with the habits of animals and birds, skilful in dissecting them and drawing them with pen and ink, often in Landseer-like postures, to illustrate his books. Some of his descriptive papers on the woodcock, the quail, the bittern and the fox were worthy of Audubon and Wilson. He was a charming writer, a lover of all things beautiful and shy, with some of the spirit and fire of the poet and the painter, whose books brimmed over with the zest of the woodsmen on lovely summer and autumn days in the brisk breezy air of the mountains and the forest. They abounded in romantic scenes: deep, dim,

secluded groves and the reedy margins of inland lakes
and ponds, fairy glens, musical brooks, misty hollows,
leafy knolls and the creatures of the wild that lived
among them.

A grandson of two English peers, a viscount and an
earl, Herbert had arrived in New York in 1831, supposedly an exile because of his gambling debts, and he
taught Greek and Latin in a school for boys near Bowl-
ing Green, where Charles Astor Bristed was one of his
pupils. He made a translation of Æschylus, for he was
an excellent classical scholar who had taken his degree
at Cambridge after going through Eton; then he wrote
several historical romances under the influence of Scott
and Froissart. These were scholarly enough but dull,
though Herbert was vividly aware of the sports and pastimes of the barons of mediæval France, reflecting his
own most active interest, for he had brought with him
from England an intimate knowledge of horses, hunting
and dogs. He defeated a professional jockey in a New
York horse-race, while his own cronies in the town were
sons of the old landed gentlefolk who shared his habits
and tastes and his prejudices also. For like them, and
like Fenimore Cooper, he disliked the odour of the
counting-house and resented the rising power of the
merchant patricians, and he was drawn to the youthful
Corinthians, the lovers of turf, stage, rod and gun, fast
horses, field-sports, duelling, boxing and leisure. As one
of their sporting fraternity, he dined at Cato's on the
Boston post-road, the old resort of Irving and the friends
of his youth, and he joined them on excursions to the
Delaware river, Seneca Lake, the Newark meadows and
especially the Warwick woodlands in Orange County.
They hunted the deer in the autumn and fished in the
spring, pursuing in winter the fiercer beasts, the bear,
the cougar and the catamount that roamed and roared
in the solitudes of the Catskill mountains. Sometimes

Herbert's fishing companions were Inman and Durand, the painters, or he went off with the poet Charles Fenno Hoffman, one of the first explorers of the Adirondacks. Sometimes he set out alone with carpet-bags and fishing-rods, creels and tackle, dram-bottle and sandwich-box, to visit some friend in the wilderness who had retired to a fishing hut with books, a little wine and a charitable heart.

His novels, based on these expeditions, in the War-wick woodlands mainly, with two or three sporting friends for his *dramatis personae,* recalled the wild beauty of the hills and dells where the woodcock swarmed, with quail and grouse, and the merry adventures and talk of these gay young men. The settlements there were still Dutch, and little stone taverns with long low porches nestled, with their stately signposts, by the winding roads, half hidden in mossy ravines that were strewn with vines, where nameless mountain rivulets flowed from the granite crags above, the huge round-headed hills and feathered ridges. At the day's end the farmers and the millers, in the barrooms of these taverns, discussed the ravages of the wolves and their own prowess in hunting, over glasses of pineapple-rum and New Jersey cider, and sometimes their talk went back to the days of the patriot partisans and the old forest warfare of the Revolution. Along with various local figures, woodsmen and hunters suggesting Cooper, these farmers occasionally appeared in Frank Forester's novels, with Frank himself, undisguised, as Harry Archer, the model sportsman, his servant Tim Matlock, the Yorkshireman, and two or three friends. One was Fred Heneage, an Englishman, another Tom Draw of Warwick, all oddities and humours, the author's favourite character, drawn from an actual Mr. Ward, a mountain of flesh who weighed three hundred pounds. Tom was a gallant figure rigged for dinner in his best swallowtail sky blue, with his grey inexpressibles and canary-coloured waist-coat. This "great American original," the king of native sportsmen, brave, honest, bold, rotund, grotesque and kind, resembled Captain Porgy in the novels of William Gilmore Simms, not least in his enjoyment of the good things which the Lord provided. As for these, Harry and Fred between them invented a venison soup, a quail-pie and a steak that out-matched the creations of Tim, who devilled his hambones to the utmost pitch of mustard, soy and oil of Aix and simmered other viands in champagne. For with preparations of buffalo-tongue and cold boiled larded grouse, and with burgundy, hock, port, sherry and curaçao, they lived very well at Archer's shooting-box, which was decked with red-deer antlers, maps of the region and Herring's portraits of champions of the English turf. Frank Forester's novels were slight enough beside his well-known treatises, which were valuable and permanent additions to the lore of sport, but, with their scenes of the field and the forest and their lively incidents and livelier talk, they were entertaining still a century later.

CHAPTER XI

WASHINGTON: LINCOLN AND WHITMAN

Towards the end of 1862 Walt Whitman went to Washington to find his brother George, who had been wounded in the war, and there he remained for eleven years until he moved to Camden, for he never again returned to live in New York. Almost at once he found himself involved as a volunteer nurse working in the vast war-hospitals with the disabled and the dying, supporting himself by a part-time task in one of the government bureaus while he slept in a shabby top room in a poor little house. With a cot, a table and a broken-down chair, he subsisted largely on bread and tea in order to spend whatever he had on the soldiers, visiting them almost every day and occasionally watching for nights together when he was concerned with some special or critical case.

In the three remaining years of the war, constantly thrown with these young men from all the states, North and South alike, Whitman measured as never before the American people *en masse,* of whom he had countless intimate and revealing glimpses. Sometimes he dressed wounds, sometimes he found that his personal presence accomplished more than medical nursing or gifts when he sat down quietly and talked a little with one of the men or wrote a letter for him or led him to talk. He discovered that friendship could cure a fever and daily affection a wound. In summer as he crossed the fields he gathered great bunches of dandelions and red and white clover, which he scattered over the cots, while he usually

223

carried a knapsack full of oranges, apples and figs, tobacco, postage-stamps and writing-paper. He had a pipe
for one, a shirt or a little paper money, for he was supplied with funds by friends in the North, or perhaps a
pocket-diary to write in or an old pictorial magazine,
for the smallest gift broke the monotony of the hospital
hours like a sympathetic turn of the eye or touch of the
hand. There were times when, finding a whole ward in
a heavy mood of listlessness, he read aloud to the men to
break the spell, Shakespeare or the Bible,—he never
read his own poems,—or the songs and sketches of Private Miles O'Reilly. This was an imaginary Irish soldier
in one of the New York regiments (conceived by an
Irish general, Charles G. Halpine), whose comic adventures and impromptu verses dealing with incidents of
the war, suggesting reforms in the army, were favourites
with the soldiers. Whitman played games of twenty questions, recited declamatory poetical pieces and sometimes
sat by a friend in perfect silence. Each case needed some
special thought, and he learned hospital wisdom, as he
called it, adjusting himself to every emergency, after its
call or kind, however trivial or solemn.

He carried a little pocket notebook and took notes as
he went along, sometimes while one of the soldiers was
telling his story, jotting down other memoranda in the
crowded streets and working them out more carefully in
the evening at home. In this way he wrote *Drum-Taps*
and many a passage in *Specimen Days,* under a big old
cherry-tree, in the hospitals, in the fields, for all he saw
and heard aroused undreamed of depths of feeling in
him and quickened his fervent faith in the future of
the country. Passionately concerned as he was for the
Union, he had no partisan feeling and was drawn to
the Confederate soldiers and the Northerners alike, impressed by their essential oneness, the basic traits in all,
their dignity, courtesy, honesty, manliness and candour.

Three qualities were always coming to the front, good nature, decorum, intelligence, with a certain animal purity and heroism, and he was struck by their frequent unworldliness and a strange spiritual sweetness at times with something in their manner that was abstracted or veiled. They made little ado, whatever their sufferings, excited as his own sympathies were, so that sometimes he found himself trembling hours later, as he recalled some case before him; and he felt he had never realized before the majesty and reality of the people in the mass, —it fell upon him, he wrote, like a great awe. Never could anyone speak in disparagement of Americans, whether of the North or the South, to one who had witnessed these hospital scenes in the war, and more than ever he felt that humanity could depend upon itself alone with its own inherent, normal, full-grown traits.

Meanwhile, he walked the Washington streets, sometimes far into the night, or lingered along the Potomac, under the stars, delighting in the silences, the exhilarating air, the "nimbus floods" of the moon that left traces in his poems. The streets struck him as prairie-like, planned on a generous scale, and he caught something American in the character of the town, an indolent largeness of spirit, quite native, a margin as it were, a flowing hem, that somehow redeemed the extravagances and vices and worse. He liked to wander in the capitol at night, under the lighted rotunda, and the grounds laid out by Andrew Jackson Downing, observing types that were new to him, the ravenous office-seekers, for instance, who were looking for Indian agencies, consulates and what not. They would sometimes accept a small post-office, as the humorist Petroleum V. Nasby said, if there was a good distillery within easy range, and they swarmed in the White House and button-holed President Lincoln, waylaying him in the corridor between his bedroom and his office. As the Democrats had been in power for thirty years when Lincoln came in, the new party was expected to make a clean sweep, and place-hunters of every type,—for Herman Melville was one of them,[1]—continued to seek security "in Abraham's bosom." [2] Artemus Ward threatened to turn his Boy Constructor loose among them if these office-seekers did not get out of the President's house, and Robert H. Newell satirized them in the *Orpheus C. Ker Papers,* comic impressions and sketches of Washington in wartime. He said it was every citizen's duty to settle in the capital during the war in order to give the cabinet the sanction of his presence. Whitman had known Newell in New York, where they had worked at adjoining desks as fellow-editors of a paper called *The Aurora.* Whitman himself fell in with soldiers who had fought in all the battles, Fredericksburg, Roanoke, the Wilderness, South Mountain, Antietam, and who told the things that never appeared in official reports, journals or books, the things that were genuine and precious. He was continually astonished by the absence of boasting on the part of these hardy, intuitive, quiet young men, and he witnessed several scenes at the front himself, where he slept with the others in the mud, wrapped in a blanket. In some of his poems and in *Specimen Days* he pictured cavalrymen crossing a ford, a surgeon at work in a hospital in the field at night, artillery in action and the six-mule wagons, bearing pontoons and square-end flatboats. He sketched the cavalrymen cleaning their sabres with their overcoats hung out to air, the tent-fires blazing, soldiers driving the poles, pots and kettles over the logs and squads of tethered horses, stamping and whisk-

---

[1] Melville had appeared in Washington early in 1861, hoping for the consulship at Florence. It was just at this time that William Dean Howells was appointed to the consulate at Venice.

[2] Or the "grand old benevolent National Asylum for the Helpless," as Mark Twain called Washington in *The Gilded Age.*

ing their tails to keep off flies. His scenes were like those of Winslow Homer, the Boston artist who had gone to New York, to work for *Harper's Weekly,* before the war, and who visited the front four times as a draughtsman-correspondent. Homer made his reputation as a painter of the war, for his earliest canvases, like many of his drawings, were war-scenes, although his chosen subjects were aspects of everyday army life, in camp, by the bivouac-fire, in hours of repose. He liked to picture the soldiers at ease with their Negro wagoners and servants. Homer had drawn Lincoln in New York at the moment when Whitman saw him first, at the Astor House in February, 1861, and his life and work were to parallel Whitman's in certain other ways, with his largeness, his occasional crudeness, his freshness and vigour.

Whitman was too late to see another correspondent whom Lowell had asked to write for the *Atlantic Monthly,* the author of *The Canoe and the Saddle,* who was killed, like another New York officer,—Fitz-James O'Brien,—early in the war. In fact, this writer of the "Siwash Odyssey" was the first Northern officer to be killed after he had marched down Broadway, with the Seventh Regiment, in a "tempest of cheers," he said, "two miles long." When Theodore Winthrop reached the capitol the spring was at its freshest and fairest, and the "boy element," so large in the regiment, lay on the sweet young grass between drills with the odour of the horse-chestnut blossoms drifting on the breeze. They talked about San Francisco bay and the smooth, graceful, treeless hills that had reminded Winthrop of the shores of Greece, where he had spent several weeks after leaving Yale, and they compared notes on Oregon, Indian life and the plains of which Winthrop had written in books that were soon to appear. For all of his novels and travels were posthumously published, brimming over as they were with his own high spirits and infectious humour and the images and apostrophes he had caught especially from Homer. His last composition perhaps was *Washington as a Camp*. Whitman, who had missed these earlier scenes, had also missed the tragic rout, which he described so well, after Bull Run, when many an officer and high official was all for striking the flag at once and the Union seemed to have been smashed like a porcelain plate. But Whitman knew Edmund Clarence Stedman, the young poet who had come, like Winthrop, from Yale,—though, like Fenimore Cooper, he had been dropped for mischief,—and who had acted as a correspondent with the army of the Potomac, sleeping in camp and in farmhouses and taverns in the field. He was one of the war-correspondents who were creating a new profession, for earlier reporters had known little of military life, and he had witnessed on horseback the first battle of Bull Run from the outset to the final headlong confusion and panic. His long and graphic description of the battle, contributed to the New York *World,* had opened the eyes of thousands to the reality of the war. Later for a while he was pardon-clerk in the Attorney-General's office, where he examined all applications for pardons, deciding which the President should see, and he and Whitman were drawn to each other, different as the older poet was from this singularly handsome young man with his air of the world. Stedman, who called Whitman a "noble fellow, despite his erratics," was one of the few living writers who recognized his greatness, while Whitman, for whom Stedman remained the best of the "New York lot," described him as honest, generous and true.

One Sunday in 1863, during a ramble in the Washington woods, Whitman fell in with John Burroughs, a farm-boy from the Catskills who was working as a guard in the Treasury building, while his great interest was natural history, and who had come to the capital really to be near him. Burroughs had heard of the poet first when he was teaching in a school near Newark and read the wondrous poem in the Bohemians' weekly, and, going into town himself, he had looked for Walt at Pfaff's, where he had met Henry Clapp and Ada Clare. Then, poor, disheartened and lonely as he was, he too had gone to Washington, magnetically drawn by the author of *Leaves of Grass*. Whitman had taken to Burroughs at once with his look of a big plain farmer and a face that he said was "like a field of wheat"; and what was Burroughs's own surprise to find that Walt was not "one of the roughs" but a sympathetic tolerant soul, immaculate and kind. Large and slow-moving, with an easy stride and a singularly good-natured air, ruddy with his full grey beard and open throat, Whitman was a curious blend of age and youth, while sometimes, benevolent as he was, one caught a look in his clear blue eyes that was more—or less—than human, as it seemed to Burroughs. At these times the younger man felt as if the earth were looking at him, at once dumb, yearning, relentless, immodest, unhuman. There was something so impersonal, so elemental in Whitman's glance that Burroughs almost shrank from him at moments, though the longer he knew him the more he loved him and the greater he felt Whitman was, as great as Emerson, though of a different type. Burroughs's task at the Treasury building was to sit in front of an iron vault, keeping track of the paper money passed in and out.[3]

This young man, born in 1837, had grown up in the true back country, fifty miles from the railroad and twelve miles from the stagecoach, in the Catskill region,

[3] The old poet John Pierpont and the young sociologist Lester F. Ward were also clerks in the Treasury Department at this time.

more or less, that appeared in the *Letters from an American Farmer,* where Crèvecœur himself had lived for seventeen years. His forbears had also been American farmers for seven or eight generations and Burroughs had only to "unpack," he said, his boyhood memories of the farm to write his first sketches and essays in the *New York Leader.* These followed in 1861 an earlier paper in the *Atlantic Monthly* that many readers supposed Emerson had written,—for he had adopted the style of his "spiritual father,"—and this had led him to decide that he must get on his own ground, where he was to flourish as an essayist for two generations. Washington as he found it lay in a vast spread of half-wild country, where nature in places crossed the threshold of the city and the primitive woods were only a step away; and he heard the whistle of the fox-sparrow on the grounds of the Smithsonian and the soft flute of the veery in trees near the White House. Buzzards on long flexible pinions sailed through the ether. Burroughs remained a farmer there, for he built a small brick house, where he kept a cow and chickens, on Capitol Hill, selling milk and garden truck, stubbornly guarding his independence, dressing, working, loafing as he pleased. Mrs. Burroughs made pies and cookies for the soldiers and Burroughs sometimes joined Walt on his hospital rounds, or sat and talked with him on the capitol steps, while, intrenched behind his high desk facing the vault in the Treasury, with two or three hours to himself in the day, he read and wrote at leisure. Burroughs knew more than anyone else of the birds and wild life of the District, as one could see in his first collection of essays, and Whitman, who helped him with his manuscripts, pruning and amending them, suggested the title, *Wake Robin,* which he used for this. It was the popular name of a plant that blossomed in the woods at a moment when the birds appeared in springtime. Whitman, who had a genius for titles and took great pains with them,[4] suggested the title of an earlier book of Burroughs, *Notes on Walt Whitman as Poet and Person*,[5] a study of his own compositions and of his life and character as a poet-prophet. Burroughs was convinced that literature was becoming petty and artificial and needed a tremendous plunge in the other direction, and he saw in Walt a mighty reaction against the puny feeble ways into which the younger poets seemed to be falling. For him the poet of *Leaves of Grass* was one of the grand primary bards whom nations could build upon, and had built in the past, and his poems were akin to the Bibles, the sacred books. Whitman worked over this study with him, reshaped passages, trimmed and cut it, and wrote one section and some of the notes at the end.

Both of these books of John Burroughs were published, and written, after the war when he and Whitman remained in Washington together, employed in government bureaus for some years still; and when Whitman wrote his great poem in memory of President Lincoln it was Burroughs who suggested the "shy and hidden bird." The lilacs were in their April bloom on the day that Lincoln died,—they were always to bring back to Whitman a memory of the moment,—and, as it happened, in the early spring just before the assassination the great star Venus in the West seemed exceptionally brilliant. Restlessly haunting the Potomac, he had watched it, far off, aloof and somehow moody as himself. The star and the lilacs connected themselves in his mind with Lincoln, and then Burroughs described to him the hermit thrush he had known as a boy, a bird that Audubon apparently had never discovered. Bur-

---

[4] In a note in *Specimen Days* he gave a list of thirty-five names he had thought of and rejected for this book.

[5] John Burroughs's first book, 1867, and the last essay in his last book, *Accepting the Universe*, 1920, both dealt with Whitman.

roughs had occasionally heard its song, a quarter of a mile away rising over a chorus of wrens and warblers, resembling no other sound that he recalled in nature, a beatitude that was religious, pure and serene. This was the bird that appeared in Whitman's poem.

Whitman had never met Lincoln, though he saw him twenty or thirty times and almost every day during one season, when the President, who was living out of town, rode by on his grey horse surrounded by a squad of cavalrymen with sabres drawn. Dressed in a somewhat rusty black, with his stiff black hat and dark brown face and the deep-cut lines and eyes with their latent sadness, he had an air, Whitman thought, of a Hoosier Michael Angelo and a look of great tenderness and goodness underneath the furrows. It was a face that offered an artist a rare study, almost as impossible to depict as a wild perfume or fruit-taste, so subtle were the superior traits that lay behind its homeliness, in the eyes, the mouth, the expression, the colour and the lines. There was a story that Lincoln in Springfield had read the second *Leaves of Grass,* which his partner Herndon had bought about 1857, leaving it on the table of the office where Lincoln listened to discussions of it and presently picked it up and took it home. As the story went, he referred to it with emphatic approval and even read passages aloud from these "chants of the prairie." [6] Whitman, who never talked with Lincoln, knew his assistant secretary, John Hay, who procured free passes to Brooklyn and back for him,—the aid of John G. Nicolay, the Bavarian-born chief secretary, who had edited a newspaper in Springfield before the war. There John Hay had also lived, returning to the West from Brown

---

[6] This story, sometimes described as apocryphal, told by William Sloane Kennedy in *The Fight of a Book for the World,* was later accepted and repeated by Carl Sandburg in *Abraham Lincoln: the War Years.*

University, reading law with his uncle, the head of a
firm of which Lincoln, his grandfather's friend, had
once been a partner, at a time when most of the leading men of the new Northwest were assembled there, so
that Hay already had many friends at court. No other
young American since Alexander Hamilton had ever
reached such a position as Hay's so early, graceful and
accomplished as he was, versatile and witty, instinctively, as if by nature, a citizen of the world. This easy-
mannered observant young man whose childhood had
been spent on the Mississippi,—like Mark Twain's,
though further to the north,—enthusiastic, sunny, fresh,
perhaps a little shallow, was to go far in literature and
politics alike. Already a constant guest in Washington of
ambassadors and members of the cabinet, he was closely
connected with the Lincolns in their family circle,
escorting Mrs. Lincoln when she drove out in the
afternoon and amusing the boys on rainy days in the
White House.

In his way Whitman had prophesied the advent of
Lincoln at the time of Frémont's candidacy in 1856. He
had said then it would please him to see some bearded
pioneer, shrewd, healthy, well-informed, appear in the
West, stride over the Alleghenies and walk into the
White House, a blacksmith or a boatman, for instance,
who might have split rails; and, as it happened, Lincoln, like Whitman, was the son of a carpenter and
farmer and had even written poems of his own. His
partner Herndon said of him that he had read less and
thought more than any other man in his sphere in the
country, but even at New Salem, where he had shared in
the talk at the tavern, he was often seen reading barefoot on the top of the woodpile. That was in the days
when Lincoln slept on the counter of the store in the
little log-village that had vanished in the prairie-grass,
when, with one suspender, wearing tow-linen panta-

loons, he had suggested the youthful Horace Greeley. He had read Blackstone under a tree, lying on his back, sometimes with his feet up the trunk, with the shiftless air that fascinated the Western frontier folk and that caught the fancy of the busy American people. He had experimented with verse, composing a poem for his sister's wedding and a number of mournful ballads in the rhythms of Watts, together with *The Bear Hunt,* modelled perhaps on *John Gilpin* and based no doubt on a memory of his boyhood in the woods. Lincoln had even planned to publish a volume of poems with one of his friends. He was also an unrivalled story-teller, like David Crockett, at the polls, at the races, at log-rollings and musters where his sweetness of nature, his child-like temper and his honesty pleased the crowd, a favourite because of his droll talk about Cousin Sally Dillard, about Becky Williams's courtship and the Down-Easter and the Bull. He knew the boatmen's lingo and the river-lore of the Mississippi, the tales about Boone, Mike Fink and Simon Kenton and the yarns about Sut Lovingood who threw the camp-meeting into fits by setting the lizards loose in the preacher's trousers. When the judges were on circuit and the lawyers moved with them from town to town, on horseback, by stage or, like Lincoln, in a shabby old buggy, there was no one more famous than he as a spinner of these yarns in the country taverns where the lawyers met for talk when the court had adjourned. Once Lincoln read aloud to a roomful of lawyers from Baldwin's *Flush Times in Alabama,*—describing scenes like those they were enacting themselves,—and he borrowed stories from Balzac too, passing them off as his own and setting them in Illinois or Indiana. He made over whatever he found in Shakespeare, the Bible or Æsop in the light of his frontier experience and the frontier people. This was one of the secrets of Lincoln's power and charm.

Later, some of his cabinet-members could never understand why Lincoln wasted their time, as they thought, with stories, reading aloud, as he also did, at the gravest moments and crises of the war, from Artemus Ward, for instance, or Petroleum V. Nasby. He largely transacted the nation's affairs with anecdotes of frontier circuits, stories about scrub hogs and border wisdom,—"Don't swap horses when you are crossing a stream,"—for, having small use for abstractions and theories, he loved the concrete, as artists love it, and spoke and taught, like a poet, in parables and fables. He liked the homespun Western humour because it relieved the melancholy, the fear of madness and suicide, that weighed on his mind, and, besides, it kept him closely in touch with the frontier people he represented, the loungers round the stoves in country stores. As Herndon observed, his nature was a blend of the "curious and amusing" with the "august and noble," and he was one of these humorists himself who had written, in dialect, letters that were much like Nasby's, Jack Downing's and Artemus Ward's. One was the "Aunt Rebecca" letter in which in 1842 he had satirized the state officials of the Democratic party, the party of Jefferson and Jackson that had since become Buchanan's party, servile to the South and favouring slavery and disunion. All these humorists, who, for the rest, spread good will and affection for Lincoln, were active and efficient in forwarding the cause of the Union, and one of the Northern statesmen said that the fall of the Confederacy was due as much to Nasby as to the Northern arms. Lincoln invited to the White House the burly uncouth editor-author, who looked like a simple old farmer, David R. Locke, the man who created in the character of Nasby, with spelling modelled on Artemus Ward's, the type of the "Copperhead" apologist for slavery and the South. In the Nasby letters in the *Toledo Blade,* which were copied and read from ocean to ocean, one saw the ignoble Democrat who opposed the war because he was willing to betray the country and give the South whatever it wished in order to preserve his own comfort, his money and his skin.

Lincoln, a Southerner by family and birth who was grafted on the West and who had remained unchanged as a man in the White House, had long since become for Whitman a symbol of the Union, which he saw as in turn a symbol of the future of mankind. In Whitman's mind the "American totality" stood for the "modern idea," the cause that hung in the balance throughout the war,[7] for the governments of Europe were against this Union,—they hoped the American experiment would fail, that the war would cripple and split the democratic republic. The ruling powers of England and France, of Germany and Spain would have helped to dismember the Union if they had dared to do so, just as they watched the Russian experiment half a century later and ardently hoped that the Soviet cause would fail. Mexico, the only country the United States had really wronged, was the only well-wisher it had in the Civil War; the others would have liked to see it compelled to descend to the level of empires and kingdoms that clung to their feudal and aristocratic regimes. It was plain to Whitman that, owing to this, Americans in the future would never trust the governments of Europe, and this was to prove true, in fact, just as it was with the Russians when their new regime was watched by a menacing world. As Whitman saw in Lincoln a symbol of the Union, he also shared Lincoln's hope for the welfare of mankind, the international feeling that accompanied his nationalism, his sympathy with peoples

[7] For this reason Whitman, like Lincoln, though both detested slavery, cared more for the cause of the Union than for Emancipation. "The Negro was not the thing," Whitman said to Traubel: "the chief thing was to stick together."

everywhere that were struggling to be free. Both had been deeply touched by Kossuth and the efforts of the Irish, the Germans and the French who had fought unsuccessfully to establish the supremacy of the people against the regimes in their nations, as both defended the right of the people to rise and shake their governments off and form whatever new governments suited them better. For both were equally followers of the "most distinguished" of American statesmen,—Lincoln's phrase for Jefferson, the idol of Whitman, who had studied his statue in the capitol "long and long"; and indeed it was to assert his Jeffersonism that Lincoln had broken with the Whigs when the party of Clay dissolved in 1855. Obliged to choose a new alignment, Lincoln had joined the Republicans, the party that continued the true Jeffersonian line since the Jacksonian Democrats, who were technically Jefferson's heirs, had come to stand for slavery and subservience to the South.[8] Money had become a political power, and money and slavery, Lincoln saw, tended more and more to become allies, and the whole social system of the country had shifted, so that the ancient watchword "Humanity" had given place to the slogan "Prosperity" and the rights of man were superseded by the rights of wealth.

In all these political matters Whitman and Lincoln fully agreed, and one might have said that in public life Lincoln represented what Whitman was expressing in poetry in *Leaves of Grass*. They stood for those "axioms of a free society" that Lincoln found in Jefferson and that Whitman touched with emotion and developed further, axioms that were "denied and evaded with no small show of success" as "glittering generalities," Lincoln said. In days to come the Republican party to which both had been drawn in 1855,—Whitman from

[8] With Andrew Jackson's name as "cappytal for us to do biznis on," as Nasby, speaking for the Copperheads, said in a letter.

the party of Jackson, Lincoln from Clay's,—was to undergo the same shift to the cause of money from the cause of man that the Democratic party of Jefferson had undergone. There had always been two great parties of feeling for which property-rights and human rights were respectively of paramount importance, and for generations the nominal parties were to switch their points of view and assume the other's position on this fundamental question. As Lincoln had written in 1859, it was like the feat of two drunken men who were engaged in a fight with their great-coats on and each of whom fought himself out of his own coat and into the coat of the other. The perennial issue had come to a head with the passage of the Kansas-Nebraska Act that opened these territories to slavery in 1854, reversing the policy that had always been followed since Jefferson established the principle that slavery should be prohibited in new territories. This it was that evoked from Lincoln, in the year before *Leaves of Grass* appeared, the first great speech that revealed him as a man of letters, the address at Peoria attacking Douglas, who had sponsored the Kansas-Nebraska Act on the ground that slavery had been nationalized by the Constitution. For this reason, Douglas said, it was unconstitutional to prevent the extension of slavery if the territories wished it,—the argument that Whitman described as "technically right but humanly wrong" when many a Southerner used it in Civil War times. Thus had begun the great debate at which twenty thousand people stood in the wind and the rain for hours at a time, so passionate and so deep was their anxiety over this question, while Lincoln warned them of the danger of cancelling the white man's charter of freedom in the greedy chase of the nation to make profit by the Negro. What man was good enough to govern another without his consent? As for himself, he hated slavery because of its monstrous injustice and because it deprived the republic of its influence in the world, enabling the enemies of free institutions to taunt the Americans as insincere, especially now when they talked of "superior races." A great party had recently risen to exclude the foreigner with the Negro among those who were not "created equal," a party that Lincoln described as the sappers and miners of despotism who tended to restore a government of legitimacy and caste. Better the Russia of the czars, he said, where despotism could be taken pure and without the base alloy of hypocrisy.

It was Lincoln's moral force that made these speeches memorable, the intensity and depth of his conviction, the religious nature that had led so many in the Western country, at a time of signs and wonders, to regard him as a patriarch Abraham returned in the flesh. An enthusiastic "unbeliever," he had written an essay in the manner of Paine against the inspiration of the Bible and the divinity of Jesus, and, revolting against the Baptist training that had left him a fatalist none the less, he had never returned to the orthodox Protestant dogmas. He had retained the belief in dreams and visions in one of which he foresaw his tragic end, a belief that led him in New Orleans in 1831 to visit one of the voodoo fortune-tellers; but, happening on *Vestiges of Creation,* struck by the doctrine of evolution, as it was expounded there, he had begun to defend it. Then, reading Channing and Theodore Parker, whom he admired and agreed with, he had reached a positive faith that was much like Whitman's, a religion of humanity that Jefferson had shared with them and that flowed through many Americans, through Emerson and through Melville. In all that Lincoln said and wrote, behind it, underneath it, ran the deep river of feeling that ran through Whitman. For the rest, Harriet Beecher Stowe observed that Lincoln's state papers suggested a devoted father's talk to his children, benign as they were, informal, undiplomatic, appealing alike to head and heart, intimate, homely, close to the soil and the pathos, humour and folklore of the vast frontier. It was known that before he was forty he had thought of himself as an old man and assumed a paternal relation to his partner Herndon; and he had become, as a multitude felt, the father of his people and his country, as no president, even Washington, had been before him.

CHAPTER XII

AFTER THE CIVIL WAR

WITH the conclusion of the Civil War, an epoch opened in American life with immediate results that were anything but reassuring, with frauds and scandals in politics and business, vulgarities scarcely known before and a general dissolution of the ways of the familiar order. As for the remoter effects of the war, they were to reveal themselves in time, whether for good or ill, in a unified nation, although one saw already that the old republic which Jefferson knew had changed into another country of industry and cities. The mountaineer president Andrew Johnson, the North Carolina democrat, who shared Lincoln's affection for the rank and file, had fought the concentration of power in the hands of the few and tried to carry out the wise policy of Lincoln towards the South. But all his efforts were over-borne by the triumphant industrialists and the often unscrupulous bankers who dominated Congress. Many could feel that the Civil War had justified democracy if only by revealing the stamina of the masses of the people, but it cost the country heavily in other respects, while factories rose and cities grew round them, immigrants poured in from Europe and chaos overwhelmed the prostrate South.

In the minds of writers Abraham Lincoln had become a national symbol, a figure that stood for the republic, its essence and aim, of all the great national heroes and statesmen the "only real giant," as the young novelist in Russia, Tolstoy, said. Melville's poem on Lincoln, like

Whitman's, was among his best, and half the writers of
the time produced a sonnet or an ode to Lincoln, a biography or an essay about him, a tribute in prose,—Lowell,
Stoddard, the young poets Stedman and Richard Watson Gilder, Bret Harte in California, Josiah Gilbert Holland. He appeared as a character in the Western novels
of Edward Eggleston and Joseph Kirkland.[1] They needed
him for reassurance in days of melodramatic crime when
spoilsmen and demagogues seemed to possess the country, when the words "boss" and "ring" first appeared in
political speech and Lincoln's own party already rocked
with scandal. Whitman, living through the war, had felt
that his own American days were more fateful than the
days of which Æschylus wrote, that men with whom he
had shaken hands were more heroic than the fighters
round Troy and models of character as astute and as
hardy as Ulysses. To one who had felt the presence of
men who seemed to him prouder than Agamemnon the
chieftains of the new age were disconcerting,—the pedlar from Vermont, Jim Fisk, the old cattle-dealer Daniel
Drew and their partner in the war with Vanderbilt, Jay
Gould the promoter. These men created the colour of
the decade of the Tweed ring, the Erie ring, the Crèdit
Mobilier scandal, the Union Pacific. Another adventurous financier, George Francis Train, was offered by
rebel miners the presidency of Australia. This owner of
a line of clipper-ships built the first English street-rail-
ways, and it was Train's voyage around the world in
eighty days that was supposed to have suggested Jules
Verne's story.[2] Gamblers on a grand scale, these Wall
Street hawks personified a new unsavoury chapter in

[1] Henry George's career as a writer began with an article in
1865 on Lincoln's assassination in the *Alta California,* on which he
worked as a compositor.

[2] Jules Verne spent a few days in the United States in 1866. He
and his brother Paul visited Niagara by way of the Mohawk valley,
where they called each other Hawkeye and Chingachgook.

American folklore: Jim Fisk with his harem and his opera-house, Jay Gould, who had once been John Burroughs's schoolmate, and the pious Methodist "Uncle Daniel" Drew. Jay Gould had written and peddled in his youth a history of the county in which he and Burroughs were born in the Catskill region. Like the others shabbily picturesque, the "merry old gentleman" Daniel Drew boasted that he could still "take a slice out of the boys," after years at the "milking-stool," at eighty-two. It was he who had first "watered stock" by feeding his cattle a quart of salt, obliging them to increase their weight by copious drinking before he sold them to the butcher, and he was grateful to the "boys in blue" who beat the waters in the war and thus provided good fishing for the boys in Wall Street.[3]

Later this epoch was described in books as the "dreadful decade" and the "tragic era," and certainly it abounded in episodes that were sordid and sorry, the Beecher affair among the rest, exposed in their weekly by the Claflin sisters, Victoria and Tennessee, the "lady brokers." These youthful Ohioans had set up shop with the aid of Commodore Vanderbilt and had presently established a magazine to defend free love, with socialism, birth control and woman's suffrage, and their only objection to Henry Ward Beecher's adventures of the flesh was that a veil of duplicity and hypocrisy concealed them. Attacking all forms of suppression themselves, they defended the flesh as the temple of God and portrayed the book of Genesis as an allegory in which the Garden of Eden was the human body. They sympathized with Whitman, as Beecher himself had also done, drawn as he was from the first to *Leaves of Grass*,—

[3] "It's good fishing in troubled waters." Daniel Drew also said, "It's the still hog that eats the most" and "The dog that snaps the quickest gets the bone."
The clever imputed autobiography *The Book of Daniel Drew* was actually composed by Bouck White.

Whitman, who was drawn to Beecher in turn, the man whom Lincoln, towards the end of the war, had described as his greatest living countryman. Beecher, most famous of orators, the most widely known American, had preached magnanimity and tolerance after the war, and the sad spectacle of the Beecher trial permanently lowered, beyond a doubt, the prestige of the Protestant ministry in American eyes. The Connecticut Yankee Anthony Comstock, appearing at this time, pursued the Claflin sisters as they pursued Beecher, attacking the Oneida community also in his movement for the suppression of vice in which he defended, he felt, the folkways of the people.[4] Together with pornographic books, he opposed the new "dime novels," those "traps for the young," as he called them, that appeared in the sixties, following at first the lead of Cooper as briefer tales of adventure and combat in which almost invariably a redskin "bit the dust." The publisher Erastus Beadle had been a printer in Cooperstown, where he built a house called Glimmerview on the shore of the lake; but only the thrills and banalities of Cooper survived in the tales that he sponsored, which had none of the vigour or the poetry of the Leather-Stocking stories. Others dealt with country boys who arrived in New York, like Horace Greeley, with a bundle on a stick on a shoulder,—the classic posture,—or girls wearing boys' clothes and following their lovers into danger and war among trappers, rangers and scouts on the Western frontier.

With all that was shabby, paltry or base, there were other notes of the post-war years that seemed to speak for progress in the nation, as in the world, where the slaves of Brazil and the serfs of Russia had been freed

---

[4] Anthony Comstock's Society for the Suppression of Vice was founded in 1872. The first use of the word "comstockery" is attributed to Bernard Shaw.

along with the slaves of the South and the Latin-American republics appeared to be advancing. The cause of reform made headway in England, the insurgents in China were gaining ground, Italy and Germany were achieving their unification, and moreover, as hopeful souls remarked, the Atlantic cable had been laid and railroads were spreading all over the United States. The first transcontinental line was opened in 1868, while bridges were built over rivers and canyons and great cities rose on the plains where the buffalo herds and the Indians were disappearing. Millions of acres of Western land were sowed by settlers with wheat and corn; copper, coal and silver poured from the mines, and for young Americans, as a writer said in 1873, the "paths to fortune" were "innumerable and all open." [5] At the same time the political corruption developed a movement of reform and a critical spirit that was active in the young men of the country. E. L. Godkin had established *The Nation,* a focus of many of the rising writers, *The Tribune* with "Greeley's young men" was full of promise and the *Evening Post* of the poet Bryant and John Bigelow, his youthful partner, continued to stand for the traditional virtues of the republic. Erect, slender, elastic, alert, Bryant, with his venerable air, was an image of the old-fashioned simplicity and sagacity of New England, and Bigelow, rejoicing that he had been born "a man and an American," was scarcely less happy that he was a "contemporary of Bryant." After grow-

[5] "If there be any place and time in the world where and when it seems easy to 'go into something' it is in Broadway on a spring morning, when one is walking cityward and has before him the long line of palace-shops with an occasional spire seen through the soft haze that lies over the lower town, and hears the roar and hum of its multitudinous traffic.

"To the young American, here or elsewhere, the paths to fortune are innumerable and all open; there is invitation in the air and success in all his wide horizon."—Mark Twain, *The Gilded Age,* 1873.

ing up on the banks of the Hudson, where his father
owned sloops and a country store, Bigelow had gone to
Haiti before the war to study the Negroes as they had
developed in freedom;[6] then his work as consul-general
in France and minister during the war-years had paralleled the diplomacy of Charles Francis Adams in England. He had exposed and defeated the plans of the
Confederacy to secure Napoleon III's effective support,
while he also contributed to the undoing of the "chromo
empire" of Maximilian, his phrase for the trumpery
adventure in Mexico. Bigelow recovered the manuscript of Franklin's autobiography and printed the
earliest accurate version of it, and he wrote studies of
the quietist Molinos, with whom he deeply sympathized,
and the author of the *Mariage de Figaro* and the *Barbier
de Seville*. In celebrating Beaumarchais, he paid a belated American homage to the man who had largely outfitted Washington's troops, the playwright who had persuaded his government to give the rebellious colonists
ample assistance in money as well as in arms. He had
employed at his own expense a fleet of forty vessels to
provide the Americans with uniforms, ammunition and
guns.

As for the literary field in general, it was "never so
barren," a writer observed, in a New York paper, the
Round Table, in 1866. It was "never," he continued,
"so utterly without hope or life"; and he had asked who
would awaken the writers, who would "show us the first
signs of a genuine literary reviving." He could scarcely
have foreseen the remarkable talents that were just beginning to appear in New England,—the Ohioan How-

[6] One of John Bigelow's books, *The Wit and Wisdom of the
Haitians*, a collection of proverbs in the Haitian *patois*, anticipated
the work of Lafcadio Hearn with the proverbs of the Louisiana
Negroes. While most of these Haitian proverbs were originally
French, the most interesting were indigenous or of African extrac-
tion.

ells, the New Yorker Henry James, with Henry Adams and others in Cambridge and Boston,—although many contributed from the first to Godkin's *Nation;* and there was little that enlivened the mind in the writings of Josiah Gilbert Holland, the editor of the new magazine *Scribner's Monthly.* Established in 1870, this was to reveal in time a number of striking new talents especially in the South, but Holland himself, the "apostle of the commonplace," who had something in common with Anthony Comstock,—opposing corruption with prudery,—was quite unpretentious. As the author of *Katrina* and *Bitter-Sweet,* long domestic story-poems, abounding in household piety and the events of farm-life, Holland was a still more popular Longfellow who was wholly local in his range of feeling, perhaps the most popular poet for a while in the country. His assistant Richard Watson Gilder, who succeeded him in 1881, when *Scribner's Monthly* was transformed into the *Century Magazine,* was one of a group of younger writers, appearing in New York, that flowered with a measure of energy in the seventies and eighties. Others were on Horace Greeley's staff, the most noteworthy editorial corps the country had ever seen, for two or three decades. Greeley, the apostle of labour-reform and the champion of a just distribution of wealth, had beggared himself and almost destroyed *The Tribune* by his fairness to the South after the war,—it was he who signed the bail-bond of Jefferson Davis; and ever since the days of Margaret Fuller, who had come to New York to write for him, he had had the keenest of eyes for new writers and writing. He had employed George William Curtis, Charles A. Dana, Albert Brisbane, the historian Richard Hildreth, Bayard Taylor, William Winter, the critic of the drama, George Ripley, his literary editor, and the socialist Karl Marx as a European correspondent. Mark Twain joined the staff in 1867, John

Hay in 1870, and Stedman was a member whose first assignment had been to report in 1859 the funeral of Washington Irving at Sleepy Hollow. Another writer on the *Tribune* staff was Rebecca Harding Davis, a Pennsylvanian, brought up in the South and the West, who had begun to publish in 1861 an unusual series of stories in the *Atlantic Monthly*. In the first, *Life in the Iron-Mills,* the hero was a furnace-tender who lived in the inferno of the rolling-mills of Wheeling, amid the caldrons of boiling fire, the slimy pools, the pits of flame, the foul effluvia and the nightmare mud and fog.

In these otherwise undistingushed tales one saw a new strain in American writing, the sometimes grim realism of a movement that was soon to gain ground, one of the notes of the post-war literature that was to prove in many ways unlike the literature that had grown through the forties and fifties. Speaking of her work as "crude and homely," rough sketches of commonplace people in a style that might be described as plebeian and trite, Mrs. Davis urged her readers to explore this vulgar American life which contained an "awful significance that we do not see." This was to become a familiar note with the growth of American realism from the days of Howells and his contemporaries to the days of Dreiser, together with the analytical approach that supplanted the kind of heroic feeling one had found in the earlier authors from Cooper to Whitman. Another post-war literary movement was that of the writers of "local colour" who set out to present the traits of the provinces and sections at a moment when the sentiment of the nation as a whole was growing with startling rapidity and the South, the East and the frontier had been unified at last. With the spread of the railroads and the industrial system the provincial life was fading out,—its local peculiarities of dialect and custom, —and a million Americans, soldiers and others, had travelled from section to section who had previously known only their farm-lands in New England or the South. But, aware as they were of the general scene, their interest had also been aroused by the unknown regions and people they had encountered, Americans of whom they had never dreamed before, and writers in all the sections became suddenly conscious of the local life, which they wished to record and describe before it was too late. Following the lead of Bret Harte in the far-away Sierras, they endeavoured to convey the regional colour and speech, Edward Eggleston in the Middle West, Cable and Joel Chandler Harris in the South, Sarah Orne Jewett and Mary E. Wilkins in New England. One of these writers, Edward Eggleston, found a support in the theories of Taine, who made so much of the environment, the race and the moment, and encouraged him to work with the materials he discovered in his own.

A third and equally important note in the literature that followed the Civil War was the rapid and general appearance of the journalist in letters, for, unlike the writers of the previous age,—with a few exceptions, Walt Whitman, for one,—the new writers in surprising numbers were newspapermen. Like the group surrounding Horace Greeley,—Taylor, Stedman and Hay, with Gilder,—Bret Harte, Mark Twain and Howells were journalists at first, in a country in which, for good or ill, the people were generally newspaper-readers[7] at a time when they read the papers as never before.[8] Many of

[7] "You see, Mr. Russell," said Dr. Bellows, "how our Yankee soldiers spend their time. I knew at once they were Americans when I saw them reading newspapers."—W. H. Russell, *My Diary North and South.*

Cf. Josh Billings's remark: "The morning paper is just as necessary for an American as dew is to the grass."

[8] "The worlds before and after the Deluge were not more different than our republics of letters before and after the late war . . . For ten years the new generation read nothing but newspapers."—E. C. Stedman, Letter to William Winter, 1873.

them had qualities of style that revealed this character for better or worse and that differed widely from the qualities of the older writers, whether in the South or in the North, in New York or New England,—the qualities of the old grand style that was always formal and sometimes pompous, the scholarly style that was based upon classic models. Bret Harte's brevity and lightness of feeling, like the mockery and wit of Artemus Ward, like Mark Twain's play of humour in decades to come were symptoms of a general change of feeling in writers and public alike that was leagues removed from the feeling of earlier times.[9] Who could have believed in later years that Bret Harte's *M'liss*, for instance, was written within seven years of *Moby-Dick?* Certain of the new Western writers were in conscious reaction against New England,[10] and theirs was the Western spirit that Melville described as the "true American" spirit,—for "no other is," he said, "or can be so."[11] Both Emerson and Whitman had called this the spirit of the future. The new writers were close to the common speech, and

[9] "The old classic splints are being loosened and taken off, and the long-cramped mental members are limbering at the joints, as it were, and striking straight out from the shoulder."—Letter of James Whitcomb Riley to Joel Chandler Harris, 1883.

[10] "That correct and sometimes narrow New England civilization and its corresponding crisp and dapper style of thought, which for years represented the North in the councils of the nation, has always seemed to me to be at best an English graft, which, if it has not dwarfed the growth or spoiled the vitality of the original stock, has at least retarded the formation of national character."—Bret Harte, *Our Last Offering.*

Cf. Whitman in *Good-Bye My Fancy:* "For future national literature in America, New England (the technically moral and schoolmaster region, as a cynical fellow I know calls it) and the three or four great Atlantic-coast cities, highly as they today suppose they dominate the whole, will have to haul in their horns. *Ensemble* is the tap-root of national literature."

[11] Writing in *Israel Potter* of Ethan Allen, Melville said, "His spirit was essentially Western; and herein is his peculiar Americanism; for the Western spirit is, or will yet be (for no other is, or can be), the true American one."

they were familiar with the whole country and readily accepted it as few had been able to accept it in earlier times.

*

*   *

Where, meanwhile, were Melville and Whitman, the two New York co-supremes, to use Shakespeare's word in *The Phoenix and the Turtle?*

Herman Melville had left Pittsfield and returned to New York during the war when his literary life had virtually come to a close, and he had lectured as far afield as Chicago, Milwaukee and Montreal in one of a number of attempts to earn a living. At last, in 1866, like Hawthorne long before, he had received an appointment as an inspector of customs. Ten years earlier, depressed and tired, with most of his writing already behind him, he had set out for Italy and the Holy Land, on one of those occasions when he took to the ship as a substitute for pistol and ball, to drive out the "drizzly November," as he said, in his soul. Nervously exhausted, he was in search of he knew not what, a philosopher's stone, some secret of religious faith, a search as vain as Taji's in pursuit of Yillah, though the long poem that recalled it later, filled as it was with darkness and doubt, ended, like *Billy Budd,* on a note of affirmation. Melville had arrived in Jerusalem when the Zionist movement was taking shape and Sir Moses Montefiore, on one of his visits, had expressed his intention to live there. Two groups of Americans had started agricultural schools for the Jews who had gathered from all over Europe on the soil of Zion, believing that the time for their prophesied return was at hand.

For nineteen years, every day, Melville was to plod back and forth between his house and the pier on the Hudson river, all but forgotten as a man of letters, for

New York seldom remembered its own and New England, now in the ascendant, had small interest in him. Melville himself had had small interest in other writers. His favourite reading was in metaphysics and authors of the remote past; he was scarcely aware of his contemporaries, aside from Emerson and Hawthorne; he had never known Whitman, who had abandoned Manhattan now, and he had nothing in common with the other New York writers. Those of the rising generation must have seemed to him shallow. So, proud as he was, he withdrew from the world in the spirit of his remark in *Mardi*, "Better to sink in boundless deeps than float on vulgar shoals." When a visitor spoke of the Polynesians, he discouraged any discussion of them, turning the subject with a word about Plato's Republic, as if he were unwilling to be reminded of his former life, and he underscored Matthew Arnold's comment in his essay on Maurice de Guérin, "To a sensitive man like Guérin, to silence his genius is more tolerable than to hackney it." For he had no gift for popular writing nor any inclination for it. Moreover, he found all the tendencies of the post-war years unsympathetic. In *The Confidence-Man*, long before, he had expressed his contempt for the over-developed commercial smartness of the time, and in *Clarel*, with its note of religious faith, he was soon to manifest an almost complete disillusionment with the future of the country. It had sunk to the rankest commonplace of an "Anglo-Saxon China," he felt, with demagogues misleading the people and freebooters robbing them, and he had no more use than Fenimore Cooper before him for what he described as the "great improvements of the age." [12]

[12] "Great improvements of the age! What! to call the facilitation of death and murder an improvement! Who wants to travel so fast? My grandfather did not, and he was no fool. Hark! here comes that old dragon again—that gigantic gadfly of a Moloch—snort! puff! scream!—here he comes straight-bent through these

"What could a sage of the nineteenth century teach Socrates?" he asked in a pencil note in one of his books, answering himself, "Why, nothing more than something about Cyrus Field, and the ocean telegraph, and the sewing-machine, etc." Then he repudiated the gospel of work, that nineteenth-century shibboleth, observing that the "dignity" lay rather in leisure and that work was merely a "necessity" of our earthly condition.[13] In *The Tartarus of Maids* he had written with horror of the dreadful "iron animals," the machines of the Berkshire paper-mill, maniacally served by pallid girls, mournful, beseeching, yet unresisting, as mutely and cringingly as ever slave served sultan. It was the "metallic necessity," the "unbudging fatality" governing them that made these machines so terrible to him, and he contrasted the girls and their fate with the "paradise of bachelors" which he had once observed in the Temple in London. There he had seen the "very perfection of quiet absorption of good living, good drinking, good feeling and good talk." In his preference of the older order and all that was humane in it, Melville spoke almost with the voice of Cooper and Irving.

For the rest, he felt neither defeated nor bitter, and, having once cherished a notion, he wrote, that he did

---

vernal woods, like the Asiatic cholera cantering on a camel . . . For two hundred and fifty miles that iron fiend goes yelling through the land, crying 'More! more! more!' Would fifty conspiring mountains would fall atop of him."—Melville, *Cock-a-doodle-doo!*

[13] "So it appears that I used in my letter to you the expression 'people of leisure.' If I did, it was a faulty expression—as applied in that case. I doubtless meant people the disposition of whose time is not subject to another. But it amused me—your disbelieving the thing as if there was any merit in *not* being a person of leisure. Whoever is not in the possession of leisure can hardly be said to possess independence. They talk of the *dignity of work.* Bosh. True work is the *necessity* of poor humanity's earthly condition. The dignity is in leisure. Besides, ninety-nine hundredths of all the *work* done in the world is either foolish and unnecessary, or harmful and wicked."—Melville, *Family Correspondence,* Letter of 1877.

not care to live very long, he frankly owned that he had changed his mind.[14] He had slowly recovered a faith in life that had been lost or clouded, and there may have been a personal touch in two of his sketches: one was the story of an inventor who failed and thanked God for his failure, the other described a fiddler who had once had fame and was now "hilarious without it." That Melville did not have the air of a man disappointed in life was the verdict of one observer of his later years, and, although he had periods of mental suffering, he apparently expressed a normal mood when he wrote, "We are all as usual—that is to say jolly." His change of feeling about civilization was like that of many another man, not only in America but in England and Europe as well. Tennyson spoke for all of them in his two poems *Locksley Hall* and *Locksley Hall Sixty Years After,* the first with its youthful vision of progress and the glorious gains of the "march of mind," the second with its older man's distrust of the future. How much there was of Melville's life, even to the "summer isles of Eden," even to the rejection of the savage's level of existence, in these poems that spanned the emotional life of an age, the feeling of an "increasing purpose," the doubts, as time went on, and progress seemed to be "halting on palsied feet." For Melville too "Reversion" dragged "Evolution" in the mud and Demos perhaps was working its own doom, while science increased and beauty dwindled in the ugliness of industrial growth and only hope and youth could still cry "forward." Later Melville was deeply drawn to James Thomson's essays and poems, to *The City of Dreadful Night,* which he called "massive and mighty," saying, "its gloom is

[14] "I once, like other spoonies, cherished a loose sort of notion that I did not care to live very long. But I will frankly own that I have now no serious, no insuperable objections to a respectable longevity."—Letter of 1862.

its sublimity," relishing "the pessimism in it," he observed, "as a counterpoise to the exorbitant hopefulness . . . that makes such a bluster in these days,—at least in some quarters." But he described himself as "neither optimist nor pessimist"; and there were many along with him who disliked the fools' paradise of the "juvenile and shallow," while the dominant note of his poems was genial and seemed to show that, in spite of all, his feeling for democracy was as clear and deep as ever. Many of his poems were suggested no doubt by the letters from old shipmates who wrote to him, like Cooper's Ned Myers, after he was famous; and was not the story *Billy Budd,* composed at the very end of his life, the glorification of another common sailor? Like Timoleon in his poem, the ancient general and patriot who had been driven into retirement by the curses of his kinsfolk, he too was estranged from "membership in the mart," but, preferring exile to reconciliation with the world that had rejected him, he was yet entirely and serenely philosophic about it. He merely, as it were, went underground and lived a subterranean life like other sensitive persons of the new generation,—like Emily Dickinson, the poetess, for one, like the historian Henry Adams when he failed, or felt that he had failed, to find favour with his country.

Melville had taken to writing "doggerel," as he called it in a letter to his brother, as early—his wife recorded— as 1859, and for more than thirty years this was virtually all he wrote, although he produced four volumes first or last. The impulse to write in verse had come to him, oddly enough, at the moment when the prose-impulse had quite run out, a reversal of the usual order; and he stubbornly continued to compose and print, privately at times, at his own expense, the rhymes that a handful of readers at best were aware of. Only his poems of the war were at all widely known, but some of these were admirable, like certain of the travel-pieces that recalled his voyage to Italy and the Holy Land. Among them were poems about Venice and Pisa, Padua and the isles of Greece that were sometimes brief and happy in the man-ner of Landor, for in *The Ravaged Villa,* for instance, as in *Lone Founts* and in *Art,* Melville was all but a master of the epigrammatic. In the longer Browning-esque poem *At the Hostelry,* the shades of Velasquez, Rembrandt, Poussin and others met for the talk he might have enjoyed so much, while the cluster of verses called *Weeds and Wildings,* which he inscribed to his wife, brought back their happy days at the Arrowhead farmhouse. Melville remembered the butterflies, the bluebirds, the chipmunks and the bright summer morn-ings when he came in from his ramble with his arms full of the clover he had gathered in the fields. As for the philosophical poems, these were too often inexpert, a marriage of wooden rhetoric and refractory thought that turned him into a still more awkward Clough, espe-cially in the ambitious *Clarel* with its jogtrot metre and its characters vaguely drifting in and out. Melville's sea-pieces, on the other hand, in their wild power now and then carried one's mind back to *Moby-Dick.* In the prose preface to *John Marr and Other Sailors,* he imagined a "lone-hearted mariner" who had settled on the prairie, living in a log-cabin there after his wife and child had died and with no neighbours or friends who spoke his language. In the blank stillness of the prairie his former shipmates had become for him like phantoms of the dead, and, gradually thrown back as he was upon retro-spective musings, they became his spiritual companions. Losing their first indistinctness, they put on a semblance of mute life, lit by the aureole that clings over objects of affection in a past towards which an imaginative heart passionately yearns. Like Timoleon, John Marr was another image of Melville himself, as he invoked his vi-

sionary former watchmates, striving as it were for some
verbal communion with them. There were Bridegroom
Dick and Ap Catesby, there were the men who had
messed with Decatur or fought beside Perry, Porter,
Hull and the rest, Top-Gallant Harry, Jack Roy and
Jack Genteel, Rhyming Ned, Jewsharp Jim and Riga-
doon Joe. Where, he wondered, were all these blades, fine
fellows, so strong, so gay, who were mingled with his
memories of "Edens in a pagan sea"? Where, if anywhere,
had they beached their boats? Had they hauled down
their colours in a lack-lustre day?

If some of these pieces were alive and moving, still
more so was the tale in prose in which, in the last
months of his life, he went back to the sea, reviving in
the character of Billy Budd all he had loved in Jack
Chase, the noble captain of the top who had appeared
in *White-Jacket*. The story was inscribed to Jack Chase,
—"wherever that great heart may now be,"—and, finished just before his death, it proved that Melville's imagination had somehow survived the débâcle of his earlier years. This tale, moreover, of the "handsome sailor"
whom crew and officers loved alike, so great was the virtue that went out from the "welkin-eyed" Billy,—who
was betrayed into a crime that left him innocent in
everyone's eyes,—was a proof of the harmony in Melville's spirit as well. It was a story, for the rest, of the
"Great Mutiny" of the Nore, in the British navy in
1797, a theme which had also attracted Walt Whitman,
forming the background of a tale of his that Poe had
described as "admirable" and that merited the praise.
For his "Richard Parker's Widow" was no other than
the widow of the leader of the mutiny. Whitman and
Melville had much in common in their feeling about the
Civil War and their sense of the equality in courage of
the South and the North, and they bore out Lincoln's
deep belief that the inmost desires of the people of the

North were magnanimous and compassionate towards the vanquished. The Southerners were "not less righteous" than the Northerners, only "less fortunate," Melville wrote,—though they sought to perpetuate slavery and even extend it,—as the "fated inheritors," not the "authors" of the curse,[15] and he hoped they might be reconciled fully to the Union while cherishing their special loyalties unrebuffed.[16] Following the war with passionate concern, he wrote poems on the great engagements whose names were to ring for decades through the American mind,—Shiloh, Antietam, Ball's Bluff, Lookout Mountain, Gettysburg, Chickamauga, Chattanooga: poems that were sometimes ponderous or forced, with the tripping measures into which he fell that were often so incongruous with the subject-matter. But sometimes these pieces were uncommonly fine, *Malvern Hill* and *The Portent,* for instance, and the poem *Sheridan at Cedar Creek* which was so much better than *Sheridan's Ride.* When the Merrimac and the Monitor fought he knew as well as Henry Adams that man had once more learned a "deadlier lore," that this "blacksmith's fray" meant the end of wooden navies and that where all went, not by passion but "by crank, pivot and screw," it placed war "among the trades and artisans." With this "plain mechanic power," he saw, warriors were "now

[15] "*'The South's the sinner!'* well, so let it be;
    But shall the North sin worse, and stand the Pharisee?

    "O now that brave men yield the sword,
        Mine be the manful soldier-view;
    By how much more they boldly warred,
        By so much more is mercy due."
            —*A Meditation.*

[16] ". . . cherishing unrebuffed that kind of feeling for the memory of the soldiers of the fallen Confederacy that Burns, Scott and the Ettrick Shepherd felt for the memory of the gallant clansmen ruined through their fidelity to the Stuarts,—a feeling whose passion was tempered by the poetry imbuing it, and which in no wise affected their loyalty to the Georges."—Melville, *Battle-Pieces and Aspects of the War.*

but operatives," and a "singe," as he put it, ran "through lace and leather." Suddenly, war had become less grand than peace.

Melville, whose fame in his own country passed into a long eclipse, continued to be read in England for a number of reasons,—among others, that the English never lost interest in the sea,—and more than one reader in England connected him with Whitman. In their sympathy with all ordinary life and common occupations, together with their feeling of brotherhood for all rough workers, James Thomson observed that the two were much alike, as they were alike in their sense of grandeur and beauty; and Whitman and Melville were also associated in the mind of the writer Robert Buchanan when he visited the United States in 1885. Buchanan, who went to see Whitman in Camden, sought in New York for the "Triton" Melville, aware that he was living somewhere in the town; but "no one," he wrote, "seemed to know anything of the one great imaginative writer fit to stand shoulder to shoulder with Whitman on this continent." Melville's obscurity in New York was like that of George Borrow in London, when Browning supposed he had been dead for twenty years, while Whitman, who was never really obscure, driven as he was to live obscurely, was rather despised and rejected almost to the last. There was a time in the early seventies when he was reduced to knocking for his breakfast, like some aged minstrel of the Irish famine years, at the kitchen door of a charitable cabin in Camden, and, when he had at last a dwelling of his own there, it was a mean little house near the railway-tracks. To the end of his life the great magazines excluded him. Dr. Holland returned his *Eidolons,* which he had sent to *Scribner's,* with a long and very insulting and contemptuous letter; he was vilified as a writer of bombast, vulgarity and nonsense; and as late as 1884 a Boston friend wrote to him, "I find a solid line of enemies to you everywhere." It was almost true, as the *Tribune* said, that his verses had "never been published at all,"—they had been "printed irregularly and read behind the door." After the first flurry of interest on the part of Emerson and the dead Thoreau, he had for years only a handful of readers,[17] although he was recognized in England in influential circles like those that proved so faithful to Melville also. "Those blessed gales from the British islands probably (certainly) saved me," he said. The Rossettis and others took him up, while for certain younger Englishmen he was a prophet and a teacher, a counsellor and guide. In the darkest hours of his own youth, John Addington Symonds later wrote, Whitman had influenced him more than Plato or Goethe, or any other book except the Bible, giving him the feeling that he could not go amiss and was playing his part in the symphony of cosmic life. Edward Carpenter was similarly affected by Whitman, while Robert Louis Stevenson, who delighted in Melville, said that at a critical time of his youth Whitman helped him to discover the right line of conduct.

Undoubtedly Whitman was warped a little, not as a writer but as a man, by some of the results of this obloquy, as time went on, by the cult that grew up in con-

---

[17] The general feeling towards Whitman in literary circles was reflected in *The Fate of Mansfield Humphreys*, 1885, a novel by Richard Grant White which also reflected their bitter resentment of the English regard for Whitman. Mansfield Humphreys, an American in England, insists that Americans are not "products of the soil,"—only Sitting Bull and the Indians being so,—and do not want a literature and art that smack of any such notion. The novel contains a savage and preposterous parody of *Leaves of Grass*.

When, in Constance Fenimore Woolson's Italian story, *A Pink Villa*, 1888, an Englishman quotes *Pioneers O Pioneers*, not one of the Americans in the party recognizes the poem as Whitman's.

James Whitcomb Riley's feeling was typical of American literary circles. As William Lyon Phelps said, "Riley recognized genius immediately, always excepting Walt Whitman."

sequence of it, surrounding him with adoring disciples, mostly of a rather small calibre, who swung incense before him. In his later years of invalidism he developed a child-like fondness for praise and a habit of judging others by their loyalty to him, the frequently tiresome egotism of a self-centred old man who never felt sure of his position as a writer among writers. But how could he have felt sure of this when he was so constantly attacked or ignored in the days when he was doing his finest work? A deep feeling of insecurity underlay this egotism, he could never feel certain of the "foothold" of *Leaves of Grass,* "its hold on the world, its place in literature," he said, indifferent as, on the whole, he was to his unpopularity, caring so much for "the people" and so little for "the public." [18] As for his vanity, at its worst, as John Burroughs said, it was "but the foible of a great nature," and moreover he steadily deepened as both man and poet after his experience of suffering in the hospitals in the war-years. He refused to "talk persons" censoriously and he was tolerant as Burroughs, for one, had never supposed it possible for a man to be, while, as his notebooks later showed, he was bent on the study of self-perfection during the war and for several years thereafter. He was resolved to inaugurate a "sweet clean-blooded body," he wrote, a "purged, cleansed, spiritualized, invigorated body" by avoiding all fats and drinking only water and milk, and he jotted down notes on the behaviour of a "superb calm character," admon-

[18] "While I stand in reverence before the fact of Humanity, the People, I will confess, in writing my L. of G., the least consideration out of all that has had to do with it has been the consideration of 'the public,'—at any rate as it now exists. Strange as it may sound for a democrat to say so, I am clear that no free and original and lofty-soaring poem, or one ambitious of those achievements, can possibly be fulfill'd by any writer who has largely in his thought *the public*—or the question, what will establish'd literature—what will the current authorities say about it."—Whitman, *Good-bye, My Fancy.*

ishing himself not to do this and that. He was not to utter "smart sayings" or "harsh comments on persons or actions" but rather to be indulgent to the ignorant and the low and silly; not to be scornful in his criticisms, to help the poor, to offer no explanations but to mind his words. He urged himself to cultivate a more uniform demeanour, gentle and cool. Whitman had never ceased to study Epictetus, who had been one of his favourites when he was sixteen,—finding him, he said, was "like being born again,"—and he underscored throughout his copy of the sage.

The writer had matured too, and some of Whitman's finest poems, *Pioneers O Pioneers* and *Passage to India*, for instance, appeared, with many another, in the post-war years, and, shocked and saddened as he was by the "measureless viciousness" of the times, he was by no means discouraged or silenced by it. He would never have chosen this kind of world, any more than Melville, —both would have preferred an agrarian to an industrial regime,—but Whitman, who was never essentially at odds with the country, was only partially at odds with this new turn of fate. He saw that the old political idealism had lapsed and fallen into opportunism, with its "ruffianly nominations and election"; he disliked the "surfeit of prosperity," the "scrofulous wealth"; he distrusted the excessive growth of commercial theories and practices, the new "vast ganglions" of mercantile princes and bankers. As he said later to Traubel, "The trouble is that we don't live in an age of public emulation, but of private greed,"—of depravity in the business classes, corruption in the state, and poverty growing side by side with wealth. It was during these years that he wrote *Democratic Vistas* largely to "admit and face these dangers," he said, to search our times and lands like a physician, and he found on all

sides hollowness of heart, small aims or no aims at all
and a shallow intellectuality that was highly deceptive.
The body of the nation grew ever larger and more thoroughly appointed while more and more it seemed to
have no soul. To expose the weakness and the liabilities
and corruptions of democracy was, he felt, a service to
the country; but he liked the new age in many respects
and hailed with joy, in fact, its oceanic and variegated
energy. Even what he called its "business materialism"
was not wholly alien to him. He rejoiced in the laying
of the Atlantic cable in 1866 and the opening of the
Suez Canal and the Union Pacific, events which he celebrated in *Passage to India* as leading to the realization
of the world unity and consciousness for which he
longed. He had been stirred by the World's Fair of 1856,
as he was to be stirred by the Centennial twenty years
later, with its vast spread of exhibits of the new age,
—of the "modern, the busy nineteenth century, as
grandly poetic as any," he observed, with its "steam-
ships, railroads, factories, electric telegraphs, cylinder
presses." On a long journey in later life, he said one
must travel to inland America "to see what the railroad
is, and how civilization and progress date from it," and
he was not disturbed by the thought that "the fact of
money's being made" was the "paramount matter in
worldly affairs." As time went on, he was more and
more troubled by the monstrous growth of the business
interests and more and more took the side of the exploited masses, but he said that "money-making suc-
cesses" and "comforts" were the *sine qua non* of "moral
and heroic (poetic) fruitions to come." If these "presuc-
cesses" were all, he added, America would indeed be a
failure. But he was convinced that worldly wealth and
products on the largest and most varied scale, with common education and intercommunication,—and in gen-

eral the passing through of "the stages and crudities we . . . are passing through,"—were the bases and prerequisites of the great nation of the future.

So, paradoxically enough perhaps, Whitman's most patriotic poems were produced in this age that drove so many to despair; his optimism was higher than ever and his faith in democracy stronger, although he expected less of the immediate future. As for the arrogant money-powers, he wished to see them disciplined, as he wished the swindled masses to be given their due, but he felt that the morbid facts of society were only passing incidents of the nation's unbounded impetus of growth. Were they not weeds, he asked, of the luxuriant soil, and annuals, not central, enduring, perennial things? He repeated that he could never doubt the future of the country after living with the rank and file of the armies in the war, and he felt that America with its institutions could absorb all elements, good or bad, and turn the worst luck into the best, curses into blessings. So he felt that America should welcome all, Chinese, Irish, Italian, German, the pauper and the criminal with the rest, without exception; for all men needed was the chance which the rulers and institutions of Europe had immemorially denied and withheld from the masses. If Whitman was always more optimistic, it was because, like Emerson, he believed that evil was not a law in itself but a sickness, a perversion of the good and its other side. At the same time his feeling for America had widened to include the world, his thinking had embraced the planet in the course of years. The word he used was "orbic,"—he called for a "race of orbic bards,"—and he was increasingly concerned for the "whole of man," for the well-being of all lands and peoples, "fraternity over the whole globe . . . the dazzling pensive dream," as he called it, "of ages." He felt that, passing beyond petty limits, the time had come to enfold the world, to inaugurate from America international poems, fixing one's verse to the gauge of the round globe; and so he rejoiced in the railroads, the cable, the press. He favoured everything that broke down fences and brought together the East and the West, creeds, classes, races, customs, colours and tongues.

CHAPTER XIII

SAN FRANCISCO: BRET HARTE

WHILE the North, the South and the Middle West were occupied with the Civil War, the regions beyond the Rockies were at peace and thriving, largely thanks to the war indeed, which had driven a multitude thither and thrown California upon its own resources. Mining had more or less given place to cattle-raising and fruit-growing, the chaos of the fifties had resulted in stability and order and the new stream of Nevada silver pouring in from the Comstock lode added to the steady prosperity of San Francisco. The days of "luck" were long since past, the "early days" of the forty-niners who were called old Californians in 1859, when Bayard Taylor, arriving again to lecture in the mining-towns, found massive piers and buildings fronting the bay. As the summer clouds of sand and dust wore off the gloss and the varnish, there was nothing new in the appearance of the gay little city, and it even had for Taylor in its mellow air of age and use the charm of some southern port of Italy or Spain. With magazines and libraries increasing through the war-years, San Francisco had become the literary capital of all the vast country west of the plains and the mountains. There a singular group of writers rose and flourished for a while. Others appeared and joined them as birds of passage.

The centre of literary San Francisco was the *Golden Era*, the "miners' favourite," eleven years old in 1863, when Joaquin Miller came down from Oregon, Mark Twain arrived from Virginia City and a number of

other writers passed through the town. Miller found no
foothold there and Mark Twain returned for a year to
Nevada,—to the *Territorial Enterprise,* an offshoot of
the *Golden Era;* but several of the New York Bohemian
circle, scattered by the war, gathered in the office of the
Era as they had gathered at Pfaff's. Charles Henry Webb
indeed was one of the staff of this pioneer weekly, with
Bret Harte, Prentice Mulford and Charles Warren Stoddard, while others contributed to the magazine as visitors and friends of the group, among them Artemus
Ward and Adah Menken. This future mistress of Dumas
and Swinburne brought one of her many husbands with
her,—Robert H. Newell, otherwise "Orpheus C. Ker,"
who continued in the *Era* the series of papers that had
begun by satirizing the office-seekers in Washington who
had pestered Lincoln. Adah,—"such a figure in tights,"
—produced a defence of Whitman, and nothing had excited the town so much since Lola Montez's spider-dance
as her frantic circus-act in the play *Mazeppa.* Presently
Ada Clare appeared, the "Queen of Bohemia" who had
followed Menken and who wrote for the *Era* until she
departed for Hawaii,—like FitzHugh Ludlow of *The
Hasheesh-Eater* who had crossed the plains with Albert
Bierstadt in a stagecoach by way of Salt Lake City.
These two, planning a book together on the Mormons
and the Western coast, had taken notes and sketched
the Rocky Mountains, passing through the Yosemite
valley which Bierstadt was to reproduce on many a canvas that harmonized with this epoch of "expansion."
Bierstadt designed a new masthead for the *Era,* and
meanwhile Mrs. Frémont commissioned him to paint
the Golden Gate, with the sun setting through it, from
the slope of Oakland. He set up his easel on the spot
where Frémont had first pitched his tent. For the Frémonts had returned to San Francisco for several years
before the war after Frémont was defeated for the pres-

idency in 1856, the candidate of the new Republicans who had come into power with Lincoln later and whose anti-slavery platform had attracted writers. Whittier, Longfellow and Walt Whitman had written poems for Frémont's campaign; Washington Irving had extolled him, with Emerson and Bryant; Theodore Winthrop had stumped for him and Stephen Foster in the *Camptown Races* had contrasted him as the "mustang colt" with the grey old Buchanan who had won the bet.[1] In the house with the great glassed-in verandah that overlooked ocean and bay, Jessie Frémont was the centre of a little salon, and she had done more than anyone else to further the fortunes of the young Bret Harte when he was setting type for the *Golden Era.* She was herself an accomplished writer, as one saw in *A Year of American Travel* and her other books of memories and impressions. She had largely composed her husband's renowned "reports."

Beside Bret Harte on the staff of the *Era,* the author of *Prentice Mulford's Story* excelled in his recollections of the mining times when he had "creviced" in the banks of a stream with crowbars, picks, spoons, scrapers and pans and lived as a solitary prospector on the Tuolumne river. The camps were mostly deserted now, the old-timers were dead or gone and the chaparral had overgrown the cabins, but no one more than Mulford felt the charm of those exciting days that Harte was soon to convey in a hundred stories. He recalled in his sketches the unclouded sky, the sunlight in the dark green woods, the feverish expectations of the hunt for gold, the sudden reports of strikes in claims, the welcome shadows of the ridges and peaks at the end of long days of grappling with bank and boulder. The roving Indians idled about regarding with wonder and scorn

---

[1] "I'll bet my money on the mustang colt.
    Will anybody bet on the grey?"

these futile agitations of the white invaders. The shy,
abstemious, self-distrusting, self-tormenting Mulford spent
much of his time in a whaleboat drifting in the bay,
with blankets to keep him warm at night and a spirit-
lamp to cook with, while he read and wrote for the
San Francisco papers. He was preparing for the hermit's existence that he was to lead in the New Jersey
swamp, in a hut like Thoreau's near Passaic, deep in
the woods, when he developed his "new thought" philosophy of the occult powers that exist in men and became a minor rival of Mrs. Eddy. Charles Warren Stoddard, another associate, who had been brought from
New York as a child, had lived in a low-roofed bungalow for a while in Oakland, a wildwood with a broad
sandy trail that parted the grove in the middle where
one had to turn out for trees and recumbent cows. Bret
Harte, who was seven years older than Stoddard,—he
was born in 1836 in the Albany of Cooper, Melville and
Henry James,—had lived in this bungalow earlier under
the live-oak and had built the white-washed fence bordering the garden. But Harte, whose stepfather was
mayor of Oakland, had stayed there only now and then
between bouts of work as a tutor, a messenger, a printer,
and much of Stoddard's childhood had been passed in
San Francisco, where his father was a member of one of
the vigilance-committees. There he observed the Bar-
bary Coast, the Chinese and Mexican gambling-hells
and the bright-coloured streets with their crazy wooden
stairs, but he was especially drawn to the wharves and
the little barques just in from Tahiti whose dark-
skinned sailors gave him shells and trinkets. A lifelong
lover of islands, he had seen Hawaii first as a boy when
he visited his sister there, the wife of a planter.

Stoddard was already writing the poems that Bret
Harte collected a few years later when he was himself
the best-known writer on the Coast, the adviser and

critic not only of Stoddard but of Joaquin Miller and Mark Twain, for he was a master-craftsman, unique in the group.[2] But these poems were derivative and unimportant beside the travel-sketches that soon revealed a writer of distinguished prose when the indolent Stoddard, a lover of Whitman and still more the Melville of *Omoo* and *Typee,* had returned to Hawaii and visited the Marquesas and Tahiti. A supersensitive young man, swayed by every influence, with a feminine shyness born of delicate pride, he had previously failed as an actor, though his voice and presence fitted him well for the stage. It was not because he disliked the theatre. He doted, as he said, on dingy tinsel, as he loved the odour of the footlights and the spangles of the circus, the clowns, the ponies, the snap of the ring-master's whip; and one of his best Hawaiian sketches, in *The Island of Tranquil Delights,* was the story of the impresario of Honolulu. This Yankee Mr. Proteus had fitted up a theatre that was like an old-fashioned New England meeting-house, where the Hawaiian kings and queens witnessed from their benches the lives and deaths of the kings and queens of Shakespeare. Lola Montez and Edwin Booth had appeared there in the fifties and many an actor of world-renown visited this tropical oasis while crossing the watery desert to Sydney and Melbourne. Mr. Proteus had brought to the Coast the hula-hula dancers whom Stoddard saw in the orange-groves of Waipio. Stoddard, who liked all exotic things, was

[2] Bret Harte was the literary mentor of the early San Francisco writers as Ambrose Bierce was of a later group. "To his criticism and encouragement," Stoddard said, "I owe all that is best in my literary efforts." Joaquin Miller also said, "Bret Harte was my mascotte, my good genius, or what you please," and Mark Twain later wrote to Thomas Bailey Aldrich, "Bret Harte trimmed and trained and schooled me patiently until he changed me from an awkward utterer of coarse grotesquenesses to a writer of paragraphs and chapters that have found a certain favour in the eyes of even some of the very decentest people in the land."

charmed by Ada Clare, with whom he fell in again at
Honolulu,—the actress who parted her corn-coloured
hair, like a schoolboy's, in the middle so that it fell over
one of her violet eyes. A convert to the Roman faith, he
was also drawn to the South Sea islands because he was
"numbed with the frigid manners of the Christians," as
he wrote in a letter to Whitman, and he longed to exchange, at least at times, the "duplicity of civilized man"
for the savagery that gave him the fullest joy of life.[3]
All the rites of savagedom found a responsive echo in
his heart, he hated civilization,—unlike Melville,—and
again and again he vainly swore never to revisit the
workaday world, although somehow or other he always
came back betimes. He loved the dreamy days of calm in
the flowering equatorial waters, the booming of the surf
on the beaches, the clashing of the palm-fronds, the twilight glow on the yellow shores and the cane-fields and
banana-thickets, the slopes of the distant headlands and
the sickle of the sea. He never tired of the winding
roads, the groves with their seventeen shades of green,
with the huts of the natives half-hidden like voluminous
nests, or the foam-girdled reefs of the great lagoons
where exquisite sea-gardens blossomed in splendour under the tranquil waves. The coral bowers caught the
light and flashed it back from their gilded tendrils and
the white sea-sand shone like a pavement of gold, while
fish of every form and hue sailed through the amber-
tinted water like fan-tailed moonbeams and sunbeams
and firebrands of gauze. He often explored the deep valleys and recesses of the mountains where league-long

[3] "I know there is but one hope for me. I must get in amongst
people who are not afraid of their instincts and who scorn hypocrisy.
I am numbed with the frigid manners of the Christians; barbarism
has given me the fullest joy of my life and I long to return to it
and be satisfied."—Letter to Whitman, 1870.

Stoddard also wrote to Whitman, "Where I go you go with me, in
poem and picture."

creepers poured over the cliffs their cataracts of flowers and the waterfalls plunged into basins of cress and fern.

For several years at intervals Stoddard returned to the tropical isles that appeared in his *South Sea Idyls* and other books in which he related his own adventures and told the stories of others he had known, the widow of Spook Hall, for instance, and islanders like the "man-fish." He never knew the Marquesas well and saw the valley of the Typees, naked and forlorn as it looked, only from the sea, but he spent three or four years in Hawaii and lived in Tahiti for a while, wandering through the green lanes enchanted. Working at first in the store of a Frenchman, he had a few dollars, a handful of books and a room in a hut by a palm-tree and a jungle of vanilla; he talked to the breadfruit trees that had sheltered Omoo and nodded to the low white cala-boose, steaming in the sun. He was followed by a sacred idiot, monstrously ugly, and he witnessed the Fête Napoleon that occurred long after the empire had gone to smash when the drummers of the tom-toms had not yet heard the news. In Hawaii, Stoddard knew the bronze-brown Kane-Pihi, the hero of his fine story, *On the Reef,* the slim, unconscious, unclad boy, steeped to the toes in sunshine, who put on vice as a garment with the clothes of the Christians. He had begun to lie and steal the moment he was slipped under cover, for he had passed out of his element and lost his bearings, and, con-demned to hew out coral blocks, as a convict, on the reef, he went to his death without hope like a bird in a snare.

Twice Stoddard visited Molokai, once before Father Damien came when the gardens were already ablaze with the scarlet hibiscus and the lepers crouched under the thick banana hedges. On his second visit the young Belgian priest prepared the supper of eggs and rice in the neat white cottage he had built when he enlarged

the chapel. It was from Stoddard that Robert Louis Stevenson first heard about this missionary whose legend
he was to spread through the reading world, but this
was some years later, in 1879, when Stevenson climbed
up to see him on Telegraph Hill. "What a background
for a novel!" he said in Stoddard's eyrie, with its litter
of battle-clubs, calabashes, masks and plumes and the
rough stone images, baskets and bowls in the midst of
which, talking with this friend, Stevenson first heard the
names of the South Sea Islands. It was from one of these
talks that he "returned (a happy man) with *Omoo* under
one arm and my friend's own adventures under the
other";[4] for Stoddard, who had first visited the islands
in 1864, had published his *South Sea Idyls* in 1873.
Stevenson had crossed the plains with Bancroft's *History of the United States,* in six fat volumes, in his rug
on an emigrant train; and he had gone first to Monterey, where Stoddard was to spend his later years, the
old capitol that was a bankrupt village now. There one
heard the harp-like tinkle of the first piano that was
brought to the Coast, and Spanish was the language of
the low adobe dwellings, with tangles of cactus and
hollyhock behind their walls, and there one saw true
vaquero riding when the Mexicans wheeled and checked
their horses, at a hand-gallop through the wandering
sandy streets. In the bay lay the bones of the little brig
"Natalia" on which Napoleon made his escape from
Elba. Stevenson tramped through the pine woods, exploring the peninsula, from which he perhaps drew
scenes for *Treasure Island,* with Point Lobos and the
ruined and roofless Carmel mission, camping out later
on the slopes of Mount Saint Helena, recalled in *The
Silverado Squatters.* Between whiles, he was in San Fran-

---

[4] Stevenson, *The Wrecker*. There Stoddard and his eyrie are described in the chapter called "Faces on the City Front." Stevenson
addressed a poem in the Scottish dialect "To C. W. Stoddard."

cisco writing his essays of American travel, *Across the Plains, An Amateur Emigrant* and others, and Stoddard saw him in his lodgings there, submerged in pillows like a half-drowned man, with Thoreau's books scattered over the counterpane. For he was preparing his essay on Thoreau as well. Stevenson, who was fond of Stoddard, pliant and winning as he was, observed that he was a type of a class of man that is "doomed to a kind of mild general disappointment through life," and true it was that Stoddard, with all his happy gifts, remained a child of unfulfilled renown.

In the early sixties, when Bret Harte met him and the two were thrown together, Stoddard had not yet begun to write in prose, and he always wrote "for the fun of it" and never when anyone saw him, he said: he had the ways of an amateur as well as the charm. His writing, occasionally mannered, was invariably graceful, and with his exacting taste and style and his lower vitality and smaller scope he belonged to the same literary family as Lafcadio Hearn. He had a horror of the ruts of life and preferred an unencumbered existence, so that only the lightest of ties bound him to the world, and later he wandered in Europe and Asia, a lover of solitude and solitary places, "going about," as he put it, "with my roots in my pockets." Meanwhile, he joined Bret Harte again on the *Overland Monthly*[5] in the later sixties with still another poet, Ina Coolbrith, the niece of the prophet Joseph Smith and the author of *Songs from the Golden Gate* whom Stedman described as the "Sappho of the Western sea." She might have suggested Bret Harte's "Susy," who had also crossed the plains as a child, drawn by a yoke of oxen, in a prairie-

[5] Named after the "Overland Mail" and modelled on the *Atlantic Monthly*. Along with the earlier California writers, Clarence King contributed to it, with Agassiz, General Sherman and John Muir. Josiah Royce's first published essay, a plea for poetry, appeared in the *Overland Monthly* in 1875.

schooner, as well as the "Sappho of Green Springs" whose poem about the underbrush in the twilight of the redwood grove made such a stir. This poetess in Bret Harte's story was popular at once; she appealed to the feverish mind of the place and the moment, and perhaps there was nothing improbable in the tale of three admirers who took so much trouble to find her in her village in the Coast range. They were as eager to see the poet as the pretty girl they supposed she was, and in this they resembled many Californians of the time. As for Ina Coolbrith, she was one of a legion of writers in verse who were appearing in every corner of the English-speaking world and whom nothing whatever particularized, delicate and skilful as they often were, aside from their choice of local and distinctive subjects. She played her part with well-turned rhymes on representative regional themes, the Yosemite valley, Alcatraz, Russian Hill, themes that served Stoddard as well for similar pieces, and even Bret Harte, whose conventional verses celebrated the giant trees, the grizzly, the coyote, the yerba buena and what not. But Harte, whose first book was a collection of poems, was better than the others even in verse, in his rhymes of the Civil War,—for instance, *What the Bullet Sang*,—and especially in his monologues in dialect with a story in them. In the poems that led up to *The Heathen Chinee* he created surprising original effects in Horatian or Swinburnian metres, humorous, fresh, revealing a lively direct perception of something new under the sun, a world that had scarcely been heard of or seen before. One might have found even there some at least of the "many things" that Kipling later said he owed Bret Harte.

It was the world of Roaring Camp, Poker Flat and Sandy Bar, of "partners," gentlemanly gamblers and lucky strikes, the new strange wild California scene that appeared in the best of Bret Harte's poems and the stories that were soon to make him famous. He had struck its more idyllic note in his first tale *M'liss* in 1860, prompted by his life as the master of a pioneer school in a little mining camp in the lower Sierras, but, busy as he was at other tasks as late as 1867, he scouted the "grand gold-hunting crusade" as a subject for writers. What he later called the heroic era of the California Golden Fleece he saw as "hard, ugly, unwashed, vulgar and lawless," while he turned his mind to other themes, legends of the Spanish past and the brilliant series of parodies that he called *Condensed Novels*. The "dying glow of Spanish glory" had something in common here on the Coast with the poetry of the old Dutch life on his native Hudson, as Washington Irving had felt it, and Bret Harte, influenced by Irving, imagined Western counterparts of the legends of Sleepy Hollow and Rip van Winkle. He wrote about lost galleons, the pirate sailors of Sir Francis Drake searching for gold they had heard the Mexicans talk of, padres wandering over the dunes by the Mission Dolores and the Golden Gate, muleteers tempted by the devil. He recounted a friar's vision on Monte del Diablo, where the devil showed him the past and the future of the country in a gay procession of cavaliers with their cross of Santiago that was followed by a swaggering horde of unshorn Yankees. The Spaniards in their phantom train defiled from the ravines, stately, with decorous tread sweeping down to the plain, while as the blue-eyed Saxons passed the trees fell down before them and the bowels of the earth were torn asunder. At haciendas near San José, where riotous fandangos were held on Sunday with fights between bulls and grizzlies near the mission, Bret Harte had seen the vestigial remains of the older civilization in scattered feudal households of the native Spaniards. Sometimes the life went on unchanged in the casa with a patio, a garden with oranges and olives and a ruinous corral,

with walls that were crumbling under the flowering
vines, where a grave major-domo ruled the lounging
Indian servants and the family occasionally bore a
Yankee name. For now and then one happened on some
Don Henrico Silsbee or a young Doña Maria Salton-
stall, the daughter of a Salem whaling-captain who had
married into a Spanish house with lands that dated from
the days of Charles the Fifth. Disputes over tangled land-
titles were a frequent occurrence of the new regime, as
one saw in two or three of Bret Harte's tales. In the
hills and cattle-ranges of the Contra Costa region there
were also traces of the old life lingering on, and there
Bret Harte, as a tutor near Oakland, made friends with
the Spanish ranchero's son who was to appear as Enri-
quez in several of his stories. He studied Spanish with
one of the fathers of the missions.

Later Bret Harte made constant use of these picturesque notes of the old regime, which appeared in some
of his earlier poems and sketches, written during the ap-
prentice-years when he composed the parodies that were
never to be excelled perhaps in American letters. In his
comic treatment of Victor Hugo, Disraeli's "first-class
conversation," Dumas, his favourite, Marryat, Charlotte
Brontë, he showed how critically he had read the masters of his craft and how highly conscious he was of their
style and their methods. He studied them even as he
burlesqued them, affirming his own independence, while
he succeeded in satirizing whatever was absurd and
banal in them without impugning any of their rightful
claims. A few continued to affect his work, Fenimore
Cooper, for instance, whose note one felt in his pictures
of the virgin forest, the sylvan glades and wilderness
clearings with their resinous fragrance of hemlock and
pine that formed the scenes of so many of his tales of the
Sierras. His woodland cabins brought back Natty
Bumppo's, and there was a hint of Cooper too in Bret

Harte's feeling for the giant sequoias that outtopped the towers of Ilium and were older than Homer. But Dickens was the decisive influence one saw at once in Bret Harte's tales, in their play of humour and sentiment, their mannerisms, their style. The mood of Dickens's Christmas stories reappeared in some of them,—with their odour of cedar boxes, evergreens, toys, glue and varnish,—and his way of repeating a stock phrase to identify a character, along with his selection of taverns and bar-rooms as settings. Bret Harte even followed the master's theatricality and drops into bathos. Dickens himself had recognized the younger writer's indebtedness to him, moved as he was by Bret Harte's bold new gift.[6]

Many of the American story-tellers of the new generation were influenced by Dickens,[7] a power as despotic as

[6] Bret Harte received from Dickens a complimentary letter that reached him in a camp in the Sierras a week or two after he heard of Dickens's death.

John Forster wrote in his *Life of Dickens:* "Not many months before my friend's death he had sent me two *Overland Monthlies,* containing two sketches by a young American writer, far away in California, 'The Luck of Roaring Camp' and 'The Outcasts of Poker Flat,' in which he had found such subtle strokes of character as he had not anywhere else in later years discovered; the manner resembling himself, but the matter fresh to a degree that had surprised him; the painting in all respects masterly, and the wild rude thing painted a quite wonderful reality. I have rarely known him more honestly moved."

[7] Henry James in *The Princess Casamassima,* Mark Twain in *The Gilded Age,* Edward Eggleston, Constance Fenimore Woolson, George W. Bagby, "Charles Egbert Craddock," etc. Bret Harte's *Gabriel Conroy* was in many ways almost a Dickens novel. Somewhat earlier, Herman Melville's *Bartleby the Scrivener* was obviously influenced by Dickens. So, later, were James Whitcomb Riley's prose sketches of local celebrities and other odd fish in Indiana.

Dickens afforded a general model for the treatment of low life, as Thackeray, in less degree, for the treatment of high life. Whenever they dealt with low types both Henry James and Miss Woolson were apt to fall straight into the Dickens manner. This was because they were not really interested in these low types and therefore made no effort to observe them. Dickens's models were ready-made for them.

Carlyle's in the previous age, and it may well have been
he who crystallized Bret Harte's feeling for the miners
and gave him a pattern to follow in presenting their
lives. Dickens had prepared the way for him in his treatment of outcasts and rough men in vividly drawn surroundings of slum and country, together with a feeling
for the goodness of heart that so often exists in the rudest and a sympathy, which the younger writer shared,
with children. But, after all, Bret Harte soon outgrew
this influence. He became the sort of writer whom others
follow,—if not the master of a school, at least the inventor of a kind of tale that numbers of others developed in America and in England. As he matured, he left
behind the more obvious traits of the school of Dickens,
his melodramatic tendencies and abuse of the pathetic,
for he had a keen eye and a mind of his own, with a
fine-grained instinct of workmanship and a style that was
natural, resilient, clear, light and quick. For the rest, the
miners were only one of a dozen aspects of the Western
life of which he was a capital observer,—politics, ranch-
ing, newspapers, schools, religion, business, lawyers and
the law and the glittering and varied scene of San Francisco. He spent less than a year in the mining region. For
a few weeks on the Stanislaus river he worked a claim
with the partners of a friend when the mining camps
were already beginning to decay, and twice, like his half-
Jewish father, he was the master of a school, an experience that he recalled in several stories. Cressy and M'liss
were suggested no doubt by girls who were almost as
old as himself but who shared the benches with little
boys of six, among them refractory and incorrigible
"Pikes" who arrived in straggling groups with anything
and everything in mind but the business of the day. Bret
Harte delighted in picturing them as they appeared
from behind the trees after vague and purposeless de-
tours along the road, relinquishing a possible truancy

only on the threshold, with the sighs and the corruga-
tions of foreheads, the scratching of slate-pencils on
slates, the cries of complaint that punctuated the morning sessions. The rattlesnake that was coiled by the
door was a memory too perhaps, with the yellow-birds
and squirrels and the woodpecker hammering on the
roof. Then Bret Harte was a village editor on the coast
of Humboldt county, the region of his Dedlow Marsh
and *In the Carquinez Woods,* and he rode for a few
weeks or months beside the driver of a mountain stage,
guarding the Wells-Fargo safe that was chained to the
footboard. He was supposed to watch the gold and
greenbacks and letters of the miners which the company
delivered to their friends and to the banks in the city.
He may have encountered a Yuba Bill, the driver of the
"Pioneer" coach to Wingdam, the imaginary capital of
Bret Harte's realm, whose stumpy shotgun "Left Bower"
was always at his feet. This warm-hearted autocrat,
gruff, sarcastic, affectionate and loyal, with his usual
expression of humorous discontent, was a master-hand
with horses on the perilous descents of the mountain
roads and a hero like Mark Twain's Mississippi pilots.
He could "feel and smell" the road when he could not
see it in the dark,—as the "lightning" pilots felt and
smelt the river,—when the coach dipped and plunged
on the steepest grades through thickets of laurel and bay
on the snow-covered slopes. Bret Harte remembered the
shadowy trees that seemed to approach in the dusk and
then move hurriedly away as the coach flew past and the
thickly-strewn pine-needles that deadened the sound under the wheels, sending up a soporific odour that be-
numbed the senses. While he was never held up himself, he must have day-dreamed many a time of the
exploits of Rattlesnake Dick, Three-fingered Jack and
the robber-band of Joaquin Murieta, imagining the per-

emptory voice on the road, the bullet through his hat and the hand that disdained to touch "passengers' fixin's." Perhaps, like his young expressman Brace, he might have bearded the outlaw in his den and run away with the niece of Snapshot Harry.

When Bret Harte settled in San Francisco in 1860, at twenty-four,—setting type and writing for the *Golden Era*,—he had absorbed in his six years of life in California the greater part of the material of a hundred stories. Already on his westward voyage in 1854, sailing on the "Brother Jonathan" up from the Isthmus, he had been storing away the impressions of the Mexican coast, torpid in the sun, that appeared in *The Crusade of the Excelsior* many years later. The ship was detained for two days at the town of Acapulco, where a local revolt was in progress against President Santa-Anna, an incident that he reconceived in his tale of the barque "Excelsior" and the revolution conducted by General Leonidas Perkins. There Acapulco was called Todos Santos, the forgotten Mexican settlement, hidden in the fog, isolated from the world and time by ocean and desert on three sides, where a half-mediæval civilization continued unchanged. His glimpse of Mexico was a foretaste for Bret Harte of the Spanish-Californian country he was soon to see, as the liberator Leonidas Perkins was a reminiscence of William Walker, who had just started his filibustering at about that time. William Walker's name was on everybody's tongue when Bret Harte arrived in San Francisco, different as he was in many respects from the courteous and benevolent Southerner who liberated Quinquinambo in the story. Both had always "some Central American revolution on hand," with the best of intentions regarding the downtrodden and the oppressed. Another character in the tale was Adah Menken, the actress and poet whose husbands were almost as numerous as her marital wrongs. She figured as Belle Montgomery, the "Euphemia" of the poems.

For sooner or later Bret Harte made use of all his impressions of the "misty city,"—Stoddard's name for San Francisco,—beginning with the semaphore that greeted the ship from the sand-hills. He liked to recall the long arms that zigzagged to and fro, announcing the approach of the brig, the schooner, the clipper or the side-wheel steamer that signified "letters from home," waving darkly against the sky, forwarding the message to Telegraph Hill, where the gambler George Dornton was pursued by the Vigilantes. Long before he settled there, Bret Harte knew the city well, crossing the bay from Oakland or on journeys northward, and it may have been there that he worked as the druggist's assistant who remembered later the "mysterious incense of the shop." This was the combined essence of scented soap, spice and orris-root that reminded his Reuben Allen of the Arabian Nights. After the Civil War began he was deeply involved in the life of the town, when Thomas Starr King[8] and the Frémonts took him up and he constantly appeared at the political meetings for which he wrote some of his poems of the war, passionately defending the seriously menaced Union. For the San Francisco editors were Southerners in large part and the town was alive with secessionist plots to cripple the cause of

[8] The Boston Unitarian minister, a member of the Transcendental Club, who preached and died (1864) in San Francisco. Like Dr. Clapp, the New Orleans minister, another disciple of Channing, he was one of the springtime apostles of the Unitarian movement, those bearers of the "Boston religion" and Boston culture which they spread through all the outposts of the country. As an orator during the Civil War, he largely influenced local feeling in favour of the North and the cause of the Union. Thomas Starr King was also known as a mountaineer whose writings on the High Sierras, the Yosemite and the "big trees" gave Easterners their first adequate impression of the great scenes of California. As a writer on Far Western scenery he anticipated John Muir.

the Union and bring the state openly out on the Confederate side. Bret Harte described in *Clarence* a circle
of conspirators, among them Colonel Starbottle, who
were working for this, or to set up a Pacific republic in
sympathy with the South; but as for the intensity of his
own feeling, which was rather out of character, it must
have been due in a measure to Jessie Frémont. He dined
with the Frémonts every week, bringing his manuscripts
with him, and Jessie Frémont, who had read him first
in a magazine-sketch on the Stockton boat, constantly
helped him and found him a place in the mint. The Frémonts were Southerners themselves, devoted as they were
to the cause of the Union, and most of Bret Harte's favourite characters were Southern, Colonel Starbottle,
Dr. Duchesne, Jack Hamlin and many another, some of
whom appeared in his stories again and again. Perhaps
he loved best of all the "personally responsible" colonel,
with his old-fashioned elegance and his neckcloth and
ruffles, the gallant veteran of the Mexican War who was
always "Southern and dialectic" and aflame for a pretty
woman and an affair of honour. Bret Harte, who had
met him in Sacramento, or someone very like him, embellished the portrait he drew in tale after tale, dwelling
on the full-breasted chivalry of this Calaveras war-horse
who had known John C. Calhoun and the lamented Poe.
He was fond of his Colonel Pendleton too, the Nashville Don Quixote whose Negro Sancho Panza supported
him in secret by working in a barber-shop when his bank
had failed, and the Creole physician Dr. Duchesne, the
brusque old army surgeon who was loved and feared for
his honesty, his precision and his gruffness. There were
countless Southerners indeed in Bret Harte's stories,—
the McKinstreys, the Blue Grass Penelope, Salomy Jane,
the Clays and the Larrabees who carried on their Kentucky feud in California, Judge Peyton, who adopted
Susy, the orphan of the plains. Jack Hamlin appeared in

twenty stories, the lonely faro-player, always alert for a green veil fluttering from a window.

Bret Harte, who was nothing if not romantic, a lover of chance and the picturesque, was naturally drawn to these types, so many of them Southern, that seemed especially characteristic of what he described in a story as the "fierce, half-grown, half-tamed city." He had encountered almost at first on the staircase of his lodging-house a handsome young man, up very early, dressed in black, elegant, slight, with a pale Southern face, a gambler who was killed a few hours later in a duel. No doubt from that moment he had clearly in mind the "knight-errant of the foothills," for the reckless Jack Hamlin too was pale and slim, one of those gamblers from New Orleans, St. Louis, Memphis, Louisville or Richmond, sometimes well-born and well-educated, who had flocked to the Coast. Bret Harte was familiar with their duelling-grounds in the glens and fields of Oakland, the canyons with elastic moss-carpeted aisles and unsunned herbs and grasses, the hillsides that were golden Niagaras of yellow poppies. The gambling saloons were the largest buildings in the city, the scene of many a tragicomedy when the "successful miner on a spree" was reduced in ten minutes to the status of a crossing-sweeper. Bret Harte knew these gaudy halls and the restaurants where the waiters were Sicilian ex-bandits or noblemen as often as not, for in San Francisco the unexpected happened as regularly as the humdrum elsewhere and the melodramatic was almost a matter of course. One could plausibly imagine there the road-agent hiding in the ginger-bread cottage, the rise of some penniless failure to a fortune overnight, the sudden confrontation of long-lost husbands, wives and sons, perhaps at some auction of unclaimed pioneers' luggage. Bret Harte's notorious abuse of coincidence, one of the weaknesses of his art, might almost have been due to the

character of the world he pictured, a chaos that crystallized in the brilliant Bret Harte heroines who expressed
as they reflected this atmosphere of excitement and risk.
These were the frank direct young women who were
always ready to "lead the way" in the "trackless, un-
charted *terra incognita* of the passions" [9] and whom
Henry Adams had in mind when he said that, alone
among the Americans, Bret Harte, after Whitman, had
insisted on the power of sex. The author of the *Education* observed that the other American writers had "used
sex for sentiment, never for force," the force that appeared in Miggles, for instance, Christie Carr, Salomy
Jane and Yerba Buena, the "ward of the Golden Gate."

The actual California scene was largely a world without women,—a world of lonely men, "partners" at best,
—and Bret Harte made the most of the "lilies" of Poverty Flat, the belles of Canada City and the Marysville
Pets. He found in the Sierras pretty schoolmarms, young
ladies with a dubious past in theatrical troupes, impulsive girls who eloped with gamblers, freckled nymphs
like Flip and shopworn Cherokee Sals and Mother Ship-
tons. There were mermaids on the beaches who turned
out to be half-white Indian girls, there were Western
Flora Macdonalds in fishermen's cabins who were bent
on saving Bonnie Prince Charlies from the South, there
were cool and well-poised Boston damsels with whom
young Spaniards fell in love and rosy country maids
in league with bandits. There were dance and song
girls too, Flora Montagues, Nell Montgomerys, there
were Fiddletown enchantresses and waitresses like Peggy
Moffatt, Spanish women with a "free, gaudy, picture-
covered style with the boys," saucy brunettes, she-devils
and real heroines of the mountains. Bret Harte's tales
were often woodland idylls, stories of courtships under
the greenwood tree, with girls who were candid and

[9] Bret Harte, *The Great Deadwood Mystery*.

sincere, audacious and fearless, types that were drawn from every sphere of this new Far-Western civilization, not merely from the limited field of the mining camps. For Bret Harte knew the settlers in the Santa Cruz mountains, where Flip met Lance in the fog that swept in from the sea, the lighthouse-keepers on the coast, the ranchers of Los Gatos, the orchard-folk and the vintagers of the Santa Clara valley. He saw cities with handsome squares rising on plains near the seashore over fever-haunted tules and sedges of the creek, with warehouses, mills and steamboat-wharves and millions for the promoter's daughters to spend in San Francisco, Paris and New York. Wherever there were "Sydney ducks" there were always women of a sort, as there were in the train of the revivalists and the exhorters at the camp-meetings around the bay where the ague-stricken and the feeble of limb assembled in the tents and shanties with their sons and daughters. A few of Bret Harte's settings were grim Presbyterian tabernacles or the zinc or wooden chapels of the frontier religion where some unlettered cowboy perhaps who had once been an Arkansas jail-bird revealed astonishing powers of eloquence. Bret Harte occasionally liked to contrast this pioneer fundamentalism with the laxities and charms of the Spanish Catholic faith. In one of his tales a circuit preacher in an old California Spanish town was converted by the organist niece of the gardener of the mission.

In one or another of his many stories Bret Harte sketched first or last virtually every phase of this social scene. But the "Bret Harte country" proper was the mining country, approached by the Stockton boat or the boat to Sacramento on which Jack Hamlin rescued the unhappy young girl. These boats appeared in several of the stories, visions at night on the desolate shore, seen from the low, flat banks of the winding stream, where the vast, airy, resplendent structures with their brilliantly lighted and gilded saloons were "floating enchantments" like the boats that enthralled Mark Twain. They were the scene of many a tale that Bret Harte might have written, with their mirrors and white-jacketed servants and lounges and colonnades,—the scene of a number he wrote, in fact, involving miners on their way to town and others ruined in town and returning to the mines. For beyond lay the land of straggling shacks, yellow ditches and crumbling roads where the Argonauts of the Sierras pursued their quest, the land of Red Dog, One Horse Gulch, Blazing Star, Lone Pine Flat, Nip and Tuck, Sandy Bar and Rough and Ready. Each camp had its winding street lined with flaring bar-rooms, gambling-halls and groggeries, a store, a hotel,—thrown together with boards, cloth and paper,—a chapel and a schoolhouse now and then, with squirrels scampering on the roof, and a newspaper-office in a little wooden building. Nests of cabins clustered on knolls and slopes. The camps themselves were scarcely more than disorganized raids on nature that had left behind battlefields strewn with waste and decay, banks furrowed by water, rocks blasted by fire, unshapely stumps of ancient pines, forgotten engines lying half-buried in the gullies. There were scarred flats on every hand, ruined flumes and debris, abandoned heaps of tailings that were worn into mounds, and the soil was everywhere fissured and broken while often the cabins were roofless with nothing but the hoards of field-mice in them. Some of the camps were moribund, others were alive with expectation, swarming with red-shirted miners and the waifs and strays of played-out gulches and bars on some neighbouring river, and occasionally a gang of bully-boys who were bent on painting the settlement red galloped in, yelling and emptying their shooting-irons. Half-lost in tangles of forest and canyon and thickets of manzanita, with the wooded mountains above and the river below, the camps were swept day and night with the balmy and resinous odours of the spruce, the juniper, the wild syringa and the bay.

There, in cabins of adobe and bark, with beds of sacking filled with moss, lived Euchre Bill, the Major, the Doctor, the Judge, Right and Left Bower, "Him," "That Coot," Union Mills and Poker Dick, the miners, mostly young, of Bret Harte's stories. Few knew their last names,—their nicknames were given them almost at random,—though some were educated men with shanties embosomed in vines and flowers, with books on a swinging shelf and a hearth swept clean. A few just out of college, living the "perfect life" in the mines, wrote letters of the purest philosophy under the hemlocks, toiling all day with a copy of Homer in their pockets, and others were frontiersmen with the roving instincts of their type,—virtually all the miners were under forty. Whence and how had they come to the mines? Often this question remained unanswered, but sometimes Bret Harte withdrew the curtain that hung between them and their past and revealed their background in Virginia, Kentucky or New England. In two or three stories, *A Waif of the Plains* and *Gabriel Conroy,* for instance, he related the adventures of his people on the overland trail, though more generally the characters of this fictional world came out of darkness and vagueness, for all the reports and rumours that were spread about them. It was not unusual to hear someone suggest, "If that man had his rights," as if much of the property and peerage of Great Britain mysteriously but justly belonged to penniless American republicans who had failed to obtain it. That these men were there at all was almost a proof that they were courageous, or adventurous and vigorous at least, high-hearted and hopeful, looking forward every morning to the stroke of the pick that might bring them a fortune, in the mood of the miner's code of honour. For, according to this, a man might accept the smallest results of his labour as long as he lived in prospect of a larger strike: he was only condemned if he was contented with a modest certainty or gold enough to pay for his daily wants. Some of the miners saw signs in nature and even heard voices in the trackless wood, others were sustained by a mystic sense of freedom, a feeling of partnership with birds and trees and beasts; and they were often characterized by a reckless generosity and the loyalty that Bret Harte described in *Tennessee's Partner*. Practically all of Bret Harte's stories were drawn from events that really happened, as most of his characters were based upon actual persons, and he was nowhere truer to life than when he revealed the deep civilization that so often underlay the rough crust of the hardened frontiersman.[10]

Along with the miners, other types that might have been found in the mountains appeared in Bret Harte's stories, road-agents and outlaws, eccentric recluses with lonely ranches and settlers who had come for the healing properties and the tonic air of the Sierras. There were monte-dealers like John Oakhurst who played an open and honest game and were connoisseurs of feminine weaknesses and charms, emigrants who built hotels in wild defiles on the highway of travel, Bostonians who opposed their tastes to those of the West. There were

---

[10] "The character of the Western frontiersman is often a singular accumulation of such strata,—the training and beliefs of his earlier days overlain by successions of unrelated and violent experiences, like geological deposits. Underneath the exterior crust of the most hardened and ruffianly nature often remains,—its forms not yet quite fossilized,—a realm full of the devout customs, doctrines, religious influences, which the boy knew, and the man remembers. By sudden upheaval in some great catastrophe or struggle in his mature life, these all come again into the light . . . and he is thrown into all manner of confusions and inconsistencies of feeling and speech by this clashing of the old and the new man within him."—Helen Hunt Jackson, *Ramona*.

highwaymen who threw in "fancy touches" on occasion and were never mixed up with anything but the highest strikes, who never broke into private houses or robbed a woman or a child or a man except with courtesy and face to face. Then there were always the Chinese, whom Bret Harte defended but who were suspected because of their secret ways, for whom somehow a basket of clothes from the wash was a library of information and a slip of rice-paper on the road was a command or a portent. Bret Harte's stories were the prototypes of all the "Westerns," with all the stock characters that appeared in the later tales,—characters, fresh with him, that were "stock" in time,—the pretty New England schoolmistress, the sheriff and his posse, the bad man, the gambler, the heroic stage-driver, the harlot with the heart of gold. His holdups, lynchings, bar-room brawls and romantic idylls on mountain ranches were the models that hundreds of writers followed in the future, few of whom ever compared with him in workmanship, style or refinement, for Bret Harte was not only original, he was an artist. His people appeared in flashes only, he could not develop a character and consequently failed when he attempted novels and plays, and sometimes he was melodramatic and often sentimental, though as often masterly in manner, subtle and firm. He ignored the demand for happy endings and in many of his tales there were none of the young heroes and heroines of conventional fiction, and this, with his clarity and lightness of touch, his abrupt beginnings and informal air, defined a new kind of story of which he was the inventor.

CHAPTER XIV

MARK TWAIN IN THE WEST

MARK TWAIN was twenty-nine years old in 1864, when he came to live in San Francisco, and he had seen much of the country already as a Mississippi pilot and a wandering printer since he had longed as a boy to "get away." A Southerner on both sides, like Lincoln,—his father was Virginian, his mother Kentuckian,—he had been for two weeks a lieutenant in the Confederate army, and before this, at seventeen, leaving home to see the world, he had visited St. Louis, Philadelphia, Washington and New York. Lodging in mechanics' boarding-houses, setting type to pay his way, he had even started for the Amazon in the land of revolutions, a dream that left him only when he met the pilot Bixby and undertook to "learn the river" himself. At loose ends when the Civil War destroyed the river-traffic, he followed his brother to Nevada across the plains, mining for a few months in Washoe, as the territory was called, and later on the Stanislaus over the California border. Then he became a journalist in Virginia City. He was soon well-known as the "Washoe Giant," the author of a series of burlesques and hoaxes who was presently also described as the "Moralist of the Main" when he censured the abuses and corruptions of San Francisco. As early as 1851 he had written short pieces for Eastern papers, the *Saturday Evening Post* and a weekly in Boston, but this was the first real public appearance of a mind as original as Melville's or Whitman's and a character as marked and complex as either of theirs.

As a reporter in San Francisco, where he spent more than two years, Mark Twain saw much of the writers who had gathered in the town, Prentice Mulford, Charles Warren Stoddard, Orpheus C. Ker, Bret Harte and Fitz Hugh Ludlow, among others, the "Hasheesh Eater." He may have met Joseph G. Baldwin as well, the Southern lawyer who had settled on the Coast, the author of *Flush Times of Alabama and Mississippi,* who was planning to write another "flush times" about Nevada and California but died, too soon, in 1864. Mark Twain owed more than a little, no doubt, to Baldwin's sketches of the thirties and forties, as to *Simon Suggs, Sut Lovingood* and David Crockett, for he was a child of the Southwestern frontier and its tall tales were in his blood with many other qualities that were typical of the West and the South. Just as Bret Harte's was an Eastern mind, occupied with Western themes but wholly in the manner of the cultivated Eastern seaboard, Mark Twain was "from Missouri,"—a phrase that arose in later years, —and something new under the sun of letters. He had to be "shown" things that others accepted on faith, he had a strong feeling for the actual as opposed to the sham. He was to write in *Roughing It* the "flush times" Baldwin failed to write, for he had lived in Virginia City in the palmy days of the Comstock lode when he and Artemus Ward had seen much of each other. Already the best-known American humorist, whom Lincoln read at cabinet-meetings, Ward had urged Mark Twain to publish *The Jumping Frog of Calaveras,* which he had heard at a bar at Angel's Camp. Mark Twain studied and presently followed the lecturing technique of Artemus Ward, who played the end-man without the minstrel-show and who had been the first to divine his own great gifts.

Mark Twain, who owed something to Artemus Ward, owed more to Bret Harte, the most experienced craftsman he had met, who "trained and schooled" him "patiently," he said in a letter. The two planned in San Francisco to publish a volume of sketches together, but they fell out later over a play on which they were collaborating and Mark Twain cursed Bret Harte in a posthumous essay. He was "bad, distinctly bad," Mark Twain said, he was "showy, meretricious, insincere," he was an "invertebrate without a country" who was "mean and base" with his son and his friends and his heart was "merely a pump" without any other function. There was much in these accusations that was obviously true. But as a writer Mark Twain humbly submitted his work to this friend as he submitted it to others, both then and later, asking Adah Menken to read it when she was playing in Virginia City as he also asked Fitz Hugh Ludlow in San Francisco. Before his wife took him in hand and read and censored all his proofs, Mrs. Fairbanks, who mothered him on the "Quaker City," edited his papers and told him what not to print, and later he always deferred to Howells, to whose training he owed as much, he said, "as the rude country job-printer owes to the city-boss." Was any other equally eminent writer ever known to accept and court so many advisers, revisers, correctors and improvers? Mark Twain was always in someone's leading-strings.[1]

When later he said that man was a "machine," moved and directed from the outside,—"from the cradle to the grave . . . under training,"—was he not describing his own docility, the lifelong habit of a boy who was "destitute," as he once remarked, "of judgment"? For, man of genius that he was, Mark Twain remained an impul-

---

[1] "His proof-sheets," Howells later wrote, "came back to the *Atlantic* each a veritable 'mush of concession,' as Emerson says."

"There has always been somebody in authority over my manuscript and privileged to improve it," Mark Twain wrote wryly to S. S. McClure in 1900. But the privilege had always emanated from Mark Twain himself.

sive boy, tractable and rebellious by turns to the end of his days, with the very special feeling for the traits of adolescence that he was to show in time in the best of his books. In these San Francisco years, meanwhile, he showed most of the other qualities that characterized him as a man and a writer later, a deep concern with religion and morals, compassion for the under-dog, humanitarian feeling and a hatred of political corruption. The tender-hearted Mark Twain, for whom hunting rabbits was a "mild thuggee" and who could not bear in New Orleans to watch a cock-fight, defended the peaceful, industrious Chinese[2] as he defended the Polynesians who were "fleeced and down-trodden," as he said, by the rapacious whites. That he was more a social philosopher than he was a humorist one of his friends observed in these early days, although he had revealed already the comic strain that was to make him the funniest man perhaps in the English-speaking world. Sometimes the humour in his early sketches ran to the macabre,— suggesting Poe,—for example, in *Aurelia's Young Man*, who was cut to pieces in an Indian fight to the point where the question arose whether there was enough of him left for Aurelia to marry[3] Other burlesques like

---

[2] See *Goldsmith's Friend Abroad Again* in *The Galaxy*, October, 1870, describing in a series of imaginary letters from one Chinese to another the experiences of Ah Song Hi in San Francisco. He had looked forward to a visit to the land "where all are free and all are equal, and none reviled or abused," when, walking from the gangplank, he was "kicked violently behind" and struck by another officer with a short club. Then some young men set a fierce dog on him. Mark Twain, who had observed these incidents, said, "Fancy is not needed to give variety to the history of a Chinaman's sojourn in America."

[3] Cf. the fate of General Smith in Poe's *The Man That Was Used Up*,—in the "late Bugaboo and Kickapoo campaign."

The flight of the balloon in *Captain Stormfield's Visit to Heaven* also suggested Poe in the tale of *Hans Pfaall*. It had the same gigantesque quality of imagination.

Mark Twain even suggested Hawthorne in *The Canvasser's Tale*, in which the "canvasser" buys and sells echoes and makes a collection of them.

The Petrified Man and *My Bloody Massacre* were satires on mining companies and local officials,—hoaxes
in certain cases that were also like Poe's,—and some of
the stories, which were half realistic, ended in melodrama or farce with all the incongruity and loquacity
of a Simon Suggs tale. This writing teemed with the
verbal effects for which Mark Twain was famous later,
the comic understatements, the equally comic exaggera-
tions, the contrasts of the unexpected with the conventional or the solemn with the profane. He spoke, or was
to speak soon, of his "nineteen injurious habits"; he
said he "went down in a state of mind bordering on
impatience" when he meant that he went down with
intent to kill; and he said that the Kanakas would "lie
for a dollar" when they might just as well have got "a
dollar and a half for telling the truth." He spoke of an
American army on the plains, sent against the Indians,
that conquered sixty in eight months "by tiring them
out," as he was to say of ancient Palestine that people
slept with their legs pulled up "because they couldn't
stretch out without a passport." At the same time in San
Francisco he investigated spiritualism as later he examined a number of panaceas and cults,—notably Christian Science towards the end of his life,—equally drawn
and repelled by this but anxious not to be taken in as
he sat on the platform at seances watching for tricks.
Most of the San Francisco writers joined in the current
debate on the spirit-rappers, the Fox sisters and the
existence of ghosts. Prentice Mulford conversed, as he
thought, with the dead John Wilkes Booth, and Henry
George, who was beginning to write for the newspapers
in San Francisco, produced three tales of the supernatural and the spirit-world.

Roughing It, written a few years later, described Mark
Twain's Far Western life, beginning with his overland
stage-drive from Missouri to Nevada, spinning through

Kansas and a part of Nebraska over the "great American desert," where one trod on a bone at every step. For the trail was littered with wrecked wagons and the skeletons of oxen. Mark Twain recalled the buffalo-hunt, the coyotes, jack-rabbits and lizards, the pony-express rider passing on the way to Sacramento, the Rocky Mountain desperado, the train of Mormon emigrants, the memorable halts at Fort Bridger and Salt Lake City. He related the oft-repeated story of Horace Greeley and Hank Monk, the famous stage-driver on the road to Placerville, whose tally-ho with six horses was the first that had crossed the Sierras and who was "always on time" at any cost.[4] The most memorable parts of the book portrayed the "flush times" of Nevada, the days of the silver-bonanza and the Comstock lode, for the California mining-camps were already in decay when Mark Twain saw them, tramping through the woods with a pan looking for pockets. They were lost in the underbrush and the miners who remained, grizzled and old at forty, were left with their regrets and their baffled pride, while Virginia City roared and flared, flushed as it was with the silver-fever and swarming with bankers, editors, lecturers and actors. Lotta Crabtree appeared there with Adah Menken and Artemus Ward, and there Sam Brown, the "chief" of Washoe, had his "private graveyard," the prototype, the first real exemplar of the

[4] Mark Twain heard this story four hundred and eighty-one times, he said, at Julesburg on the Platte, at Fort Bridger from a Colorado man, from a wandering Mormon beyond Salt Lake, etc. Drivers told it, conductors, inn-keepers, chance passengers, lone Indians, Bayard Taylor told it, Artemus Ward referred to it and Joaquin Miller made it the subject of a poem and a play. Horace Greeley was especially popular all over the Far West because he had written strongly in *The Tribune* in favour of a Pacific railroad.

The story illustrates the homogeneity,—along with the diversity and chaos,—of the far-spreading Far-Western life of the time. Writers, travellers and settlers alike repeated it in a similar spirit over an area as large as Central Europe.

"bad man" of the movies. The town was an unsightly hodge-podge of frame shanties and tents of brush, of blankets, old shirts and potato-sacks as often as canvas, with empty whiskey-barrels piled up for chimneys and crates and boxes on rocks, in the mud, in the snow.

Mark Twain revealed in *Roughing It* a masterly grasp of an American scene, and his tale of Buck Fanshawe was one of a number in which he consciously reproduced the story-telling manner of Jim Gillis and similar frontiersmen. Others, written then or later, were the story of the Jumping Frog, the Jaybird and Acorn story of *A Tramp Abroad* and the stories of Jim Blaine and his grandfather's ram and Dick Baker's cat, which he tried to tell exactly as he had heard them. Later he developed this art in *Huckleberry Finn.* Along with his chapters on the mining days he included a few on the Sandwich Islands, for he had gone to Honolulu to report on the sugar-industry there, a town that suggested, vividly indeed, New England. The streets were lined with white frame houses with picket fences and green blinds and the little white wooden churches that one found in Vermont. In the dwellings of the missionaries, the traders, the whalers, smothered in tropical vines and flowers, one found the same objects that one found in Nantucket or New Bedford,—sea-shells carved with biblical texts, whales' teeth with full-rigged ships, glass paper-weights with miniature pictures of rural snowstorms. The Hawaiian king sat on a barrel fishing on the wharf. Charles Warren Stoddard had visited the islands two years before Mark Twain with feelings and a point of view that were totally different, for he was wholly charmed precisely by the pagan elements that shocked this "brevet Presbyterian," as he called himself. Mark Twain spoke up for the Protestant missionaries, the "devoted old Puritan knights" who had broken the tyranny of the chiefs over the people, while, relishing the voices of the island girls, so liquid, free and joyous, he found their native dances "strange and unpleasant."

This little touch of prudery recurred in other books in which Mark Twain was to record his impressions of travel; he could not contain his fury, for instance, at one of Titian's Venuses, which he called the "vilest," the "obscenest" picture in the world.[5] He described this lady as "Titian's beast" because of the position of one of her hands, for he was a very prudish man, "demonstrably more prudish than Howells," in the view of one who had read his unpublished papers.[6] He had grown up in a different world from Stoddard's or Bret Harte's, children of cultivated families who had come from the East with its liberal traditional standards of the old European culture. Mark Twain was the true frontiersman, like David Crockett, in an earlier day, who was shocked by the mild goings-on in the theatre in Philadelphia[7] and "blushingly retired," in a phrase of the time, as Natty Bumppo would have done and many another grave American woodsman. One and all had absorbed the atmosphere of the evangelical Protestant sects that were strictest in their taboos in the sexual sphere, the simple old frontier religion that dominated Mark Twain's mind long after he had consciously ceased

---

[5] *A Tramp Abroad.*

[6] Bernard De Voto in *Mark Twain at Work.* "His squeamishness was greater than Howells's," Mr. De Voto repeats, observing that he did most of his own bowdlerizing.

[7] "We started for the theatre, and found a very full house . . . What a pity it is that these theatres are not so contrived that everybody could go; but the fact is, backwoodsman as I am, I have heard some things in them that was a leetle too tough for good women and modest men . . . Folks pretend to say that high people don't mind these things. Well, it may be that they are better acquainted with vice than we plain folks."—*Col. Crockett's Tour to the North and Down East*, 1835. What David Crockett heard in Philadelphia in 1835 must have been very mild indeed.

to accept its creed.[8] His favourite poems were *The Burial of Moses* and *From Greenland's Icy Mountains*,[9] he was always drawn to ministers, though he liked to shock them, and his delight in Robert Ingersoll, whose writings he "devoured," was a measure of the depth of his early religious faith. Like the popularity of Paine's *Age of Reason* and Volney's *Ruins*, on the frontier, decades after these books were obsolete elsewhere, it bore witness to the presence and pressure of the old religion and the "limitless fire and brimstone" that he recalled. He had shared this to the point where, at the age of twenty-three, he regarded himself as a "lost and ruined sinner," [10] and his mind retained the impress of it, like untold thousands of American minds that had lost their belief in its dogmas and in heaven and hell.[11] The sabbath and the Sunday school constantly recurred in his stories and jokes, with the old celestial imagery of harps, haloes and hymn-books, reflecting the culture of the frontier,—almost exclusively biblical,—where the Holy Land was always and everywhere a subject of interest.[12]

[8] Cf. Augustus Longstreet, *Georgia Scenes:* "The waltz would have crimsoned the cheek of every young lady who attended a ball in my day."

[9] He called the latter "my favourite poem" in *Following the Equator*. His biographer Albert Bigelow Paine said that *The Burial of Moses* was his "literary touchstone."

[10] See the letter to his sister Mollie, June 18, 1858, written at the time of the death of his brother Henry.—Mark Twain's *Letters,* I, 39-40.

[11] Towards the end of his life Mark Twain several times addressed the younger John D. Rockefeller's Bible class. He called himself an honorary member of it.

[12] Even at Virginia City this interest flourished. Mark Twain lectured twice there on the Holy Land after his return from the voyage of *The Innocents Abroad*. One might multiply examples indefinitely. James Whitcomb Riley wrote a few years later that at Rossville, Michigan, the Holy Land was the subject in most request for a lecture.

The stamp of this old religious faith went very deep in Mark Twain, and how much was not the fatalism of his later thinking a result of the predestinationism he had heard as a child? His contempt for the "damned human race" had largely a Calvinist origin too, his notion that God made man "because he was disappointed in the monkey," and Mark Twain's first important book, *The Innocents Abroad,* was a singularly complete expression of the frontier culture. He wrote, or rewrote, this in San Francisco for a San Francisco paper, for he returned there after the voyage, the first modern "luxury cruise," in 1867, on the "Quaker City." He wished to "squeeze some of the wind and water" out of the letters he had written on the ship. While the "innocents" had seen much of Europe,—France, Italy, Spain and Constantinople,—they had "cared nothing much" about it, as Mark Twain observed, and it was the Holy Land that brought out their enthusiasm,—the "pet feature" of the excursion, he said, was the "pilgrimage part." In Italy Mark Twain himself marvelled over the great railway stations, the smoothness of the road-beds of the railways, the magnificent turnpikes, hard, level, straight as a line, as white as snow,—which pleased him because he understood them, as he frankly said,—while, convinced of the superiority of his own country in everything else, he confronted the European scene in the mood of a "debunker." For he was the "man from Missouri" who had to be "shown" there. With his fellow-travellers, as he described them, he "galloped through the Louvre," he observed that Lake Como would seem only a "bedizened little courtier" in the august presence of Tahoe,[13]

---

[13] In Mark Twain's "debunking" mood, he debunked the American Indians too. "People say that Tahoe means 'Silver Lake'—'Limpid Water'—'Falling Leaf.' Bosh! It means grasshopper soup, the favourite dish of the Digger tribe—and of the Piutes as well. It isn't worth while, in these practical times, for people to talk about Indian

the Sierra lake, and this ex-Mississippi pilot remarked that the Arno, a "historical creek," would have to have water pumped into it to become a river. Amused by the English that appeared in the guide-books,—he was always amused by foreign tongues, Portuguese and the "awful German language," [14]—he found the new copies of the old masters invariably "handsomer" than the pictures themselves, as he found that Italy was full of female beards. The frowsy unwashed peasant girls who had fooled so many poets were, he had always known, a glaring fraud, and as for Petrarch, who had loved another man's Laura, was not this a "clear waste of the raw material" of love? Besides, who ever said a word for poor Mr. Laura? How did one suppose *he* liked this state of affairs? Thus Mark Twain galloped through Europe too, as well as through the Louvre, feeling the need of a "tourist for breakfast" when he saw how the travellers' books had deceived him—until he came to Palestine, which was another story. Like the other pilgrims he was all excitement over the sea of Galilee, Samaria, Nazareth, Tabor and the mouth of the Jordan. The Holy Land was the "grand feature of the expedition,"

---

poetry. There never was any in them—except in the Fenimore Cooper Indians . . . I know the Noble Red Man. I have camped with the Indians; I have been on the war-path with them, taken part in the chase with them—for grasshoppers; helped them steal cattle; I have roamed with them, scalped them, had them for breakfast. I would gladly eat the whole race if I had a chance."—*The Innocents Abroad.*

Elsewhere Mark Twain ridiculed the "Fenimore Cooper Indians," though, regarding the poetry of the Indians, Fenimore Cooper was ten times closer to the truth than Mark Twain.

But Mark Twain was too tender-hearted to maintain for long a grudge against any variety of under-dog. It was a Piute Indian he had known in Tulare County who received Captain Stormfield when he visited heaven.

[14] "Whenever the literary German dives into a sentence, that is the last you are going to see of him till he emerges on the other side of his Atlantic with his verb in his mouth."—Mark Twain, *A Connecticut Yankee in King Arthur's Court.*

he said. The taste of the frontier triumphed in *The Innocents Abroad.*

Mark Twain's intention in this book was to see the old world with his own eyes, not as other and earlier American tourists had seen it, to tell what he had seen, not what he had read.[15] The guides in Italy were delighted, he found, to secure an American party because they were usually so full of emotion and wonder, expressing a delight and admiration that he could have envied when it was real but that struck him as too often conventional, sentimental and false. He tried to be honest about his feelings, he tried to distinguish, both then and later, between his own and those he had borrowed from others, and he once remarked that he had visited Niagara Falls fifteen times before he got his imaginary Falls "gauged to the actuality." Only then could he "begin to sanely and wholesomely wonder at them for what they were, not what I had expected them to be." [16]

---

[15] Two other "debunkers" from the West had seen the old world with a similar purpose, one a few years before him, J. Ross Browne, the other J. Franklin Swift, whose sketches were appearing in another San Francisco paper at the same time. Browne, who lived near Oakland in a Chinese-Moorish-Indian pagoda that was also Italian, Russian, Gothic and what not,—like Mrs. Trollope's bazaar in Cincinnati,—had anticipated *Moby-Dick* in his *Etchings of a Whaling Cruise,* as he anticipated Mark Twain's *Roughing It* in *A Peep at Washoe.* Earlier, in 1853, he had visited Europe and the Holy Land on the journey that he described in *Yusef,* in which, with the hope of starting a "crusade against the mists of Fancy," he tried to tell not what he had read but what he had seen. He was tired of what he called "this systematic way of lionizing Europe." Similarly J. Franklin Swift set out in *Going to Jericho* to represent "what I saw as I saw it" and to comment "from my own standpoint," as he said in a preface. He refused to look with veneration on ancient objects "because they are ancient," and his approach to Europe was boisterous too, the fruit "of an education," he said, that "demands proofs to sustain averments," a roundabout way of saying that he too was "from Missouri." In point of fact, he was,—Swift was a "Pike."

[16] *Following the Equator.* See, in the same book, his remarks about the Taj Mahal. He could not "keep down," he said, his enthusiasms and emotions about it, although he knew they were not his but

n his efforts to "get a natural focus" on things that he
observed, he struck the first note perhaps of the tourist
mind that flourished in American writers fifty years later,
when they were determined not to be fooled by "culture," but he also resembled too many of them in throwing out the baby with the bath, in rejecting the "truths"
of culture along with the "shams." Really believing, as
he later wrote, that a "chromo" was as good as a "Raphael,"—or equally important, at least, to civilization,—
that the "august opera" was no better than the hurdy-
urdy,[17] he attacked the legitimate claims of culture
along with its illegitimate claims as equally a "supersti-
tion . . . imposed upon the world." So, teaching writers to be honest in their vision, he also sanctioned the
bad taste, the provincialism and philistinism and ignorance of the American masses.

Yet just in this, oddly enough, Mark Twain performed
an essential role, distressing as this was at the moment
to cultivated people. Had not Emerson looked to the
"rank rebel party," the Western Jacksonians and their
heirs, to root out the "dilettantism" of American culture? He hoped these berserkers would have their way
that the "new" might start with greater promise, the
"genuine growths" of the American mind that had begun to appear already in the Western stump-orators, for
instance, and David Crockett. Thus Emerson had written

---

belonged to the writers whom he had absorbed. In order to find out
what his own genuine feelings were, he carefully itemized his in-
debtednesses to the descriptions of others.

[17] "The critic has actually imposed upon the world the supersti-
tion that a painting by Raphael is more valuable to the civilizations
of the earth than is a chromo; and the august opera more than the
hurdy-gurdy and the villagers' singing society; and Homer than the
little everybody's poet whose rhymes are in all mouths today and
will be in nobody's mouth next generation; and the Latin classics
than Kipling's far-reaching bugle note; and Jonathan Edwards than
the Salvation Army; and the Venus de Medici than the plaster-cast
peddler."—Letter to Andrew Lang, 1889.

in 1843; and was not Mark Twain, the "Vandal abroad," as he called himself in an early lecture, precisely the kind of berserker that Emerson had hoped for? Did not Mark Twain, in his negative way, do almost as much as Walt Whitman had done to clear the path for an American culture of the future, as the Vandals of old prepared the way for another new culture in the north of Europe because they were insensitive to the Mediterranean culture? For ignorance and incomprehension are the womb and the cradle, as often as not, in which new states of mind are conceived and sheltered, new cultural variations, new human types. Ignorance, *not* independence, was Mark Twain's contribution, in *The Innocents Abroad,* to the growth of an American culture, for if he had been prepared for Europe as he was prepared for the Holy Land would he not have been moved there too to the conventional raptures? As Huck Finn said in *Tom Sawyer Abroad,*[18] "There ain't anything that is so interesting to look at as a place that a book has talked about," and the Bible had aroused Mark Twain's interest in the "holy places," [19] whereas he had inherited the immunity from Europe of the settlers who had crossed the Alleghenies and who shared the feeling of the later "isolationists" in advance. If he had inherited the feeling for Europe of the usual good little Boston boy,—quite comparable to the Westerner's feeling for the lands of the Bible,—would he have shown the independence of Emerson, the author of *English Traits,* or the author of the *French and Italian Notebooks,* Hawthorne? Not so, to judge by the conventional thrills, the appropriate tourist's emotions that Mark Twain actu-

[18] It was symptomatic that Tom Sawyer's "abroad" in this story of Mark Twain's later life did not include Europe at all. It was an old-fashioned Western Sunday school "scholar's" romantic dream of the Biblical "land of Egypt."
[19] Mark Twain carried a Bible with him on the tour of *The Innocents Abroad.*

ally registered at Versailles and at Milan. Mark Twain's impressions were stereotyped as Emerson's and Hawthorne's seldom were, and *English Traits* and Hawthorne's *Notebooks* were both independent and mature beside the infantilities and banalities of *The Innocents Abroad*. But Mark Twain's active ignorance[20] was nevertheless on the side of growth at a moment when the national feeling was awakening in letters and when the "best people," as an English traveller observed in a novel of William Dean Howells, talked with admiration "only" of Paris and Rome. If this defiant Americanism encouraged the Philistine frame of mind and the frontier fashion of regarding "history" as "bunk," it also destroyed the subservience of Americans to the local ideals of the mother-lands,—it broke the umbilical cord that attached them to Europe. This was an indispensable step in the process of building ideals that were not derivative but native and in time universal.

Thus Mark Twain with his fathomless naivety prepared the ground, as Whitman did, for a new and unique American art of letters, in a negative way with *The Innocents Abroad,* in a positive way with the Western writings in which he contributed to establish and foster this art. For *Huckleberry Finn,* with *Tom Sawyer* and the first part of *Life on the Mississippi,*—books that were all composed before 1885,—were germs of a new American literature with a broader base in the national mind than the writers of New England had possessed, fine as they were.[21] As the literary centre of gravity of

[20] Like his humour, which often abetted this ignorance and all the more effectively because he was really so funny. See, for instance, in *A Tramp Abroad,* his comic praise of the "Hair Trunk" of Bassano as "approaching even to the boldest flights of the rococo, the sirocco and the Byzantine schools." While this instantly rendered unreadable all the more fatuous writers on art, it somehow had the effect of discrediting all serious discussion of art as well.

[21] There was thus a measure of justification in Ernest Hemingway's remark (in *Green Hills of Africa*) that "all modern American literature comes from" *Huckleberry Finn.*

the country shifted slowly westward and the Western writers in time came into their own, one found traces of Mark Twain in their rhythms, in their vision, in their choice of themes, in their mode of seeing and recording what they heard and saw. *Huckleberry Finn* with its panorama of river-towns and river-folk was the school of many a later Western writer: the imaginative world of Sherwood Anderson was largely based upon it and the style of Ernest Hemingway owed much to it as well. By his recreation of the frontier life in the great central continental Mississippi valley, by his skill in recapturing its speech and its turns of mind,—the accent and the manner of the world he had known as a child,—Mark Twain preëmpted for later writers a realm that was theirs by right of birth but might never have been theirs for literature if he had not cleared the way.

For Mark Twain made the Mississippi a focus of the national mind, as Washington Irving earlier had made the Hudson, on a scale incomparably larger and richer than Irving's. Through him this greatest of the American rivers became a dwelling-place of light, one of the enchanted countries of the imagination, a world, uncolonized hitherto, where the mind had never been at home and where henceforth it was always happy to rest. There wonderful steamboats floated by, with chimney-pots like sprays of plumes, as one lay on the bank in the woods on summer mornings, gazing over the vast brown stream that reached around the points where the trees looked smoky and dim in the soft blue distance. Broad-horns from Pittsburgh floated past and enormous rafts, acres of boards with long sweeps and flagpoles fore and aft, with wigwams scattered over the expanse of white sweet-smelling timber and a campfire blazing in the middle. They moved so slowly that a boy could swim out and ride with the fiddling, dancing crew, listen to their Crockett-like stories and tremendous talk and watch them crack their heels together as they jumped up and crowed like cocks, bragging of the whiskey and the alligators they had consumed for breakfast. Sometimes the raft shaved the bank and flowing creepers with red berries and swinging grapevines littered the deck with leaves. Gleaming bars of gold and crimson stretched over the river at sunset and fairy archipelagoes reflected their foliage in the stream. The sounds came from afar over the water as one lay on the raft on moonlight nights: one heard the voices of the people at the ferry-landings and fiddle and song from distant trading-scows. But the heart of the magic for Mark Twain had always been the steamboats. He had been enchanted as a boy by their white wooden filigree work, their gilded acorns and deerhorns and chandeliers and pictures; for the stateroom doors had paintings on them that might have been by Audubon or Catlin. The pilots were treated with exalted respect whenever they appeared in the village and they always expressed their wishes in the form of commands. Their skill was a legend along the river, for they followed blind channels that were choked with logs and grazed invisible wrecks in rushing water. That was "gaudy" piloting, "gold-leaf, kid-glove, diamond-breastpin" piloting, and Mark Twain had finally rivalled the best himself. But before he aspired to this he had longed to be a cabin-boy so that he could emerge with a white apron and shake the tablecloth over the side where the other boys of Hannibal could see him. He loved the river in a hundred ways, and, sailing to New Orleans, like Lincoln before him, he had found employment on the levee watching the freight.

This was the summer world, bright and fresh, brimming with life, where Mark Twain had hunted wild turkeys and squirrels as a boy, where the locust-trees, as he recalled them, had always been in bloom and the fragrance of the blossoms filled the air. Thoreau was living in his hut at Walden and Cooper was writing *The Deer-slayer* in the days that Mark Twain brought back in *Huckleberry Finn,*—before the Mexican War and the great Western migration,—when he had spent part of every summer away from the village on his uncle's farm where he made friends especially in the Negro quarters. His great ally and adviser there was Uncle Dan'l,—"Nigger Jim,"—and one old woman had talked with Moses and lost her health in the desert, she said, coming out of Egypt a thousand years ago. In the quarters Mark Twain learned how to ward off witches and nip spells in the bud, as he learned the many bad-luck and the few good-luck signs; he heard the stories that were later told by the Georgian "Uncle Remus" and tales that he was to recount about runaway slaves. He knew the deep woods and their mysteries, the earthy smells, the wild strawberry plants, the muffled drumming of the pheasants in the remoteness of the forest, the far-off hammering of the woodpeckers, the sound of wild creatures scurrying through the brush and the great stretches of the prairie and their loneliness and peace.

Before his piloting days began Mark Twain had seen much of the river-life in Hannibal, along the Missouri shore, in the little one-horse Arkansas towns where the mud in the lanes suggested a village in Russia. There were ash-piles everywhere in these towns, a litter of curled up boots and shoes, pieces of bottles and rags and played out tin-ware, the hog-wallows and broken-down fences and the gates with hinges of old leather or none that Mark Twain later deplored in the American scene. The town drunkard slept with the pigs in the tan-yard and only returned to life at the sound of a dog-fight. Old worm-eaten boards staggered over the graves on the hillside, and the gardens were full of jimson-weeds with sunflowers here and there and watermelons sunning their rotundity among the pumpkin-vines. All these scenes appeared in the books that Mark Twain wrote about the river, along with the camp-meeting, the funeral, the circus, the auction and the characters, drawn mainly from the Hannibal people, who were to suggest in turn innumerable figures in later books by others. Mark Twain was the serio-comic Homer of this old primitive Western world, its first pathfinder in letters, its historian and poet.

CHAPTER XV

EXODUS TO EUROPE: NEW YORK

WITH the opening of the Overland railroad in 1869, a brief bright epoch ended in San Francisco. It no longer stood for the unique frontier that captivated the mind's eye, it had lost its earlier appeal to the imagination, and one by one the writers who had reached it by clipper or steamship, by stagecoach or covered wagon, left by the train. Within two or three years Bret Harte had vanished, Prentice Mulford, Charles Warren Stoddard and still another, Ambrose Bierce, better known in later years, who had settled in San Francisco after the war. Like Mark Twain, who had also left, and the Oregonian Joaquin Miller, all these writers presently appeared in England, where one, Bret Harte, was to stay for the rest of his life. The historian Hubert Howe Bancroft was the only writer of any importance who remained as it were to tell the tale. He had retired from the publishing business in 1869 to record, with his twenty assistants, the history of the Coast, from Central America northward to Bering Straits, while he spent a fortune ransacking the world for manuscripts and books and collected pioneer narratives of the Pacific region. It was to him that Captain Sutter, who had retreated to Pennsylvania to live with the Moravians, related his story, and this Western Bancroft won the regard of Parkman, Lowell and Herbert Spencer, who quoted him at length or reviewed him with fervent applause.[1] Prosaic as his mind was, he had

[1] On the other hand, Henry Adams described Bancroft's *Native Races* as a "disgrace to American scholarship," and Lewis H. Morgan

310

assembled for all time a prodigious body of knowledge that was wholly new.

In later years Charles Warren Stoddard, Ambrose Bierce and Joaquin Miller, who had all met in London, returned to San Francisco, and only Bret Harte remained abroad whither he was the last to go after the unhappy fiasco of his adventures in the East. He had visited Boston and Cambridge, where Longfellow and Lowell gave dinners for him, and walked in Concord with Emerson round Walden pond, struck by the nearness to the village of the wilderness hut of Thoreau, who had sometimes heard the dinner-bell in Emerson's garden. It was very unlike the wilderness he had known in the Sierras. He lectured in the South, where he was touched by the fallen grandees who were trying their best to be business-like and seldom succeeding; then, going to Germany first as a consul and later to Glasgow for five years, Bret Harte had faded forever from the American scene. All the others had left England before Bret Harte arrived, although a large public there, prepared to like frontiersmen, relished Mark Twain as much as Artemus Ward. The creator of Artemus had died in England, a special favourite of the readers of *Punch,* who enjoyed the old showman's comment on the standard sights, Shakespeare's tomb, for instance, which he called a success, amused when he observed that Chaucer was a man of parts but could not spell and when he addressed policemen as "Sir Richard." The English had to admit, he said, that it "rained rather numerously" there, though whether this was owing to a monarchal

---

attacked his uncritical use of Spanish documents as a "crime against ethnological science."—See *Lewis H. Morgan,* by B. J. Stern.

This change of feeling in regard to Bancroft followed the new scientific trend in the writing of history in the eighties. Unliterary as Bancroft's ways were, he was highly competent in style and form and this had been largely the criterion in earlier days. Later, accuracy in facts was all that mattered.

form of government or not he left all candid and un-
prejudiced persons to say: and he talked much about
the Mormons,[2] who had had a revelation bidding
them to go to his lecture without paying for their tickets.
Mark Twain, who called the *Book of Mormon* "chloro-
form in print," regarded Ward's American "irreverence" as a safeguard of freedom. Charles Warren Stoddard lodged with Prentice Mulford and Joaquin Miller
and acted as Mark Twain's secretary in England, while
he saw something of the old poet Richard Hengist
Horne, whose *Orion* had once been extravagantly admired by Poe. Ambrose Bierce spent a good part of his
three and a half London years as a sort of press-agent
for the exiled Empress Eugénie.

As for Joaquin Miller, he was a nine days' wonder in
England, where he wore a sombrero and a red shirt
open at the neck with a flowing sash and trousers tucked
into his boots to show the British what a frontiersman
was like. It tickled the duchesses, he said, but it gave
less pleasure to some of the other frontiersmen.[3] Rossetti,
who had taken up Walt Whitman, took this other wild
Westerner up and seemed to see small difference between
the two, while Swinburne and others, among them Lord

[2] The sinister reputation of the Mormons and their "destroying
angels" was reflected in stories and plays for a generation. Fitz-James
O'Brien's *My Wife's Tempter* and Joaquin Miller's play, *The Danites
in the Sierras*, were cases in point. Bayard Taylor's play *The Prophet*,
1874, had higher pretensions than most of these other writings. The
story of this prophet, Joseph Starr, his proselytes and his Western
trek followed closely the story of Joseph Smith.

[3] See Mark Twain's recollection of Joaquin Miller at a dinner in
London: "He was a discordant note, a disturber and degrader of the
solemnities. He was affecting the picturesque and untamed costume
of the wild Sierras at the time, to the charmed astonishment of conventional London. He and Trollope talked all the time, and both at
the same time, Trollope pouring forth a smooth and limpid and
sparkling stream of faultless English, and Joaquin discharging into it
his muddy and tumultuous mountain torrent,—well, there was never
anything just like it except the Whirlpool Rapids under Niagara
Falls."—*Mark Twain in Eruption*, edited by Bernard De Voto.

Houghton, who helped him to revise his work, were delighted with the "Poet of the Sierras." He told them tales
of buffaloes running down Beacon Street in Boston, while
smoking three cigars at once,—"as we do it in the States,"
—relating his life with the Indians and the "peerless dark-
eyed girl" with whom he had shared his adventures in the
woods round Mount Shasta. The musical word Sierras
pleased English ears as the word Susquehanna had once
pleased Coleridge, and, as Whitman observed of Joaquin
later, he struck a chord in the English breast that "vi-
brated to the wild horse business." He had been born to
the saddle and rode like the wind, and riding bareback
and neck to neck he left Anthony Trollope and his friends
behind and most of them—or so he said—unhorsed.[4] He
tried to teach the young Prince Napoleon, the son of
the empress for whom Bierce was working, how to cling
to his horse and climb into the saddle as he ran, after
the fashion of the Indians and vaqueros, and although
the prince thought this method scarcely becoming for
a soldier he placed a large diamond ring on Miller's
hand. The success of the *Songs of the Sierras* was not
unconnected with this personal success. Bizarre as Miller's costume was, his talent was deeply conventional,
—his idols were Byron, Scott and Burns,—but he grafted
on the Byronic stock new scenes, new characters, a
whole new world, wild as the first and for Englishmen
also exciting. His mountains, plains and gulches were
peopled with outlaws, Indians and scouts, Kit Carson,
William Walker, the Comanche and the Sioux, and his
atmosphere and properties, poncho, serape, sombrero,
lasso, savoured of courage and a new variety of danger.
When the *Songs* appeared in London in 1871, they were

[4] "One morning Trollope hinted that my immunity was due to my
big Spanish saddle, which I had brought from Mexico City. I threw
my saddle on the grass and rode without as much as a blanket; and
I rode neck to neck, and then left them all behind and nearly everyone unhorsed."—Joaquin Miller, note in *Collected Poems*.

greeted with extraordinary praise by distinguished reviewers who said that Miller had far outstripped all his
rivals across the Atlantic, including presumably Emerson, Whitman and Poe.

Up to this moment Joaquin Miller had been virtually
unknown at home, although he had made two visits to
San Francisco. He had arrived in moccasins on the Oregon steamer, having previously asked Stoddard to review
in the *Overland Monthly* an obscure little book of his
poems that was published in Portland, but he had not
impressed the "bards of San Francisco bay" whom he
invoked in a poem that he brought in his pocket. Bret
Harte told him that his choice of subjects fostered and
developed a theatrical tendency and a feverish exaltation that ought to be restrained, and in fact whatever
merit the published *Songs of the Sierras* had was largely
due to the criticism and assistance of others. Lord
Houghton was not his only helper. Two young Irish
writers,—one of whom suggested his title,—retouched
the poems, just as Prentice Mulford in London rewrote
his *Life Among the Modocs* and, as Miller said himself,
"did all the work." For Miller, who was all but illiterate,
was frank about it, although, as Ambrose Bierce said, he
was the greatest liar living and borrowed from the new
dime novels in describing his past. Yet he had had such
uncommon adventures that he need never have invented
them. He may have been in Mexico, he may even have
seen William Walker at the time when the filibusters
were making their plans, and he surely knew some of
the secrets of the Indians and their way of finding water
by following over the desert the flight of a bird. In Oregon he had been a judge, administering justice, as he
said, "with one law-book and two six-shooters," as well
as a pony-express rider between Walla Walla and the
mining regions of Montana and Idaho. Carrying letters
in and gold-dust out, he followed some of the old trails

of Lewis and Clark on the matchless night-rides under
the stars when Indians held the plunging horses waiting
at the relay-stations till he galloped up. He recalled his
adventures crossing the plains, his childhood in a covered wagon and in camps along the trail from Indiana,
—where three silver dollars had been the family nest-
egg,—the trek west when the wagon stalled in quick-
sand on a swollen stream and his father abandoned the
load of Connecticut clocks. They had crossed the Missouri on frail rafts, the women and children huddled together while the brawny men swam with the bellowing
cattle that whirled and swirled and spun about calling
to their young with their bright horns shining in the
sunlight. On the further bank painted savages leaned,
watching, on their bows and let the white men pass on
towards the Western horizon, the land where the sun
and the moon lay down together and, as their fables
told, brought forth the stars. At the Dalles, Captain
U. S. Grant, who commanded the military post, sent his
father a yoke of strong fat oxen with two soldiers to see
them to the summit of the Cascade range, and they had
settled at last in the mild valley of the Willamette, surrounded by snow-covered mountains, glorious with flowers.

Of all that Joaquin Miller wrote, *Overland in a Covered Wagon,* a plain direct recital of this journey of his
childhood, remained the best composition in prose or in
verse, but he had a strong spontaneous gift, a vigour,
dash and freshness that carried the day for a few of his
narrative poems. He was an improvisator, always at his
worst in the shorter pieces that required a measure of
subtlety and a tincture of art, while in some of his descriptive tales in simple ballad or Swinburnian metres,—
The Arizonian, for instance,—he was happy and stirring.
His verse had a certain melody and swing and he seemed
to express with his new scenes all that was wildest and

woolliest in the little-known West, as a counterpart in poetry of Bret Harte and Mark Twain and their prose sketches and stories of the Sierras and beyond. Verbose and banal as he often was, rough-hewn and melodramatic, he evoked the romantic, heroic life of the plains and especially the mountains that appeared in the popular pictures of Albert Bierstadt. Here were the great open spaces, the dust and taste of alkali, the giant California trees, the miners and their cabins, the wigwam and the outlaw's camp, the gambler, the vaquero, the white buttes flashing in the light of the moon. One saw the coyote in the chaparral, the rattlesnake in the manzanita, the fleet-footed mustang, the hawk, the deer and the bear, the prairie fire, the Indian lodge, the Spaniard's hacienda, the pack-train stringing round the mountain its long grey line. This was the world, with its picturesque settings and vigorous primitive life, that Bayard Taylor had touched in his *California Ballads.* In Joaquin Miller's livelier poems it stretched from Nicaragua and the cities that John Lloyd Stephens had discovered in the jungle to the thundering river canyons of the far Northwest.

Leaving London, Joaquin Miller, returning to Oregon for a while, set out for South America where he visited Brazil, composing a long poem there with effective descriptions of tropical scenes which the emperor Dom Pedro translated into Portuguese. For this highly intelligent monarch was doing his best to bring the Americas together. He had translated Longfellow too, brought Agassiz to Rio de Janeiro and welcomed the composer Louis Moreau Gottschalk, who had sailed round from San Francisco in 1865 and died in the Brazilian capital four years later. As for Joaquin Miller, he joined Charles Warren Stoddard in Rome, where the two frequented the Caffé Greco, once the resort of Irving, Cooper and Morse, while Miller wrote one of his

vague weak novels in which the "half-savage" artist-hero
falls in love with "Annette," who was Mrs. Frank Leslie.
For, just as the blond Murieta, who had grown up in
the wild West, with his "abundant hair," was the author
himself, so in the "One Fair Woman" of the title Miller
had in mind the lady who had married the well-known
editor-engraver. This glamorous and brilliant New
Orleans girl who had also married E. G. Squier and who
was to marry the brother of Oscar Wilde had written
a book about California also. Charles Warren Stoddard, who thought it was a duty to be picturesque, said
that Miller's mannerisms were natural to him. Both
these two made journeys to the East, to Constantinople
and Palestine, like Bayard Taylor, George William Curtis, Herman Melville and Mark Twain. Joaquin Miller
in later years wrote a romance that opened in Jerusalem at the time when Melville was there and Montefiore
had come to establish the new Zion in the old home of
the Jews. The young man in *The Building of the City
Beautiful* fell in love with a beautiful Jewess, but they
finally built their city of God on the mountain slopes
of the American West. Stoddard in turn described Jerusalem in *A Cruise under the Crescent,* one of a number of his books of travel, the casual fruits of a restless
life that carried him hither and thither around the
planet. He had previously visited Egypt in 1876 on the
tour that he recorded in *Marshallah,* when, starting from
Paris and Marseilles, he had ascended the Nile and
spent a most memorable night on the island of Philae.
With his feeling for colour and the charm of life, he
wrote many a beautiful passage on Venice, Damascus,
Baalbek, Nubia, Malta, although only the South Seas
had touched him deeply. He was incapable of writing an
ungraceful page.

Meanwhile, Joaquin Miller, who tried his hand at
everything, turned out several plays, naïve and crude,

melodramas that might have been parodies of Bret
Harte's tales and owed their considerable success to the
vogue of these. All the stock figures appeared in them,
the genteel gambler of '49, the Chinaman who was
known as Washee Washee, pards, heavy villains, destroying angels and the baby born in the mining camp,
with the ever-present bowie-knife and rope. The miner's
first thought on making a strike was to hasten to New
York and "buy the Astor House, bar and all," while the
bespectacled Boston man who strayed into the picture
could always be known by his fear of women and bears.
Joaquin Miller, going to Washington, lived in the woods
along Rock Creek where he built a log-cabin arranged
as a mountaineer's home, with bows and arrows nailed
up outside, bear-skins and elk-horns within and the pro-
prietor himself dressed as a frontiersman. Miller, who
was half a mountebank and all the time a showman, was
one of the sights of the capital for a number of years
before he went back to the Western shore where he had
attracted settlers from England by calling attention to
the scenery and the climate there. Building his house on
the Oakland slope where Frémont was supposed to have
pitched his tent, he cultivated olive-trees as a poet-
farmer, occasionally limping with the wrong leg, as Ambrose Bierce observed, when the memory of the famous
arrow grew dim in his mind.

Before they returned to California both Miller and
Stoddard had stopped in New York, where they spent a
winter camping as it were together, but this was a day of
literary small things when the metropolis, big as it was,
had little that attracted writers and still less that held
them. Stoddard, who idolized Herman Melville and
had followed his footsteps about Tahiti, visiting every
spot that he mentioned in *Omoo*, had carried Whitman also on his travels, while Miller, to whom Rossetti

in London had introduced *Leaves of Grass,* enthralled by the book at once, venerated Whitman. He regarded him as the "one lone tree that tops us all." [5] But these writers who suggested a heroic age had vanished from the New York scene and the talents that were emerging seemed small beside them, while the atmosphere of the new generation, the rush for money, the corruption, the noise repelled the imaginative mind. The great hegira had begun that was to take so many abroad, Bret Harte, Henry James, Whistler and others, among them Charles Godfrey Leland, along with the Californians, although Leland never returned to America to stay. He expressed a feeling that others shared when he wrote, "I have found nothing to keep me here. There is nothing to engage my ambitions." Since as a boy in Philadelphia he had heard David Crockett speak, he had always longed for a glimpse of the woolly frontier, and he had gone West after the war, in which he had served briefly, to report the progress of the surveys of the Western railroads. In Duluth he had counted six houses, with twenty-six wigwams, and, stopping at Fond du Lac, he had added the Chippewa language to the dozen or more that he already knew. He was living across the Atlantic again in 1872 when he and Emerson happened to meet in Egypt and witnessed a dance of howling dervishes together.

In the matter of this general migration abroad, Emerson and Whitman felt much alike, although neither was in the least dogmatic about it. The argument was "not all on one side," as Whitman said, but for him Europe with all its glories was in many ways a "vast abnormal ward or hysterical sick-chamber," while he found Amer-

---

[5] I often think of you as the one lone tree that tops us all, battered by storm and blown but still holding your place, serene and satisfied."—Letter of Joaquin Miller to Walt Whitman, 1876.

ica always enlivening and a spectacle not to be missed, tumultuous as it was and oceanic.[6] Others who could not weather it hankered for the repose of England, which they found grateful and comforting after the restlessness of home. They delighted in the landscape there, the thick and uniform turf of the fields, the streams that flowed so placidly and full, the foliage that made our own seem dishevelled and thin, and England especially charmed the minds of countless American writers in the four or five decades following the Civil War. Many of them fought a losing battle against what Henry James described as a "superstitious valuation" of it, for the tastes and the outlook of the frontier West had not yet dominated the national mind and cultivated readers were not interested in *The Innocents Abroad.* England was restful to the American eye, as John Burroughs said, weary as this was of disorder and violent contrasts, and as Burroughs wrote of the flowers and birds, so others, following their prepossessions, found them deeply gratified in the English scene. William Winter, a typical pilgrim, looked for theatrical associations, visiting literary shrines and graves of actors, as Joaquin Miller's first act in England had been to go to Nottingham to lay a California wreath on Byron's tomb. Winter's *Gray Days and Gold, Old Shrines and Ivy* and other books with a vein of Shakespearean interest running through them resembled scores and hundreds of others in a sentiment, fresh with Washington Irving, that grew more and more insipid and sterile as the years went on. Then all the questions that were so important to Henry James's char-

---

[6] *"Travel.* The argument for travelling abroad is not all on one side. There are pulses of irresistible ardour, with due reasons why they may not be gainsaid. But a calm man of deep vision will find in this tremendous modern spectacle of America at least as great sights as anything the foreign world, or the antique, or the relics of the antique, can afford him . . . Shall I not vivify myself with life here, rushing, tumultuous, scornful, masterful, oceanic—greater than ever before known?"—Whitman, *Uncollected Poetry and Prose.*

acters, the problems of the American abroad, came to
the fore, more pressing than ever, as it seemed to many,
with the growing mixture of races at home that made
the Anglo-Saxons more conscious of their blood. There
were thousands of Americans, besides Henry James, like
Richard Grant White's Mansfield Humphreys, who fell
in love with English country-houses,—and the names of
Timmins the housemaid and the butler Wraggs,—while
their hearts trembled over the question of what the English thought of *them* and whether they would be accepted as social equals.[7] In their displeasure at the
Americanization of so many slum-Europeans, they clung
to every shred of their English birthright, eager to prove
in the land of their forbears that, though Americans
born, they were of English descent, and the best, themselves. They bitterly resented the queer, coarse, grotesque slang that passed as what "the Americans say" in
England,[8] happy as they were to accept the statement of
E. S. Nadal, the Virginian, that "the longitude of character and custom is reckoned from Greenwich."

There was much in the state of affairs at home, the
deterioration of morals and manners, the decline of political decency that explained this migration, and only

[7] "I am painfully struck, by the way, with the amount of discussion
going on just now, which somehow implies a certain consciousness
of inferiority on our part as compared with our English cousins . . .
I think we were less conscious when I was a youngster. Nowadays
Europe, and especially England, seems a glass of which everybody is
uncomfortably aware, an horizon which, instead of suggesting something beyond itself, cuts us all off with reflections of (perhaps I
should say on) our unhappy selves. We are all the time wondering
what is thought of us over there, instead of going quietly about our
business."—James Russell Lowell to William Dean Howells, 1879.

"While I think our present consciousness [of England] is a fashion,
we certainly are more conscious than we used to be, and are less dignified."—Howells to Lowell, in reply.

Lowell had written to Howells apropos of Henry James, who, like
his own Mrs. Headway, had "taken a great fancy to this old Europe."

[8] There have never been more fastidious purists than some of these
Americans, such as Logan Pearsall Smith, for one example.

the stoutest hearts perhaps could look ahead with confidence, unchanged and firm in their faith in the future
of the republic. The political world had lost the standing it had once possessed in the mind of the country, in
the aristocratic past or with Webster and Clay, when
politicians were statesmen whom the masses revered,
and Americans were forming the habit now of looking
down on legislators as they had looked up to them in
the good old days.[9] The Congressman became a byword
in the writings of Mark Twain and others, while the feeling for great causes largely vanished, for the Poland and
Greece, the Hungary and Italy of old.[10] For the faith
in republican institutions had grown dim in many
minds, and not alone the minds of the women who appeared in so many of the novels and who longed for a
court and a king and queen at home. (Always on the
understanding that *they* were to be duchesses, as Mr.
George said in *Rollo's Tour of Europe*.) As for more
fundamental matters, Whitman grieved that so many
young men were hungry for loaves and fishes and fat
berths, that they seemed always ready to obey, and John
Burroughs, a keen observer, noted the disappearance of
the picturesque, large and original characters of the
past. As the virtue, he felt, had gone out of farming, a
tamer, inferior race of men had supplanted the pioneers

[9] "Some story now and then is told which discloses the vast reverence in which Hamilton and Jefferson, and later Clay and Webster,
were held by the Americans of their time . . . I remember to have
heard my father, who was an old-time Whig and an adherent of
Webster, say that Webster admired Isaiah. The impression made
upon me at the time was very distinct. I thought how conceited the
prophet would be were he only aware of the great man's eccentric
partiality."—E. S. Nadal, *Impressions of London Social Life*.

[10] "Hardly a vestige remains of that enthusiastic sympathy which
the people of that day gave to Greece and Poland. It is but twenty
years since Kossuth, it is but ten since Garibaldi and the impulse
of Italian unity. So that only in the last decade of years (1865–1875)
has the change of which we speak come over society."—E. S. Nadal,
ibid.

who created the farms, the shaggy, gnarled, primeval types that had once suggested forest trees, so forcible and sizable they were and so pleasing to the mind. What a contrast too were the old preachers to the flippant and polished men of today. As Burroughs said in *Signs and Seasons,* the city rapidly used men up. They tended to become feeble and sophisticated as families ran out, and the fresh stream of humanity that flowed in from the country brought back from the city a humanity that was jaded and pale. It flowed in as arterial blood and came back venous, and nations began to rot first in the cities.

Elsewhere Burroughs continued his argument, applying it to literature, which died, he believed, with the decay of the unliterary in men, the human and heroic traits of simple manhood, and became a "mere skin of elegant words blown up by copious literary gas," a parade of its verbal acquirements and technical merits. He was afraid that American literature might lose its connection with the viscera and the blood and become an expression merely of intellectual quickness,[11] for, as he wrote to Edward Dowden, the Irish admirer of Whitman, the rising writers ran to "mere refinement." They seemed to him of the superficial sort, knowing, quick, bright, deft and smart, but without port, bowels, carnality, sexuality or stomach, unlike the first crop of American writers, Cooper, Emerson, Hawthorne and

[11] "Speaking of Thoreau's dry humour reminds me how surely the old English unctuous and sympathetic humour is dying out or has died out of our literature. Our first notable crop of authors had it,— Paulding, Cooper, Irving and in a measure Hawthorne,—but our later humorists have it not at all, but in its stead an intellectual quickness and perception of the ludicrous that is not unmixed with scorn . . . As the voice of the American has retreated from his chest to his throat and nasal passages, so there is danger that his contribution to literature will soon cease to imply any blood or viscera, or healthy carnality, or depth of human and manly affection, and be the fruit entirely of our toploftical brilliancy and cleverness."—John Burroughs, *Birds and Poets.*

Bryant, who had so much more force, manliness and body. There were things, he wrote, in Stedman that had the old generosity and breadth, but there were not enough of them, for the new poets and critics were lacking in timber and mass, like the new pleasure-vehicles and buggies. The novelists lacked body too,—their workmanship was admirable, but how little they had of Turgenev's grasp of the fundamental human traits, not to mention the power and the heartiness of Scott and Dickens.[12] Certain it was that the younger writers were shallower and smaller on the whole and had less creative energy than Melville and Whitman,—Bret Harte, Stedman, John Hay, Aldrich and Howells, for instance, who seemed somehow thin and lacking in weight beside them. It was as if the "un-literary" part that had been so active in the older men had been more or less left out of their composition, as, moreover, they had experienced so little of the elemental life that lay behind *Leaves of Grass* and *Moby-Dick*. For Whitman himself these writers were mostly "scintillations" of other writers and the "literary needs of other lands," while many solicitous observers noted the disheartening change in the literary scene, the absence of boldness and power in the new generation.[13] Bayard Taylor found no new writers who conquered by their daring or even provoked the reader by offending his tastes;[14] and it struck the young South-

[12] John Burroughs, *Indoor Studies.*

[13] "The era of genius and vigour that seemed ready to burst upon us . . . has not been fulfilled. There is a lack of boldness and power. Men do not seem to strike out in new paths as bravely as of old . . . We have very little strong, original writing."—Editorial in the New York *Round Table,* May 12, 1866.

[14] "Don't you feel, with me, that our imitations become more and more difficult as we take the younger authors who give us sentiment, fancy, pure metres,—in short, very agreeable and meritorious work,— but who neither conquer us by their daring nor provoke us by offending our tastes?"—Bayard Taylor, *Diversions of the Echo Club.*

erner Sidney Lanier that none of the new American
poets even thought of attempting anything great.[15]

It was probably true, as Stedman said,[16] that American poets in the immediate past, in the generation before the Civil War, had inspired the historic movements of the country more than the poets of England,
on their own ground, had inspired them during these
decades; and if the poets were smaller now it was partly
because the great causes had passed and nothing had appeared to replace them in the general mind. The old
cause of the Revolution had lost its magic in these
latter days, while the great issues of national unity, abolition and popular rights, which had filled the minds
of poets, had been settled by the war. These causes had
evoked and focussed strong native American feelings
that had given the poets an indigenous character of their
own, fostering a certain independence that the poets appeared to be losing again in this day of minor issues
and smaller things. They could not withstand the despotic power that Tennyson especially exercised over all
who wrote in English,—with Browning and Swinburne,
—and after apparently taking root in their own soil for
a generation the American poets were reverting to the
sway of England. So it seemed in New York, at least, if
not in New England to the same extent. There Emily
Dickinson retained the native tang.

How far a cause could vitalize and magnify a talent

[15] "In looking around at the publications of the younger American
poets, I am struck with the circumstance that none of them even
attempt anything great. The morbid fear of doing something wrong
or unpolished appears to have influenced their choice of subjects.
Hence the endless multiplication of those little feeble magazine-lyrics
which we all know, consisting of one minute idea each, which is
put in the last line of the fourth verse, the three other verses and
three lines being mere sawdust and surplusage."—Sidney Lanier,
Letter to Bayard Taylor, 1876.
[16] *Poets of America.*

one saw in the case of one of these younger poets, the Jewish Emma Lazarus, whose first book, published in 1867, was a typically accomplished collection of minor verse. It was true that this interested Emerson, at whose house Miss Lazarus stayed in Concord, where she might well have reminded him of Margaret Fuller as the daughter of a cultivated family in New York who was deep in the study of Goethe, about whom she wrote a romance called *Alide*. Feeling a kinship with Heine too, she translated a number of his songs and ballads in a way that rivalled Charles Godfrey Leland's, while many of her other poems were suggested by Chopin, Schumann and Wagner, by musical themes or incidents in the history of art. But she was an undistinguished writer, one of a legion of the poets of culture who abounded in the nineteenth century in a dozen countries, until towards 1880 she was suddenly aroused by the anti-Semitic movements in Germany and Russia. She threw herself into the study of the history, literature and language of the Jews, visited the immigrants who were crowding into the port of New York and exerted herself for the restoration of a Jewish Palestine. In this she was quickened by *Daniel Deronda*, George Eliot's last novel, in which the hero discovered he was a Jew by birth and resolved to devote his life and wealth to the settling of his people as a nation with a political centre in their ancient home.

No one was better aware than Stedman, a friend of Emma Lazarus, that she had struck her true note in this crusade for the Jews, that, after reflecting the Greek ideals of so many minor poets, her talent had expanded with this vital cause and theme. A number of lyrics in her *Songs of a Semite,—The Crowing of the Red Cock* and *The Banner of the Jew,*—were moving and memorable as nothing she had written before, and especially the drama *The Dance to Death,* her finest work undoubtedly, a study of the persecutions of the Middle

Ages. Causes alone have never made poets, and the greater poets have owed their power to other sources and elements of a very different sort, but, when there is no question of these involved, a cause can sometimes lift a poet above his accustomed level of the middling good. Stedman and Richard Watson Gilder, like Bayard Taylor and John Hay, by no means undistinguished, were not poets of power, and they would have profited, as Miss Lazarus did, by the kind of cause that before the war had expanded the talents of some of the New England poets. They were all public-spirited men, inspired by Lincoln and the war itself, supporters of "good government" and the various movements of reform, and many of Gilder's poems especially were on patriotic subjects and on Sherman, Grant, Sheridan and other heroes of the North. In the national emergency during the war when the Southerners invaded Pennsylvania, Gilder had enlisted with Burroughs and Charles Godfrey Leland, and later he was a close friend of Grover Cleveland, who was Stedman's cousin and a leader of reform in Buffalo, in Albany, in the White House. Gilder was a valiant fighter for a higher standard of civic life, in a sense more political than literary in his sympathies and interests,[17] albeit an "authors' editor," as Cable said,—one of the successors of Bayard Taylor as a sort of semi-official poet, a writer of odes and inscriptions for public buildings. For "Barnum's poet laureate," Taylor, who wrote the national Centennial ode and the

[17] "I take another sheet to scold you on. Is there nothing interesting to you but art and literature? Now let me tell you—I would rather have one article by Grant on a battle won by him—I would rather read it—print it—publish it—than twenty articles by Daudet on Mistral. And yet I know all the Provençals—one of the happiest times of my life was the few days spent among them. Daudet is enthusiastic, but not enough for me. Provence, Avignon—they are among the magic words for me. But Heavens! a great world, changing heroic events told by the hero of it!"—Letter of Richard Watson Gilder to Edmund Gosse, 1885.

Gettysburg ode in 1869,[18] was a constant observer of public occasions as Gilder and Stedman also were,—but this was by no means the same as possessing a cause. So, having no great force themselves, these poets of a sterile time wrote little or nothing that interested readers later. With Richard Henry Stoddard, they suggested merely a *diminuendo* of the relatively important poetry of the pre-war years.

Strictly as a poet, no doubt, Stedman was the best of these and better than the somewhat colourless Bayard Taylor, the gifted, driven, laborious Taylor who wore himself out with lecturing and travelling, the "most hard-worked man in the United States," he said. Too busy to retain his spontaneity, toiling for his great house and farm, reviewing, drudging, pouring out books of travel, he was to be remembered only by his version of *Faust* in the original metres, a standard translation, a triumph of knowledge and skill. John Hay's poetry was rather a flash in the pan, although his *Pike County Ballads* were highly influential and, with Bret Harte, set the tone of much writing of the time.[19] Several of Bret Harte's characters were Pikes,—Uncle Jim, Tennessee's partner, Sandy,—with a disregard for grammar that was contagious at the moment,—a contempt for "diction-

---

[18] Bayard Taylor was the orator of the day at the dedication in 1877 of the monument to Fitz-Greene Halleck in Central Park, New York. This was the first monumental statue that was ever raised to an American author.

[19] With very unfortunate effects, in the opinion of Stedman: "Cultured as are Hay and Harte, they are almost equally responsible with 'Josh Billings' and the 'Danbury News' man for the present horrible degeneracy of the public taste . . . The whole country, owing to the contagion of our American newspaper 'exchange' system, is flooded, deluged, swamped beneath a muddy tide of slang, vulgarity, inartistic bathos, impertinence and buffoonery that is not wit."—Letter of Stedman to Bayard Taylor, 1873.

Elsewhere Stedman referred with regret to this "outburst of gulch-and-canyon minstrelsy."

ary hogwash" and the language of Boston;[20] and Hay, whose childhood had been partly spent in Pike County, Illinois, knew these types that were fascinating so many writers. For John Phœnix, Bayard Taylor and Theodore Winthrop had also described them before they became the heroes of Bret Harte and Hay, in whose ballads Jim Bludso and Little Breeches showed, like so many of the characters of Harte, the goodness that often exists in the least prepossessing. These improvised frontier sketches in verse were John Hay's freshest and most virile work, accomplished and graceful as he was in much that he wrote, and he ceased to think of himself as a poet, though he published at intervals during his life translations of Heine, Baudelaire and numbers of others. His *Castilian Days* was more interesting than any of his poems. Hay, the typical prairie boy, as E. S. Nadal called him, in his keenness for fame and for making the most of himself, had spent a number of years abroad in the diplomatic service after the war and before he joined *The Tribune.* An attaché in the Paris legation first, under John Bigelow, he had gone on to Vienna and then to Madrid, influenced still in his feelings abroad by the long association with Lincoln that he was to commemorate, with Nicolay, in years to come. He was full of scorn for Napoleon III, the Hapsburgs and the Bourbons, the "curse of kings," and horrified by the corruption and fraud, the wretched misgovernment and injustice of Spain, where the Inquisition had been only

---

[20] "We ain't hankerin' much for grammar and dictionary hogwash, and we don't want no Boston parts o' speech run in on us the first thing in the mo'nin'. We ain't Boston—we're Pike County—we are."—The leader of the strike in Bret Harte's *The New Assistant at the Pine Clearing School.*

Speaking of the popularity of the Pikes, Josiah Gilbert Holland in 1871 said it began to seem "as if the ordinary decent virtues of civilized society could stand no chance in comparison with the picturesque heroism of this savage in dialect."

recently abolished. The post-war misrule in America was trifling beside it. He shared the contempt of Mark Twain, John Muir and Richard Henry Dana for the taste that rejoiced in the bullring and found it amusing when old cabhorses were taken out and their gaping rents were plugged up with tow and sewn together roughly for another sally.[21] Hay made a collection of Spanish proverbs and wrote well of Spanish art in this age of Murillo-worship when Velasquez was scarcely known as yet, when the king had just sent out his pictures to the Prado museum. For the rest, *Castilian Days,* lively, natural and direct, was singularly picturesque and winning in its manner.

As for Edmund Clarence Stedman, the Connecticut poet who had settled in New York, where he lived at the Unitary Home before the war, he had published earlier in his country weekly poems by Stoddard and Bayard Taylor, who were later his friends and associates in the "Echo Club." The broker-poet of after times, —a phrase that he detested,—the son of one of Griswold's "female poets," Stedman had written society verse before the French forms came into vogue with Swinburne,[22] Gosse and the neat bright Austin Dobson. His serious poetry was sometimes mannered. He adopted the "olde Englysshe" note that seemed so insupportable to readers later, but, along with traces of Tennyson and Poe, whose writings Stedman edited, one found among his poems fine pieces like *The Carib Sea.* Stirred perhaps by Taylor's *Faust,* he collated the existing texts of Theocritus, Bion and Moschus, whom he also translated, partly in excellent hexameters, partly in prose, while he deplored the reduplication of the psuedo-classical mod-

---

[21] Mark Twain, who never saw a bull-fight, drew his description in *A Horse's Tale* directly from John Hay's *Castilian Days.*

[22] Theodore Watts-Dunton said in 1909, referring to the letters of Swinburne to Stedman, that they were "by far the most interesting letters that Algernon ever wrote."

ern poems that reproduced the Grecian myths and legends. The simplest home pastorals would be better, he said, than these. But Stedman, a sort of lesser Lowell, —for Lowell was his favourite New England author, as Emerson was Whitman's favourite and Hawthorne was Melville's,—lacked the native touch and flavour that was always the strength of the New England poets and gave them, although otherwise indifferent, an interest and value.

Thus one could only say of Stedman that he never "drew very deep water" as a poet, a phrase of Walt Whitman, who admired and loved him as a man, personally grateful as he was to him, as to Richard Watson Gilder, in the "literary fiddle-faddle" of the rest of New York.[23] As a critic, with a lifelong interest in poetry, Stedman was the best since Poe, the best of the Americans since Lowell had begun to write, although he was too immersed himself in the atmosphere of Victorian verse to see it in the light of history or the right perspective. In the eyes of Stedman the New England poets, who had been famous in his youth, and in whose shadow he developed, were larger than life,—Bryant, for one, who seemed to him, in his own unsettled later age, as permanently monumental as a Doric temple. He was too close to these older poets, or too much their disciple, too near -sighted as it were in his judgments of them, and his criticism was full of distinctions that ceased to have a difference when readers could no longer accept his weights and measures. When he greatly preferred Elizabeth Stoddard to Emily Dickinson's "half-formed lyrics," which he called "intellectual diamond chips," he showed, as also in the case of Whitman, that a

[23] "I always found Gilder and Stedman in a group by themselves in that New York art delirium—two always sane men in the general madness."—Quoted in Horace Traubel's *With Walt Whitman in Camden*.

totally new poetic vision was not the one thing necessary
from his point of view. But some of his critical essays
were capital, the study of Landor, for one example,
which Swinburne described as the best that had yet been
written, and the highly intelligent Stedman defined a
critical standard in one of his letters that anticipated
Benedetto Croce and the American Spingarn.[24]

[24] "In criticizing a work of art, the question should be, How is
this done from the author's standpoint? Has he carried out his own
purpose? *How is it of its kind?* . . . The only true critic . . . pro-
nounces neither the rose, the violet, nor the lily to be the superior
flower, but asks, How is this rose *as* a rose? How does this lily compare with other lilies? etc., etc."—Letter of Stedman to Josiah Gilbert
Holland, 1872.

CHAPTER XVI

THE SOUTH: CONSTANCE FENIMORE WOOLSON

A NUMBER of writers from the South, unknown or famous, old and young, had appeared in New York immediately after the war, finding that there was no place at home for men of their complexion in the general devastation of the Southern plantations and towns. Among them was John R. Thompson, the poet, who had edited *The Index* in London, the journal of Confederate propaganda, during the war, and who had returned to Richmond from England in 1866 in the vain hope of finding employment there. Within two or three years he was literary editor of Bryant's *Evening Post,* and he and the poet of *Thanatopsis* toured Cuba together. George Cary Eggleston soon arrived, Edward Eggleston's Virginian brother who also became a literary editor in New York, with Dr. George Bagby, who observed, "Baronial Virginia is dead. Ilium, nor Carthage, nor Thebes is more so." John Esten Cooke appeared as well, and the young poet Sidney Lanier came up from Alabama, where he was teaching, with the manuscript of a novel called *Tiger Lilies,* while at about the same time the veteran William Gilmore Simms was trying to reëstablish his career in New York. The metropolis was tolerant as it was large: two laudatory lives of Stonewall Jackson had been published in New York during the war, with several other books by Southern writers, and there had been no protests from the government about it. Then, as Whitman said, while New York

was a bad place for literary farming, it was a good market for the harvest.

Other Southerners flocked to Baltimore, "that almost
sole harbour of refuge," as a later writer called it,—the
town was half Southern,—where "Little Aleck" Stephens was to live for a while, the Confederate vice-presi-
dent whose career was so far from finished. Richard
Malcolm Johnston, who had lost the whole of his large
estate, settled there as a schoolmaster in 1867, and Sidney Lanier and Basil L. Gildersleeve joined him there a
few years later when both were teaching at the new university, Johns Hopkins. The novelist and poet Maurice
Thompson moved from Georgia to Indiana, and the
geologist Joseph Le Conte, after teaching in Georgia
and South Carolina, joined the hegira to California in
1869. There this old student of Agassiz opened his
well-known career as a teacher in Berkeley. The great
diaspora had begun in the desperate South. Thousands
of ex-Confederate soldiers thronged to the Pacific coast,
drawn by the appeal of cheap land and the spirit of adventure that were bred by the war and the ruin of the
farms of the South, while others, in the disorganization
of institutions and property alike, emigrated to various
foreign countries. There were those who went to Paris
or to London, where the former Confederate Secretary
of State, Judah P. Benjamin, established himself as a
lawyer and Robert Toombs also lived for a while as an
exile. Five ex-Confederates became officers in the Egyptian army. Many left for Mexico, Brazil and Venezuela,
which had offered them land and the hope of prosperity with it. A colony of Southerners settled in the coffee
region of Brazil and another from Alabama went to
Honduras, where some were so shocked by the intimate
relations of the Negroes and the whites that they were
happy to return to the United States. The great ocean-
ographer Matthew F. Maury, who had gone to Mexico,

nade plans for the establishment of a new Virginia
here. As imperial commissioner for Maximilian he pic-
ured the good fortune of prominent ex-Confederates
who had already joined him.[1]

But with all these movements hither and thither the
vast majority remained at home, for all the misery and
havoc and waste of a time that was worse in many ways
than the years of the war, following the example of the
great-hearted Lee, who discouraged Maury's plan and
who never knew "one moment of bitterness or resentment." His only answer when English noblemen offered
him houses and large estates was that he could never
leave Virginia in her time of trial, and, urging "silence
and patience on the part of the South," he looked for
some quiet little dwelling with a farm in the woods.
Then, mounted on "Traveller," he rode off to the Valley
of Virginia where he had accepted the presidency of a
half-ruined old college. He was only too happy to play
his part in educating the future South, while he advised
his sons on the problems of farming, admiring and hon-
ouring his fellow-officers, affluent once, who were cheerful now as porters perhaps or as farmers who did their
own ploughing. One of them was grateful that, having
lost one of his arms, he had a chance to use the arm that
was left. There were many other sons of planters who
drove pie-wagons and warehouse-drays, peddled wood
for fires and moulded bricks, while their plantations
went back to forest or were reduced to two-mule farms
and the broomsedge and the scrub-oak grew over the
fields and the ruins.

[1] See also the character of Colonel Fontaine Flournoy in Joel
Chandler Harris's *On the Wing of Occasions,* a member of an old
adventurous family, a Confederate officer who, after the war, thinks
of himself as a man without a country. He goes to Florida with
Robert Toombs and thence to Cuba and South America, where he
lives for five years as a soldier of fortune. The old instinct of the
buccaneers and filibusters revives in him as he shares in revolutions
and rebellions in the South American republics.

From Harper's Ferry to New Market the country wa
a desert, virtually eighty miles without a fence or a
horse, with roofless dwellings, burned barns and chim
neys without houses, while vast regions of other state
were scorched, dilapidated, trodden by war, and the old
mansions had vanished or were tenantless wrecks. One
saw them in South Carolina and Georgia, battered, with
windows fallen in, rifts in the bricks and plaster lying
on the steps, perhaps with a wing that was occupied by a
swarm of gaunt poor whites who greeted the passer-by
with a vacant stare. As for the destitute "quality folk"
who had never thought of money in their lives, they
were unable to think of it even now, though they did
not know how in the world to get on without it, and
powerless as they were to improve things, they could
only endure. They had been quite content to leave the
shipyards and the foundries and the coal-mines to the
North, proud that the South had few arsenals, factories
machine-shops, proud that Southerners had never
stooped to trade, mechanics or engineering and had
never been anything but soldiers, planters and states
men. They could no longer be soldiers now, and simple
farming was all that was left to the lords of the soil who
had ruled the Southern world,—who had all but ruled
the nation, at Washington, for decades,—and politics
were closed to them by laws that gave votes to
their former slaves and disfranchised all ex-Confederates
whether soldiers or civilians. The "bottom rail" was "on
top" and the struggle to restore the top rail to its former
position was to form the "Solid South" in these years of
unrest,[2] when the spoilsmen of the North and the car
pet-baggers, with the liberated Negroes, repressed the

[2] According to Thomas Nelson Page, the harsh treatment that
Jefferson Davis received also went far to "solidify" the feeling of
the South. Dr. Craven's record, *The Prison-Life of Jefferson Davis*
aroused intense resentment throughout the region and destroyed all
previous feeling against the Confederate president.

political life of the old master-class. The Southern whites were helpless in the presence of this alien horde, together with their own bushwhackers, deserters and outlaws, and the Ku Klux Klan inevitably rose to provide them indirectly with political work and reëstablish, if possible, the supremacy of the whites. With its emblem of the fiery cross, its uniform of sheets and pillow-cases, its masks and infantile mummery that frightened the Negroes, it undertook to "regulate" a region it could not control by law and retrieve for the disfranchised overlords the power they had lost.[3] The force of the revolt was proportional to the strength of a thwarted political sense that was almost a primary instinct with the people of the South.[4]

In a future that was not too remote the South of broken fortunes was to bring forth writers far better than those of the past,—with the exception of Poe and two or three others,—proving again that, as Ernest Renan observed about this time, "Discomfort is the principle of movement." The old South of the articulate class had been too happy, too satisfied merely to exist, to bestir its mind. On the other hand, these violent years of chaos, ruin and destitution, these years that preceded reconstruction, were too much for the writers. Many

[3] The Ku Klux Klan spread from Tennessee, where a group of young men started it, to break the "drab dullness" of their lives, in 1865. The "chief justice" of the Klan was Albert Pike of Arkansas, the poet who had written one of the versions of *Dixie,* and the "grand chaplain" was another poet who was also a Roman Catholic priest, Abram J. Ryan, the writer of songs of the war.

[4] "Little Compton observed that the young men [of Hillsborough, Georgia, before the war], no matter how young they might be, were absorbed in politics. They had the political history of the country at their tongues' ends, and the discussions they carried on were interminable. This interest extended to all classes: the planters discussed politics with their overseers; and lawyers, merchants, tradesmen, and gentlemen of elegant leisure discussed politics with each other. Schoolboys knew all about the Missouri Compromise, the Fugitive Slave Law and States' Rights."—Joel Chandler Harris, *Free Joe and Other Georgia Stories.*

had been Confederate soldiers,—Timrod, Hayne, George
Eggleston, Lanier, George W. Cable, Gildersleeve, Maurice Thompson,—and many were adrift after suffering
the miseries of war. Some were even homeless, and a
were obliged to construct again a basis on which to exi
before they could hope for any calm of mind. Simms
plantation-house The Woodlands had been destroye
by fire, though in this case the Northern general ha
given orders for the place to be spared, saying, "Simm
and his fame belong to the Union." The house and th
great library had been burned by the Negroes after th
Federal troops had left the region, but gone it was, lik
Paul Hamilton Hayne's fine house in Charleston, whic
had been burned to the ground in the bombardment o
the town. Maurice Thompson's house was in ashe
Richard Malcolm Johnston was poor and Henry Tim
rod was walking the streets in 1866, "weak for the wan
of a good meal," as he wrote to a friend. He had tried t
open a school in Charleston, but no one could pay hi
tuition-fees, and he had asked Hayne what were th
prospects in New York,—was there any chance of hi
finding employment there? His family was reduced t
"beggary, starvation, death," and he was willing to be
grocer's clerk or a hack-writer on a third-rate pape
Timrod was "swallowed up in distresses," Simms wrot
to Hayne, lonely and dying of consumption,—the manu
script of his translation of Catullus had been lost,—
while Hayne was scarcely better off, camping out as h
said he was in the "shanty" he had built in the wood
not far from Augusta. He could not send his son t
school, a Christmas turkey was a dream of the past an
the children saw plum-puddings only in visions, but a
least he was able to work on serenely while his wif
papered the little house and made chairs, tables, book
cases, benches and lampstands. He cherished the auto
graphs on the walls of Simms and Timrod, who cam

to see him, enraptured by the sight of new books in this literary dwelling,—so few had been seen in the South during the war-years. For Hayne was in touch with the publishers and continued to write: some of his best verse was written on this windy hill. In much of this, he followed Tennyson, the poet whose idylls of the feudal world appealed as deeply to the Southern mind as Scott, exhaling as he did the feeling of caste, revelling in traditions of knights and chivalry and the splendour that fell on ivied castle walls. It was there Hayne collected the poems of Timrod in 1873 when he was himself the oracle of the younger writers. He inspired Lanier with a faith in his own vocation.

But the veterans Hayne and Simms were exceptional cases. As Lanier wrote to Bayard Taylor, "With us of the younger generation of the South . . . pretty much the whole of life has been merely not dying," and most of them were a long time getting under way. The magazines of the South were dead, readers were fewer than ever and writers were driven to work for quick returns, and they were therefore apt to resort to rapid, shallow story-telling and the hasty historical writing that was required at the moment. For they were asked and they naturally wished to justify the Southern cause and uphold the ideals of the Confederacy for the world of the future. This was the motive of John Esten Cooke in his lives of Lee and Stonewall Jackson and the novels *Mohun* and *Surry of Eagle's-Nest* in which he continued his earlier work as a romancer. As a literary descendant of Sir Walter Scott,—like the more important writer Simms,—he had always cared for the past more than for the present, and he mingled idealized pictures of an older Virginian scene with his tales of Jackson, Lee, Stuart and Longstreet. One realistic theme in his romances was the conflict of relatives on both sides in the war, suggested perhaps by the fortunes of his own cousins and uncles, against one of whom, General Philip Cooke, he had all but fought himself with General "Jeb" Stuart, his uncle's son-in-law. For, like "Porte Crayon" Strother and George Henry Thomas, Virginians both, Philip Cooke was a general in the army of the North.[5]

With a present that one could scarcely face and without any visible future, only the past was tolerable to the Southern mind, and this came to seem all the more wonderful in contrast to the sordid facts that were virtually identical with reality in these years of trial. The so-called "plantation tradition" had been clearly established before the war, partly by way of defence of the cotton regime, and it bloomed afresh with the younger writers and with Southern novelists for decades to come who were under the spell of the cause that was lost with the war. It was scarcely checked by the critical mind that carried weight with the Northern writers who developed the methods of realism during these years, for, unlike Howells and Henry James, the Southerners were not open to the thinking of Europe or Matthew Arnold's ideas of the "provincial" and the "centre." In its dearth of new books the South missed Matthew Arnold, whose essays were appearing in the war-years and immediately after,[6] and it remained quite unaware of its own provinciality and the fertilizing doctrine of seeing things "as they are." The Southerners, moreover, had not been given to travelling as much as the Northerners travelled;

[5] Farragut, the great Northern admiral whose father was a Spaniard, had been also altogether a man of the South. Born a Tennessean, he had lived as a boy in New Orleans and was married and living in Virginia when the war broke out.

[6] "The current literature of those three or four years was a blank to most Confederates. Few books got across the line."—Basil L. Gildersleeve, *The Creed of the Old South.* Arnold's *Essays in Criticism* was published in 1865 and many of his other important prose writings appeared in the years following the war when the impoverished Southerners bought few books.

they seldom saw their country in the light of others, while, as for their own past, the cynosure of the Southern mind, they knew this mainly through personal memories alone, through household stories that were handed down by fable-loving aunts in place of the impersonal records, for example, of New England. St. George Tucker had pointed out that the lives of the old Virginian worthies had never been observed by their contemporaries, by diarists and thinkers: their talk had never been recorded, no "chiel" among them had taken notes or even collected their speeches in time to preserve them. Hayne made the same remark in Charleston, speaking of the times of Hugh Legaré, when he wrote his sketch of this worthy in 1869, referring to the "fast-waning traditions" of the days of the fame and prosperity of the town through whose streets he "shrank," as he said, "like a stranger and alien." Culture, refinement, hospitality, wit, genius and social virtue had seemed to have taken up their lasting abode there; and he saw that Legaré had prophesied truly when he said, "We are, I am quite sure, the last of the race of South Carolina." But what Hayne regretted most, now that the orators and statesmen were gone, was that their names and fame were perishing too, for their words had scarcely been recorded and their lives were unwritten. Calhoun lived in his writings still, but Legaré was the only other exception,—his works alone had ever been gathered together. A generation later, Boston men were also to lament the passing of the prestige of their city, but at least the Bostonians had amply attested their progress and were always to know whereof they spoke. In the South much of the reality of the past was utterly forgotten or swallowed up and blurred and confused by legend. Because it was not really known, it was idealized the more and lent itself to a singularly deceptive treatment.

Thus for years the Southern writers were marked by a curious unreality that led to a kind of revenge on the part of their successors, who seemed to take a savage joy in tearing the veil from the picture of life that others had created so fondly in this heyday of illusions. What Mark Twain called the "Sir Walter disease," [7] which had, he said, so large a hand in making the Southern character before the war,—so that "in great measure" Scott was "responsible for the war,"—this disease raged still in the unreconstructed South in manners, names and customs as well as in books. Mark Twain, a Southerner himself, in full revolt against the South and its "maudlin middle-age romanticisms," as he described them, poked fun at its "absurd chivalry business" although to the end of his life he retained the peculiar sensibility that characterized it. For was not his feeling for Joan of Arc the chivalrous feeling precisely and quite in the vein of a man of Joan's own time? He said the South needed another Cervantes and attempted the role several times, when he pictured in *The American Claimant,* for instance, the Rowena-Ivanhoe College where Sally Sellers was known as Gwendolen. The South was full of these castellated buildings with towers, turrets and an imitation moat and with everything redolent of royalty and names out of Scott. As for Colonel Sellers, who thought of himself as the Earl of Rossmore, he was a Southern mediævalist on the Western frontier.

---

[7] "Against the crimes of the French Revolution and of Bonaparte may be set two compensating benefactions: the Revolution broke the chains of the *ancien régime* and of the Church and made a nation of abject slaves a nation of freemen, and Bonaparte instituted the setting of merit above birth.

"Then comes Sir Walter Scott . . . sets the world in love with dreams and phantoms, with decayed and swinish forms of religion, with decayed and degraded systems of government . . . sham grandeurs . . . He did . . . more real and lasting harm, perhaps, than any other individual that ever wrote."—Mark Twain, *Life on the Mississippi.*

Mark Twain liked to contrast this "chivalry" with the facts of life as he saw them in the South,—in the newspaper-clippings he took such pleasure in assembling,—the duels with butcher-knives fought in Virginia, the braining of a man with a club, the murder of a general and his son on the street in Tennessee. Later in *A Connecticut Yankee in King Arthur's Court* he attacked these mediævalist notions directly. Meanwhile, in *The Galaxy*, he described in 1870 a tournament that was held in Virginia during that year in which knights of the Shenandoah and the Blue Ridge with tinsel decorations and broomstick lances exhibited, he said, an "absurdity gone crazy." What could he think of modern men who accepted the mailed and plumed knight of romance while rejecting the unpolished verdict whereby history exposed him as an ignoramus, a ruffian and a braggart?

Perhaps only a Southerner could have been so angry with all these illusions of the Southern mind. But in satirizing day-dreams that replaced realities at a time when so much that was real was far too distasteful for many to look in the face, Mark Twain anticipated the feeling of a later generation. Even the Confederacy had been a kind of day-dream,—except in so far as it spoke for the interests of cotton,—for the states, Virginia, South Carolina, Louisiana and all the rest, were the real objects of the passionate devotion it aroused. Its vision of the future had scarcely more substance than Sidney Lanier's vision of Macon as a great art-centre whose streets were to be lined with statues. Lanier was one of a host of Southerners who lived in a world of make-believe and his peculiar fantasies typified the South, from the days when he organized the Macon Archers and drilled them as Froissart said he should to the days when he shared in a tournament in 1879. When, two years before his death, he addressed the "knights" in the Shenandoah valley, charging them "to do after the good and leave the evil, and ever to live nobly in the service of their fair ladies," was he not still living in the fantasy-world in which he had drilled the Macon boys who thought of themselves as English bowmen of Crécy?[8] When Burke felt, during the French Revolution, that the age of chivalry was gone, his feeling was closely connected with historical fact, but with what did the feeling of Lanier connect when he repeated this remark at another historical juncture seventy years later? In convincing himself that he was descended from a family of Laniers who were court musicians and artists of the Stuart kings, was he less willingly duped than Colonel Sellers, who held his supposititious earldom by as good a right? The biographers of J. E. B. Stuart, the "Flower of Cavaliers," who asserted that he was a lineal descendant of Prince Rupert revealed a type of the will-to-believe that flourished like broomsedge in the South, where the aspect of things "as they are" was so generally ignored. Was it not ignored because the Southerners had lived apart and remote from the world, unvisited, unvisiting, rapt in their impracticable dream?— at the core of which lay an ugly fact, which sensitive people could not face, and had never faced, "as it was," with its ramifications. When by chance in Alabama Mrs. Chesnut of the *Diary from Dixie* saw a Negress sold on the auction-block, the spectacle made her, as she said, "faint" and "seasick." She had to sit down to discipline

---

[8] Another Southern poet, Maurice Thompson, and his brother were the principal agents in the revival of the modern sport of archery. Thompson, who wrote *Alice of Old Vincennes*, was the author of several books about it, *The Witchery of Archery* among them, which led people to welcome archery as a real sport at a time when croquet was the only outdoor game.

Maurice Thompson's poems, like Lanier's, were full of images drawn in all probability from his reading of Froissart,—cross-bows, old yew-bows, "the flaunting flag and the crashing lance," tournaments and troubadours, Crécy and Agincourt.

her "wild thoughts." How far had she realized what slavery meant when one glimpse of the naked reality could have shaken a mind as clear and firm as hers?

Thus the "plantation tradition" had thriven in the days that made the old South an "unfinished fairy-story," as a later writer called it,[9] and it continued to thrive in days when the fairy-story was finished indeed but no new theme had arisen to possess the mind. Southern society in many respects still suggested the masquerade that W. C. Falkner described in *The White Rose of Memphis,* a vastly popular mystery-story about a voyage down the Mississippi from Memphis to New Orleans a few years after the war. The steamboat-company had organized it to amuse the passengers, who wore masks and fancy costumes, concealing their names, picnicking on the banks at landings while the cotton was loaded on the boat, strolling in the beech-groves and dancing on the greensward. The queen held her court on board and young ladies who knew *Lalla Rookh* by heart acted scenes from *Mazeppa* with the young men, while they were all disguised as Ingomar, Ivanhoe, Sir Walter Raleigh and other knights and ladies of chivalrous times. Behind the masks a real drama went on that involved a murderer and a desperado who were disguised with the others in the general rout, and here too the masquerade suggested the actual Mississippi that one saw when the author's great-grandson stripped away the masks. One could not say that William Faulkner saw only the murderer and the desperado,[10] but he saw more than one *might* have seen of old men who nail themselves up in attics and aunts who slide down rain-pipes and run off with horse-traders, and this would never have been the

[9] William Alexander Percy, *Lanterns on the Levee.*

[10] In *Absalom, Absalom,* for instance, a novel of a period and setting closely corresponding with those of *The White Rose of Memphis.*

case, perhaps, if the South had been more realistic in earlier days. In those times Southern gentlewomen were almost invariably pictured in fiction with exquisite hands always folded in their laps, when they were often as busy in fact as Eliza Pinckney of South Carolina who at sixteen transacted the business of three plantations. This was the lady two of whose sons were generals in the Revolution and who changed the whole face of the province when she discovered that indigo could be grown there with profit, when, versed in the difficult art of raising it, she distributed seeds to the other planters whose houses she visited on the rivers in her long canoe. Six Negroes swung the paddles, singing in cadence. Eliza Pinckney experimented with ginger, observed the habits of the mocking-birds and showed a fine taste in music and in poetry too, happy to find that, writing for Italy, Virgil had many times over written in a way that suited Carolina as well. For, entertained by his charming pen and what she called his pleasing diction, she studied agriculture also in this Roman poet. He would have delighted in turn in such a reader.

There were never many Eliza Pinckneys, but there were countless women in the South who were far more stirring than the phantoms that appeared in the romances, in which the men were so often Byronic like the gloomy and world-weary Mordaunt, with his taste for Arabic, in *Surry of Eagle's-Nest*. Mysterious and grand, with his dark proud eyes, Mordaunt was another St. Elmo Murray, the hero of the romance that bore his name. The author of this was Augusta J. Evans of Mobile, where Henry Timrod met her when he was a war-correspondent with General Beauregard's army in Alabama. St. Elmo, fierce, cynical, morose, had a basilisk's eye, and his midnight orgies and habitual excesses had stamped his Mephistophelean face, while his evil charm was as powerful as his unhallowed mind. The costly *bizarrerie* of his house in Georgia suggested Lucanian Sybaris, opulent and vast as it was, with its Egyptian museum, its vaulted passages, high Gothic windows, Moresque frescoes, rotunda and park that was filled with rare animals from Lapland, India and Peru. His favorite horse, called Tamerlane, had been brought by him from the Kirghese steppes on one of the long journeys that led him to the back of beyond, and the whisperings of his conscience were as faint and unexpected as the dim reverberating echoes from Morella's tomb. But there was a core of nobility in him, as one might have guessed, which Edna, the precious little prig, brought out in the end. Edna, a prodigy of learning too, with her Greek, Hebrew and Chaldee, was a mistress of Norse myths, runes, scalds and sagas as well as the writings of Machiavelli,—so like St. Elmo in his way,—and of archæology, ethnology, philology and what not. She became a great and famous novelist whom amorous baronets pursued at intervals when infatuated editors left her alone.

Of all the Southern romances of the time *St. Elmo* was the hugest success,—towns, hotels, steamboats and plantations were named for the book,—the Cinderella story of the little barefoot Tennessee girl who won "all this and heaven too." For Edna was a prodigy of virtue as well as of learning, and the fantasy, which recalled *Jane Eyre,* was obviously Southern: there was something of John Randolph as of Rochester in the character of the hero. In his Gothic madness he even suggested Poe's Roderick Usher. Moreover, the picture of the Georgian village with its coterie of "blues" was a Southerner's reply to the claims of triumphant New England,[11] to which,—or New York,—her countrypeo-

---

[11] As St. Elmo scornfully remarked, "Not even egoistic, infallible 'Brain Town,'—that self-complacent and pretentious 'Hub,'—can show a more ambitious covey of literary fledglings."

ple had been taunted with having to resort for their French and German books, for the opera and for pictures. St. Elmo himself preferred to read the London papers, having no use whatever for *"soi-disant* republics." The story had been shaped in every way to please the Southern public in the year that followed the defeat of 1865, when few would have welcomed the pictures of life that sprang from the realities of the local scene which other writers were to produce in time.

It was true that already a few writers had begun to recall these realities,—so many of them swept away by fire and sword,—and Dr. George Bagby was perhaps the first, the Virginia state librarian, who wrote his most moving sketches after the war. He liked to portray the rambling old homesteads, under their immemorial oaks, with moss-grown shingles black from the rain and the sun, that had grown by the adding of a wing here and the tucking on there of a woodshed until the first building was lost in a crowd of additions. In *The Old Virginia Gentleman* he described the "five types" of country squires, not all of whom were stout, bluff and fond of juleps, the company that was always coming, with beaux to see the grown-up girls, the neighbours, the friends, the strangers, the visiting kinsfolk. He brought back the days when the high-swung coach with its great C-springs set out for "Uncle Randolph's" or "Cousin Tom's," the old mansion that stood in its clearing in the forest surrounded by gently swelling knolls and the broad lapping leaves of the mottled tobacco. Some of the famous great houses survived, Westover, Gunston Hall, Kenmore, Chatham, designed by Sir Christopher Wren, with many that were humbler, the Rosewell of the Pages and the Stratford of the Lees, rebuilt in part from Queen Caroline's privy purse. While Bagby was the first no doubt to picture Virginia as it was, others were fondly dwelling on these scenes already, happy that so many of the gentlefolk clung to their devastated farms, though sometimes their houses let in the winter winds. With courteous old-fashioned manners and hearts that were often both stout and kind, they hugged their ancestral customs, living simply, putting up with ruined barns and gates that would not swing, loving as they did the sight of growing tobacco. In a corner of the barn-yard or the orchard perhaps the old family coach was going to pieces, with its pale yellow body buried in bri-ers and weeds, the refuge of the brooding hen and the roosting turkey, a mute survivor of the day when the commonwealth was a cousin-wealth, as Gildersleeve, a visitor from South Carolina, remarked.

In these homesteads, with their pictures by Herring and Morland, with two or three dogs by every chair, one found bespectacled doctors with spurs and stocks, and old fox-hunters, familiar with the language of their hounds, who despised the false tales of their former lux-ury and splendour. All this had really amounted to was an abundance of home-grown food, a julep before breakfast and a black boy to pull off their boots, with no engagements that need interfere with anything else one had in mind, fishing, backgammon or gunning for turkeys or squirrels. In one of these houses, with its air of repose, Edward Eggleston as a boy, visiting his grand-father, had learned his Latin and Greek, and Jessie Frémont had been born in another, in the Valley of Vir-ginia, her grandfather's Lexington house in a fine old park. She recalled the buzzing of the spinning-wheels, the sewing-rooms, the weaving-rooms, the dyes that were taken from the sumac and the green bark of the walnuts, and the day when her mother, for reasons of conscience, along with the Fairfaxes, freed her slaves and promised to maintain them until they were self-supporting. Her father, Senator Benton, refused two large inheritances because he would have to take the slaves with the land.

The senator, who had read his Greek Testament at eight, taught his children their Plutarch and Homer in the travelling-carriage in Virginia, in the house at St. Louis, on the decks of Mississippi steamboats sailing down the river. As Mrs. Frémont later wrote, "The gods and goddesses descended on us everywhere."

Many books, as time went on, recalled these ante-bellum days, but few appeared immediately after the war. The defeated South indeed seemed all but voiceless, and years passed before Southern writers returned to the period of "reconstruction" and its lawlessness, demoralization, corruption and fraud. Then, in books like *Gabriel Tolliver* by Joel Chandler Harris and the *Red Rock* of Thomas Nelson Page, they pictured the insolence of the carpet-baggers who passed laws to suit themselves and the chaos and general injustice of the conquerors' regime. Meanwhile, Northerners swarmed over the South, journalists, agents of prospective investors, speculators with plans for railroads, sportsmen, artists, business men looking for marble-quarries, promoters of new health-resorts, invalids who were ordered by their doctors to St. Augustine and Charleston. Some were sent to the pine woods of North Carolina or Georgia. There were others who, like John Hay, bought a Florida orange-grove or, like Whitelaw Reid, a plantation in Louisiana, or who, like Harriet Beecher Stowe, made their home on the St. John's river and shared in imagination the feelings of their neighbours. Mrs. Stowe did not agree with the former abolitionists who wished to impose Negro suffrage by force on the South, and she grieved over the corrupt politicians who played with the Negroes fast and loose and filled their heads with delusions. There were many kinds of invaders from the North and even the Yankee tombstone-cutter whom Albion W. Tourgee imagined [12] might have been real,

[12] In *The Grave of Tante Angélique*.

the man who set out with a horse and wagon and a box
of letter-stencils planning to re-cut the old stones in the
Southern graveyards. Tourgee himself, who was also
a Northerner, a lawyer from Ohio, was the first to describe these evil days, though he was himself a carpet-
bagger, a judge who had settled in North Carolina,
with a fascinated but rancorous aversion to most things
Southern. Cocksure, censorious and unfair, he was am-
bushed by the Ku Klux Klan; he was ostracized and his
life was in constant danger, while, as an ardent Negro-
phile, jealous on behalf of the former slaves, he invariably sided with them against the whites. He had his
rough and ready reply to the question of miscegenation
which Anna E. Dickinson discussed in her novel *What
Answer?*, a reformer's sympathetic tale of the marriage
of a rich young man to a Negro girl who might have
been Toinette. This was the heroine of Tourgee's first
novel, the story of a slave-girl with whom her young
owner falls in love, a book begun in 1869, ten years before *A Fool's Errand* appeared, and suggesting the same
answer that Miss Dickinson gave to the question. The
"fool's errand" of the better-known novel of reconstruction times,—unreadable later, exciting when it first appeared,—was the whole endeavour to impose on the
South the ideas of the Northern outsider which Tourgee had been the first to champion in earlier years.

Another Northern observer of the South who was
vastly more gifted than Tourgee was Constance Fenimore Woolson, a young woman from New Hampshire,
a grand-niece of James Fenimore Cooper who had also
lived for a while in Ohio before she visited the Southern coast and mountains. In the West she had seen the
Zoarite community, the subject of her first sketch, which
appeared in 1870 in *Harper's Magazine,* and she had
spent several summers in the family cottage at Mackinaw island, in the straits between Lake Michigan and

Lake Huron. Later she had travelled and lived with her mother at various places in the Carolinas, in Tennessee, Georgia and especially St. Augustine and Charleston. With her singular gift of minute observation and a talent for analysis that was just appearing in other New England writers, she studied the relations of the Southern people with the visitors from the Northern states who were flocking to the South in the years following the war.

Miss Woolson, stirred by Bret Harte and the movement of regional consciousness to which his tales of the Sierras had given rise, studied with an eager eye and a constant feeling for the picturesque the peculiar qualities of the regions where she lived in turn. In her last phase she wrote about Italy, in her best phase about the South, while she began by writing of the Great Lakes region, preceding her novels and stories by travel-sketches in every case, studying the background before she filled it in. The country around the Great Lakes, the setting of Cooper's *The Pathfinder,* appeared in twenty-three of Miss Woolson's tales, in one of which, *Castle Nowhere,* she suggested her great-uncle; for the log-fortress floating in the lake where the old wrecker lived with his adopted daughter, hidden away in the fogs, was like Hutter's castle. Others were influenced by Bret Harte, of whom one of the characters wrote in his diary, "He shows us the good in the heart of the outcast,"—one of the secrets of Bret Harte's prodigious success,—a touch that was most clearly marked in the story *The Lady of Little Fishing,* in which the rough lumbermen's lives were transformed by a woman. The events of the stories all occurred in the years before the Civil War when the Western forts were kept up with military state and the "goat-like craggy guns of lofty Mackinaw," as Melville called them, dominated the crescent-shaped harbour. The little white stronghold, perched on the brow of

the cliff, overlooked the moss-grown relics of the old
French village, the handful of cottages that remained
on the beach beside the desolate warehouses where the
trappers had been fitted out for their journeys westward.
Memories of the merry fur-trading times lingered about
their ancient frames and the peaked roofs that had
echoed with the voyageurs' songs, and the old Indian
agency had still been there when Miss Woolson was a
girl, surrounded by a heavy stockade pierced with loop-
holes. There Schoolcraft had collected his Indian legends[13] and there a French veteran lived, a grenadier of
Napoleon, in one of her stories, like the heroine of her
first novel, *Anne,* the daughter of an army-surgeon who
had grown up in the woods of the wild little island. The
French note of the trading-post still clung to Mackinaw,
where one could easily find or imagine a priest like Père
Michaux who recalled the seventeenth century and Père
Marquette.

When later she wrote about the South, Miss Woolson
was glad of any excuse to bring her characters back to
the Great Lakes region with its tangle of islands, channels, wilderness and marshes, bordering the vast wild
northland where dog-trains moved over the white expanse and the forest was thick and dark, pathless and
soundless. Mackinaw, with its high bracing air, had impressed her imagination deeply, the pines and the aro-
matic cedars, the silvery fogs, the well-trodden Indian
trails, the larches and the tall spruce-spires, the bald
Northern cliffs bathed in sunshine. She caught the
beauty of the short fierce summer in her pastoral romance of Anne and Rast, a *Paul and Virginia* placed on
this boreal island, while there as well as in the story of
Jeanette, the half-breed French-Indian girl, she stud-

---

[13] Miss Woolson's first piece of original writing was a poem in the
manner of *Hiawatha,* which was intimately connected with Schoolcraft and these early associations of hers.

ied the conflicts and the mingling of races in the region. Always interested in the remains of European cultures that were to be found lingering on the fringes of the country, she observed in Florida the relations of the Americans and the Spaniards that had struck Bret Harte in California two decades before. The Catholic and Protestant traditions were opposed there also. But she was more concerned in the South with the contrast and connections of the old American Southerners and the invaders from the North. So many were the visitors, especially consumptives, who flocked to Florida during these years that the poet Sidney Lanier wrote a guide-book about it, or rather a collection of travel-sketches and historical essays with facts for tourists, advice for the ill and details of farming for investors. In order to prepare for the book he penetrated into little-known regions of the state, with the Indian river country and the Silver Springs, the haunts of egrets and alligators and water-turkeys that had once delighted Audubon and Bartram.[14] He wrote well of the great pine-forests. One of his passages on the pines of the lowlands paralleled Ruskin's tribute to the pines of the mountains.

Many Northerners like Miss Woolson were drawn to the unhappy South by affection, compassion, admiration or the charm of the life there, among them Bret Harte, who lectured there before he went abroad and who excelled in picturing Southern people. Colonel Starbottle and Jack Hamlin, his favourite characters, Southerners both, were to reappear in his final collection of stories, and in *Sally Dows* he caught the atmos-

---

[14] Inevitably the great Southern swamps offered opportunities to writers for some of their finest bits of descriptive composition. There were many such passages in the stories of George W. Cable describing the marshes and bayous of Louisiana. See also Lanier's *The Marshes of Glynn* and Miss Woolson's decription in *East Angels* of the "South Devil" swamp near St. Augustine, with its steaming, swarming tropical life, intoxicating perfumes, dank watery aisles and beautiful, venomous plants, vines, snakes and insects.

phere of a Georgian plantation and village almost as well as Joel Chandler Harris. In this tale a young man from the North appeared with capital to invest, but it was Sally, the "Southern belle," with her deep knowledge of agriculture, through whom the restored plantation flourished again. Bret Harte, with his pleasure in types that recalled the spell of old deeds and historical names, was impressed by the frank and easy manners of the South, the spacious, dawdling Southern ways, the unbounded faith in yesterday, the indifference the Southerners continued to feel for the morrow. Half wishing he could live there, he wrote to his wife from the Virginia Springs describing the dowagers and gouty old uncles in white flannel, people he had not supposed could be found anywhere out of the theatre and who were within four hundred miles of New York. There was one octogenarian, for example, in the dress of the early century, with ruffles and a bag-wig complete, with whom he sat down to dinner in 1873,—who had visited the springs for the last forty years and remembered "President Madison, sir" and asked what he thought of the poems of Matthew Prior. Bret Harte looked back upon Colonel Starbottle as an utter failure beside this reality. Miss Woolson relished these types too and drew them in her stories, the young ladies with their old-fashioned accomplishments and notions of deportment, the old gentlemen who were so careful and correct in their way of speaking.[15] Every sentence that fell from their lips had a beginning, a middle and an end, and at home they fondly turned the

[15] "There is nothing so majestic and slow-moving today in all our quick America as an old South Carolina gentleman, for instance, making a few remarks to you in your parlour, or on the Charleston battery. His words, his periods, his very thoughts are all old English. There is no use in trying to hurry him, and much loss. For, if you will only lay aside your modern impatience, and listen, your ears will soon be charmed by the very language of Johnson and Addison."
—Constance Fenimore Woolson, in the "Contributors' Club" of the *Atlantic Monthly*.

pages of their Plutarch and Montaigne and quoted
choice passages from them on every occasion. Miss Woolson liked to describe ladies who read the letters of
Horace Walpole while they dwelt on their own children's "English traits," along with old gallants with
memories of the belles, each a toast far and wide, who
had reigned in the low-country manor-houses. They
never discussed American news,—in "polite oblivion"
since the war,—and they joined with others in sub-
scribing to the London weekly papers, preferring their
tone to that of the American journals. Paul Hamilton
Hayne was one of many in regretting, in a sonnet, that
his forbears had not remained in England.

Miss Woolson's imagination lingered over the relics
of the ancient South, the tumble-down battered houses
and forlorn plantations, the little churches, lost in the
woods, with low stone doorways overgrown and often
with high pews and mouldering funeral hatchments.
The woodland graveyards of these sanctuaries appeared
in her stories again and again, the quaintly emblazoned
tablets and colonial tombs and sometimes the royal in-
signia in faded gilt, with the wrecked old mansions that
stood near by, perhaps in ruined rice-lands, amid deso-
lated fields and broken dykes. Such was the dwelling
on the Georgia sea-island that sidled and leaned in *Ju-
piter Lights* with one of its roofless wings falling into
the cellar, while the massive kitchens underground were
still to be seen, with remains of the Dutch flower-garden
and the terraces and fishpond. After St. Augustine,
Charleston especially attracted Miss Woolson, crumbling
as it was but aristocratic still with the watchman aloft
on the tower of St. Michael's calling through the night,
"Ten and three-e quarters! A-all's well!" She had the
keys of "neighbourhood libraries" that stood where two
roads crossed, lonely and forsaken now, out in the country, and she spent many an afternoon with the French

and English classics that filled the shelves in dusty morocco editions. She had been predisposed to love the Southern world of the "better days," the "golden age," the times "before the war," because she had inherited Fenimore Cooper's conservative temper and feeling for caste, his inborn liking for the old agrarian order. She shared her great-uncle's strong distaste for the causes and practices of the new generation, his hatred of divorce, his scorn of woman's rights, in this resembling the Southerners themselves, the brightest even of the younger minds, who were almost as conservative in temper and taste as their elders. For one, the poet Sidney Lanier, addressing the graduates of Furlow College, a school for girls, in 1869, warned them against the feminist cause and said that men would cease to love them if they forgot that the home was their true sphere. How sure was the paragon Edna in Miss Evans's *St. Elmo* that woman's rights were an affair of the "old maids of New England," the "ridiculous clamour" of a few unamiable wives.[16] Miss Woolson was deeply in sympathy with this turn of mind. She would have liked the Atlanta people who showed their contempt for modern inventions by describing the railroad station as the "car-shed" and the "old gentleman with the black stock" for whom Thomas Carlyle was "not a gentleman," who looked upon this as the principal fact about him. She felt at home with ladies for whom it was despicable not to be poor when all Southerners of "our class" were impoverished as a matter of course and for whom the future, so anxiously viewed by the restless Northern mind, never assumed a place of supreme importance. She felt above all the "charm and hold" that fused together the

[16] "America has no Bentham, Bailey, Hare or Mill to lend countenance or strength to the ridiculous clamour raised by a few unamiable and wretched wives, and as many embittered, disappointed old maids of New England."—Edna Earl, in Augusta J. Evans's *St. Elmo.*

separate parts—the "wonderful interpenetration"—of the old feudal order of which Walt Whitman wrote so well and the want of which he so deplored in the new democratic world that was taking its place.[17]

With her quick intelligence and her feeling for shades, for delicate points of language and tone, Miss Woolson caught the relations of the Southern men and women with the Northerners of a score of types in Virginia, Florida, North Carolina, whom she had herself observed with a curious eye. In a later novel, *Horace Chase,* one of the best of all her books, she anticipated Thomas Wolfe in describing Asheville, in which the young capitalist from the North who falls in love with the Southern girl sees the "Lone Star" of future mountain-resorts. The admirably realized Horace Chase was one of the bold post-war promoters who were building railroads and exploiting the now unified country, tender and kind to his family and friends, as hard as flint in business, a millionaire many times over at thirty-nine. He had made one fortune in baking-powder, another in a mine, another in lumber, and was making a fortune in steamers when he appeared in Asheville, and he meant to turn into a watering-place this little hill-village that was reached only by a stage in 1873. He foresaw that Northerners would flock to these mountains that made the Catskills look like a suburb, the White Mountains like ornamental rock-work and the Adiron-

[17] "So far, our democratic society . . . possesses nothing . . . to make up for that glowing, blood-throbbing, religious, social, emotional, artistic, indefinable, indescribably beautiful charm and hold which fused the separate parts of the old feudal societies together, in their wonderful interpenetration, in Europe and Asia, of love, belief and loyalty, running one way like a living weft and picturesque responsibility, duty and blessedness, running like a warp the other way. (In the Southern states, under slavery, much of the same.) . . . What is more terrible . . . than the total want of any such fusion and mutuality . . . between the comparatively few successful rich and the great mass of the unsuccessful, the poor?"— Walt Whitman, *Collect.*

dacks a woodlot, and he liked, as he said, to "work a big deal through": he might have been Henry James's Christopher Newman before this hero of *The American* retired with his pile. Some of the characters in *East Angels,* Miss Woolson's finest novel, were also concerned with the material development of the South, planning canals and the draining of swamps, dredging the everglades, raising fruit or surveying, like Lucian Spencer, for the railroad that was coming. Others had been ordered to St. Augustine for neuralgia or consumption, while others still had come down as teachers, tourists, winter visitors who regarded themselves as the discoverers of a new Riviera. The little old town on the coast had much of the charm of San Remo or Nice for them. They found the blue over the silver beaches as languorous as the sky over Capri, and the old Spanish houses with their thick coquina walls had for them a flavour of tradition and legend. They delighted in the orange-walks like tunnels through the glossy leaves, the hedges of Spanish bayonet, the magnolias and the date-palms, and their affairs were soon involved with those of the Spanish population and the indolent Minorcans and the Seminoles who were natives of the region. It was the strictly American Southerners in their unworldly seclusion, in their walled gardens with live oaks and Cherokee roses, simple, stately, innocently proud, calmly convinced of their own importance, towards whom the invaders from the North were mostly drawn. Miss Woolson like to contrast these women, brooding in their ruined houses, with the more mundane New Yorkers and the Vermonter Mrs. Thorne, who supported life as best she could on a diet of Emerson and *Paradise Lost,* permanently exiled as she was in this Southern world. To the fierce and scornful Gardis Duke, the enchantingly beautiful Southern girl, all the young men from the North were despots and vandals.

Miss Woolson was a highly conscious writer, careful, skilful, subtle, with a sensitive, clairvoyant feeling for human nature, with the gift of discriminating observation that characterized Howells and Henry James and the talent for analysis that was also appearing in New England. A reader and follower of James,—and Turgenev,—she cared mainly for "motives" and "mental states,"—"why a man or woman," as she said, "does . . . so and so,"—and her later stories with Italian backgrounds reflected her walks and talks with James whom she knew in England and Italy, and especially in Florence. Like James's own Italian stories, they all contained American characters, art-students from the West and especially mothers and daughters, perplexed by the problems of living in a strange milieu, and most of them had the fine traits for which in *Partial Portraits* James praised the writings of Constance Fenimore Woolson. But, while she was good in other surroundings, she was surely best in her stories of the South, for which she had a deep and genuine feeling, fascinated as she was by its splendour and carelessness, its tropical plants, flowers, odours and birds and the pathos and beauty of the old order as she saw it in decay.

CHAPTER XVII

THE SOUTH: LANIER AND JOEL CHANDLER HARRIS

WHEN General Lee died in 1870 with three of the older Southern writers,—William Gilmore Simms, Augustus Longstreet and John P. Kennedy, the author of *Swallow Barn*,—the South was finding its voice again, a voice that was to grow in strength till it reached the remotest corners of the national mind. The struggles of the war had roused the local consciousness and fertilized and quickened the thinking and feeling of the region, while slavery had passed with the exactions and problems to which it had more and more given rise, an obsession that had largely absorbed the intellectual forces. The young poet Maurice Thompson, rejoicing over its disappearance, expressed a thrill of relief that others shared,[1] thankful as he also was that the South had ceased to battle "against the nineteenth century" and the "whole phalanx of progress." For the first time since Jefferson's days its mind was in rapport with the general

---

[1] "I am a Southerner;
    I love the South; I dared for her
    To fight from Lookout to the sea,
    With her proud banner over me:
    But from my lips thanksgiving broke,
    As God in battle-thunder spoke,
    And that Black Idol, breeding drouth,
    And dearth of human sympathy,
  Throughout the sweet and sensuous South,
      Was, with its chains and human yoke,
  Blown hellward from the cannon's mouth,
      While Freedom cheered behind the smoke!"
                    —Maurice Thompson, *To the South.*

mind and movement of the rest of the world, free and open to criticism and the exchange of ideas, and it responded rapidly to the new conditions. What Sidney Lanier said of himself might have been said of the South as well: "Day by day a thousand vital elements rill through my soul. Day by day the secret deep forces gather, which will presently display themselves in bending leaf and waxy petal and in useful fruit and grain."

At the time when Lanier was writing this,[2] he was launched already in his career, Richard Malcolm Johnston had written his first Georgian sketches, George W. Cable was deep in the study of Creole life and Joel Chandler Harris was working on a paper in Savannah. Three years later, in 1873, the editor of *Scribner's Magazine*, Dr. Holland, sent the journalist Edward King on a mission of discovery through the South to gather materials for articles on the effects of the war. He was also asked to look for new Southern writers. Edward King, who had gone abroad to report the Franco-Prussian war, had previously described in *My Paris* an earlier visit to the city to which all good Americans went when they died, one of those collections of lively sketches in which they have always liked to recall the first or the last time they "saw Paris." Now, preparing for another book on the economic South, he met, among various writers, George W. Cable, working at the stories of New Orleans life that he gladly offered King, who passed them on in turn to Dr. Holland. The immediate result was the publication of *'Sieur George* in *Scribner's,* the opening in 1873 of the long connection of the magazine with the story-tellers and poets of the South; for, first or last, along with Cable, *Scribner's* published Maurice Thompson, Irwin Russell, Richard Malcolm Johnston, Sidney Lanier and Thomas Nelson Page,—a student of law at the moment in Charlottesville,—together with John

[2] In a letter to his wife, 1870.

Esten Cooke, the old irreconcilable,[3] who was otherwise a gentle and kindly man of letters. At his home in the Shenandoah valley Cooke seemed as unwarlike as his old charger grazing on the lawn. The Southern writers could no longer complain that they were unsupported, as Hayne complained both after and before the war,[4] for they now had a national public that was eager to hear about Southern life and the Negroes, the mountaineers, the Creoles and the crackers. Northern readers were delighted to find that the country abounded in worlds of romance that were wholly unconnected with the Knickerbockers and the Pilgrims, worlds of picturesque adventure and odd or spacious ways of life they had either known nothing about or had forgotten. Responding as it were to the invitation, the Southern writers developed soon a professional, disciplined attitude that few had assumed in the easy-going earlier days when criticism scarcely existed in the South, rarer even than it was in the North at present. The day had passed when, as Bagby observed, any and every Southern writer was said to have shown "genius of no common order." The new writers no longer pictured preposterous dreamlands of romance that professed to represent Southern

[3] "Grand humbug of celebrations!—in which the South having no independence to celebrate takes no part! Singular how completely we rebellious ones have come to despise the United States, their flag and all concerning them."—John Esten Cooke, July 4th, 1870.

[4] "In my section, all Litterateurs are (*generally*) despised. A fourth rate lawyer, a *hundredth* rate Politician would rank above the truest and noblest of Poets . . . Thank the beneficent gods who appointed *your* birthplace northward of the 'great line' . . . In *my* most unfortunate section, Literature has never had room or air to breathe . . . I have worked for 20 years without advice, sympathy or help of any kind."—From letters of Paul Hamilton Hayne to Bayard Taylor and John T. Trowbridge, 1869–1877.

In 1875, Hayne says in his native city of Charleston the people "with *tremendous* effort have succeeded" in ordering fifteen copies of his poems. He had previously said in 1855 that he was "almost utterly alone . . . so far as mental sympathies are concerned" in Charleston.

life. They recreated the true Southern scenery and people.

The first real voice of the emerging South was the Georgian poet Lanier, who settled in 1873 in Baltimore, always a centre of Southern writers since the days of Francis Scott Key, Edward Coote Pinkney, the poet, and William Wirt. The Austrian poet Lenau had stopped there on his way to a farm in Ohio, and there "Horse Shoe Robinson" Kennedy had lived and Poe had lived and died, while the *Southern Review* was published in the seventies there. Basil L. Gildersleeve was connected with Johns Hopkins, at which Lanier himself was a lecturer later, and Richard Malcolm Johnston for a while had a school in the town. John B. Tabb lived near by, the poet of the future who had been sent to Baltimore to study music just after the war and remained to become a Roman Catholic priest. It was their common feeling for music that had brought Tabb and Lanier together when they were prisoners of war, after serving in the Confederate navy,—they were scarcely more than boys,—and they had been captured with their ships running blockade. Both had been gravely ill when Tabb heard Lanier's flute in a distant corner of the camp at Point Lookout prison and thenceforth for a number of months they were constantly together. Lanier, hiding his flute in his sleeve, had smuggled it into the prison-camp, for he was a musical prodigy who as a child was an organist, a pianist, a violinist and a guitarist also. It was his gift as a flute-player that had brought him to Baltimore, where he was first flute in the orchestra and a notable performer, one of the most notable performers no doubt of his time, whose playing Joel Chandler Harris, hearing him in Macon, described as "ravishing, enchanting, mysterious and weird." Lanier, already known as a poet, was a victim of the tuberculosis that he had caught in the war as a result of exposure, and his

life was a desperate race with death,—he was to perish
at thirty-nine,—as well as a dreary struggle to make a
living. Between bouts of work as a lawyer in Macon, a
schoolmaster and plantation-tutor, he had sought all
over the South for a favourable climate, in Texas, Florida, Alabama, the Virginia springs, the Tennessee mountains, the pines of North Carolina and his native scene.
Georgia always remained his homeland, the setting of
his finest poems and the subject of his most devoted
thought.

For Lanier was a Georgian bred in the bone and one
of the Georgian group of writers who dominated the
Southern mind in letters for a while, as Georgia, which,
of all the states, had received the harshest treatment in
the war, was also the first to recover and rise from its
ruins. It was, moreover, the first state to sink the local
in the national spirit, as the so-called "New South"
was first conceived in Georgia, for the problems of the
post-war readjustment were less grave there than elsewhere and the burdens of reconstruction were less
severe. Unlike the states of the great plantations with
their long tradition of aristocracy where the middle class
had had no chance to grow, Georgia was largely democratic, with small plantations and humbler planters who
rather resembled the prosperous farmers of the North.
The sons of the richest men, as Joel Chandler Harris
said, were put to work in the fields beside the Negroes
and the sort of cordial understanding had existed between the owners and the slaves that one saw behind
the tales of "Uncle Remus." Young men had been
taught the necessity of effort, so that work had never
been despised in Georgia and the poor whites were therefore less degraded, and Georgia was prepared to lead
the South for these and other reasons when the new
conditions bewildered the other states. The "spokesman
of the New South," who pleaded for harmony between

the sections, the "Pacificator" Henry W. Grady was a
Georgian, while Middle Georgia was the birthplace and
setting of the older Southern humour in Longstreet's
realistic *Georgia Scenes*. This, followed by William Tappan Thompson's *Courtship* and *Travels* of Major Jones,
had established the region as a centre of American folk-
life.

Georgia, with its local characters and types, had had
an early start in letters, which Joel Chandler Harris was
soon to carry further,—Harris who worked with Thompson on a paper in Savannah,—while Colonel Richard
Malcolm Johnston, in *Dukesborough Tales* and other
books, continued the line that began with Longstreet's
sketches. The son of a fox-hunting planter in Georgia
who had taught there himself in the fifties, Johnston
had begun to write professionally when he settled in
Baltimore after the war and remembered the scenes
and the people of his village boyhood. Neither as terse
nor as lively as Longstreet, he was yet an artist in his
way with a shrewd eye for all that was characteristic in
the rural Georgian life of the thirties and forties,—the
old-time schools, the country doctors, the planters who
worked their own small farms with half a dozen or at
most a score of Negroes. He pictured courtships, law-
suits, weddings and oddities of every kind among the
rural folk of this fertile region, where the class feeling
was so slight and the religious feeling so strong, Methodist mainly in the towns, Baptist in the country. He
recalled the great camp-meetings when villages of tents
rose in the woods with booths and hawkers by day and
bonfires by night,—the "grand barbaric picnics" of
Moncure D. Conway,—and he liked to show the high
qualities of honour and delicacy of feeling that often
subsisted in the people with the rudest of speech. They
constantly discussed knotty points of religious doctrine
in a way that suggested the New England country peo-

ple, while the biblical character of their names was similar also,—Absalom Billingslea, for instance, and Solomon Pringle,—so that these hardworking ministers and farmers seemed very like the Yankees in Mrs. Stowe's *Poganuc People* and *Old Town Folks.* No wonder the Georgians soon made their peace with the North.

As for Lanier, he was loyal to Georgia, the scene of *The Marshes of Glynn* and *Corn,* amply as his mind outgrew all sectional bonds, and the writing of Richard Malcolm Johnston owed much to his encouragement when the two Georgians were Baltimore neighbours and friends. They found in the town the companionship that Lanier had missed further South where there was "not enough attrition of mind on mind" to "bring out any sparks from a man," he said, although he had also felt as a casual visitor in New York "like a solitary stone in . . . a torrent, mute and lonesome." Speaking for the younger generation in the South, he observed that his life was a "drought and famine . . . as regards that multitude of matters which I fancy one absorbs when one is in an atmosphere of art," but Baltimore with its men of letters writing for the *Southern Magazine* afforded him the good conversation for which he had longed. The great Charleston Hellenist was there, the witty Princetonian Gildersleeve, the professor of Greek at Johns Hopkins after 1876, the new university at which Lanier was also a lecturer for two or three years on English poetry from Beowulf to Ben Jonson. John B. Tabb, not yet a priest, was later a professor outside the town at a college where Colonel Johnston lectured as well, when he had been converted to Roman Catholicism also,— like Joel Chandler Harris at the end of his life,—but he never lost touch with Lanier and Gildersleeve, with whom he corresponded on problems of Greek syntax and grammar.

Gildersleeve had studied in Germany, which Lanier

himself had hoped to do,—they had both been intro
duced by Carlyle to the German writers,—and he fully
shared Bayard Taylor's Goethe-worship, while he found
the war, in which he had served in the Confederate
cavalry, an occasion for the study of the conflict between
Athens and Sparta. For this editor of Pindar deeply
felt the connection of scholarship and history with life,
which accounted for his incomparable success as a
teacher of the classics whose students filled chairs of
Greek all over the country, and Gildersleeve had the
feeling of an artist for the physical beauty of Greek
that made him a superlative champion of classical stud
ies. The essays of this "passionate classicist," as he called
himself, were singularly eloquent and winning, while as
a Southerner he defended in *The Creed of the Old
South* the sentiment of place that gave colour to the life
of the nation. Had not the local life of the old French
provinces greatly enriched the national life and mind?
His austere monastic correspondent, the tall thin Father
Tabb, was an unreconstructed rebel, a professor of Eng
lish who could never be persuaded to travel north of
Mason and Dixon's line, though he outlived his friend
Lanier by a full generation. The son of a Virginia
planter, born near Richmond, he began to publish his
poems in 1877, and seven of these he inscribed to Lanier,

---

[5] "I went from my books to the front, and went back from the
front to my books, from the Confederate war to the Peloponnesian
war, from Lee and Early to Thucydides and Aristophanes. I fancy
that I understood my Greek history and my Greek authors better
for my experience in the field."—Gildersleeve, *The Creed of the
Old South.*

[6] "I am enough of a heathen to recognize in physical beauty the
only true incentive of love. It is the physical beauty of Greek that
constitutes its intimate attraction . . . and I could still rhapsodize,
as I did forty years ago, on the sequences of vowels and the combinations of consonants, the concert of mute and liquid, the clear-
cut outlines of every word in Greek, clear and sharp as the sky-line
of the mountains of Greece, as the effigies on Greek coins."—Gildersleeve, *Hellas and Hesperia.*

whose language and thought he echoed at times, dry as he was where his friend was so vaporous and lush. No two poets were more unlike,—the clear, brief, hard, sharp, desiccated Tabb and Lanier, so spongy, so vague, so loose and soft, so diffuse and so tortured where Tabb was laconic and simple, over-ingenious as he also was, for his wit was occasionally a little forced, while generally his poems were delicate and firm in texture. Admiring his fellow-Virginian Poe, he had taken to heart the admonition in *The Poetic Principle* against long poems, and, ceasing to experiment with forms in which he had never succeeded, he worked at the quatrains and epigrams in which he excelled. A fastidious craftsman in miniature verse, he recalled at times the contemporaries of Herrick, whom he read apparently only in a cursory way, and he also suggested Emily Dickinson in his closely packed lines on flowers and birds, although he was quite without her magnetism. Fine as his little poems were, *Fern-Song,* for instance, and *Evolution,* he lacked a certain intensity and magic, yet it seemed not unlikely that he might outlast Lanier.[7] For, original as Lanier was, this admirable spirit, the friend of Tabb, struck one in later times as more important in the role of a personage and thinker than he was as a poet.

But, pale, dark, slender, nervous and eager, with a passionate belief in his mission in the world, Lanier was the ideal of the bard to many in his time, a realization of the hero as poet of whom Carlyle had written, with an overflowing romantic sense of life. Brought up in a strict Presbyterian household at a time when the Calvinist faith was stronger in the South than it was in eastern New England, Lanier was in grain as much of a

[7] "Spiritual senses are the poet's heavenly privilege. Though I will not claim for Father Tabb such rapturous senses as those of Coleridge for example, I find in him the extreme sensitiveness of poetry . . . I perceive in him the pierced and contrite heart of the poet."
—Alice Meynell, *Selections from the Verses of John B. Tabb.*

Puritan as Emerson ever had been, while he shared belatedly the New England delight in Carlyle. As much as the Concordians of the Transcendental age, he had felt the power of the German romantic writers, and before the war destroyed his plan he dreamed of studying at Heidelberg religious philosophy, literature, poetry and music. His novel *Tiger Lilies* was all compact of Novalis and Richter, suggesting in certain ways the *Meister Karl's Sketch Book* of Charles Godfrey Leland, whose circumstances had been so much more fortunate than his. He made translations from Herder and Heine while passing through other phases of thought that characterized him as a Southerner of the pre-war years, especially those fantasies of the age of chivalry that he never quite outgrew and that were nourished in his boyhood by Froissart and Scott. Thinking of himself as a knight and minstrel, he imagined that the new Confederate nation would embody all that was finest in the chivalric life, and later his prose and verse abounded in figures of paladin and paynim, the tournament and the battle-axe and cross-bow. He drew from Froissart's Chronicles the story of *The Jacquerie,* the long poem on which he worked off and on. Then his old admirer Paul Hamilton Hayne was deeply impressed by his knowledge of Early and Middle English and of Chaucer and Gower, with the later Elizabethan writers about whom he wrote and lectured and whose influence often appeared in his own compositions. Among the several books that he edited for boys were simplifications of Malory, Froissart and Percy.

With these tokens and tastes of the older South, Lanier combined more recent notes that gave him distinctly the character of a voice of his age, in some respects an important voice of the nation as well as the South with a faith in America as a whole that suggested Whitman's. Interested at all times in science, he read Darwin, Tyn-

dall and Huxley with care and accepted the evolutionary creed of the new generation, studying biology and
chemistry too, mineralogy, botany and the physics of
sound, the scientific aspect of the music he loved above
all. When he wrote his book on prosody he called it *The
Science of English Verse* in the mood of a moment when
science was triumphantly advancing, when historians
were talking of historical science and scientific method
and Christian Science was the name of a new religion.
Aware of economic problems and deeply concerned for
the South, he studied its social conditions with his usual
zest, collecting statistics about cotton and cattle and
gathering clippings from country papers that gave him
the neighbourhood news of the Georgian farmers. Eager
for their welfare, he wished to keep closely in touch with
the actualities of small-farm Southern living, struck by
the rise of the small farmer since the Civil War and convinced that the South of the future required small farming. With the nation as well as the section in mind, he
felt that the republic needed large farms in order to
achieve its "mighty works," but that it needed the small
farm too to foster manhood and self-reliance, the farming that was not a business but a way of life. Let the
Northwest have its great farms, the heirs of the old
plantations of the South, but let the Southeast have its
counter-balance with small farms and a village life developed as it might be, with village orchestras, libraries,
theatres and schools. In order to prosper the Southern
farmers must cease to plant cotton for ever and ever
and diversify their crops with corn and wheat. This was
the thought that underlay Lanier's first long poem *Corn*
and some of his dialect verses of the Georgia crackers.

Lanier was one of the earliest Southerners to use the
phrase the "New South," to the problems of which he
devoted much shrewd thinking, after brooding over the
abandoned farms and deserted Georgian hills that bared

to the sun, as he wrote, their seamy breasts. He had seen how the over-production of cotton had bankrupted the region while the farmers continued to produce it, and he wrote *Corn* near his birthplace Macon among the cornfields there, feeling that their growth assured the salvation of the state. Then, fighting King Cotton in the South, he fought the greater evil Trade, which he saw supplanting all that was human in the country, destroying in the interests of capitalism the ancient prestige of the farming life, a change that Melville and Whitman were also deploring. As much as Melville, Lanier detested the "hell-coloured smoke of the factories" and the business and industrial regime that had risen since the war, side by side with an unheard-of political corruption; and as early as 1870, in his Confederate Memorial address, he attacked the "boisterous god" of the century, Trade. It was the idol of an age, as he said, that was not grand but adroit, not strong but supple, not large but keen, and, fearful of cities along with trade,—the "terrible towns" of *The Waving of the Corn,*—he rebuked in *The Symphony* the growing capitalist system. He spoke with contempt of the "flimsy houses" that were built on the "shifting sands" of trade, while he satirized the new business world in a lighter poem *The Hard Times in Elfland,* which Santa Claus, now pale and thin, had been obliged to mortgage. A "stock-thief" had ruined him, he had had to give up everything,—even his reindeer,—and plod through the snow on foot, for this smooth-tongued railroad man had come to his house with a project that suited the nineteenth century better than the reindeer. This was to build a Grand Trunk railway through to earth's last terminus, touching at every chimney-top, an elevated railway, of course, that presently failed. It was trade that had overthrown chivalry, and Lanier saw chivalry rising again, with its scorn of the small advantage, to overthrow trade, for his criterion was vaguely mediæval. But, aside from the spirit in which he attacked the rising power of the business world,—a spirit that in certain ways resembled Ruskin's,—the attack in itself made him a voice of his age, with Whitman, Bellamy, Henry George and Howells.

What made Lanier, for the rest, important, especially for the South, even more than his poems, was his feeling about them, the sense of the high vocation of the poet and the dignity of poetry in a region where it had been previously regarded as a pastime. It was this that made him a symbol and example for Southern writers in times to come who had never been affected seriously by Poe or by Timrod, poets who had reacted earlier against this Southern attitude by similarly dwelling on the "science of English verse." No regional group of American poets has studied prosody indeed as the Southern poets were to study it for four generations, from Poe to Allen Tate and John Crowe Ransom, and one might be excused for supposing that this was due in part at least to the relatively late development of poetry in the South. That poetry was an accomplishment merely was a view that prevailed below the Potomac years after the appearance of real poets destroyed it in the North, and this way of taking it seriously was compensatory.

Lanier was important as well in attempting to turn the attention of poetry to the actual problems of his troubled world and time. He was an original poet, moreover, whether a good or a bad one, not just another Victorian like Timrod or Hayne, and in this he had something in common with Whitman, who shared his feeling for science too and especially his lofty conception of the poet's role. His poet was one who leads the

> timid time
> And sings up cowards with commanding rhyme,—

another phrase for Whitman's "literatus,"—while both were striving in different ways for new and freer forms of verse and Lanier's experiments were almost as bold as Whitman's. In this respect they were unlike the other American post-war poets, who were more than commonly conventional and artificial. Lanier suggested now and then the range and sweep of Whitman, and he too was a passionate lover of the American soil; for this ex-Confederate blockade-runner, whose sectional feeling was both deep and wise,[8] expressed as whole-souled a feeling for the nation as Whitman. Lanier, discovering Whitman in 1878, delighted in the "bigness and bravery" of his "ways and thoughts" and his "strong and beautiful rhythms," as he wrote the poet, so different from those of the "plentiful mannikins" who generally spoke for American verse and whom he scorned himself as much as Whitman. Later, in his lectures on *The English Novel,* he turned against the poet, taking too seriously some of his earlier phrases, saying that he mistook the body for the soul, offended by Whitman's animality and his rude display of physical health, which filled him with all the resentment and distaste of the consumptive. Lanier was tender-minded, to use the expression of William James, in spite of his protestations of a love of science, and he hated the naturalism of Zola too and said he could blot from the face of the earth the novels of Richardson, Fielding, Sterne and Smollett. Seeing in Lanier a beautiful spirit, Whitman surmised that he himself was far too rough a dish for so delicate a palate. As for Lanier's "extreme sense of the melodic," his "over-

[8] As early as 1869 Lanier denounced what he called the "insidious evil" of the South,—"the habit of inviting purchasers to buy artists' works, simply because they happen to be Southern artists. I mean the habit of regarding our literature as *Southern* literature, our poetry as *Southern* poetry, our pictures as *Southern* pictures. I mean the habit of glossing over the intrinsic defects of artistic productions by appealing to the Southern sympathies of the artists' countrymen."

tuning of the ear," he felt it detracted seriously from the value of his work.[9]

Lanier himself had said in a letter that poetry for him was a "tangent" merely into which he shot at times from his true line, music, and this partly explained the weakness of his work, which seemed somehow abortive in later times and all but unreadable in spite of its largeness of feeling. Its "lavishness and looseness of adjectives," the fault Lanier found in the poems of Hayne, its diffuseness and vagueness and lack of finality and precision were all in part attributable to an over-dependence on his sense of music, which he called the "characteristic art-form of the modern time."[10] So, while in a way he invented a style, it was therefore not a good style, it was seldom or never natural, direct or simple, and it abounded in errors of taste and verbal effects that were constantly forced and suggested a kind of archaism that was false and hollow. This was the result of his early reading of the oldest English poets, together with the isolation of his formative years: indeed he never sufficiently lived within the literary current of his time to learn what a writer could and should not do. His language, too often over-wrought, was sometimes silly or namby-pamby, with too much of the mawkish adolescent in the quality of the feeling, and there were elements in his writing as well of the high-flown Southern oratorical style and the feverish exaltation of tubercu-

[9] "This extreme sense of the melodic, a virtue in itself, when carried into the art of the writer becomes a fault. Why? Why, because it tends to place the first emphasis on tone, sound,—on the lilt, as Rhys so often puts it. Study Lanier's choice of words—they are too often fit rather for sound than for sense . . . He had genius—a delicate clairvoyant genius: but this over-tuning of the ear . . . reduced the majesty, the solid worth, of his rhythms."—Quoted in Traubel's *With Walt Whitman in Camden.*

[10] In his book on Florida now and then he expressed himself in a passage of music just as Samuel Butler did in his *Alps and Sanctuaries.*

losis. Yet, good or bad, his poems were new, or some of them at least, where most of his American contemporaries were shadows and echoes, in all that made them poets aside from their themes, and he was at his worst in the shorter poems where one looked for the perfection he was always so far from achieving. There was much that was moving and beautiful in the longer poems, *The Psalm of the West, The Symphony* and, above all, *The Marshes of Glynn,* with its real feeling for the Southern scene, the winding creeks, the marsh and the sea, the live oaks with their clouds of hanging moss.

Meanwhile, in some of his dialect poems one heard for the first time the actual talk of Negroes on the printed page, for his earliest verses of this kind appeared before those of Irwin Russell, in the same year with Hay's *Pike County Ballads.* He had previously written dialect poems of the Georgia crackers also that reminded one of Longstreet's *Georgia Scenes,* for, as one saw in his *Music and Poetry,* he had been struck by these poor whites shouting *The Old Ship of Zion* in their piney-woods churches. Irwin Russell followed him with dramatic Negro monologues that were almost certainly suggested by the ballads of John Hay and that played their part in launching Thomas Nelson Page, the Virginia novelist later, on his career as a writer. Russell, a young Mississippian who lived in New Orleans, shared Stephen Foster's Bohemian taste for the slums, and before he died at twenty-six he wrote in a sailors' boarding-house a number of the poems that gave him a name in the South. One represented a Negro sermon, another an old Negro's advice to his son, who was going to be a waiter on a steamboat, though the most important of these compositions was *Christmas Night in the Quarters,* a dialect poem half narrative and half dramatic.

Russell was rather over-praised for his treatment of

the old plantation Negroes, whom he was the first no
doubt to present at length in a way that suggested them
as subjects for other writers, largely because of the curiosity the Negroes were exciting in these years of their
emancipation after the war. Since Thomas Wentworth
Higginson had written about their spirituals in the *Atlantic Monthly* in 1867,[11] Winslow Homer had painted
them and Eastman Johnson had travelled South to study
the Negroes for his "Old Kentucky Home." Winslow
Homer was the first to paint them not in a comic spirit
but seriously, with a feeling for their emotional amplitude and warmth. An interest in their folk-tales and
folk-songs had spread far and wide. This followed the
vogue of the Negro "narratives" of the Abolition era
that were read by tens of thousands in America and England, the scores and even hundreds of stories of slaves
who had escaped, that served as anti-slavery propaganda.
One was the narrative of Frederick Douglass, the Abolitionist orator whom Garrison compared to Patrick
Henry, a literal picture of slavery as it was, in all its
barbarity and squalor, in Maryland, where one saw its
brightest side. Another was the narrative of Sojourner
Truth, whom Mrs. Stowe called the "sibyl," the proph-
etess who had also belonged to Garrison's band. Mrs.
Stowe herself used several of these narratives as source-
material for *Uncle Tom's Cabin,* but Negro literature,
properly speaking, was not to begin till the eighteen-
nineties with the appearance of the poems of Paul Laurence Dunbar. There had been a scattering of earlier
writers since the days of Phillis Wheatley, who learned
to compose so skilfully in the manner of Pope, the
young slave-girl, a pet of the family of a rich Boston
merchant, who had been taken for her health on a voyage to England. There she had been an honoured guest

[11] In a paper later included in his book *Army Life in a Black
Regiment.*

of the pious Countess of Huntingdon's circle. These earlier writers, religious mainly, had been followed by the political writers who laboured for the freedom of their people, so that Negro literature in its evolution passed through the same phases that characterized the general literature of the country.

It was just at this moment when an interest in the Negroes was rapidly rising on every hand that Joel Chandler Harris first appeared, the other Georgian who, as a boy, had heard Lanier perform on his flute and who was to charm the world with the "Brer Rabbit" stories. These Negro tales of the "animals and creeturs" were universally known in the South, where Audubon, for one, had heard them in the Louisiana bayous, while Opie Read, the novelist, later said he had heard them "all" from an old Negro shoemaker in Tennessee. Mark Twain recalled them from his boyhood in Missouri, where "Uncle Daniel" told them in his Negro cabin, and Theodore Roosevelt was brought up on them by his Georgian mother and aunt in New York, where one of his uncles had published them in *Harper's Magazine*. There they "fell flat," as he remarked, for this later friend of Harris was aware that it required a "genius" to make them immortal.[12]

Born in the region of Longstreet's stories, the poorest of the poor, Harris had lived with his mother in a one-room cottage, a shy little homely stammering red-

---

[12] "My aunt Anna, my mother's sister, lived with us . . . She and my mother used to entertain us by the hour with tales of life on the Georgia plantations; of hunting fox, deer and wildcat; of the long-tailed driving-horses, Boone and Crockett . . . and of the queer goings-on in the Negro quarters. She knew all the 'Brer Rabbit' stories, and I was brought up on them. One of my uncles, Robert Roosevelt, was much struck with them and took them down from her dictation, publishing them in *Harper's,* where they fell flat. This was a good many years before a genius arose who in 'Uncle Remus' made the stories immortal."—Theodore Roosevelt, *An Autobiography*.

headed boy who looked like one of the piney-woods Georgia crackers. Later he described himself as "poor, small and insignificant," morbidly sensitive, with an absolute horror of strangers, a boy who forgot to be shy with the Negroes and was unconstrained with children too unless he was asked to tell them stories. Even as an older man he never liked to do this because it made the children look up to him and he could no longer be one of them, as he wished to be. He made friends with the Negroes, with whom he always felt at home, hunting 'coons, 'possums, rabbits and foxes with them, spending much time as a little boy with Uncle Bob Capers, a teamster, who told him tales of the creatures of wood and field. At Forsyth, as a young reporter, he knew an old gardener named Uncle Remus, and he had had a great friend called Uncle George, a widower who lived in his cabin alone and told him stories by the evening fire in which Brer Fox and Brer Wolf were usually the villains. From Uncle George he heard the "Tar-Baby" story. This was in Harris's later boyhood when he was an apprentice-printer on the weekly periodical, *The Countryman,* on a neighbouring plantation, a paper that was edited by a Mr. Turner, a cultivated planter, who took the boy to live in his own house.

It was a stroke of great good luck that introduced Harris, who was then fourteen, to this planter-editor, Joseph Addison Turner, whose name was a symbol of his tastes and who modelled his little weekly sheet on Addison's *Spectator,* the *Rambler* and Goldsmith's *Bee.* In a region where most of the planters were like the characters in *Dukesborough Tales,* unpretentious farmers with a handful of slaves, this Turner was a lover of nature with a serious interest in literature who took a strong personal interest in the sensitive boy. His plantation-newspaper, the only one of its kind in the South, was quoted all over the Confederacy as enlightened and lively, and Turner, who was always discussing literary matters, gave Harris the run of his library of four thousand books. He was looking for new Southern writers to reflect the scenery and manners of the South and the life and ways of the Negroes without being provincial, or only "provincial in a large way," in Henry W. Grady's sense, for he disliked all narrow sectionalism.[13] Encouraging Harris to write for the paper, he read, revised and talked over his work, careful not to dishearten the eager boy, as the author of *Major Jones's Courtship,* William Tappan Thompson, encouraged Harris later on his paper in Savannah. Between extracts from Percy's *Reliques* and the maxims of La Rochefoucauld, Harris set up little essays of his own in type,— paragraphs, sketches and verses,—just as Howells, in his village in Ohio, in the country printing-shop, working over the type-case, had set up his stories. At this little plantation-office the squirrels ran over the roof and the bluejays brought their acorns and hammered at the shells there, and Harris dropped his work once to watch a partridge and his mate building a nest that was just outside the window. It was like the sylvan printing-office that Bret Harte, who had known it well, described in his story *The Poet of Sierra Flat,* and the sympathetic Turner talked to the boy about birds and trees and spoke of his own horses as if they were people. It was easy to imagine there that all the "creeturs" were just

[13] Harris interpreted as follows Grady's feeling: "He perceived that all the talk about a distinctive Southern literature, which has been in vogue among the contributors of the Lady's Books and annuals, was silly in the extreme. He desired it to be provincial in a large way, for, in this country, provinciality is only another name for the patriotism that has taken root in the rural regions, but his dearest wish was that it should be purely and truly American in its aim and tendency."—Joel Chandler Harris, *Life of Henry W. Grady.*

This was Harris's feeling also. He wrote in 1882: "My idea is that truth is more important than sectionalism and that literature that can be labelled Northern, Southern, Western, Eastern, is not worth labelling."

like folks, as they were to appear in the Uncle Remus
stories, swarming as the plantation was with wild life,
Negroes and children in an atmosphere of fairy-tales
and folk-lore. Harris, who read Grimm and the *Arabian
Nights,* knew every by-path in the woods, hunted foxes
with the hounds, treed 'coons with the Negroes, and,
lingering in the quarters, spent hours and hours watching the dances and listening to the songs and the stories
that had come from Africa more often than not. The
Negroes played on their fiddles and the quills, pipes cut
from the reeds of the canebrakes, cleaned and lashed together with cobbler's twine,—found mostly in the trackless swamps of the Oconee, near by,—and Harris picked
up ploughman's songs, Christmas and corn-husking
songs and the melodies and spirituals that Higginson
had been the first to gather. He heard stories of the
"patter-rollers," the neighbourhood policemen who were
busy catching disorderly Negroes at night, and tales of
escaped slaves like his Daddy Jake the Runaway and of
old Zip Coon and Sandy Claus. Harris heard how the
mountains were made, how the fox got rid of his fleas
and the stories of Brer Rabbit and the overcoat and the
crayfish and the Deluge. The plantation Negroes played
the fiddle, as he later wrote, a hundred times for once
that they played the banjo.

So he said in *The Old Plantation,* a record of this
Georgian life, for Harris wrote many books besides
Uncle Remus, a number of which were meant especially
for children. In this charming chronicle he described
the deserters who left the army, because their families
were starving, towards the end of the war, and the runaway Mink, whom he befriended as Huck Finn sheltered Nigger Jim,—a Negro, mistreated by the overseer,
whom everyone admired. This episode recalled Mark
Twain, who delighted in Harris's writings and who had
grown up with the Negroes as a boy in Missouri, where

he heard the oft-told tale of the "Golden Arm." Harris wrote other stories of Negroes to express his admiration for the loyalty and devotion, for instance, of Ananias, the ex-slave who supported his former master by foraging among the neighbouring farms when the rascal who had once been the overseer had acquired the plantation. In another story an ex-slave called Jesse, finding his master's family in want, attached his fortunes to theirs and kept them alive, while in still another, the faithful Balaam clung to his rogue of a master and even broke into a prison-cell to save him. *Blue Dave* was the story of a runaway Negro who lived scot-free for years in the woods, wandering foot-loose, a terror to women and children, a giant supposedly with evil powers but really noble in his gifts and traits as he was able to show by the end of the tale. In *Free Joe,* Harris's best perhaps, one saw the tragedy of the Negro who was free in the queer world of slavery before the war, with every man his master, since he had none to call his own, despised by the other Negroes and more helpless than they were. It was one of Harris's wishes to write a novel of Georgian life, and he attempted two or three, the best of which, *Gabriel Tolliver,* was a story of "reconstruction" times in a village that was known as Shady Dale. It described the spoliation of the South, the bayonet rule, the carpet-baggers, the Negroes who became the tools of adventurers from the North; but Harris, with his fanciful poet's mind, had none of the novelist's constructive power and was always best in his tales, whether of Negroes or of whites. Little Compton, in one of these, was the Yankee storekeeper in the Georgian village who went off to fight for the Union and returned to the store where Harris as a boy had listened to the men reading their mail and their papers, discussing the war, under the china trees. As they talked they sat about on crackerbarrels and dry-goods boxes: it might have been rural New England or the Middle West. Some of Harris's good stories dealt with the Confederate secret service, others with the mountain folk of northern Georgia,—*At Teague Poteat's,* for instance, in which the moonshiners of Hog Mountain, unionists in the war, resisted all efforts to ensnare them. The revenue-officers and Confederate authorities were powerless in the fastnesses of the beautiful Sis Poteat's father and friends.

When the Turner plantation had been ruined by the war, Harris, who was turned adrift, worked as a printer or a journalist all over the state, at Macon, Forsyth, Savannah and Atlanta, where he settled in 1876 as Henry Grady's colleague on the *Constitution.* He had even spent a few months in New Orleans, where he fell in with Lafcadio Hearn. Atlanta was full of north Georgian crackers and East Tennesseans who had dropped their "you-uns" and "we-uns" and joined with the Yankees in building and pushing " 'Lantama-tan-tarum" forward,—Uncle Remus's name for the town where there was nothing but "dust, mud and money" from the point of view of a Negro of the old regime. Harris assisted Grady in making the Atlanta *Constitution* the most influential paper in the state: they worked together to bring in industry and immigrants and reconcile the feelings and interests of the South and the North. The name of Uncle Remus appeared in the paper in 1876 in one of the sketches that Harris had begun to write, containing the old man's remarks and dialect songs, the plantation and camp-meeting chants that Harris had transcribed, a series of papers that was finally collected as *Uncle Remus: His Songs and Sayings,* the first of a number of volumes, in 1880. Harris was retelling the Negro myths he had heard as a boy and continued to gather from old-time Negroes who worked for him, from correspondents, from his children, who kept their ears open for stories, all of them tales that had

been told in the kitchens and cabins of the old plantations and that poured in upon Harris from all over
the South. Other letters contained suggestions that
led to important discoveries. Ethnologists and philologists
wrote to him from Asia and Europe, for identical stories
had been found among the Indians of South America,
among the Kaffirs, among the Hottentots, in the Philippines, in India, in Siam. The stories alone appealed to
Harris, for he scarcely shared Charles Godfrey Leland's
interest in the study of the folklore of his Gypsies and
Algonquins; but he was tireless in collecting these,—
though they grew thinner as time went on,—and among
them the coast legends of the old Pierce Butler estates.
Fanny Kemble had once lived on these sea-island plantations, where many of the older Negroes still spoke
Gullah, the lingo that Daddy Jack talked in *Nights
with Uncle Remus*. This was sometimes meant to be
unintelligible and therefore impressive. Daddy Jack
was a genuine African, brought in a slave-ship to
Georgia, who had lived himself on one of the sea-islands
and had since become the foreman of another plantation of the "little boy's" family who visited the "Home
Place" once a year. This was at the Christmas holiday-
time when old man Plato with his six-mule wagon drove
up with his bugle and the Negroes from the "River
Place."

Daddy Jack was more interested in "haunts" and
witches than Uncle Remus, the venerable, reasonable,
masterful, noble old man, the Æsop of the plantation-
world, nearly eighty, still hearty and hale, whom the
little boy thought of as a partner. In old times he had
been a leader among the Negroes, ablest with the hoe,
at the plough, at logging, at the corn-pile, and he still
spoke and sang with the vigour of youth and was stout
enough to load the wagon and drive home the corn. In
the war, when the men of the big house left and he had

charge of the plantation, he proved himself faithful and responsible as a deputy-master, taller and keener as he was than the other Negroes, and well before the Yankees came he had got the cattle and horses together, driven them off and corralled them in a secret place. Collecting all the corn, fodder and wheat, he had placed it in cribs in the woods, building a pen as well for the hogs in the swamp, and, forgetting about his own chance of freedom, he had shot a Yankee, who was fighting for it, in order to protect the master's house. Then he had helped Miss Sally to nurse the Yankee back to health, whereupon, needless to say, the two were married. Now the old man liked to sit in the sun making fish-baskets with white-oak splits or sharpening his knife and cutting out shoe-pegs, preparing decoctions of wild-cherry bark to cure his rheumatism and telling stories in the evening to the little boy. He had the vaguest notions about Phillimerdelphy and the world outside and he did not "choke" himself, as he said, with names,—the Mexicans were Moccasins and Mackersons by turns to Uncle Remus; but he had a wonderful gift when it came to explaining why the guinea-fowls are speckled and the turkey-buzzards are bald. Sometimes he had to be coaxed to go on, as the little boy was well aware, and his tales were "just so stories" that could not be questioned: they had come to him as he passed them on and it did not do to ask him how the goose had hands and who were Miss Meadows and the girls. For Miss Goose took in washing and all the creatures, horn, claw and wing, did everything that people did in those days: they cooked their breakfast, washed the dishes, went out for a walk with their parasols, sauntered round, gave parties and carried pails. They had barbecues and camp-meeting times, when the weather was agreeable, and Uncle Remus thought they probably kept store. Old Brer B'ar had a cotton-patch and the ram slung a fiddle under his chin and struck up old-time tunes when they had a frolic. In short, the creatures, who carried on exactly as the Negroes did, reflected the old plantation life and mind.

Brer Rabbit was always the hero of the tales, a mighty man in those days, as Uncle Remus called him, much bigger than at present, whom nothing could scare and no one could fool and who always got away, for nobody was brash enough to catch up with Brer Rabbit. His mind was quicker than anyone else's and there was nothing he could not do, from outwitting Brer Fox to dancing a double-shuffle: he hoed potatoes, chopped cotton, fetched brushwood, split kindling, smoked, sat by the fire and read the paper. He would fling off his coat, grab an axe, spit on his hands and cut down a tree, go to town for a dram and a plug of tobacco or to get his old woman a coffee-pot with tin cups for the children, and he was a great performer on the quills who could jump into the middle of the floor and shake the eyelids off the other creatures. When they tried to be smart and laid traps for him, they were always caught in the traps themselves, for he was the fullest of tricks and the shrewdest of all, the most adroit at fooling the others and playing them against one another, inasmuch as Brer Rabbit knew how to take care of himself.

But all the creatures, said Uncle Remus, had to look out for themselves, especially if they had no horns or hoofs, since, like the Negroes, they were helpless, Negroes themselves as they were in disguise, just as Brer Rabbit was the Negro Hercules. He was as much their mythical hero as Paul Bunyan was of the lumberjacks, and indeed the rabbit had always been in African mythology the great central figure and wonder-worker. The weaker creatures, in every case, discomfited the stronger, as the Negroes wished, by their mischievous arts and cunning,—the cow killed the lion, the rabbit got the better of the wolf and the terrapin of the bear; and Brer Rabbit was permitted to strut about as if he were the king of the patter-rollers when he humbled Brer Fox before Miss Meadows and the girls. Brer Rabbit, the hero, was unique in this, for nobody else could give himself airs without being taken down a peg or two, like the uppity little Jack Sparrows who were always bothering other folks and the Lion who set up as the boss of the other creatures. When Miss Meadows and the girls gave a candy-pulling and the neighbours began to talk biggity, little Brer Tarrypin showed even Brer Rabbit that he was not the swiftest, while he showed how much cleverer and stronger he was than Brer B'ar. The other creatures thought they were bigger than the crawfishes when they 'lectioneered and agreed to have an assembly, spoke speeches and hollered and flung the language round, and the crawfishes drew up their preamble with wharfo'es in it, but these others were drowned for their vanity when the Mud Turkle and the Spring Lizzard bored holes and went down and unloosed the fountains of the earth.

For the motto of the tales was St. Augustine's, to "spare the lowly and strike down the proud," and the Negroes in these fables got even with their overseers and masters. Along with their cunning, their kindness appeared,—like their hatred of tattlers and tale-bearers,— as when Brer Rabbit forgathered with Brer Possum and Brer Fox and they all arranged their provisions in a single shanty. Once even Brer Fox was sorry enough for Brer Rabbit to give him a load of firewood from sheer compassion. Sometimes the creatures were free and easy, as when Brer Hawk in his flight said Howdy to the sun. More often in their intercourse they behaved with "monstrous" politeness, the ceremonious courtesy of the well-bred Negroes of old.

CHAPTER XVIII

THE SOUTH: MISS MURFREE AND CABLE

In a story called *Up in the Blue Ridge,* published in
1878, Constance Fenimore Woolson had written of the
people whom Mary Murfree,—"Charles Egbert Craddock,"—began to describe in a series of tales the first
of which appeared in the very same year. Miss Woolson
had observed them at Asheville, the scene of her novel
Horace Chase, when they straggled into the village for
the Saturday market and the mountain-women in their
deep sun-bonnets rode up and down the street while the
men sat on their heels in a row by the store. These were
the people whom she had seen on a journey in a wagon
through the Great Smoky Mountains that lay to the
west, the country of the moonshiners where the high
thickets of rhododendron formed solid walls of blazing
colour. Sometimes young men from the lowlands who
were fond of hunting and rambling round penetrated
to these "ragged mountains," like Mr. Bedloe, the Charlottesville valetudinarian in the tale of Poe, for the
"chain of wild and dreary hills" was all one mountain
system in Virginia, North Carolina, Tennessee and
southward. All one as well were the people who dwelt
there, the "uncouth and fierce races of men" of whom
Mr. Bedloe had heard strange stories and who lived in
their little clusters of cabins, with walls of rough logs
and chimneys of mud, mysterious, unkempt, lank and
unknown outside. Theirs was the wilderness of cliffs
and crags and tumbling flashing mountain streams that
had once appeared in "Porte Crayon's" pleasant
sketches.

Occasionally a naturalist travelled there, attracted by the wildness and grandeur of the hills and the orchids, ferns, lilies and laurels in the glades and glens. Asa Gray, the botanist, in a journey of twenty miles there, discovered a greater variety of indigenous trees than one found in the whole of Europe between England and Turkey. The region had enraptured William Bartram on his plant-hunting trip through the "Cherokee country," and the blaze of azaleas that he described there had presently appeared in Wordsworth's *Ruth,* where they were said to have "set the hills on fire." But no one had observed the mountaineers,[1] who were living in the eighteenth century still a life that was even more timeless than that of the plantations, with their diminutive garden-patches, fenced in with chestnut rails, and a few emaciated hogs as lean as greyhounds. They might almost have been wild clansmen in Scotland still, and nothing had changed in their manners and ways since they had come down from Pennsylvania, where they had been Indian hunters on the colonial border. With their bony figures and strong drawn faces, they had remained the frontiersmen who were known at a critical moment as the "whiskey boys" and they kept up their "whiskey rebellion" as moonshiners, for grain, distilled into portable form, was their only salable product in these roadless mountains. To tax it was like taxing their currency and they flouted the law. In settlements with names like No Pone, Long Hungry and No Fat, they lived by barter largely, without trades or professions,

[1] It is true that in *Fisher's River,* 1859, and the sketches collected in *Carolina Humor,* the Baptist minister H. E. Taliaferro described with a measure of skill their more humorous aspects. More or less in Longstreet's manner, he pictured these isolated mountain folk with their stills and their hunting and fishing in the wild Blue Ridge. The stories abounded in Munchausen-like frontier extravagances. Taliaferro's account of the discovery of copper in Duck Town, Tennessee, recalled Mark Twain's Nevada and Bret Harte's Sierras.

with every man his own cobbler, carpenter, gunsmith and miller, as in David Crockett's time and Daniel Boone's. Retaining Thomas Jefferson's beliefs which the rest of the South had abandoned, they submitted to laws they had inherited, and those alone, speaking a language, half obsolete elsewhere, abounding in ancient Scottish words and English words that were found only in Chaucer.

Miss Murfree, the daughter of a Tennessee planter, had seen them first in the Cumberland mountains at one of the springs where her family spent fifteen summers, a resort of people like themselves from Louisiana and Mississippi, where her father had acquired three plantations. At a similar resort in the Tennessee mountains, Sidney Lanier had spent a summer,—his grandfather had built a large hotel there,—hunting and fishing in the forest, in 1860, observing the society that gathered there in the cheerful days before the war, horse-racing, talking politics and reading Scott. In his youthful novel *Tiger Lilies,* Lanier had described the mountaineers in the characters of the Smallin brothers, Gorm and Cain, reproducing their dialect as carefully as Miss Murfree was to do it in her long series of novels and stories about them. Eight years younger than Lanier,—she was born in 1850,—Miss Murfree was drawn to the mountain folk when she heard others ridicule their outlandish manner of speaking and their barbarous ways. She foraged in their hilly retreats on the outskirts of the town for butter, vegetables, chickens and fruit for the table, talking in their poor little dwellings with the gaunt bearded men and the sad-faced, pallid women in calico and homespun. From the rafters hung bunches of medicinal herbs, brown gourds and little bags of seed, strings of bright red pepper-pods and ears of popcorn, and the rush-bottomed chairs, the spinning-wheels and gunracks, the floors and the walls were scrupulously clean as they seldom were in cabins of the lowland people. Later with her father Miss Murfree went on a horseback journey far into the mountains, visiting huts that were deep in the woods and little log meeting-houses perhaps on some rugged spur of a massive range. They found their way into moonshine caves in tangled labyrinths of forest and valley where one heard the hunter's horn winding from afar, following deep paths, where foxes barked, along the edges of cliffs and streams, and shanties stood with hop-vines clinging to the porch. Together they fell in with groups of teamsters gathered at a blacksmith's forge, parties of road-menders, farmers with bull-tongued ploughs, sometimes drawn by oxen driven by the farm-wife, girls weaving and spinning, boys watching their stills, witch-like women smoking pipes, hovels with a pack of a dozen or a score of hounds. They might have met the patriarch Miss Murfree described in one of her stories who continued to vote for Andy Jackson, out of respect for his memory since the old critter died, and they shared on occasion the fare of the mountaineers,— buttermilk, honey, corn-dodgers, fried chicken and bacon. Miss Murfree could feel that in many ways she knew them.

In the straitened years that followed the war, Miss Murfree's father urged her to write, for he himself wrote stories and delighted in them. Brought up as she was on Dickens and Scott, she had also read Longstreet's *Georgia Scenes,* with their realistic pictures of events that still happened in the mountains, gander-pullings, revivals, shooting-matches, and she may well have seen too, as a reader of the current magazines, a story about North Carolina by Rebecca Harding Davis. It described the experience of a Northern woman who met a family of mountaineers and could not make head or tail of the language they spoke, the mountaineers whose lives Miss Murfree began to chronicle almost at once after previ-

ously writing sketches of fashionable people. Like all the
world, she had read Bret Harte, who set an example
for so many writers by focussing his mind on a regional
scene and its people, and she must have noted at once
the surface similarity between his domain of the Sierras
and her Tennessee mountains. There too were settlements in forest clearings with a blacksmith's shop, a
cluster of huts, a store and perhaps a whitewashed court-
house, with clumsy wagons standing about, rough men
in rougher clothes and wild streams and wilder peaks
always in the distance. This much, at least, Bret Harte's
Sierras had in common with Miss Murfree's world, and
her stories constantly recalled his groupings and settings, far removed as her Tennessee folk with their deep-
running passions and ageless ways undoubtedly were
from the mobile California people. She dealt,—far less
successfully,—with a much more stable human scene,
marked by fierce pride and customs as old as the hills.

In her many stories, long and short, the same characters reappeared that one met in her first book, *In the
Tennessee Mountains,* but this and *The Prophet of the
Great Smoky Mountains* revealed an unknown human
sphere in a way that was singularly real, impressive and
poetic. One of the recurring themes was that of the cultivated stranger who meets the unsophisticated mountain
girl, and many of the stories dealt with the conflicts of
the mountain folk and the world outside which the
revenue-officer and the sheriff represented. Among the
other local types were the blacksmith and the horse-
thief, who mysteriously disappears, like the revenue-spy;
for one of the unwritten laws of the moonshiners was
that the informer should perish, and outsiders in general
were the enemy in the moonshiners' minds. For the rest,
they knew nothing of social classes and their speech was
full of poetry, and especially the biblical metaphors of
Old Testament people for whom dancing was more sin-

ful than killing a man in a quarrel and who bore such
names as Abednego and Jubal. The preacher was omnipresent and one of the best of Miss Murfree's characters
was the infidel prophet Kelsey with his second sight who
thought he was the only unbeliever in a Christian world
and whom Satan hunted through the mountains like a
partridge. A few of the other mountaineers were admirably drawn, the fugitive Rick Tyler who was falsely ac-
cused and who looked like a hound in the middle of the
hunting season, and Groundhog Cayce and his giant
sons, the moonshiners with their forest arts, who recalled
the Tennessee brood of Cooper's Ishmael Bush. Some of
the scenes were idyllic and many abounded in fine descriptions of the forest, the flowers and the mountains
that towered over all. The stories were vibrant as often
as not with the violent feelings of the mountain folk,
whether anger, love, loyalty, resentment or the thirst for
revenge.

Now and then Miss Murfree's stories were marked by
great dramatic power, *The 'Harnt' that Walks Chil-
howee*, for example, the tale of the fugitive cripple who
was taken for a ghost; and some of her historical writing was interesting also. She was stirred by memories of
the old Cherokees, the great Chief Oconostota who
visited King George in London and the Indian sibyl who
was known in her time as the Evening Cloud, and one
of the novels, *In the "Stranger People's" Country*, dealt
with the mysterious aboriginal Indian mounds. From the
Tennessee graveyards of the ancient pygmies all manner
of relics had been retrieved, six-slab stone coffins, curiously woven shrouds, feathered mantels, pearl beads,
rugs, mats and weapons, the objects that the youthful
Paul dicovered in the mound that was shaped like a sugar-
loaf in another story, *Mamelon*, by Albion Tourgee. In
Miss Murfree's novel the mountain folk, wishing to protect the ancient race and enable them to assemble their

bones at the Resurrection, did everything they could to thwart the archæologist who was bent on opening their graves.

But, interesting as much of it was, the best of this writing was scarcely readable, two generations later, for the very same reason that many other gifted writers were unreadable also, because of their abuse of dialect, so typical of the time, and as fatal as the abuse of bitumen in the work of the painters. It was a time that seemed willing to swallow unlimited doses of dialect from *Hans Breitmann's Ballads* to the tales of *Uncle Remus,* from John Hay's *Pike County Ballads* to Thomas Nelson Page's *Marse Chan,* an unbroken Negro monologue phonetically spelled. While the great flood of this dialect literature followed the success of *Uncle Remus,* the vogue went back as far as *The Biglow Papers,* and Bret Harte, Mark Twain and James Whitcomb Riley were only a few of the writers who were producing it at present. As Bret Harte had taken pains to convey the mixed dialects of the forty-niners, so Mark Twain was scrupulous in his rendering of the Pike County speech, the ordinary dialect with four modified varieties and the dialects of the backwoods Southwest and the Missouri Negro. He observed that the shadings were not done by guesswork, in a haphazard fashion, but with the trustworthy guidance of personal knowledge.[2] Just so Thomas Nelson Page wrote a preface for *In Ole Virginia* explaining the difference between the dialects of the Southern Negroes and the Eastern Virginia Negroes who appeared in his book, while Richard Malcolm Johnston reproduced with the utmost care the Middle Georgian dialect in his *Dukesborough Tales.*[3] As for

[2] See Mark Twain's "explanatory" note in *Huckleberry Finn.*
[3] In one of his stories in the volume called *Mr. Absalom Billingslea,* Johnston went to the length of taking more than half a page to reproduce exactly the sound of a lisp.

James Whitcomb Riley, the most popular poet of his time, he took the greatest pains with his Middle Western language, following Dickens's use of cockney and defending in one of his essays "this dialectic country cousin" of literary speech.[4]

There were many reasons for this study of dialect,— the spread of the philological mind and especially the wish to commemorate the local life and preserve the local speech that seemed destined to be lost with the growth of the industrial system and the national feeling. The literary discovery of Negro English excited the writers of the South, moreover, as the Irish were excited by the discovery of their own idiom later. If it went to their heads at times, so fresh and picturesque it was, there were those like Harris who knew how to use it with discretion,[5] as Bret Harte and Mark Twain were artists

[4] "For his dialect poetry he kept notebooks as accurate as a scientist's. Not only was the euphony of the dialectics a careful study with him, but he knew some children, for instance, say 'thist,' instead of 'just,' and why others say 'ist.' There was nothing haphazard in any of his work. The philologist of the future, studying Middle Western colloquialisms of the late nineteenth century, may depend on Riley's transcription of them as the most exact ever made."—Clara E. Laughlin, *Reminiscences of James Whitcomb Riley.*

Riley warmly praised Richard Malcolm Johnston's "minute obeisance . . . to dialect." See also his letter of advice to Miss Lucy S. Furman, 1893: "Reading your sketches I could but note the natural oversight of many dialect writers—namely, lack of vigilance in the detail of speech, pronunciation and the rest. Then, too, the (natural again) failure to consist in all details. Never—on penalty of *death!* —must any word not in the vocabulary of the unlettered be used." —*Letters of James Whitcomb Riley.*

[5] Harris's way of doing so was to keep his stories very short. It was the length of *Marse Chan,* Thomas Nelson Page's story, that made it insupportable in a later generation.

It was characteristic of this time that Sherwood Bonner, Mrs. Mac-Dowell, called her volume of stories *Dialect Tales* (1883). This was one of many books depicting "Southern life and character," the humours of village life in Mississippi mainly. Sherwood Bonner, a Mississippian, went to Boston in 1872 and became for a while Longfellow's amanuensis.

in this way also. It was the pains that writers took to reproduce dialect exactly that blighted many books which
might otherwise have survived if the writers had used a
little more tact, less science and more art, and suggested
the dialect merely by occasional touches. The attempt
to convey it literally defeated its own end because what
was intended for the ear was presented to the eye. Unable to see the sound, one resented the obstruction.

The New Orleans writer George W. Cable was one
who cared deeply for the local life and used the Creole
dialect, on the whole, discreetly, although he made every
effort, after the most patient historical research, to convey its finest shades in the precisest fashion.[6] He was enchanted by the musical patois of the French-speaking
ruling class, which had its effect in the shaping of his
own literary style, as well as the language of the French-
speaking Negroes, with whom he took great pains to
talk, and the speech of the Acadians who had come from
Nova Scotia. Cable, whose mother was of New England
descent while his Virginia father owned steamboats on
the Mississippi before he failed, had enlisted in the Confederate army like Henry M. Stanley, the explorer of
the future, who had come to New Orleans from England
as a cabin-boy. The adventurous Stanley had assumed
the name of the merchant who adopted him there and
sailed up the river in a flatboat at the end of the war,
after working as a clerk in the town, to Vicksburg and
Natchez; then, crossing the plains, he fell in with General Hancock on his expedition against the Kiowas and
Comanches. Cable, who became an engineer, joined a
surveying party in the swamps and bayous of the Atcha-
falaya river. Later his adventures as a soldier appeared

---

[6] Thus, speaking of Narcisse, the young Creole in *Dr. Sevier,* Cable
interrupted his narrative to remark, "It is hard to give his pronunciation by letter. In the sound 'right' he substituted an a for an r,
rounding it almost in the same instant with the i, yet distinct from
it: "All a-ight, ole hoss!"

in *Kincaid's Battery* and *The Cavalier,* while his observations in camp in the delta country figured in many of his
novels and shorter stories, scenes in which he had roamed
surveying the great gulf marshes and reedy isles, the
haunts of alligators, wild-cats, raccoons and serpents.
There were the tangled waterways, familiar to smugglers, slavers and pirates, with their memories of the old
buccaneers and the brothers Lafitte, the vast green
wastes and narrow channels between the luxuriant hummocks where Audubon had delighted in the sea-snipe,
the plover and the curlew. One saw the pirogue of the
hunter still and the lateen sail of the oyster-gatherer in
this maze of marsh-islands bordering the half-drowned
mainland as one followed the Mississippi out to sea.

Cable, who had begun to write,—he was a reporter on
one of the papers,—had visited the Acadian villages
that lay to the west, the parishes with the names of saints
where lakes and plantations bore French names and
French was the language of the whites and the blacks
alike. He had spent hours as a boy on the levee watching the half-naked Negro gangs that sang as they pressed
the cotton-bales, and since then he had studied the un-
canny side of the Negroes too, the side that especially interested Lafcadio Hearn. This other reporter was drawn
to Cable when he published the story of *Jean-ah Poquelin,* attracted as he was by everything that was horrible
and gruesome: Hearn and Cable together collected Afri-
can-Creole folk-songs and Hearn wrote an article about
Cable and the scenes of his romances. Later Joel Chandler Harris, who had come to New Orleans a second
time in search of Negro spirituals and hymns, went to
prayer-meetings with Cable in the Negro churches,
piqued as he also was by the "vague and mysterious
danger" that had lurked on the outskirts of slavery, as
he said. It had always seemed "ready to sound a shrill
and ghostly signal in the impenetrable swamps," Harris

observed, in the spirit of Marion Harland, who recalled in her *Autobiography* the old slave days and the story of Nat Turner's insurrection. She was told as a little girl that the signal of attack was a "trumpet blown long and hard" and for the rest of her life she was conscious of a stricture of the heart that stopped her breath at the sudden blast of a hunter's horn at night. Cable had picked up the story of the Negro chief Bras-Coupé which he related afterwards in *The Grandissimes,* the giant, like Harris's Blue Dave, who had escaped to the swamp and become the terror of hunters, slaves and children. He had chosen his name to signify that the arm which no longer might shake a spear was virtually a useless stump for anything else. As for the Acadians, in their villages in western Louisiana, they did not like to be reminded of their Canadian past, for the proud Creoles had looked down upon them, laughed at them and lorded it over them when they were peasants and the Creoles were slave-holding planters. The Acadians were small farmers still, illiterate and poor, though, for good or ill, they were catching the spirit of progress, acquiring school-houses with the English language, a free paid labour system, Cincinnati furniture, melodeons and sewing-machines. The swamps had been cleared of their rushes, flags, cypresses and willows for the building of the railroad that followed the public school. Cable soon pictured these people in *Bonaventure.*

But, with all his feeling for the Acadians and the Negroes, Cable's great interest was the Creoles themselves and their setting in old New Orleans, which always charmed him, the city whose history he explored for sketches in the *Picayune,* reading old newspapers, ransacking the municipal archives. Working as a clerk in the Cotton Exchange of which Degas painted a well-known picture,—during his months in the town, visiting a brother,—he followed in the footsteps of Charles

Gayarré as a student of the Louisianian past from the days of the Jesuit explorers. A lover of Creole antiquity, he dug up strange true stories that exhibited the romance and picturesqueness of the New Orleans life, stories of the twice-married countess, the haunted house in Royal Street, the young aunt with white hair and the white slave Salome. With small concern for its obvious aspects, the lotteries, the gambling, the races, the notes of New Orleans that appealed to more commonplace writers, his imagination dwelt on everything that gave its uniqueness to a town where one felt "further away than elsewhere from everywhere else in the world," he said. In the outskirts he knew the plantation-houses that lined the river and the bayou-front, the pillared porches half hidden by laurustines, the moss-draped live-oaks with shadows a hundred feet across, the colonial villas with avenues of oleander. The roofs, red and grey by turns, rose out of orange and magnolia groves or the deep shade of mighty willow jungles that were often surrounded by fields of sugar-cane. As for the French quarter and its balconied façades and cool flagged flowery inner courts, Cable had known it from his earliest boyhood in the town, with the dazzling white walls of the St. Charles hotel where the nabobs of the river-plantations had come in the heyday of the quadroon balls at the Salle de Condé. Though the city was a hundred years younger than Boston, it seemed already decrepit with age as it basked in a Mediterranean picturesqueness, for many of the great doors were grey with cobwebs, the ironwork was begrimed and rusty, the corrugated red-tiled roofs were overgrown with weeds. Old Franco-Spanish piles of yellow adobe or stuccoed brick were faced with showy shops and gay with flowers, with battered brass knockers highly burnished, hinges on the gates a yard long and the graceful scrolls of the balconies freshly painted. One could almost touch with a walk-

ing-stick the overhanging eaves of many of the low adobe
houses, and streets and alleys abounded with archways
through which one caught glimpses of the garden
within, blossoming parterres, dark palms and pale ba
nanas. There were gardens on every side. Scarlet pome
granates hung over the walls, orange-boughs and lemon
and the climbing jasmine. Cable, long after he left New
Orleans, recalled them in his book, *The Amateur Gar
den,* a fruit of Frederick Law Olmsted's "garden gospel.'

Here dwelt the Creoles of whom Cable was writing
when Edward King appeared in the town and accepted
his work for *Scribner's* in 1873, delighted to find a South
ern author who was doing with the New Orleans folk
what Bret Harte had done with the argonauts of the
Western shore. One of Cable's friends had urged him to
go to California in search of the local colour he had
found at home in the streets, the cafés, the records of
the city and the memories of townsmen who recalled
the first quarter of the century and the years before the
war. He was full of the scenes of the past and the present that appeared so soon in his novels and tales, the
days when Napoleon sold the Mississippi valley, when
the Creoles branded with infamy all who held office in
the new regime or sympathized with the American occupation. Those times of Edward Livingston, Governor
Claiborne and the two Lafittes were the period of his
finest novel, *The Grandissimes,* in which one heard the
monotonous chants and machine-like tune-beats of the African dances at night in the future Congo Square. The
rattling of mules' jaw-bones mingled with the sounds of
the gyrating dancers and the tom-toms, wild Negro songs
and wooden horns. Foreigners like the Dutchman Kris-
tian Kopping and Frowenfeld the German had appeared from every corner of the commercial world, after
the purchase of Louisiana, to pick up fortunes, and indigo at that time was a staple of the countryside, where

one still saw the abandoned fields and vats. The best people went for advice to voodoo priestesses and fortune-tellers like the barbaric beauty Palmyre Philosophe. A few years later the town was filled with West Indian exiles from San Domingo, Martinique, the Barbadoes and Cuba, refugees in many cases from Negro insurrections with tales of fire and blood, captures and flights. Cable himself might almost have remembered William Walker's filibusters who swarmed in the streets and the rotunda of the St. Charles hotel and whose lawless enterprise caught the fancy of the young men of the city as it captivated young men in San Francisco. They talked about Spanish-American misrule and the golden rewards that would fall to those who supplanted it with a stable government, as young men had talked in earlier days of Texan annexation and the chances of the war with Mexico that rapidly followed. Then New Orleans had swarmed again with Zachary Taylor's victorious soldiers whom Whitman had watched so curiously in 1848. Cable was all eyes and ears for these shifting phases of the life of the town, as he was for the Choctaw squaws who sold sassafras and bay, the Spaniards and Cubans in the cafés, the Sicilians with their violent gestures, so energetic when they worked, so composed when they were at rest.

Of all these types the New Orleans Creoles were the most important in Cable's stories, with the women of the quadroon caste whose golden age was the half-century before the Civil War, those modern hetairae who achieved such varied styles of beauty and such fascinating manners, such elegance, vivacity and wit. Their faultless features and nymphean grace were the fruits of a long cultivation, and Cable recurred in several stories to their often tragic fate in a world where the line of colour was so sharply drawn. *Madame Delphine* and *Tite Poulette* were tales of the devotion of mothers

to daughters whom they tried to shield from the conse
quences of their mixture of blood, and there were times
when Cable seemed to justify miscegenation, although
he opposed it strongly in his political essays. There,
speaking as an ex-Confederate soldier and a son and
grandson of slave-holders, he defended the right of the
Negroes to education, to legal equality, to be "citizens
in every sense," while he insisted that he himself no
more believed in "social equality" than "the most fer
vent traditionalist of the most fervent South." His feel
ings in this matter were undoubtedly ambiguous, which
partly explained the unpopularity that sent him North
in 1885 to live for the rest of his days at Northampton
in New England, although he was also attacked in New
Orleans for misrepresenting the Creoles, for writing
about them "inaccurately," "unjustly," "untruly." [7] His
errors were invisible to the outside reader, who could
only account for these attacks by Dr. Keene's theory
in *The Grandissimes* that, owing to their fantastic,
their suicidal pride, the Creoles were almost always
"on the defensive." Perhaps they also felt that Cable
would have stirred up trouble, as Frowenfeld did, or at
least urged others to do, in the old slave days when this
young German pleaded with the quadroon cousin of the
Grandissimes to rouse the minds of his people to a noble
discontent. But the real wonder was that Cable ob
served so sympathetically a world that was often loose
where he was strict, Presbyterian deacon that he was and
a sabbatarian like Stonewall Jackson who refused even
to go for a stroll on Sunday. He thought it was wrong

[7] Grace King and Kate Chopin, later writers of Creole stories, both
began with the purpose of "correcting" Cable. When Richard Watson Gilder asked Grace King why the New Orleans people objected
to Cable, she said he proclaimed his preference of the coloured to
the whites, assuming the superiority of the quadroons over the Creoles. He "stabbed the city in the back" to please Northern readers.
Gilder was "cold" to this argument of hers, Grace King observed
in her *Memories of a Southern Woman of Letters.*

for young ladies to read novels and as late as 1883 wondered whether the theatre was not immoral, and he obliged Mark Twain to "hunt up new and troublesome ways" of dishonouring the Sabbath when they were on a lecturing tour. For blemishless piety and limpid innocence, Mark Twain said, the Apostles were "mere policemen" to George W. Cable.

In fact, it was the goodness of the Creoles themselves that Cable especially singled out, that he treasured and extolled in his novels and tales about them,—the strength of heart of generous natures like that of Dr. Sevier, who concealed an immense benevolence under his "war-paint." In another story a taxidermist, winning a fortune in the lottery, devoted it all to building a home for orphans; in another Jean-ah Poquelin, once an opulent indigo-planter, kept his leper-brother at the expense of his name. Old 'Sieur George, with his miser-like air, also cherished a merciful plan, and one felt in *Madame Délicieuse* an equal affection on the author's part for the fiery, flamboyant old general and the son he had estranged. No one could ever have doubted that Cable admired the Grandissimes, the formidable Creole clan, "legion" but "one," with its choice spirits and others less choice, held together by family pride, by the name and "heroic good manners" of a warm-hearted race. He humoured their drowsiness of mind, their instability and scorn of toil, easily inflamed and discouraged as many of them were, as one felt his fondness for Narcisse, Dr. Sevier's secretary, whose head was as handsome as Apollo's. There was something of Hawthorne's Donatello in the animal innocence of Narcisse, gathering his honey from every opening flower, with his full round arm and strength of limb, his well-cut chin and almond eyes, his infantile amiability and butterfly charm. As for the Acadian Bonaventure, in the far-away village of Grande Pointe,—so like the Grande Pré of *Evan-*

geline, which the story continued by relating the life of the Acadians in their new home,—Cable treated with the warmest regard this saintly half-starved schoolmaster who loved his thankless work better than his life.

Cable's feeling for the Louisianians was ampler than the feeling of his rivals and critics, for he saw their life in its larger relations and contrasts, the contrast, for instance, in *The Grandissimes* of the French and American civilizations, the contending races, the old and the new regimes. Many of the characters in his shorter stories were both types and individuals, representative figures in opposition, like Jules St. Ange in *Posson Jone* and the Protestant preacher from Florida and the elder and younger De Mossy in *Madame Délicieuse.* In the old romantic general and the young doctor-scientist son, whom the father disinherits for refusing to become a soldier, the lover of peace and the lover of the sword, both equally proud and intransigent, he characterized two generations of the Creole world. One missed these notes when he became an expert professional novelist and the magic and most of the flavour vanished from his work, when he had lost the French traits that were as if innate in him, quick and elastic as he was, vivacious and alert. His style was half French in his earlier books, light, precise and epigrammatic, with an air that seemed to mirror the Creole mind.

CHAPTER XIX

WEST OF THE APPALACHIANS

ON THE wide prairies of Louisiana, beyond the bayous, lakes and swamps and the turfy Acadian villages with their hedges of roses, the South merged into the West and the corn-fields and the cane-fields gave place to great flat stretches of grazing country. There, towards the border of Texas, the herds roamed far and near at will and mustangs were begotten and foaled in the unfenced spaces, a land of horsemen where black-hatted herders rode with lariats of plaited raw-hide coiled and ready at the bows of their Mexican saddles. In this world of Cable's *Bonaventure* they talked about horse-thieves and rustlers and other affairs of the widespread "cattle kingdom,"—which had elements in common with the old "cotton kingdom" of the South,—for cattle and minerals were the only interests of the vast unsettled regions that stretched to the Canadian border and the Sierras to the west.

From the Rio Grande across these plains the cowboys drove the cattle sometimes to Montana,[1] sometimes to the market in Chicago,[2] where the young Irishman Frank Harris, who spent one year on the long trail, acted as a hotel-manager during part of another. After working as

---

[1] The long drive to Montana, in 1882, was the subject of Andy Adams's *The Log of a Cowboy*. This five-months' drive covered nearly three thousand miles. Its purpose was to fulfil a government contract to supply beef to the Indians at the Blackfeet Reservation.

[2] Frank Harris described a drive to Chicago in 1871 in *My Reminiscences as a Cowboy*. Although Harris was a notorious liar, this lively account of his early adventures bears every evidence of being substantially true.

a sandhog in New York, digging for the new Brooklyn bridge, he had lived on a ranch in the West, breaking in colts, acquiring there perhaps the look of a bad man of the mining camps, a gambler and ruffian that clung to him for the rest of his life. Before he gave up cow-punching for Kansas University and Heidelberg, he witnessed the Chicago fire of 1871, the fire that destroyed the house of the Newberrys with all their family papers and letters from Washington Irving, Cooper and Aaron Burr. This was the house that for Julia Newberry was "worth all London, Paris and New York," fiercely loyal as she was to her native Chicago, the frontier town and trading-post, still on the edge of the wilderness, where one found already the amenities of the Eastern seaboard. The diary that Julia Newberry kept from 1869–'71 brimmed over with the charms and the gaieties of civilization, engaging as this young girl was, all gallantry and courage, intelligent, perceptive, warm-hearted, witty and frank. With her ardour and her gift of observation she might have been a novelist. Her diary abounded in subtle and discerning remarks on the people she met in Homburg and in Paris as well as the guests in her father's house, such as General Sheridan and Goldwin Smith, whom she studied with eager interest and clairvoyant eyes. As a winter visitor in St. Augustine, sketching the gate and the fortress, she suggested one of the heroines of Miss Woolson's novels, and she might have been a young girl in a Henry James story of Rome, where she died,—like Daisy Miller,—in 1876.

If one saw the extremes of Western life in Julia Newberry's diary and Harris's *My Reminiscences as a Cowboy,* written years later, one found its most typical note perhaps in Edward Eggleston's homely novels, which reflected the common life of the northern frontier. Eggleston, born in Indiana, the son of an emigrant Virginia lawyer, may well have read Bret Harte's California sto-

ries, but he owed his interest in regional writing largely
to the influence of Taine, whose lectures on *Art in the
Netherlands* stirred him deeply. The Dutch painters, as
Taine showed, produced nothing of serious value as
long as they resorted to Italy for their style and their
subjects instead of painting, as they learned to do, their
own rude native themes, their often unlovely interiors,
vistas and people. Eggleston had this in mind when he
wrote about the West, which he knew as a farmer's boy
and a Methodist preacher. He had tramped all over
Indiana, sleeping in haymows and fence-corners, while
he learned to set type in a rural newspaper-office, studying the Hoosier dialect and the manners of the backwoods when he jogged through the country later as a
circuit-rider. Sometimes he travelled the circuit on foot
in a pair of Indian moccasins, sometimes he virtually
lived on a lazy old horse, reading his Greek and Latin
books and his works of devotion and history like Bishop
Asbury, who had studied on horseback before him. Indians, trappers and half-breed voyageurs formed his con-
gregations with the settlers from the East and from Europe who were clearing the woods. Before he abandoned
the ministry and went to New York in 1870 he had also
spent several years in Minnesota, observing the rise of
the mushroom towns in the land-boom of the fifties
when the cottonwood stumps stood everywhere in the
sprawling streets. Some of them, sod-towns with grandiose names from romantic novels, grew when times were
flush and were soon deserted, like Lincoln's little New
Salem in Illinois; and where the grass flourished on the
site of the short-lived emporium or city hall the former
court-house was used to stable sheep. Perhaps the town
bore the name of an Indian chief who had traded his
land for a white man's annuity of powder and blankets
and who walked away with his gun over his shoulder,
while the walls of the tavern that looked out on the roll-

ing prairie landscape bristled with engravings and maps of the metropolis-to-be.

This frontier world of Indiana, Minnesota and Illinois appeared in several of Eggleston's homespun novels with the sharp contrasts of a settlers' life that witnessed camp-meetings and barbeques, corn-shuckings, revivals and the raids of desperados. They were full of characteristic scenes of the works and days of the pioneers, the spinning, the weaving, the quilting, the great feasts in the forest where half a dozen oxen were roasted in halves, the target-shooting and jumping at the tavern with the deer's horns over the door, the suppers of venison, hoecakes and sassafras tea. Occasionally some big boy in buckskin pantaloons took to the wilderness when he had been crossed in love, joined the border-ruffians and became a horse-thief, but young men of unusual force were apt to enter the ministry, a profession that was generally reverenced along the frontier. For everywhere religion was a marked concern of the pioneers. In the towns especially the Methodists predominated, though the Presbyterians rivalled them here and there, regarding them with a certain disdain because their preachers were often illiterate and because they received without scruple all manner of men. The hardshell Baptists pressed upon them close although they abstained from the Methodist evangelism, for, fatalistic as they were, believing they were either saved or damned, they felt no call to interfere with God's arrangements. So it was mainly the Methodists who carried on the camp-meetings in the thronged recesses of the woods. It was usually in August after the summer harvesting that the great platforms rose among the tents, and the hurricanes of religious excitement swept multitudes before them and seemed to fan even the bonfires that blazed at night. Thousands were infected with the "jerks," the "dancing disease" of the Middle Ages, while the gypsy life and the shouts and songs delighted the growing boys and girls for whom these occasions were jolly religious picnics. Yankee clock and tin pedlars mingled with the crowds and the devil had his innings on the edge of the darkness, where the general ferment prompted other encounters. The "camp-meeting baby" was proverbial in stories of the West. The older New Englanders had preferred revivals of the quiet, awful and pervasive kind, but these were impossible with the inflammable Western people, who felt at home with sons of thunder like Peter Cartwright of the Sangamon country, the preacher who was still active until 1872. Cartwright often left his pulpit to thrash some heckler in the crowd, then mounted to the platform again and finished his sermon. But many even of the wild-fire Methodists were steadfast in their faith and learned, like the dutiful Roxy, in religious lore. This heroine of Eggleston knew by heart the experiences of Mrs. Jonathan Edwards as she knew all the Methodist calendar of saints.

Eggleston's deep religious vein reflected the frontier, though his Methodism changed greatly after he left it. Like Lincoln, he was touched by Channing and Theodore Parker. Later he wrote *The Faith Doctor* to show that city people were more credulous in religious matters than the simpler Hoosiers. His best novel, *The Hoosier Schoolmaster*, published in 1871 and based on his brother's adventures as a pioneer teacher, was a crude provincial classic of a sort, full of Dickensian mannerisms, with a pungent local quality that was sometimes impressive. It pictured in Flat Creek a rough Hoosier settlement with considerable differences already in wealth and education,—but without any class-demarcations as yet,—overrun with border-rowdies, with a school where the pupils were in chronic rebellion and the master was obliged to develop the bulldog in himself. One found the witch-doctress there, disseminating herbs and gossip, dispensing the blood of black animals in the dark of the moon, and the typically homesick Eastern woman whom everything reminded of something she had previously known in the neighbourhood of Boston. In *The Graysons,* another of Eggleston's novels, a story of central Illinois, Lincoln appeared as a young lawyer defending a friend, as he was also a minor character in Joseph Kirkland's *The McVeys,* where the setting was the mining region of the upper Mississippi. In a preface to *The Mystery of Metropolisville,* 1873, Eggleston defined his purpose in writing these novels: it was "to represent the forms and spirit of our own life" and "free ourselves from habitual imitation of that which is foreign." He wished to contribute, as he said, to the history of American civilization by portraying certain aspects of American manners, and he was the first of a long line of Middle Western realists who were truthful and honest as he was and sombre as well.

For neither Eggleston nor Hamlin Garland nor Edgar Watson Howe denied that the frontier life was difficult and dark,—notwithstanding the excitements and the pleasures of a settler's existence,—with its paltry politicians and the solitude and silence in which the pioneer women so often lost heart. In *The Story of a Country Town,* E. W. Howe was soon to show how hard and loveless the pioneer life could be, where the women were pale, fretful and always overworked and the men were too often surly, rough and harsh. This picture was corroborated by Hamlin Garland's recollections of the plains of Iowa in 1871–'75 and the frontier hamlets of the Middle Border where the Garlands also lived in the lake-bound region of Wisconsin and in Minnesota. Garland, happening on *The Hoosier Schoolmaster* when it first appeared, observed the similarity between Indiana and his own backwoods Western farming country, but, stirred as he was by Eggleston's wish to interest the West in its own life, he was moved still more by the novelist Joseph Kirkland. This other Western realist, a Chicago lawyer who did not begin to write until he was fifty, had lived as a child in Michigan and Illinois, and Garland, in Boston for several years, reviewed his *Zury* there and presently went to see him on his return to the West. *Zury*, a story of the thirties and forties, told the tale of Wayback, a pioneer settlement built around a grist-mill, from the day when the prairie-schooners arrived with the horsehair sofas and the Franklin stoves, and the rag-carpets were laid in the first log-houses. When Zury married a second time, his wife was a Lowell mill-girl, a reader of Fourier who had come to the village as a schoolmarm. His first wife, faded and as thin and sad as one of the women of E. W. Howe, was a symbol of the toil and aridity of the frontier existence, its loneliness and charmlessness, the poverty that destroyed romance, the gracelessness that weighed on the mind of Garland. Kirkland urged him to "tell the truth" about this farming life, and Garland was to do so more skilfully than his predecessors. But the older writer gave him too a feeling for the tragic note in scenes that had earlier struck him as dull and petty.

The adventurous mood of the pioneers seldom appeared in these grimmer books, the zest which the men experienced more often than the women, free as they were to wander, to hunt, to explore; nor did the charm of Mark Twain's Mississippi or the magic of a dozen aspects of life in the West. Here and there in real life one still met sons of the Revolution whose fathers had carried swords at Valley Forge and ancient Nimrods who had penetrated swamps to kill some terrifying beast and bore henceforth a title like Panther Jim. There was the West of the mighty rivers where the boat-whistles heard from afar filled the air with poetry and romance, and there was the levee at St. Louis, for instance, where picturesque types of a dozen kinds moved through the perfume of spices among bales of cotton. From the broad galleries of the older houses one saw French workers in peasant dress, files of Indians stepping silently by, priests in long gowns, soldiers on horseback and hunters and trappers in deer-skin shirts who had once visited Senator Benton there. For among them were some of the mountain men who outfitted themselves in St. Louis before they returned to the plains and the Rockies beyond, the closest friends now and then of John C. Frémont's father-in-law, who had been so passionately interested in the further frontier. There was the West of the riverboats where one often saw a prayer-meeting in progress with gambling at the other end of a gaudy saloon, while the legends of Paul Bunyan had thriven, especially since the Civil War, in the lumbermen's West of the lakes and the northern regions. This bellicose bearded forest warrior, as powerful as Hercules, had first become known in New Brunswick about 1837, and he was the mythical inventor of the art of making logs from trees who had camped and logged all over the northwestern country. Moving on constantly to log off the virgin woods, Paul Bunyan had appeared in Dakota, in Iowa, in Kansas, even for a while in Oregon, even in Utah, and at least a hundred tales about him spread from camp to camp, hatched by the bunk-house bards and story-tellers. He was said to have lived in a mammoth cave with raw moose-meat for his favourite food and the barrels of his shotgun were used as smoke-stacks in his saw-mill, while he brushed his beard with a young pine-tree that he had pulled up by the roots and spent his Sundays planning inventions and speeches. He was always busy with his cogitations while the loggers shaved and greased their boots, calked soles, trimmed their beards and sewed on buttons. He caught clouds of black ducks in the ample tarpaulin that he carried on his shoulders back to camp, where the Big Swede was paramount in the crowd of loggers and cooks. Paul Bunyan was a legendary rival of Davy Crockett and Daniel Boone, Kit Carson and the Buffalo Bill of a later time.

In the Mississippi valley states, in the years just after the Civil War, the intellectual life was especially active, more so, as Mary Austin thought, than it was in the decades that followed her childhood, when "culture" had been to the fore in Illinois. Debating societies were omnipresent, Lyceum lectures and literary circles that obliged their members to keep up with the movement of mind, and people were as much concerned about their cultural qualifications as once they had been regarding the state of their souls. Outside of Bret Harte and the new dime novels the West was scarcely literary ground,—it harboured few writers as yet in any part,— and Boston and the Yankee authors largely ruled the Western mind in regions where many of the settlers had come from New England. There were multitudes for whom Bunker Hill, the Common and the Old South Church were invested with sacred memories and associations, as they were for Howells and for Hamlin Garland, who followed him to Boston in the mood of the Moslem pilgrim to the sanctuaries of Mecca.

Few writers of the Middle West thought for a moment of remaining at home, where there was little to meet their special needs, and while a few settled on the Pacific slope, like Joaquin Miller, John Muir and Bierce, they made their way in the main to New England or New York. There Edward Eggleston for many years was a literary editor. The founder of American sociology, Lester F. Ward, whose father had been a millwright in Illinois, settled after the war in Washington, where he spent most of his later life employed in one or another of the government bureaus. He had grown up with McGuffey's readers in a little red schoolhouse, working in the West as a farm-hand, harvesting and haying, roaming the Iowa prairies during much of his boyhood with a special eye for animals, insects and birds. As a soldier in the Civil War he had been wounded at Chancellorsville; then, like John Burroughs, a clerk in the Treasury, he had mastered seven languages and made himself at home in the world of science. Familiar above all perhaps with botany, zoology and anthropology, while he kept his diary in French, he shared in the Darwinian controversies of the eighteen-seventies and gradually developed his own sociological system. An American member of the family of minds that included Spencer, Huxley and Comte, he greatly admired Condorcet and his faith in the future, although he knew it would require a longer time than Condorcet thought for the world to "get its growth." All the races of men must first be blended into one race, and for this a millennium might be necessary, or ten thousand years,—"but not so long as it took to develop the horse,"—for he was an ardent believer in evolution, though he never supposed that this was automatic. Far from regarding it as a merely natural or unconscious process, he thought of it rather as voluntary, according to law, a conscious striving for a higher goal, for the individual as well as the race, a great continuous flow of human effort. The idea of continuity was central in his thinking. As an equalitarian, with a lifelong sympathy for the submerged, he attacked monopolistic privilege and the laissez-faire system, and his *Dynamic Sociology* was the only American book that was ordered to be burned officially in the Russia of the czars. Ward was one of the obscure great men of an age that knew little of Willard Gibbs and forgot whatever it knew of Melville and Whitman.

While most of the other Western writers took flight for distant parts, a number of the Hoosiers remained on their own home-ground, among them Maurice Thompson, born in Indiana, who had returned to live there after the war. In most respects a Southerner who had known Kentucky and Georgia as a child, he had settled as a lawyer in Crawfordsville near General Lew Wallace, and his verses recalled the Georgia rivers, the bayous and the shores of the Gulf he had skirted on long canoe-voyages as an adventurous boy. In one of his poems the fragments of Sappho, most happily translated, were woven in true mocking-bird manner into the text, while others revealed his Lanier-like taste for Froissart's mediævalism and the tournaments that appealed so strongly to the fancy of the South. It was Maurice Thompson who wrote later the romance of *Alice of Old Vincennes,* and he had steadily opposed the realistic tendency that Eggleston represented in the Middle West.[3] As for Lew Wallace, also a lawyer who had fought on the other side in the war,—for Maurice Thompson served with the Confederate army,—he had lived as a boy in Indianapolis when his father was governor there and the capital was a straggling village in a wooded morass. Drawn early into army life,—his father was a West Point man and his mother, a Virginian, was a niece of John Paul Jones,—he had served as an officer in the Mexican war and spent two years in Mexico, where he studied the history of the conquest. With a taste as a boy for historical novels, *The Scottish Chiefs* and others, he had started one of his own on the invasion of Cortes, a favourite theme of American writers from the days of Charles Brockden Brown to the days of Robert Montgomery Bird and Prescott. In the land of Montezuma he followed the clues that Prescott left, visited temples and palaces and investigated the Aztecs, the remains of their

---

[3] Maurice Thompson's first little book, *Hoosier Mosaics,* 1875, was a group of sprightly sketches of rural types, specimens of Indiana character, old-time pedagogues, Hoosier farmers and county fairs, country auctions and minstrel-shows.

civilization and the records of their past, then, returning to Indianapolis, he continued the novel that he had begun but was not to finish for more than twenty years. The story purported to be told by a converted Mexican scholar, a noble Tezcucan who had served as interpreter for the viceroy,—a device that recalled Irving's *The Conquest of Granada*,[4]—and the romance was full of minute and varied pictures of the Aztec world, the Spaniards and the fall of Montezuma. It was published as *The Fair God* in 1873.

This adroitly told historical novel with its skilful local colour remained a popular classic for two generations, and Wallace was perhaps the best of all the American writers of a type that was soon to lose its magic for critical readers. He had great vitality as a story-teller, though his last romance, *The Prince of India*, a name for the Wandering Jew, was inferior to the others, *The Fair God* and *Ben-Hur*,—the best of them all; but this tale of the fall of Constantinople revealed his careful documentation and the breadth and depth of his scholarly interests and tastes. As minister to Turkey he worked in the archives in Constantinople with an eye for Oriental statecraft and domestic life and especially the history of religious faiths and comparative religion, always for him the central field of thought. Writing *Ben-Hur* in the later seventies,—the book was published in 1880,—he studied in the libraries in Washington and in Boston, collecting circumstantial knowledge of the Holy Land, the desert, the Arabs, the first century of the Christians and the history of Rome. The western Bible-worship that found much to like in *The Innocents Abroad* accounted for the prodigious success of this book as well, with the classical note that it also struck, the sea-fight and the chariot-race that exhibited Lew Wallace's soldierly feeling for horses. Then, along with its biblical

[4] Mark Twain used a similar device in his *Joan of Arc*.

character and its early-Christian atmosphere, the author was always on the side of the under-dog: his sympathies were obviously with the Jews against the Romans as they had been with the Mexicans in his earlier story. *Ben-Hur* had very substantial merits aside from the energy of the story-telling and was not without subtlety moreover here and there, in withholding, for instance, the appearance of Christ, whom one felt in the depths of the book but who did not emerge as an actor in any of the scenes.

In the Hoosier poet James Whitcomb Riley, the Middle West meanwhile expressed the "folksy" note that characterized it, the neighbourly spirit of so many of the settlers, their genial optimism, their homely domestic affections, their pastimes and tasks. This "poet of the people," as he came to be called,—or "poet of the school-children,"—reflected the tastes of a thoroughly settled West, a village world which was very unlike the wilder world of the Mississippi that appeared in Mark Twain's *Tom Sawyer* and *Huckleberry Finn*. It rather resembled in many ways the rural New England of Whittier's poems with its husking-bees, barn-raisings and barefooted children. Riley continued, in point of fact, the line of the popular New England poets and Longfellow for thirty years was his travelling-companion, the mascot he carried in his bag on all his reading-tours, the poet of childhood as Whittier was the poet of the farm. He had read early *The Task* of Cowper, contrasting the allurements of urban life with the charms of the country and the village, which remained his field, and he was influenced by Dickens as well, his child-characters and feeling for children, by Tiny Tim, Oliver Twist and Little Nell. He shared the cheery sentiment that was sometimes false in Dickens too,—his sentimentality was utterly unabashed,—and his prose sketches of pathetic children and older human oddities, his eccentric accountant, for instance, reminded one of Dickens. There were echoes of Dickens in *The Raggedy Man,* in *Little Orphant Annie,* in the travelling professor of phrenology, an American type that one found in Henry James, Mark Twain and Melville, and Riley perhaps had Dickens in mind when he became a public reader who was almost as famous and as versatile in his actor's role. This was in the days of the "platform kings" who appeared in Indianapolis,— Wendell Phillips, Josh Billings, Mark Twain and Alcott. Riley was described as a great comedian impersonating some little girl, a boy in a watermelon patch or a Hoosier farm-hand. Like Dickens he felt that his hearers were all personal friends.

Riley, born in a log-cabin in 1849, had lived as a boy in a pioneer farming village in an atmosphere of McGuffey's readers with which his poems were later in tune, for they perfectly expressed the mind of the pioneer schoolboy. He had travelled with a patent-medicine vendor who toured Indiana and western Ohio and employed him as an advertiser and entertainer, and he painted signs on fences and the sides of barns. He roamed about in farm-wagons, talking to ploughmen at work in the fields, loitering with weavers at their looms, sleeping in cabins, beginning in 1874 to publish the poems, in dialect often, that revealed so fully the feeling of his place and time. Finding the material for all of them within a short radius of his early home, he usually looked backward for his subjects to the village childhood that was so like the childhood of hundreds of thousands of others, reviving accurately in image and phrase the barefoot days, the old swimming-hole and the joy of being for a moment "a boy again." Caring really for poetry only,—he rarely talked about anything else,— he recalled the "summertime of youth" and the chums at school, strawberry time, the magic days when the frost was on the pumpkin, the fireplace with the crane

swung out, the old mulberry-tree. Studying his Hoosier
dialect with care,—the "country cousin" of literary
speech,—to be closer to the inner character of the people
he spoke for, he was a favourite reader always at old settlers' meetings, where he vividly evoked the ways of the
pioneers. There was no one like Riley for conjuring up
the well-sweep by the loghouse, the spot where the tavern used to stand, Saturday's chores in the good old
days, the sociable stove in the country store and the year
when the first grist-mill was erected in the village. His
poems were all of old times, old favourites, the rustic
beauty of the Western scene, pets and children, happiness, friendship and grief, with a constant reference to
"you and me" that made the reader a confidant and a
plain "blue jeans" philosophy that won him still further.
With his prodigious facility, Riley combined a remarkable skill, and the "Indiana Burns" might also have been
called a Herrick, while he resembled Stephen Foster in
the note of a constantly personal feeling that explained
his vogue with a multitude of homespun readers.

CHAPTER XX

THE PLAINS AND THE MOUNTAINS

ON HIS first real visit to the West in 1879, Walt Whitman crossed "bread-raising" Indiana, rejoicing in the golden belt of wheat that stretched from Ohio a thousand miles, always at home as he was in a farming country. Then he sped over Kansas and Colorado through herds of cattle and buffalo grass and stayed for a while in Denver, facing the Rockies. In the limitless sea-like spread of the plains, the untrammelled play of nature, in chasm, gorge and crystal mountain stream, in their broad handling and uncramped forms and the large, calm, able men he met he seemed to discover the law of his own poems. He found his earlier thoughts confirmed in the boundless prodigality and amplitude, in the pure breath and the primitiveness of these farm-lands of the future, in the presence of the swarthy cowboys, bright-eyed as hawks, who were always as it seemed on horseback, swinging in their saddles. This continental inland West was fated to be the home, he felt, of America's distinctive realities and distinctive ideas.

It was virtually a *tabula rasa* now in its further-western stretches where traditions were forgotten and conventions were all but unknown, where there had lately been "no law west of Kansas City" and there was little "beyond the Pecos" still. The agricultural frontier had leaped across this region and established itself long since on the Pacific slope while the plains themselves were only beginning to be settled, because new methods of pioneering had to be found for a waterless

country with very little timber for the building of fences
and cabins. Farming was scarcely feasible there before
the invention of barbed wire made possible the enclos-
ing of the land in 1874. Meanwhile, when the railroads
enabled the cattlemen to meet the Eastern markets, the
longhorns had swarmed out over the plains from Texas,
from the Mexican border to Montana and the Dakotas
to the north, and the years that followed till the middle
eighties were the great epoch of the cattle kingdom
when the cow-towns, the boom-towns rose at the ends of
trails. From Abilene and Dodge City to the west, to the
north beyond Cheyenne, the Indians were disappearing
from the buffalo-ranges. The advance of the settlers, following the railroads, roused them to fight for their lands
and their ways and they were to hold out longer in the
southwestern regions, but the victory of the Sioux over
General Custer in 1876 served merely to quicken the
forces that were putting them down. Custer was among
the last to see the ancient plains life of the Indians as
the painter George Catlin had seen it forty years before in the Mandan villages, for example, that had formerly stood on the site of Bismarck, where Custer camped
for a while across the Missouri. He saw the Sioux in all
their glory of war-bonnets and beaded shirts, necklaces
of bears' claws, embroideries of porcupine quills, capes
fringed with ermine, armlets of burnished brass, while
Mrs. Custer, in *Boots and Saddles,* written after her husband's death, described the campaigns against the Indians as the army saw them.[1] Henry M. Stanley, as a corre-

[1] High-spirited, full of romantic feeling, Mrs. Custer in *Boots and
Saddles* recorded especially the domestic life of the army-posts on
the Western plains. Usually the only woman who followed Custer's
regiment in Indian Territory, Kansas, Colorado and Nebraska, she
was often in the saddle riding beside her husband, and she did much
to enliven the dead calm of barrack life which Custer found less
endurable than danger. She taught the soldiers to dance and wrote
letters for them. Their fare, as she described it, consisted largely of
beaver-tails, black-tailed deer, buffalo tongues, elk and plover, and

spondent, learned much from these campaigns that he found indispensable in Africa a few years later. Leaving New Orleans after the war, following his nose for adventure, joining Sherman on one of his expeditions, he observed the general addressing the Indians now as warriors, now as children, and this taught him the art of dealing with savage races. He had General Sherman and his methods in mind in 1871 when he tramped in search of Livingstone through the African jungle.

The plains were the scene of a struggle now to establish law and order that brought peace-officers and bandits to the fore alike, and these were the days of the famous plainsmen, the heroes of novels and movies later, who followed Kit Carson, Jim Bridger and the men of their time. Some of the bad men, like Jesse James, the first train-robber, were graduates of the border banditry of the Civil War, when guerrillas were licensed to commit all manner of crimes. A young man might have been excused, in the unsettled after years, if he did not realize that circumstances alter cases, if he went on committing these crimes when they ceased to be sanctioned, especially if, like Jesse James, he had grown up on the Kansas border in the days when John Brown was "above the law." In these conditions, as in Billy the Kid's, in the vast vague region round Santa Fé, outlaws who were skilful and courageous, light-hearted and cool were often as much admired as the heroes of the law on whose efforts to break them society and the future depended. But even the desperados honoured the peace-officer Wild Bill Hickok, Bigfoot Wallace, the intrepid Texas ranger, Deadwood Dick of South Dakota, the express-guard of the gold-fields there, and the great

---

for her there was no bit of colour like the delicate blue line of smoke that rose in the evening from the campfire. So constant was her dread of the summer campaigns that it made her shudder to see the grass grow in the spring.

"gun-fighting" marshal, Wyatt Earp. It was Earp who
"cleaned up" Tombstone, the "howling wonder of the
Western world," the toughest of the frontier towns, in
1880, where the brilliant lights of the mahogany bars
and the Brussels carpets of the gambling saloons recalled the early days of San Francisco. All the mule-skin-
ners knew Wyatt Earp, all the bull-whackers and trappers; he had fished with Jim Bridger, the old scout and
mountain man, and he was a friend of Wild Bill
Hickok, who had once been Frémont's wagon-master
and a spy, sharp-shooter and scout in the Civil War. Usually dressed like a Mississippi steamboat gambler in a
long-tailed cutaway coat and fancy vest, with high-
heeled boots and ivory-handled pistols,—the "white-
handled guns" that were copied in so many stories,—
Wild Bill was the deadliest shot that had ever been seen
on the Western plains, or so at least Buffalo Bill, his follower, said. Two of Wild Bill's far-famed feats were
driving a cork through the neck of a bottle and splitting
a bullet against the edge of a dime. His own idol Kit
Carson, whom he had known as a young man, had never
seen Wild Bill's equal for fearlessness, and he was one of
Frank Harris's three lifelong heroes. After Harris had
accompanied him on the long drive to Chicago, Wild
Bill ranked in his mind with Cervantes and Shakespeare.

In the dime novels even now some of these men were
the heroes of boys who were agog with stories of the
plains, shooting and trapping, Indians, buffaloes, bad
men and life in the open; and these, with Buffalo Bill
and others,—Pinkerton detectives, Calamity Jane,—were
the setting and the *dramatis personae* of the "Westerns" later. The so-called Western story as a type had
not begun to appear as yet,—it was waiting for Owen
Wister and Stewart Edward White,—but Mark Twain
and Bret Harte especially had largely established the

pattern for it in their tales of the Far-Western mining world. In this young man's country the outstanding figures were Bret Harte characters who often recalled John Oakhurst and Yuba Bill: Wild Bill Hickok was even described as an "Oakhurst of the plains" and he and Bigfoot Wallace were stage-drivers for a while. Calamity Jane of the pony express was one of Bret Harte's less savoury types, and the Western stories, when they appeared, recalled at almost every point Bret Harte's California ranches and wind-blown Sierras. Meanwhile, the plains were already appearing in a kind of drama, the Wild West show that Wild Bill organized himself in 1870 to appeal to the interest in the buffalo-hunting and the cowboy and Indian life that were rapidly passing into their final phases. It was in Omaha, where Henry M. Stanley in 1868 had found a flimsy settlement of the overland trail, that Wild Bill opened his show for the emigrants who were crossing the plains with ox-teams, with wheel-barrows, usually in covered wagons. There were ex-manufacturers and bankers among them, sportsmen and actresses from New York on their way to the City of the Saints where Brigham Young had built the first important theatre in the West. It was in Omaha thirteen years later that William Cody, Buffalo Bill, who had ridden the pony express with Wild Bill from St. Joseph and who as a boy at Fort Laramie had met Kit Carson and Jim Bridger, opened the Wild West show that went round the world. A scout for Sherman, Sheridan and Custer, a Rocky Mountain trapper, a buffalo-hunter, stage-driver, despatch-rider and ranchman, Buffalo Bill was to become, as James Gordon Bennett said, the "beau ideal of the plains." [2]

---

[2] He was first so presented in the "dime novels" of "Ned Buntline," who also introduced him on the stage in a melodrama, *The Scouts of the Plains,* 1873. The adventurous Ned Buntline, Colonel Judson, who ran away as a boy to sea and fought in the Seminole,

The real stories of the West were still to come. Andy Adams's *The Log of a Cowboy* was not to appear for another twenty-five years, the more or less permanently valuable account of the long drive when western Kansas was still a part of the great American desert. On the "sod-house frontier," as it was called, there were few newspapers even as yet, and it was not many years since the buffaloes had trampled the corn-patch of the editor of the *Huntsman's Echo* in the middle of Nebraska. In the monotony of their lonely cabins the settlers' wives lost their minds, and the pioneer farmers were beset by outlaws and horse-thieves, with the nearest sheriff three days' ride away, yet Germans and Poles had poured into the country ever since the Civil War, Bohemians like "My Ántonia's" family, educated Swiss. The medical student who became "Old Jules" Sandoz did not arrive until 1884, but the cousin of the Swiss philosopher Amiel, the young idealist Edward Lyanna, had become a Nebraska farmer before 1860. Coming to America ten years before, he had joined Cabet's Icarian colony and remained energetic and hopeful when the colony failed, active and happy for fifty years in the "country of the Sioux," where Amiel rejoiced in having a correspondent.

Meanwhile, the desert lands to the south were inspiring studies of Indian life and Major Powell had explored the Colorado river. His *First Through the Grand Canyon* was the record of the expedition through the only region west of the Missouri river that had never been investigated by trappers before 1869, the thousand-mile series or chain of canyons, the river so-called of mystery and fear, that led by falls and rapids to Arizona. Wonderful stories were told of this river in hunt-

---

Mexican and Civil Wars, born in the Catskills, was a woodsman, angler and scout and a mighty hunter of Rocky Mountain game. He was a comrade on the plains of Wild Bill Hickok and Buffalo Bill. As a prolific writer, a follower of Cooper at long remove, he produced sea-tales and tales of border life.

ers' cabins and prospectors' camps, and no one was known to have passed alive through the underground chasms one heard of and the whirlpools into which one was carried with fearful speed. When, in John W. De Forest's *Overland,* Thurstone entered the Grand Canyon, he felt like another Orlando in the magic garden as the gate vanished the moment he entered and there was no choice for him but to pass on from trial to trial. Thurstone, who was on his way from Santa Fé to California, was engaged in a life-and-death race with the ferocious Apaches, shielding the delightful Miss Van Diemen from these Tartars of the American desert, which gangs of wild raiders haunted from end to end. For in 1870 the great plateau of New Mexico and Arizona was still the raiding ground of four large tribes, the Utes, the Navajos to the north, the Comanches, the Apaches; and the taste of the Apaches especially for capturing and torturing girls was a favourite theme of romancers and writers of novels. These hair-raising tales of abductions appeared not only in De Forest's book but in J. Ross Browne's *Adventures in the Apache Country* and in *Across America and Asia* by Raphael Pumpelly, who had travelled a few years earlier through Arizona. Pumpelly had found the country full of ruffians and gamblers whom the vigilance-committees had driven from San Francisco.

Virtually more distant than China or Norway from San Francisco or New York, Arizona had been wild enough in 1868, when Ross Browne discovered that a trip from Germany to Iceland and back was easier and cheaper than a journey from San Francisco to Tucson. There were no mails in the territory, no newspapers, no printing-press, although one had existed in New Mexico since 1834; one saw fresh Apache tracks on the main roads everywhere and felt the constant presence of murderers and robbers. Even the bones of the dead were seldom left to tell the tale in this country where no one travelled without a shotgun, a revolver, a bowie-knife and two derringer pistols, for America could vie with Italy now when it came to murdering, robbing and stabbing, if one threw in Montana and Idaho, as Ross Browne said. He found Tucson a town of mud-boxes, dingy and dilapidated, cracked and baked into a composite of dust and filth, littered with sheds and broken corrals, dead dogs and shattered pottery, parched, naked and grimly desolate in the glare of the sun. Approached through thickets of mesquite and sage and beds of sand and cactus, it swarmed with speculators, traders, gamblers and horse-thieves, and there was not a farm to be found in this region of pueblos and ranches although there were millions of acres of arable land. Billy the Kid was often there before he was killed in 1880 after killing a man for each of his twenty-one years, the last notable outlaw of the Southwest whose lightning-like quickness and coolness were the theme of laudatory ballads in both Spanish and English. "Straight as a dart, light as a panther," as one admirer, a sheriff, said, this child of the gambling-houses and mining-camps lived mainly in New Mexico, where his adventures with Mexicans and Indians made most of the popular dime novels seem meagre and tame. He had spent his boyhood in Santa Fé, where General Lew Wallace, the governor of the territory from 1878–'81, invited him for an interview and offered him a pardon if he would give up his wild ways and settle down. Wallace, who was finishing *Ben-Hur* in the governor's palace, working at night, was warned to close his shutters so that the light of his lamp would not be a mark for Billy, who had threatened to kill him.

At this time, 1878, the "father of American anthropology," Lewis H. Morgan, visited the pueblo country, driving a thousand miles by wagon, stopping at Indian villages, studying their social organization and system of kinship. He had just published his *Ancient Society* with the theory of social evolution that made the book one of the scriptures of the socialist movement when Kautsky translated it into German, Marx favoured its ethnological views and Engels produced a work that was based upon it. Born on a farm near Lake Cayuga when the Iroquois Indians were all about, he had early been adopted as a member of the Seneca tribe, and his work was a marked advance over Schoolcraft in the scientific method with which he recorded the customs of primitive people. As a devout Presbyterian he was deeply concerned in the great contemporary conflict of religion and science, while, convinced as he was by Darwin, whom he saw in England, he was one of the founders of evolutionary anthropology. A constant friend of the hounded Indians in the border warfare of these later years, he had visited them in Kansas and Nebraska before the war, and he observed that Indian studies had always been perverted by the use of such words as king for sachems or chiefs. Their communal houses were falsely called palaces, their villages were described as cities and their confederacies as kingdoms.[3] Lewis H. Morgan stayed at Taos, where Kit Carson had had his ranch. Frank Harris had bought cattle there for the long drive northward.

At just about this time too, in 1879, John Muir was visiting one of the wildest of the states, the "battle-born"

[3] In a letter to Lewis H. Morgan in 1877, referring to his *Ancient Society*, Henry Adams said that "the portion relating to our Indians . . . must be the foundation of all future work in American historical science." Adams, writing what he called "my poor ponderous life of Gallatin . . . my own ewe lamb or prize ox," asked Morgan in 1878 what he should say about Gallatin's ethnological and philological studies of Indian languages and races. What was the value of his work and what was its present standing? "I shall of course," Adams wrote, "rely on your opinion."—H. O. Cater, *Henry Adams and His Friends.*

Nevada, admitted during the Civil War and already strewn with grey and time-worn ruins. On every hand dead mining towns stood forlorn amid broken walls, with their chimney-stacks, furnaces and machinery half buried in sand, towns in which coyotes wandered now through the sage-brush in the streets where churches and hotels had flourished ten years before. John Muir had already seen the California mining camps. A few survivors whom he found in the washed-out gulches had shown him round the old Calaveras diggings, but he had been tracing the channels of pre-glacial rivers and the mines were only picturesque for him. He saw the Sierra gold-region as a "rose-purple zone" consisting of low, tawny, waving foothills, roughened with brush and trees and outcropping masses of slate, coloured grey and occasionally red with lichens. Muir, a naturalist, was also a writer whose first paper in the *Overland Monthly* had aroused immediate interest in 1872. It described an unusual snow-storm in the Yosemite valley.

John Muir had arrived in San Francisco in April, 1868, with a wish to go, as he said, "anywhere that's wild," and presently set out for the Yosemite on foot, camping along the way, ignoring the roads. It was the blossoming time of the year over the lowlands and the coast-range and the valley of the San Joaquin was drenched with sunshine, one vast level flower-bed, a lake of colour, perfume and light, with the meadow-larks and the streams singing together. Muir wandered enchanted through this glorious garden in long wavering curves, knowing by his map that the Yosemite lay to the East. There, during the last few years, two or three settlers had wintered and one of them had even planted an orchard in the valley. Muir, at last arriving there, found employment as a shepherd for a while. He was to spend many years in the heart of the Sierras.

A few weeks before this he had finished his "thousand-

mile walk to the Gulf," a botanical excursion from
Louisville through the Southern states, not the first of
his expeditions, for he knew the Northern wildernesses,
but one that took him to Florida and even to Cuba.
Pushing southward through deep woods, by the leafiest
and least trodden ways, with a small rubber satchel and
a plant-press, he had followed the course of the migrating birds, finding Kentucky, as Audubon had found it,
the most favoured province of all for the lover of wild
life. In the great bedroom of the open night, he slept in
this paradise of oaks, with its rapid streams and flower-
bordered canyons, travelling only with a loaf of bread,
living for weeks on crusts and water, wandering as free
as the wind in forests and bogs. He had little to fear
from the bands of guerrillas roaming the Cumberland
mountains, long accustomed to plunder in the recent
war, who thought nothing of murdering a traveller for
a handful of coppers. As for plants, he had looked for
them even in the Chicago streets, finding a few between
the paving-stones, and he discovered rare varieties in
the river-lands of Georgia, where William Bartram had
botanized long before him. Penniless when he reached
Savannah, he built a shelter of rushes and moss and
camped in the Bonaventure cemetery, the old forest
graveyard, spending five nights among the tombs that
suggested so many of the poems of Poe under the silver
streamers waving from the live-oaks. He searched the
swamps and pine-barrens of Florida and the creeks with
water as black as ink, watching the pelicans fill their
baskets and the herons, blue as the sky, winnowing the
warm air on quiet wings. Other lonely old white herons
drowsed between tides in their favourite oaks, curtained
by long skeins of Spanish moss. Once he dined on venison and milk, after a ramble through the flowery woods,
with a former Confederate officer who had become a
planter; then, sailing to Cuba for a month, he gathered

shells and plants in the sunflower bogs and wild gardens along the shore. He longed to go on to South America, visit the basin of the Orinoco and float the whole length of the Amazon on raft or skiff, a dream that Mark Twain had shared a few years before him. Then his imagination turned to California and its wonders and he sailed thither by way of Panama.

In the Yosemite, Muir's first task was to watch over sheep in the pastures near by, then he was employed to build and run a sawmill; but, able as he was to live on three dollars a month, he was not obliged to sacrifice much of his freedom. He put up a little shanty of sugar-pine shingles that stood near the foot of the lower Yosemite fall, digging a ditch for a stream from the creek that passed through the cabin and gave him society and music as well as water. For it fell enough to ripple and sing in low sweet tones that made delightful company, especially at night. There was a floor of rough slabs and a bed suspended from the rafters, while ferns climbed over the window by the writing-table. It all cost less than four dollars: it was cheaper than the hut where Thoreau had lived in a similar spirit at Walden. Muir roved by day through the trackless forest crossing the pathways of ancient glaciers, tracing mountain streams through lily-gardens, learning the habits of the squirrels and the birds in the redwood groves and among the rocks, camping for the night at the foot of some wild cascade. With resinous firewood from a storm-beaten thicket, he boiled the water for his tea, sleeping in chambers as snug as a chipmunk's nest, well-ventilated and full of spicy odours, enchanted in the wilderness of shattered crags, ridges and peaks, botanizing, geologizing, sketching and writing in his notebooks. During his first year he explored much of the Divide between the Tuolumne and the Merced basins, while he climbed Mount Dana and Mount Hoffman and penetrated the

Bloody Canyon to Mono Lake. In winter, with its wondrous storms, snow-bound in his cabin he ranged
through Humboldt and Agassiz by the cozy fire, through
Lyell, Tyndall, Darwin and Emerson's essays, considering his discoveries of the summer in the light of their
minds. He had become convinced that a vast ice-mantle
had once covered all this mountain region, grinding and
sculpturing it into the forms that one saw today as it
followed rock-cleavages and faults in its slow descent.
This was the "glacial erosion" theory of the origin of the
valley which he presently expounded in articles in Greeley's *Tribune*, the first of all his writings for publication,[4] a theory that was scouted by Josiah Whitney,
who conducted the survey of the valley, along with his
assistant, Clarence King. Whitney and King rejected the
views of "that shepherd,"—who was right,—believing
that the valley originated in a cataclysm. Muir even
found living glaciers in the Sierras that were unknown
before 1871. In the autumn of that year he discovered
the Black Mountain glacier in a shadowy amphitheatre
between two peaks. He had never expected to find an
active glacier as far to the south as this in the land of
sunshine.

Thus began the explorations that he carried on for
forty years in the mountains of California, in Nevada, in
Alaska, recorded in books that were published later,
many of them after his death, but largely compiled from
his journals of these earlier days.[5] Towards the end of
his life, as a student of trees, he visited Australia and
Africa and realized his early dream of the forests of
Brazil by sailing for a thousand miles on the Amazon
river. Meanwhile, for ten years he wandered alone
among mountains and storms, exploring all day long in

[4] 1871.
[5] Muir's first book, *The Mountains of California,* was not published until 1894.

the high Sierras, setting out as a rule before daylight with a bundle of bread tied to his belt and striding away with his notebook in the bracing air. Going to the woods was like going home for him. It pleased and amused him to sleep on rocks, curled like a squirrel round a boulder, when he could not find a fragrant bed of fir-plumes, and he was as happy as Daniel Boone in his sunny forest garden in these calm, vast, measureless mountain days. He lived without animal flesh, for he never carried a gun with him and even left the rattlesnakes unmolested,—after killing two, for which he felt sore and sorry,—rejoicing in the glorious landscapes about him, the serene assemblage of ice-born peaks and the immense domes and ridges that shone below them. In their wide-sweeping belts and beds covered and dotted with forests and groves, the moraines that looked so barren were full of life, composed in a wild harmony, moreover; and the lakes scattered on the table-lands, linked together by shining streams, glowed for him like pleasant human faces. He bathed in the floods of light, watching the sunbursts over the peaks and the radiance of noon on ledge and cliff, with the pure, blue, bell-like sky brooding over all. In the forests, ponds and meadows in the hollows, there were always new crystals and plants for him, arctic daisies, lilies higher than his head, and to him the rocks seemed talkative and friendly, with warm blood gushing through their granite flesh. He never tired of the valley itself, a paradise for him that made even the loss of Eden seem unimportant, with its groves of pine and oak strewn over the grasslands and the river flashing in the sun as it swept between them. But he found no one to share his feeling about the trees until Emerson visited the Yosemite in 1871. The silver firs and the sugar-pines filled Emerson at once with delight and awe, and, riding up to the sawmill on horseback, he was immensely interested too in Muir's collec-

tion of Sierra plants and sketches. Together they rode
out to the Mariposa grove, and Emerson seemed to be
pleased when Muir, who was thirty-three years old, proposed an immeasurable camping-trip in the depths of
the mountains. Muir pictured the fire he would build in
the woods, the beautiful fragrant sequoia flame and the
great trees transfigured in the purple light, while the
stars looked down between the mighty domes; but
Emerson, already old, was a child in the hands of his
friends and their indoor philosophy held him to the
hotels and trails. It was Emerson's afternoon of life, but
Muir remembered later that no one before him had
properly seen the valley, while Emerson, happy in his
visit to this mountain tabernacle, found Muir the right
man in the right place.

For the better part of six years Muir lived in the Yosemite. He often scrambled about the brink or went for
a ramble along the walls, which were sculptured into
an endless variety of spires and gables, of battlements
and mural precipices, all trembling with the thunder
tones of the falling water, cascades that were so subordi-
nated to the mighty cliffs over which they poured that
even while their voices filled the valley they seemed like
wisps of smoke or floating clouds. Sometimes he made
discoveries, as when he first found Shadow Lake, hidden
in the glorious wildness like unmined gold. He spoke
of this charming lake only to a few friends, fearing it
might come to be trampled like the Yosemite valley, and
visiting it year after year he never found traces of humanity there beyond the remains of a camp-fire and the
thigh-bones of a deer. The Indians had broken these to
get at the marrow. Occasionally an Indian would suddenly appear, standing silent and grim before him, as
motionless and weather-stained as an old tree stump,
with that wonderful art of walking unseen and escaping observation which his people had slowly acquired

in their forest life. Once he was startled by a group of queer, hairy, muffled creatures that came shuffling and stumbling towards him out of the woods, with a boneless wallowing motion like that of bears. They were Mono Indians wrapped in blankets made of the skins of sage-rabbits with dirt on their faces that was fairly stratified,— old and thick enough to have almost a geological mean-ing, it was divided into sections by furrows that resem-bled the cleavage-joints of rocks. Strangely blurred, with a worn abraded look that suggested exposure in a cast-away condition for ages, they were travelling to the Yosemite to gather acorns. Often Muir was out in storms. He made rather a point of being so, for even at the open-ing of the winter season, when he hastened down to his valley den, it was not to "hole up" and sleep the white months away. He was abroad all night at times and every day as well, wading, climbing, sauntering amid calms and gales, when the snow-laden summits were swept by a wild norther and the snow-dust on the exposed slopes, caught by the winds and tossed into the sky, was borne from peak to peak in resplendent banners. He had seen these snow-banners nearly a mile in length, and once when the whole Yosemite fall was torn into gauzy shreds and blown horizontally along the face of the cliffs, he saw the peaks of the Merced group waving banners against the sky, as regular in form and as firm as if woven of silk. He found himself once enjoying an avalanche-ride. After a heavy snowfall he had set out early to climb by a side canyon to the top of a ridge when he was swished down of a sudden to the foot of the canyon. It hap-pened as if by enchantment, and Elijah's flight in a chariot of fire could scarcely have been more exciting than this flight in a milky way of snow-stars. Once when he was out exploring a tributary valley of the Yuba river he was overtaken by a Sierra windstorm and found himself, as it were, blown on through the midst of its passionate music and motion across many a glen from ridge to ridge. In order to have a wider view, it occurred to him to climb one of the trees and get his ear close to the music of the topmost needles, and, choosing a tall Douglas spruce, he mounted about a hundred feet while the tree swirled round and round and rocked in the torrent. He clung to the lithe, bushy top, braced like a bobolink on a reed, while his eye roved over the excited waving forest, watching the light that also ran in ripples and swelling undulations across the wild sea of pines from one ridge to another. The shafts of the trees were brown and purple, tinged with yellow here and there, with masses of grey, chocolate and vivid crimson, and he listened to the click of leaf on leaf, the deep bass of the branches and the tense vibrations of the pine-needles, whistling and hissing. He kept his lofty perch for hours, frequently closing his eyes to enjoy all the better the waterlike flow of the wind or to feast on the delicious fragrance streaming past him.

In later years, extending his travels, Muir went on a rambling mountain journey of eighteen hundred miles across Nevada. He reconnoitred Utah and studied the northwestern states, and he made several trips to Alaska, beginning in 1874, especially to see the stupendous glaciers there, pushing as far as the Arctic ocean, on one of these expeditions, visiting northeastern Siberia and the Aleutian chain. He had spent years in the Sierras studying the action of ancient glaciers that had created new landscapes with their tremendous pressure, and, aside from this interest, he found sea-voyages inspiring as a change, with water hills and dales in motion instead of the permanent waves of the rocks. Alaska was a wonderful country for a lover of pure wildness. There one could travel thousands of miles without seeing any mark of man save some little aboriginal village now and then, or the faint smoke of a camp-fire, and Muir was de-

termined to get into the heart of it,—trusting to his
usual good luck,—with his bag of hard-tack. He spent
weeks of rapturous speculation canoeing through the
intricate channels of the coast, between the small islands of grey granite, closely observing the Stickeen Indians, the Chilcats and the Chilcoots, sharing their dinners of salmon and the fat of a deer. For dessert they
boiled with seal-grease the hips of wild roses. Muir was
almost too happy to get any sleep in Glacier Bay, where
the thunder of the icebergs rolled through the solemn
stillness. Some of the bergs were purplish by day and
some were of pure blue crystal throughout, while all of
them had azure caves and rifts of ineffable beauty in
which exquisite tones of light pulsed and shimmered.
New bergs were constantly born from the ice-cliffs, falling from the sides or top or emerging with a grand com-
motion from below, springing up with tremendous voice
and gestures, while tons of water poured down their
sides and they plunged and rose again and again before
they settled in perfect equipoise. On dark nights when
the winds were blowing and the waves were phosphores-
cent the glaciers stretched through the gloom with an
unearthly splendour. The luminous torrents streamed
from their sides like long robes of light and they roared
in awful harmony with the waves and the wind. Deep
called unto deep and glacier to glacier all over the wonderful bay. Muir witnessed unheard-of auroras in Alaska
also. Magnificent upright bars of light appeared in
bright prismatic colours and swiftly marched in close
succession along the northern sky. On another occasion
a silver bow, colourless and steadfast, majestically
spanned an inlet between two peaks, as intense in its
solemn white spendour as if all the stars had been raked
together and fused and welded to make this celestial
bridge. More than once Muir was in peril of his life in
these regions, canoeing on ice-floes, caught in the midst

of charging bergs or scrambling over glaciers enveloped in grey flying clouds and crossing crevasses hidden under the snow. But he felt that, as compared with death from some shabby lowland accident, it would be a blessing to meet one's fate on a glacier or a mountain.

All this was in the later years when Muir had become a public man, the father, as the newspapers called him, of the national parks, who had seen the great California trees, the oldest and largest of living things, blasted for commercial ends by dynamite. He awakened the nation to the importance of saving them. Meanwhile, he had taken up fruit-ranching not far from San Francisco, where he shut himself up in a room in a hotel to write, leaving the ranch from time to time to compose from his journals the series of books that did not begin to appear till he was almost sixty. In these he conveyed an exhilaration that was often ecstatic, like Thoreau's and like no other American nature-writer's, and he resembled Thoreau again as a lover of all things wild who did not "mould in," as he said, with the rest of the race. It pleased him to discover that even wild wool was finer than tame, that the wool growing on the mountain sheep in northern California was more delicate in texture than ordinary cultivated wool. If there had been a war of races between the bears and civilized man, he would have been tempted, he said, to side with the beasts, for he had a certain disdain of humanity that sprang from his native Calvinism and preferred the "less vertical" creatures, at least at moments. "Rough as the rocks," as he said of himself, "and about the same colour," congenial with mountains, glaciers, snows and storms, he often wrote well of animals too, detesting the anthropocentric notion that the world was especially made for the uses of man. Every crystal, bird and plant controverted this and proclaimed that it was made for itself, and its uses, alone, yet man's enormous conceit went unchallenged. Muir detested equally the notion of the behaviourists that animals were merely "machines in fur and feathers," for he had been deeply impressed by their intelligence and courage, by the fresh mountain vigour and valour of the Douglas squirrel of which he wrote and the loyalty, constancy and prowess of the dog Stickeen. This was the small black beast of most uncertain origin that followed him week after week through the flying snow on one especially perilous Alaskan journey. Nor could Muir praise the deer enough, at home as they were the continent over, whether in the Florida savannahs or the Canada woods, roaming over the northern tundras, crossing canyons and roaring streams, adding beauty moreover to every landscape.

CHAPTER XXI

FARM AND COUNTRY

JOHN BURROUGHS had cast about for a fruit-farm on the Hudson, and he found one on the west bank of the river at West Park, near Esopus, where he built a half-wooden house that was half of stone. Still connected with the Treasury department, he spent a good part of the year driving through the country as a bank-examiner and receiver, farming in the other months, raising grapes, peaches and currants for the market, reading and lounging when he could under the trees. In winter he wrote down what the summer had brought him. His new farm Riverby was not too far from the ancestral home to which he usually went back twice a year, at saptime when the maple sugar was made near the rock-maple grove and in midsummer when haying was in progress. To build his house he scoured the Catskills for butternut, cherry and ash trees which he took a hand in sawing and hauling to the mill, and he quarried into blocks a limestone ledge near by. This was the house where Walt Whitman visited Burroughs three times within the next few years. Whitman was to draw from his farmer-friend many of the detailed observations,—more than a few at Riverby,—in *Specimen Days*.

It was at Amenia across the river, in a valley not far from Poughkeepsie, that Burroughs had first read *Leaves of Grass* on a nutting expedition with the rural poet Myron Benton, who produced this odd-looking book during their tramp. They read it together aloud in the shadow of a rock. Benton, who remained for forty years

Burroughs's friend and correspondent, was one of a "set-fast" family with a farm called Troutbeck[1] who had "hugged the soil close," as he wrote in a letter, "an un-broken line of farmers" with none of their countrymen's usual roving ways. In their dell with its meadows and venerable trees, with the Webatuck flowing between, they had long been interested in farming and poetry alike, and Benton with his brother Charles, who had read Thoreau's *Week on the Concord,* had planned a similar voyage on this other river. Theirs too was a voy-age of discovery that led to the junction with the Housa-tonic, for the stream had never been seen that way be-fore, not, for once, looked down upon, but as it were looked up from, up the trunks of the trees and up the banks. Rowing through lands of old Dutch farmers who had mingled with the Yankees, past meadows where the Indians had met for their dances and powwows, they uncovered new secrets of vegetable life, castles of musk-rats, colonies of swallows, while they sketched and hunted for specimens to study and stuff. Charles Benton had written a charming essay that recalled the note of the Concord brothers, with whom the Bentons were deeply connected in spirit, and in fact it was to Myron Benton, the author of *Songs of the Webatuck,* that Thoreau wrote his last letter in 1862. Thanks to them and their cousin Joel, whose birthplace adjoined theirs, Amenia was a New York outpost of the Transcendental circle, and Joel Benton, who conducted the local lyceum, had arranged with Margaret Fuller to lecture there. Wendell Phillips and Horace Greeley, who supped on bread and milk at home and sometimes left his axe under the sit-ting-room sofa,—a special admiration of the hero-wor-

---

[1] "The most beautiful farm I have ever seen," Burroughs wrote to Joel E. Spingarn, the critic and poet who bought it and lived there later. It was on this farm, where Spingarn did much of his own writing, that he published the "Troutbeck Leaflets."

shipping Joel Benton,—had shared the hospitality of
their Amenia friends. Joel Benton liked to think of
Greeley's farm at Chappaqua, where the great man
usually spent one day a week, always ready to discuss his
theories of farming, indulging his hobby for deep ploughing and the foresting and reforesting of refractory and
obstinate fields and stony knolls.

Of all this family, Joel Benton was the most gifted by
far, the author of *Emerson as a Poet* and *Persons and
Places,* but the poet-naturalist Myron Benton was John
Burroughs's closest friend who had camped with him
one summer in the Adirondacks. This was in 1863, when
Burroughs had begun to study birds and expected to see
new varieties in these primitive woods, the paradise of
fish and game that was still known as "John Brown's
tract," where the old abolitionist had lived with the Negro settlers. But Burroughs found, like Thoreau in
Maine in the course of three excursions, that usually the
birds preferred the settlements and clearings. Myron Benton had written to Burroughs praising his sketches of
rural life, the first appreciative letter he ever received,
and Burroughs, happy to find one who was travelling the
same road with him, was charmed with the Bentons and
their flavour of the farm and the country. They were
lovers of picturesque paths and streams who liked to
gather local relics, preserve old crumbling cottages and
plant trees and vines, some of whose feeling of local
attachment was born, said Burroughs, of their native
spring, which one reached by a flight of stone steps under an elm. It was a spring that was large enough to
cool the milk of forty cows where trout from the river
made themselves at home. Myron Benton was somewhat older and more scholarly than Burroughs, but
they had almost everything in common, with the *Atlantic*
as a "university," a taste for Emerson, Thoreau and

Whitman, and a passion for farming, for plants and for animals and birds. They had countless talks in forest and field, by river, lake and mountain, and Benton many times appeared in the writings of this friend of his, now and again as "Richard" by way of disguise.

Meanwhile, Amenia, the home of the Bentons, had witnessed for several years a notorious and singular experiment in plain living and high thinking, one of the many communities that throve in the United States with the Zoarites and the Rappites and the Owenites, Brook Farm and Oneida. There Thomas Lake Harris had carried on his Brotherhood of the New Life from 1863 to 1867, establishing a grist-mill and a bank; and Laurence Oliphant joined him there before he moved on to Lake Erie, working as a labourer on the farm, hoeing in the vineyard. Harris, "America's best-known mystic," as William James called him, had preached as a regular minister in the Mohawk valley before he came under the influence of Andrew Jackson Davis and adopted the "harmonial philosophy" as a lecturer at large. Wandering to England, a Swedenborgian, he fell in with Oliphant, a member of Parliament, a diplomat and the cleverest of writers, a brilliant and charming man of the world who was also a friend of the Prince of Wales and always in the centre of excitement. Oliphant had once set off to join William Walker in Nicaragua, and after meeting Harris this sybaritic young man suddenly withdrew from Parliament and vanished from Mayfair. It was known that he had become a labourer on a far-away farm in America where presently his mother, Lady Oliphant, joined him, for Harris had a taste for "key people" that was much like Dr. Buchman's later. There, at the "Use," as they called the community, Oliphant was put to gruelling work, like the neophytes at Gurdjieff's community at Fontainebleau, intended to crush the old Adam in him and prepare him for a second birth, a spiritual reëducation directed by "Father." Up at 4:30 on winter mornings, he cleaned the boots of the other members, Dovie, Dimple, Seedcorn, Viola and Ernest, Golden Rose and Tiny Funnyhorns, washed their clothes, carted rubbish, curried the horses and swept the stables, living in a shed, silent, forbidden to speak. With the others he followed Harris's methods of "demagnetizing" and "energizing," practising "counterpartal marriage" and "internal respiration," while the master, engaged in his life-long mission to regenerate man and society both, dispensed revelations and composed oracular poems.

Harris and Oliphant had left Amenia,—the Use had moved further north and moved to California again in 1875,—and Joel Benton went to Poughkeepsie, where he became an editor in this early home of Andrew Jackson Davis. There Henry W. Shaw lived, the town auctioneer, who was known as Josh Billings, the humorist, all over the country and who looked the farmer and thought as a farmer quite as much as Benton and spoke for a world that was still overwhelmingly rural. He even made fun of Horace Greeley's *What I Know about Farming*, observing that Horace was only a "dictionary farmer," while he professed to live in Pordunk, the home of all the Billingses, as Artemus Ward was a denizen of Baldwinsville. The son and grandson of members of Congress, Shaw was a child of the Berkshires whose father had been a good friend of Henry Clay and, graduating from Hamilton College, he had knocked about the West, wandering for ten years in Illinois, Missouri and Kansas. He had owned and piloted a steamboat on the Ohio River, first appearing in the West as a comic lecturer who toured the country later with Mark Twain. He had adopted, like Artemus Ward, the spelling of an unlettered farmer and was famous for his *Farmers'*

Allminax and "sayings" [2] that satirized the foibles of his countrymen from the farmer's point of view.

For, with all the growth of city life and urban ways of thinking and feeling, the mind of the country retained its rural habits, although, partly because of the new machines, farm-life, as John Burroughs thought, had lost so much of its virtue and picturesqueness. Winslow Homer was a type of the time, the country-minded artist who dwelt by choice on rural themes and liked to think of hay-makers in meadows, the farmer's wife at the kitchen door, a girl giving a farmhand a drink of water. Homer lived in New York for twenty years without painting a single city theme, much as his eye delighted in women's fashions, and half the people who lived in the towns were homesick for the old rustic life, from which their imagination had never been weaned. They relished the humour of Billings and Ward that took one back to the country store where the wit was all at the expense of the man from the city. The horrors of metropolitan life were the subject of many a novel and poem, like the jog-trot *City Ballads* of Will Carleton, for example, a Western editor who lived for a while in Boston and in Brooklyn and expressed the disgust of the farmer in the Bowery and Wall Street. Carleton saw only poverty and squalor, despair and vice, the sinister "drunken and devilish pursuits of power, pleasure and gold" that Joaquin Miller saw in *The Destruction of Gotham.*

As for John Burroughs on the Hudson, he was a farmer for good and all, a countryman dyed in the wool, bred in the bone, a solitary man who mingled best with

[2] "It is better to know less than to know so much that ain't so."
"Fools are the whetstone of society."
"I never knew an auctioneer to lie unless it was absolutely convenient."
"Early genius is like early cabbage, don't head well."

his own kind and was never at home in the city or with men of business. Making his living from the soil, he kept in close touch with the old family farm in its broad grassy valley in the western Catskills, a land of open sunny fields and rugged wooded ranges, of round-backed hills and flowing mountain lines. One felt as if the muzzle of the cow might have shaped the landscape. Burroughs returned there every summer, for he loved to revisit the clover meadow, the bush-lot, the sheep-lot, the burying-ground, the barn on the hill, and he wrote many of his later books on this farm where, as a boy, he had cradled the oats and dug out rocks for fences. His family were plain uneducated folk who never read these books of his, and his father, like William J. Stillman's uncle, had been one of the "down-renters" in the anti-rent war when Cooper,—and even Walt Whitman,—had sided with the landlords. (For Whitman, later Burroughs's friend, was at the time an editor who followed the Democratic party-line.) This father was an old-school Baptist whom Burroughs remembered, Bible on knee, holding a tallow dip, flushed and shouting, hurling St. Paul's predestinationism at the free-salvation Methodism of one of his neighbours. Burroughs had cleared fields, tended the maple-sap kettles in April, driven the cows to pasture, built stone walls and carried the butter over the mountains to Catskill on the Hudson, a two-days' autumn journey in the lumber-wagon. He recalled the vast armies of passenger-pigeons that Cooper had described in *The Pioneers* and that disappeared forever about 1875, when the naked woods in early spring were suddenly blue and vocal with them and their dense moving masses filled the sky. The half-mile's journey to the far-away pasture was a chance for all manner of rambles and excursions and for glimpses of birds and birds' nests, woodchucks and squirrels, for berries and the fragrant wintergreen and the beechwoods with their treas-

ures in which the cows so loved to wander and browse.
As for the sugar-bush, nestled in a spur of the hills,
Burroughs knew every tree by its quality and look:
each one of the whole two hundred was unique for him.
There he had noted the coming of the bluebird, the
lines of swans etched on the sky and the twitter of the
first spring swallow in the air overhead.

All the associations of farming had for Burroughs a
lasting charm, the care of the crops, the cattle, fowls and
bees, the orchard, the building of the barns and coops,
watching the clouds and the weather, the ways of the
insects and the birds, the growth of the plants. Feeling
that a man could never exhaust the natural history of a
single farm, he clung to his own tenaciously for nearly
nine decades, for Burroughs was a stubborn man and a
lover of continuity, a note of his life that one felt in the
character of his work. He cherished the companionship
and silence of an old farmer-brother, while he maintained the ancestral homestead where he was first
drawn to the birds as a boy on a Sunday walk with his
brothers in the woods. Gathering black birch and wintergreen, he had suddenly caught sight of a yellow-backed
warbler, astir with its white-spotted wings among the
flickering leaves, so curiously marked and so new to
him that it was like a fairy bird, a vision of the woods
of which he had never dreamed. He had not seriously
studied birds until 1863, however, when he was teaching
near West Point and was deeply moved one day in the
library of the military academy by a set of Audubon's
pictures of the birds with the flowers. He always wondered that Audubon's errors were so few: there was
only one observation that he knew was mistaken. He
counted it a triumph to find a bird that Audubon had
missed. He had seen only two.

This was the beginning of Burroughs's lifelong interest in birds. He was looking for them in the woods on

the day of the battle of Gettysburg when James Russell Lowell in Cambridge was getting in his hay, and on Lincoln's second inaugural day, March 4th, in Washington, he was out for his first ramble of the season. That was the day when he first heard the song of the Canada sparrow, and he found the flowers of the houstonia under a bank. In the summer in the Catskills, looking for a trout-lake, he lost his way twice in the trackless forest, but he discovered rare yellow-bellied woodpeckers breeding in an ancient beech and a downy woodpecker's nest in an old sugar-maple. June was the month he tried never to miss when the birds were in full song and plumage and visitants from Latin America and the islands of the sea held their reunions in the branches over one's head. Then he observed the muskrats and the bumblebees, the insects and the tree-toads that also appeared in his essays. He had seen a partridge drumming, the next thing to catching a weasel asleep, standing by a log erect, expanding his ruff. The wing-tips scarcely brushed the log, while he struck faster and faster till the sound became a continuous unbroken whir, mainly produced by the force of the blows on the air and the body of the bird itself as if he were flying. Deeply interested in geology too, he had delighted as a young man in lingering about the ledges of his native hills, attracted by their curious forms and the presence of geologic time that looked out from their gray and crumbling fronts. But he was not a naturalist, nor did he wish to be one. He only wished to know the facts to see how animals and birds were related to nature in general and to human beings, for his mind was more or less of the order of Thoreau's while his aim was altogether that of a writer. But he was not conscious of any debt to Thoreau, of whom he wrote well in *Indoor Studies* as "a character crisp and pearl-like, full of hard, severe words and stimulating taunts and demands." Burroughs had begun to

write on out-door themes before he happened upon
Walden, and this was partly to break the spell of the
master-enchanter of his youth, whom he had seen at
West Point, Emerson. It was Emerson who had prepared
him for Walt Whitman. The *Atlantic* had largely shaped
his taste when he was a country schoolmaster, attracted
especially by books of the essay kind. He had contributed to the *Knickerbocker*, like most of the other New
York writers, and to Clapp's Bohemian weekly, the
Saturday Press.

Settled in the valley of the Hudson now, he found it
was a natural highway for the birds, a road as it were already graded for them, like all the large rivers running north and south, and there between times on the
farm he wrote through the autumn and winter,—writing for him was irksome from April to August. As the
fall approached, the currents mounted to his head again,
—his thoughts opened best like the burrs when there
was frost in the air,—and he stayed close at home, occasionally ploughing and boiling sap, while he raised small
fruits and potatoes for the market. First or last, however,
he travelled widely in forty years, recording his journeys
in various essays and books, and he envied Alexander
Wilson his famous walk in the winter snow from Niagara to Philadelphia through the woods. He explored
the Catskills and the Adirondacks and returned to the
Pepacton, his native stream, on which he voyaged in a
boat he built himself, visiting also the cotton states and
the prairie states and Maine, and even Hawaii and
Alaska. The birch in Maine delighted him, the tree from
which one made canoes, tents, buckets, torches, cups and
candles and even cloths for a table and paper for a
journal. What interested him in the Southwest was the
geology scattered there, crying aloud to be read, all
over the landscape. In the East the forces of erosion had
passed the meridian of their day's work and the grass

and the verdure hid their footsteps, but the vast naked flood-plains here and the painted deserts and dry lake-bottoms suggested a world that was still in the making. Many of the mountains might have been just blocked out, and one found close to the surface there the petrified remains of the great army of extinct reptiles and mammals, the three-toed horse, the sabre-toothed tiger, the fin-backed lizard, the brontosaurus, the imperial mammoth, the various dinosaurs. As the great Philadelphia paleontologist Edward Drinker Cope found, the book of earthly revelation lay open on the plains. Burroughs disliked tropical nature, as he saw it in Jamaica, rank and barbaric for him, without poetic appeal, largely because it knew neither winter nor spring, but he felt deeply at home in England, where he made two visits, in 1871 and 1882. On the first he was despatched with two other clerks from the Treasury department to convey fifteen million dollars in government bonds and his only pleasure on the voyage was to watch the little land-birds that followed the ship and rested on the decks and rails. He was told that more than fifty varieties of common American birds that were naturalized in Ireland had crossed that way. His papers on England in *Winter Sunshine* had much more character than most of their kind because they were free from derivative and second-hand impressions. The interior of Westminster Abbey reminded him of an ancient dilapidated forest and London seemed to him also like a natural formation. It suggested a forest of brick and stone of the most stupendous size that one traversed as adventurously as the mountains and the woods.

Yet what pleased Burroughs most in England was a certain domesticity,—it put him in mind of a "seat by the chimney-corner,"—and this defined Burroughs himself as a lover not of the real wild who was never at home in the forest as Audubon and Muir were. If, as he showed in *Riverby,* he delighted in Kentucky, it was because this too was a husbandman's land, and the farmer in him was all eyes as the train approached the blue-grass region, charmed by the unbroken fertility and verdancy of the scene. It was as if the long line of thrifty yeomen from which he had sprung had prepared him to respond so quickly to the well-kept landscape. How fat and smooth the country was, the soft and lovely fields, the long, even, gentle, flowing lines, the peace and plenty of the blue-grass farms that were dotted here and there with herds of slowly grazing and ruminating cattle. He had seen later the Illinois prairies and the vast level stretches of the farm-lands of Ohio and Indiana, but they were never so beautiful, so productive or so human. Then the blue-grass region appealed to the evolutionist in him. It was one of the oldest parts of the surface of the earth, a land that had seen and nourished the great monsters and dragons, and he thought of the millions and millions of years it had taken to ripen the soil for this delicate little blue-grass plant to grow to perfection. He loved to dwell on his own beginning, trying to picture to himself the long road he had travelled through the geologic ages to the first pulse of life in the primordial seas, embracing the eternity between that moment and the present. His essays on philosophical themes resembled John Fiske's, while in feeling they suggested William James's; for Burroughs, along with his distaste for theology, disliked an explanation of life that savoured too much of chemistry and the laboratory. Repelled by Spencer, he was drawn to Bergson and his non-mechanical view of life, which was redolent for him of the atmosphere of creation itself.

For many of Burroughs's later essays dealt with the nature and origin of life, and he had been prepared for Bergson by Emerson and Whitman. That was in the day when he had become a popular writer, with the rapid and general growth of the study of nature, the multiplication of nature-clubs and societies for the protection of birds and the spread of the interest in wild life in the schools. A farmer, happy only at home, like Thoreau in Concord or Gilbert White, who never exhausted the wealth of his own little parish, he liked to feel that he could find all nature in the Catskills and the sylvan retreat he had built on the bank of the Hudson. The rabbit and the jay brought the woods to his door, the gulls and the fish-hawk brought the sea, as the wild swans brought Labrador, and he felt the Canada lakes were also there when he saw or heard a loon on the river. Occasionally opinionated, he was an objective writer who kept himself as a rule out of his essays, and these accordingly lacked the charm of a vivid evident personality, abounding as they were in observation, felicitous and clear. His papers on Matthew Arnold, Emerson, White of Selborne, Thoreau and others were equally acute and poetic and sometimes profound, while in general he conveyed the feeling of a mind that was really in love with the world, large, alive with curiosity, perceptive, alert. Perhaps it was true that Burroughs's writing had little of the tang or power of another disciple of Emerson, John Muir, at his best, but one could open virtually at random any of his multitudinous books and count upon finding something memorable and happy.

More than once Burroughs gave Walt Whitman observations that he used in poems,—for instance, the poem that was called *The Dalliance of the Eagles*,—and Whitman at Riverby, in 1878, and later, jotted down notes of his own that suggested Burroughs. He picked his own currants and raspberries for breakfast, and, sitting at the open bay-window, he watched Burroughs ploughing and grafting trees, always deeply at home as he was in the atmosphere of farm-life and the patriarchal simplicities of the rural world. While he liked to have people in the

scene, differing in this respect from Burroughs, who was
altogether a child of the woods and fields, he had recovered of late the tastes of the farm-boy on Long Island
and rambled with Burroughs through the country as
if he belonged there. Together they listened to the
meadow-lark and looked for the early wild flowers, as
Whitman presently recalled in *Specimen Days,* visiting
a waterfall, deep in the woods, a greenish-tawny stream
that plunged over broken rocks amid shaggy old trees.
It was a savage druidical spot such as Thomas Cole had
painted in the days when he explored these woods with
the poet Bryant. Whitman sometimes ranked Bryant
highest among all the American poets, the severe old
man with the gnarled and knotty mind who had finished
his simple and faithful translation of Homer; and he
went to the poet's funeral in 1878 with Richard Watson
Gilder and the inseparable Burroughs. The two friends
later visited the seaside together. They spent long autumn days on a New Jersey beach, where Walt struck
Burroughs as ample for such a setting. He seemed to be
in harmony with the sand and the shore, with his grey
hair and blue-grey eyes and the grey clothes that blended
so well with the surroundings, while his thoughts had the
same broad sweep and the elemental grandeur and force
together with the all-embracingness of the impartial sea.
His voice too suggested the sea as he moved slowly
along the beach or sat in some nook that was sheltered
from the wind and sun. Sometimes his talk was confused
and choppy, then a long splendid roll of thought would
bathe you from head to foot or swing you from your
moorings. Out of these joyous ocean days came Burroughs's essay *A Salt Breeze* and Whitman's *With Husky-
haughty Lips, O Sea.*

On that occasion, Walt was a realization of Homer
for Burroughs, crippled though he was, half paralyzed
since 1873, at the time when he left Washington for

Camden, very unlike the young man who had gone to
Staten Island with Moncure Conway once for a sunbath
and swim. Whitman might have given rise to the myth of
Bacchus, Conway felt, so graceful and shapely he seemed
that afternoon. Now he had what another friend described as a "wild hawk look," while he left the impression of a vast vista or background in his personality. One
often saw him in Philadelphia ambling through the
streets where the founder of Germantown, Pastorius,
had walked before him,—the mystic who wrote with a
quill from an American eagle,—carrying a basket on his
arm filled with copies of *Leaves of Grass,* occasionally
leaving one at a purchaser's door. In some ways Philadelphia had become another New York for Whitman. He
relished the sparkle on Chestnut Street as he had rejoiced in Broadway once, the gayly-dressed crowds, the
china-shops, the pedlars, the toy-men, the flowers, the
pictures and the poultry and fish in the windows. Sometimes he sat in a big chair by the fruit-stall at the foot of
Market Street, with the soft grey hat that suggested both
the Quaker and the cowboy, eating peanuts, gossiping
with the Italian peanut-vendor, shaking hands with the
conductors and the horse-car drivers. Charles Godfrey
Leland fell in with him once, home on a visit from England himself and out for a walk with the Gypsy Britan-
nia Lee, and there were those who felt they owed a debt
of gratitude to Walt for the strength they drew from his
"godlike face and mien." [3] His Brooklyn ferry had become the Camden ferry, where he knew the pilots and

[3] "The very best thing about Walt was his godlike face and mien,
and this will die with the generation which was blest with the sight.
I once went up to him when I saw him on Chestnut Street and said
that I must personally thank him for being so handsome, adding
that I hoped he didn't mind. 'No, Horace,' he said, 'I like it.' "—
Letters of Horace Howard Furness.

The Canadian psychiatrist, Dr. R. M. Bucke, who wrote an early
study of Whitman, felt there was something in his personality that
was "clearly and entirely preternatural."

deck-hands, the gate-keepers, bootblacks and newsboys by name, all of whom knew him and hailed him with affection. He often went for an evening sail, sometimes recrossing hour after hour, absorbed in the pictures and poems that he found in the river when the powerful boat with its wide firm deck on a clear cold moonlit night resistlessly crushed through the marbly glistening ice. He never tired of watching the sea-gulls and their broad, easy, spiraling flight, oscillating, peering at the water and dipping for a fish.

The Delaware had become his Hudson,—he knew it all the way down to the sea,—the river on which Thomas Eakins was born, that other lover of the out-of-doors who painted Whitman's portrait a few years later. The painter and the poet had much in common, a preference of character over physical beauty, a delight in the solid and the real, the natural and the free, and Eakins was another victim of the prudery of his time and place when he used the nude figure for study at the Academy art-school. It led to his virtual dismissal and ostracism, rewarding as he found Philadelphia nevertheless. Studying for three or four years in Paris, he had returned in 1870 deeply convinced of the need of a native art, feeling that painters should remain in America, "peer . . . into the heart of American life" and study and portray the native types.[4] In this he felt as Whitman felt, and Winslow Homer too, that other believer in a "thoroughly

---

[4] "If America is to produce great painters and if young art students wish to assume a place in the history of art in this country, their first desire should be to remain in America, to peer deeper into the heart of American life, rather than to spend their time abroad obtaining a superficial view of the art of the old world. In the days when I studied abroad conditions were entirely different. The facilities for study in this country were meagre . . . Far better for American art students and painters to study their own country and to portray its life and types . . . Americans must branch out into their own field, as they are doing. They must strike out for themselves, and only by doing this will we create a great and distinctly American art."—Quoted by Lloyd Goodrich in his *Thomas Eakins*.

native art" who was also described as "unaesthetic,"—
again like Whitman and Melville as well, two writers
who resembled these painters in the bigness of their style.
In their energy, their simplicity and their spaciousness
the four were alike, and all lived deeply into their world
and were spiritually sustained by it, while Eakins had his
own specifically Philadelphian stamp. For he shared the
interest in medicine and science,—his own chief avoca-
tion,—that had characterized the Philadelphia mind for
a century and more. He wrote a treatise on anatomy, his
favourite reading was in works of science, he painted
many physicians and scenes in clinics, and his photo-
graphs of the movements of horses, an outgrowth of his
anatomical studies, contributed much to the development of the motion-picture. But with all this he never
lost that feeling for elemental life which he shared with
Winslow Homer, with Melville and with Whitman, who
had turned largely in his invalidism to an out-of-doors
existence.

For ever since 1876 Whitman had spent parts of several summers in a farmhouse ten miles from Camden on
a road to the sea, a short stroll from Timber Creek, a
primitive, winding, wooded stream where he went every
day for a water-and-air bath. He reached it by a farm-
lane that was fenced by old chestnut rails, grey-green
with moss and lichen and with briers and weeds over-
growing the stray-picked stones at the bases of the posts,
where the horses and cows had left their tracks and the
odours of poultry and pigs were mingled with the perfumes of the apple-blossoms or the August buckwheat.
The lane led into an upland field, where he walked for
sky-views and effects, sometimes in the morning, sometimes at sundown, but he spent most of his time at the
creek and the pond it opened into, hanging his clothes
on a rail or a branch near by. Already hobbling down the
lane and crossing the field in the good air he could feel

nutriment and peace filtering through him, with the solitude, the woody banks beyond and all the charms that birds, flowers and squirrels, old oaks, willows and walnut-trees could bring him. Free from ligatures, buttons and boots, from all but his old broad-brimmed hat, he rasped himself with the bristle-brush, arms, breast and sides, stepping about barefooted in the black ooze of the brook, pulling away at a hickory sapling, swaying and yielding to its upright stem, or the strong tough-timber bough of an oak or a beech. He pulled, pushed, wrestled with the tree, working the muscles of his chest and trunk till he felt its young sap welling up and tingling through him, while he shouted passages from Shakespeare and army refrains and wild tunes of the Negroes he had heard in the South. He rinsed himself in the clear running water and rubbed himself with the fragrant towel, strolling over the turf in the warm sun.

With his Adamitic air-baths in this natural gymnasium, his health in two or three years was largely restored, while he did most of his writing by the pond, sometimes under an old black oak or seated on a log or a stump or leaning on a rail. Wherever he was, in city or country, winter or summer, travelling or at home, taking notes had been a ruling passion with him, and this was still strong, he found, in his disablement and age. So in these woods he jotted down most of the memoranda of *Specimen Days,*—moods, sights, hours, traits and outlines,—carelessly pencilled as it were in the open air, and he even arranged a new edition of *Leaves of Grass* at Timber Creek, sifting it out and giving it some final touches. He had always chosen to try his pieces by the play of lights and colours in the sun, the plentiful grass, the song of a thrush within hearing and the trees with their leaves and branches in relief against the sky, amid all the negligence and freedom of primitive nature, the only permanant reliance, he felt, for sanity of book or human life that brought out one's natural affinities from their torpid recesses. He made lists of trees he knew by the pond, with the birds and flowers too, the slate-coloured dragon-flies, the water-lilies, the flitting insects, the calamus, shaped like a sword, while he watched the swallows for hours together, sailing, darting, circling, cutting their figure eights close to the ground. He observed the butterflies, white, yellow and purple, and a great moth that knew him and liked to perch on his extended hand, delighting in the woodpeckers tapping their bark, the fresh earth-smells, the bumblebees and the kingfishers on their evening frolic over the stream. For he often lingered at the pond long after the sun had set and even occasionally till midnight, perhaps with a friend, listening to the velvety rustle of the migrating birds overhead and their long-drawn-out chirps and calls. Then, with everything so cool and still, under the refulgent starry show, merged in the scene, like Emerson in the woods at Walden, he shared, as often under the sun, lying on the summer grass, what Melville had called and experienced as the "all" feeling.

CHAPTER XXII

MARK TWAIN IN THE EAST

FOR several years before 1880, Mark Twain had been living at Hartford,—with the factory of the "Connecticut Yankee" across the river,—half way between New York, where he was to live in later years, and the "Indian summer" Boston of William Dean Howells. He had married, he had visited England twice, he had taken the journey of *A Tramp Abroad,* he had written Mississippi sketches and the romance *Tom Sawyer,* and in collaboration with Charles Dudley Warner, his neighbour, he had pictured the post-war years in *The Gilded Age.* He appeared as a public entertainer at a time when humour was much in demand.[1] With Josh Billings he toured the country, as later he gave readings with his fellow-Southerner from New Orleans, George W. Cable, for, "desouthernized" as he said he was, Mark Twain kept many of his Southern traits,[2] with a special delight in Cable and in *Uncle Remus.* He read Harris's tales aloud in a voice that recalled the Missouri Negroes who had told him the wonderful stories when he was a boy. He loved the Negro spirituals, the Negroes in his books were invariably good, and he made a lifelong effort, in his affection for the race, to repair the wrong that had always been done them by the whites.[3] As for George

[1] This was the period of the rise of the American comic papers, *Puck,* 1877, the first that had ever been really successful, *Judge,* 1881, and *Life,* 1883.

[2] Only a Southerner perhaps could have presented so understandingly the Grangerford-Shepherdson feud in *Huckleberry Finn.*

[3] By way of the reparation which he said was "due from every white man to every black man," Mark Twain sent two Negro students through college.

W. Cable, another child of the Mississippi, one of his novels[4] was a detailed account of a voyage from New Orleans to Louisville five years before his friend had "learned" the river.

Long before he was forty-five Mark Twain was world-renowned. Letters reached him quickly that bore his name as their sole address, and "as Mark Twain says" was a universal phrase. In Washington, where he had spent a few months after the voyage of *The Innocents Abroad,* all the members of the cabinet had read his book: both Grant and Sherman had laughed over it till their bones ached, as they told Mark Twain, and Sherman and the younger Grant had used it as a guide-book. Senators gathered about Mark Twain and offered him appointments as minister or consul. For this new writer had somehow struck the key-note of his epoch, the boisterous geniality and self-confidence of the triumphant nation, unified by the Civil War, aware of the resources it was rapidly exploiting, good-naturedly contemptuous of the Europe it had once revered. He stood in the centre of the new national feeling, he expressed the singular homogeneity that Fenimore Cooper and Howells discovered in a country that was otherwise so varied and chaotic, a country where all had somehow "been there" and had felt and experienced much in common, though this was no longer to be true in another generation.[5] In his large, loose, easy-going way he

---

[4] *Gideon's Band.*

[5] "We are doubtless the most thoroughly homogeneous people that has ever existed as a great nation. There is such a parity in the experiences of Americans that Mark Twain or Artemus Ward appeals as unerringly to the consciousness of our fifty millions as Goldoni appealed to that of his hundred thousand Venetians. In our phrase, we have somehow all 'been there'; in fact, generally, and in sympathy almost certainly, we have been there. When [our humour] mentions hash we smile because we have each somehow known the cheap boarding-house or restaurant; when it alludes to putting up

seemed to speak for the pioneer West, the frontier that had found an earlier voice in Lincoln, and he dramatized its point of view, actor and showman that he was, with a relish for personal effect that recalled Tom Sawyer. For, much as he distrusted Scott, he was a lover of pageantry too, he liked the picturesque trappings of the Middle Ages,[6] and if he had been an ancient Briton he would not have contented himself with blue paint,—he would have "bankrupted the rainbow," he said on one occasion.

Always by choice in the centre of the stage, Mark Twain was a symbol of the new America, fresh and arresting as he was, for the world outside, incomparably funny[7] and in countless ways in his tastes, feelings and interests a type of the feelings and interests and tastes of the nation. He was irreverent, like many Americans, but only irreverent regarding things which the mass of Americans agreed were not worthy of respect,—old masters

---

stoves in the fall, each of us feels the grime and rust of the pipes on his hands. In another generation or two, perhaps it will be wholly different."—Howells, *My Mark Twain*.

Compare J. Fenimore Cooper in *The Sea-Lions:* "The world cannot probably produce another instance of a people who are derived from so many different races, and who occupy so large an extent of country, who are so homogeneous in appearance, character and opinion."

[6] See with what pleasure he described them in *The Prince and the Pauper* and *Joan of Arc.* See also, in *Following the Equator,* Mark Twain's delight in the "Oriental conflagrations of costume . . . The walking groups [in Ceylon] of men, women, boys, girls, babies—each individual was aflame, each group a house afire for colour . . . Such rich and exquisite minglings and fusings of rainbows and lightnings." Observing them, Mark Twain felt "ashamed to be seen in the street with myself . . . We go to the theatre," he added, "to look at [such costumes] and grieve that we can't be clothed like that."

The well-known white suit of Mark Twain's old age was a modest expression of this taste.

[7] Mark Twain could scarcely speak without uttering some such phrase as that he would rather "decline two drinks than one German adjective."

they did not understand, kings[8] and the "cruel and infamous shams" that Mark Twain hoped, as he said, to "laugh into the grave." Believing that irreverence was the "champion of liberty" and its "only sure defence," [9] he respected, on the other hand, plenty of things and persons,—the old sea-captain Josiah Mitchell, the Indian widows who committed suttee and whose courage he was later to praise in *Following the Equator*. He revered, above all perhaps, General Grant,[10] whom he saved in the eighteen-eighties from financial ruin, as in earlier days he had venerated Horace Bixby and other "lightning pilots" he knew in the West. In his warm-hearted Southern way a champion of women, he expressed an American feeling toward Harriet Shelley,

[8] "The institution of royalty in any form is an insult to the human race . . . The kingly office is entitled to no respect. It was originally procured by the highwayman's methods; it remains a perpetuated crime."—*Mark Twain's Notebook*.

"Another throne has gone down, and I swim in oceans of satisfaction. I wish I might live fifty years longer; I believe I should see the thrones of Europe selling at auction for old iron . . . The grotesquest of all the swindles ever invented by man—monarchy. It is enough to make a graven image laugh, to see apparently rational people . . . still mouthing empty reverence for those moss-backed frauds and scoundrelisms, hereditary kingship and so-called 'nobility.' "—Mark Twain, Letter of 1889.

His feeling about kings was much like Thomas Jefferson's: "It is enough to make a body ashamed of his race to think of the sort of froth that has always occupied its thrones without a shadow of right or reason."—*A Connecticut Yankee in King Arthur's Court*.

[9] "To my mind a discriminating irreverence is the creator and protector of human liberty." So says the "essayist," expressing Mark Twain's feeling, in *The American Claimant*. He defends as the most valuable trait of American journalism its "frank and cheerful irreverence towards 'nobilities' and kings, monarchy and its attendant crimes," ecclesiastical slaveries, etc.

[10] When it was suggested that General Grant might welcome his opinion on the literary quality of his memoirs, Mark Twain said, "I was as much surprised as Columbus's cook could have been to have learned that Columbus wanted his opinion as to how Columbus was doing his navigating."

when Edward Dowden traduced the poet's wife, as he defended Joan of Arc, as earlier in *The Innocents Abroad* he defended the memory of Eloise against the "dastardly seducer." For to Mark Twain, Abélard was merely an "unprincipled humbug." His impulsive humanitarianism was typically American, so was his respect for Germany and his contempt for France,[11] in this age when Germany was the "go-ahead" nation of Europe,— although in the first of his travel-books he had found in Napoleon III the American "genius of energy, enterprise, persistence." Delighting in their material progress, he saw none of the traits that were to make the Germans a planetary nuisance in the world-war epoch to come.

In dozens of other respects as well Mark Twain's personality was an all but unparalleled emblem of the country and the time, to such a degree that his name evoked in the minds of his contemporaries a picture of America itself in this post-war age. He was the natural democrat who wrote the story of the prince and the pauper to show that they were identical when one removed their clothes; and who was more interested than he in money-making, inventions, machines at a moment when the capitalist system was approaching its zenith? With the instinct of the born promoter or the gambler who had acquired his taste in the "flush times" of Nevada and the Sierra mines, he was driven to invest in a dozen schemes for making money quickly, a patent steam-generator, a

[11] The one race-prejudice that he admitted in his defence of the Jews as "peculiarly and conspicuously the world's intellectual aristocracy" was his prejudice against the French. He expressed this often, e.g., in *What Paul Bourget Thinks of Us*. His humour was often directed against the Frenchman, "the most ridiculous creature in the world," he said.

See, for example, in *A Tramp Abroad*, the comic account of the duel in which Gambetta assumes an attitude "which for sublimity has never been approached by man and has seldom been surpassed by statues."

new process of engraving and what not. With all the buoyant hopefulness that was also a typically American note, he was drawn to these money-making schemes as a fly to a jam-pot, although he lost fortune after fortune, and he negotiated with another inventor, an Austrian with a new machine, when he had been struggling for a year to pay his debts. He hoped to control the carpet-weaving industries of the world. He was the first author ever to use a typewriter and he had the first telephone that was used in a private house. This house was like Beecher's Boscobel, the spreading edifice with the broad verandahs, the cupolas and columns and acres of rare shrubs and trees,—it was almost a rival of Barnum's Iranistan. For the rest, Mark Twain had become a national pet.

These personal traits of Mark Twain suggested his literary character as well, for he was the greatest American folk-writer of the time. He regarded himself as a journalist who had planned for a while to settle down as a newspaper editor and owner before he went to Hartford, already in 1869 $22,000 in debt and expecting to earn and repay this by his work on a paper. He was not going to "touch a book unless," as he said, "there was money in it," and he was accustomed from the first to the largest returns, for his motives were seldom those of an artist whose primary concern is to do good work and accept whatever rewards may happen to follow. His commercial and his literary motives were inextricably mingled; he used his literary name in money-making schemes,—in the "Mark Twain Scrap-book," for example,—and when, referring to his literary work, he spoke of its "possibilities," he meant possibilities in dollars, not in form or in style. He had little pride in himself as a writer. In *Life on the Mississippi* he said he had loved his profession as a pilot "far better than any I have followed since . . . and I took a measureless pride in it," [12] because pilots were "unfettered" and "independent" whereas writers were "manacled servants of the public" and could never be fearless and frank as the pilot was. He did not respect his writing, in fact; he called himself a "jack-leg" beside the "born-and-trained novelist," the "other kind," [13]—and nothing was ever more haphazard than Mark Twain's ways in composition, the hit-or-miss methods that resulted so often in failure. He never knew when he was writing well. He seemed all but indifferent to *Huckleberry Finn* when he was at work on this best of his books, partly because his mind at the time was full of a worthless experiment to be called "Simon Wheeler, Amateur Detective." He threw away his energy on "blindfold novelettes," he "started sixteen things wrong," he said, one summer,—he had so little of the inner control of the artist,—and there were hundreds and thousands of pages of undistinguished journalism in the final collected set of Mark Twain's books. Then how many of these books were confused and involved, infantile, half thought-out, inane,—*A Double-Barrelled Detective Story, Those Extraordinary Twins, Pudd'nhead Wilson,* an absurd and unholy mixture of tragedy and farce. There was no pretence of unity in this, whether in feeling or style. Even Mark Twain's great books, with their brilliant beginnings, ended badly,— *Tom Sawyer* in the commonplace melodrama of juvenile fiction, *Life on the Mississippi* in a welter of statistics. *Huckleberry Finn,* the finest, was the most disappointing of all, in a way, with its long-drawn-out story of the

[12] On the farm at Elmira where he spent his summers Mark Twain built his hilltop study in the shape of a pilot-house with windows on all sides.

[13] See the foreword and epilogue of *Those Extraordinary Twins.* At the beginning he wrote: "The reader . . . has been told many a time how the born-and-trained novelist works; won't he let me round and complete his knowledge by telling him how the jack-leg does it?" At the end he added, "The reader already knew how the expert works; he knows now how the other kind does it."

rescue of Jim. Indeed, as an artist, Mark Twain was just what Arnold Bennett called him: he was the "divine amateur" whose two great stories, "episodically magnificent," were inferior as "complete works of art." What was he then?—for Mark Twain was without doubt a writer of genius. He was the frontier story-teller, the great folk writer of the American West, and he raised to a pitch unrivalled before him the art of oral story-telling and then succeeded in transferring its effects to paper. One could see in his *How to Tell a Story*[14] the pride that he took in this old folk-art,—as great indeed as the pride he had felt as a pilot,—an art he had learned as a boy from the Negroes, with their ancient inherited folk-skill, and later in the further West from various frontiersmen.

This was Mark Twain's peculiar note, the craft that he exhibited in the stories of Buck Fanshawe, Dick Baker's cat and others, the art that reached its highest point in *Huckleberry Finn* with its note of the extempore frontier teller of tales. Others had practised this art before him in a rudimentary way, the authors of the cycles of Sut Lovingood and Simon Suggs, with David Crockett, for instance, and Augustus Longstreet, frontier humorists and realists of an earlier day; but Mark Twain touched their line with genius and established a form and style that were later to be vastly influential in American writing. There alone Mark Twain was great, in reliving the scenes of his youth in the Mississippi valley that appeared in so many of his stories, though often the vil-

---

[14] Note here the pains that Mark Twain took to tell the story rightly, to pause in the right places just long enough, to enunciate each word with just the right emphasis and spring the final effect in just the right way. In all this he showed a craftsman's conscience that was seldom or never in evidence in his references to writing. Howells spoke of his "carefully studied effects" as a public performer, calling him a "great and finished actor" on the platform.

lage was disguised in one way or another,[15] the village that remained for him the measure of humanity, in which his mind was always at ease and at home. In this recollected atmosphere his genius flowered freely as it never could in the atmosphere of the world he lived in, —the world of which he wrote in *The Gilded Age,*—as he was never successful either in the orthodox role of the novelist, the writer who is also an artist in the traditional way.

It was true that in *The Gilded Age* Mark Twain was also a pioneer, for the book was one of the earliest novels that tried to come to grips with the movements and events of the post-war American years. This was a difficult field and theme, since the change from the older agrarian world was too sudden and confusing for anyone easily to grasp and the scene was one of demoralization in which the heroic spirit of the past was lost in a chaos of vulgarity, snobbery and corruption. One had to invade the formidable realms of American politics and business, scarcely interpreted hitherto in fiction, and moreover Mark Twain and his comrade Warner attempted a canvas on a national scale with episodes and characters of the East, the South and the West. This was the West of Colonel Sellers[16] where fortunes were "lying

[15] As Eseldorf in Austria in *The Mysterious Stranger,* as Hadleyburg, St. Petersburg, Dawson's Landing and what not in *Pudd'nhead Wilson, The Man That Corrupted Hadleyburg, The Adventures of Tom Sawyer, Huckleberry Finn,* etc. *Life on the Mississippi,* another great book, was drawn from the same circle of associations.

[16] This favourite character of Mark Twain reappeared in *The American Claimant,* where he planned to "buy Siberia and start a republic," in the spirit of the "Connecticut Yankee," who started a republic in King Arthur's England, and numbers of actual Americans of an earlier day. William Walker was one of these, with other filibusters who planned to establish states on the American model, as the Mormons really did in the forties and fifties, as presently the Confederates did in the states of the South. Compare the vague plan of Joaquin Miller and his friend De Bloney to establish an Amer-

round loose" and young men of spirit had merely to pick them up. The Missouri frontier appeared in the book, the Mississippi, a Western mine, the Washington of post-war politics that Mark Twain had seen, Broadway and Wall Street in New York, youthful Eastern speculators, senators, promoters, miners, farmers and what not. Few writers at that time imaginatively grasped the nation as a whole, the conception of a unified America was still vague in men's minds, and the new writers, for this reason partly, were regionalists in the main, as Mark Twain too was a regionalist of the Mississippi valley. Turning away from the national present, which they found too difficult to comprehend, they dealt with the regional past in New Orleans, in Georgia, in Bret Harte's mining country, on Eggleston's frontier, as Mark Twain dealt with the past of the Mississippi; and this made the venture of *The Gilded Age* all the more courageous, while some of the characters in the book were at least well drawn. One of them was Sellers, with his "Rothschild's propositions," who always had "prodigious operations" of some kind on foot, buying up wildcat banks perhaps, building a system of railroads, a plan for selling mules that had "millions in it." Yet the novel was a failure, as Mark Twain felt, when he gave up writing about the present and returned to his books of travel and stories of boyhood. It had, like other books of his that were far from successful as works of art, a largeness of conception and feeling that was Mark Twain's own,—a "magnificence" of imagination, as Howells called this; but it was crude and melodramatic and especially vague in its point of view, for its object was to satirize and condemn the speculative spirit. This was the source of the evils of the time

---

ican Indian "Mount Shasta republic." This state-building mood was a typical note of the nineteenth-century American mind, with its unlimited confidence in American institutions.

and Mark Twain was too involved in it, too busy living his age, to see it with detachment. In the name of *what* could he attack the speculative spirit when he was up to his neck in speculation? Eager as he was for his own share of the spoils of this age of exploitation, he could satirize this spirit only in its superficial aspects, condemning it in one way or another in Sellers and Senator Dilworthy and praising it in the youthful Philip Sterling. The book, as a result of this, was without a focus.

Later in *A Connecticut Yankee in King Arthur's Court* the "capitalistic" Mark Twain had his innings, the inventor, the promoter who hoped to control the carpet-weaving industry, the lover of machines and schemes for making money. He was out and out for the "gilded age" in this glorification of Yankee smartness, which had none of the mental reservations of his earlier novel, while it showed much of the "great burly fancy" that Howells spoke of and admired and that somehow redeemed the infantility of much that he wrote. There was something indubitably large in the very conception of the Connecticut Yankee who set out to make mediæval England a "going concern," although questions of taste were involved in this that Mark Twain did not understand and that virtually destroyed in the end the value of the book. It celebrated without reserve the dominant views of this business epoch and the "booming" nineteenth-century civilization,—the "plainest and sturdiest and infinitely greatest and worthiest of all the centuries," as Mark Twain called it in one of his letters. It ratified the "Boss's" notion that his factory in West Hartford "turned groping and grubbing automata into men," and Mark Twain squared accounts with Scott and his magnification of the Middle Ages by sharing the Boss's attitude in King Arthur's realm. The Yankee was a "giant among pygmies, a man among children, a master intelligence among intellectual moles," rejoicing in the "opportunities here for a man of knowledge, brains, pluck and enterprise to sail in and grow up with the country." He was sure that in this "midnight world" they needed newspapers and a patent-office, together with the match-factory and the soap-factory that he presently established, feeling that he must do anything and everything to convince the nobility that soap was harmless, even to the point of catching a hermit and seeing if he could survive a bath. He set knights in "hardware,"—his name for armour,—going about as sandwich-men working up a sentiment for stove-polish, toothpaste and tooth-wash, and he hung the saddle of one of them with leather hat-boxes containing plughats which he forced in his travels on other wandering knights. For he regarded it as part of his mission to extinguish "this nonsense of knight-errantry" by making it,—"grailing" and all,—absurd and grotesque. He had his advertisements painted on cliffs, boulders and walls, and with his total eclipse of the sun he put poor old Merlin to shame and reduced his art to the status of parlour-magic. Then he kept Merlin in the weather-bureau to "undermine his reputation."

While this book might well have been suggested by the vogue of Tennyson's *Idylls of the King* and really owed much to Malory and his tales of King Arthur, it was also in part indirectly evoked by Andrew Carnegie's *Triumphant Democracy*, another whole-souled eulogium of the business world. Mark Twain was a friend of Carnegie, who kept him supplied with Scotch whiskey and whom he once thought of involving in his publishing business, as he was the friend of H. H. Rogers, the Standard Oil magnate, who later became his financial adviser and saviour. There was even a day when Mark Twain saw himself in prospect as "one of the wealthiest grandees in America, one of the Vanderbilt gang, in fact." Whether he approved of them or not, he was

drawn to the "Holy Speculators," the name he gave to a well-known Hartford church, and he suggested in his utopia *The Curious Republic of Gondour* that a man's votes should be increased as his property grew. He seemed to share wholeheartedly the feeling of a time when poor boys became multimillionaires and the gambling spirit of the frontier raged through the country, and the fact that he had to write something popular to maintain the credit of his publishing house was all of a piece with his pleasure in delighting the masses. He had always consciously written for them since he had refused to consider a book that did not have "money in it," and a great deal of money, and few books could have promised more than this exaltation of the Yankee mechanic who threw Malory's enchanted realm into the shade. It even offered a repetition of *The Innocents Abroad* by sacrificing beauty and distinction to the taste of the groundlings, by ridiculing along with the evils of the mediæval world all that was splendid, noble and lovely in it. To exalt the plug-hat above the plume was a way of burning down the house in order to roast a pig for the philistine public, and did not Mark Twain, in doing this, violate his own taste, his passion for beautiful costumes and picturesque trappings? Was he, in fact, as whole-souled in reality as he seemed to be in writing thus for what he described as "this great big ignorant nation," he who had objected in *A Tramp Abroad* to the painted advertisements on boulders and cliffs that defaced, as he said, the scenery of the country? The man who made King Arthur and his court appear so ignominious was the same man who read Malory with "reverence," one is told,—Malory was one of Mark Twain's passions and delights,—and, drawn as he was to plutocrats, did he like plutocracy, which he saw leading to monarchy in another generation? In his private papers Carnegie appeared with a "foxy, white-whiskered,

cunning little face" and Senator Clark of Montana was the "disgusting creature" with whom he chose, nevertheless, to dine, while he was all against the tariff and in favour of trade-unions and organized labour, the principle of the strike and woman's suffrage. He consistently favoured the union of labour as the workingman's only present hope of defending himself against money and the power of it, and this "sansculotte," as he called himself, bitterly regretted the formation of the trusts as tending to create a monarchical presidential succession. For the rest, did Mark Twain really admire the "booming" nineteenth century, sturdy and great as he sometimes said it was,—the civilization the "Connecticut Yankee" stood for? Privately he said it was shabby and mean, cruel and hypocritical, and he wished he could see it in hell, for it belonged there. Was it not the moral of *Huckleberry Finn* that all civilization is a hateful mistake, something that frustrates life and stands in its way, something that did not "work" for Huck, the hero of the tale, who had to return to his barrel to save his life? Was not this one of the reasons for the vast vogue of *Huckleberry Finn* in the disillusioned years that followed the first world war, when the very conception of civilization lost all its charm for countless minds for whom honesty implied a reversion to a primitive existence?

As it happened, dual personality was an obsession of Mark Twain and one that recurred in many of his anecdotes and stories. He constantly spoke of the Siamese Twins and changelings in the cradle, a theme that appeared not only in *Pudd'nhead Wilson* but in *The Prince and the Pauper* and *The Gilded Age*. The schizophrenic story *Those Extraordinary Twins* concerned two incompatibles who were bound together, the good young man who followed his mother's injunctions, the wild young man who defied the taboos of the town. This idea in its various forms obsessed Mark Twain to

such an extent that a reader was driven to look for the cause of the obsession, and in fact Mark Twain was a dual personality, a seriously divided soul, as one saw in the letters he wrote on public questions. It became a regular practice with him, when his feelings differed from the popular view, to write,—and suppress,—a letter expressing his feelings, and then to write another letter, which he permitted to appear in print, that placed him more or less on the popular side. His strong instinctive feelings were all for "lost causes" and the under-dog, for the Boers against the British in South Africa, for the exploited in China, but, as he said on a certain occasion, he had a family to support and he could not afford "this kind of dissipation." He appeared on the side of the winner in public, affirming that nothing succeeds like success, that the hand of the strong must be upheld, that success was a fatality and nothing could oppose it. Just so, he continued to vote for the party that stood, he felt, for "monarchy" because, he said, nothing could unseat this party, although it was unseated within five years of Mark Twain's death when the long reign of the Republicans came to an end.

This habit of suppressing his beliefs and feelings had begun far back in Mark Twain's life, and his passionate personal loyalties largely explained it. He had planned a book on England after his first visit there and had written hundreds of pages before giving it up, finding he could not continue it, as his biographer Paine observed, without running the risk of offending his hosts and friends there. If Emerson had felt the same way, we should have had no *English Traits;* if Fenimore Cooper had been checked by any such fears we should never have had his frank, free comments on England; but these earlier Americans, brought up in the East, with a long intellectual tradition behind them, instinctively adjusted their feelings to an impersonal ideal. There was no such tradition in the frontier West, where "neighbourliness" and personal relations governed the mind, and Mark Twain, so largely unconscious as an artist, had scarcely dreamed of literature as a cause that demanded the writer's allegiance and good faith. He never thought of it indeed as a great impersonal spiritual force that asked him to seek for perfection and to tell the truth,— although he had twinges of conscience when he was "dishonest";[17] and accordingly his personal relations and loyalties had settled from the first the question of what he was to publish and almost to think. He had promised the supporters of the Buffalo paper which his father-in-law had financed for him not to "make trouble" or introduce reforms, though his mind was bubbling with satirical and trouble-making thoughts, as he suppressed and locked up in a safe for more than forty years a book that his wife loathed and shuddered over. This was the germ of the private "Bible" that he was always tinkering with, that he felt it a duty to publish and still withheld, in deference to what Howells called his wife's "ladyhood limitations" and because its "blasphemous" tendency might shock his friends. Or because it would certainly have shocked the larger public. How could he risk offending this when he was committed to writing for money, when, in fact, he had staked his life on the pursuit of success? He had given too many hostages to

[17] "Am I honest? I give you my word of honour (privately) I am not. For seven years I have suppressed a book which my conscience tells me I ought to publish. I hold it a duty to publish it. There are other difficult tasks I am equal to, but I am not equal to that one."—Letter of 1904, apropos of *What is Man?*

When finally he published the book anonymously he said in the preface, "Every thought in them [these papers] has been thought (and accepted as unassailable truth) by millions upon millions of men—and concealed, kept private. Why did they not speak out? Because they dreaded (*and could not bear*) the disapproval of the people around them. Why have not I published? The same reason has restrained me, I think—I can find no other."

the established order. He had so involved himself in the popular context of the "gilded age" that he could not strike out freely in any direction.

No wonder Mark Twain loved Robert Ingersoll, as he liked Saint-Simon and Casanova, whom he constantly praised, in private, for their "unrestrained frankness," and inevitably he came to look upon writers as "manacled servants of the public" who "write frankly and fearlessly" but "'modify' before we print." He came to speak of "writing for print" as if it were something unthinkable, something that, when he could afford it, he was going to stop,—as if Walt Whitman had never existed, or Emerson, or the free Thoreau, or Cooper, who published whatever came into his head. He repeated in his note-books, "None but the dead have free speech," "None but the dead are permitted to speak the truth" and that "Be weak, be water, be characterless, be cheaply persuadable" was the only command that Adam would never be able to disobey. Perhaps, he said in *What is Man?*, there is something a man loves more than peace, the approval of his neighbours and the public, as he dreads their disapproval more than he dreads pain, while he observed that man is a machine, moved by exterior influences only, a creature of his environment, a chameleon, a slave. All this reflected the mind of a writer who was only an artist now and then, who could scarcely have felt this way if he had lived as an artist,—for is not the artist the man whose mind is "free"?—but who remained a great folk-writer and especially a great folk-personality, like Benjamin Franklin, Lincoln and David Crockett. It was certain that a few of Mark Twain's writings were destined to live with the best in America, and the man was to be remembered also as the type of his epoch, the humorist and the gambler, dramatic, shrewd, compassionate, impulsive and boyish, the "man from Missouri" who became an American legend.

CHAPTER XXIII

TRANSITION

MORE and more, as the eighties advanced and the cities grew larger and larger, the old life of the farm receded in the national mind, the immemorial rural life that had formed the American point of view and seemed to be losing its hold over the imagination. The earlier writers had loved the forest,—Cooper, Bryant, even Irving, whose *Rip van Winkle* was a tale of the primitive woods, Thoreau, at home in the depths of Maine, Emerson, whose "woodnotes" were characteristic, even the author of *The Scarlet Letter*, with its "wild heathen" forest scenes. The forest, which had covered the face of the country, had filled its imagination too in the days of the woodsmen and naturalists Audubon and Wilson, and now the rural type of mind, fashioned on the farm, in the village, was fading along with the woodsman's into the background of the picture. In the fifties, Greeley, Barnum and Beecher, the three great worthies of New York, had all maintained the character of the *rus in urbe,* as the humorists of the school of Artemus Ward had assumed as their standard and measure the point of view of the farm and the country store. Old showmen had dreamed of retiring to farms in the evening of their days, and the typical American adolescence was Lester F. Ward's, for example, the sociologist who began as a Western farmhand. But the life-hungry natives of the backwoods communities, the sons and daughters of the

476

farms were pouring ·by hundreds of thousands into
the cities, caught by their glamour and their lights, their
crowds and shows. The rural life, like the life of the sea
in Cooper and Melville and Dana, had lost its preëmi-
nence and its magic in the minds of the masses.

With the growth of the cities the power of money had
also grown in a sinister way and poverty was increasing
along with this. The day had long passed when Anna
Mowatt in *The Fortune Hunter* in 1844 could speak of a
"cool hundred thousand dollars" as a fortune, and a
feeling was growing up in the nation that a group of
Titans had come to the top who were setting out to en-
chain and enslave the people, who had no human feelings, no sympathy with the rank and file, and despised
the bucolic mass as fools and yokels. The millionaire
appeared in fiction in Howells's Silas Lapham, in
James's Christopher Newman, in Horace Chase,—
Constance Fenimore Woolson's roving promoter,—
though these on the whole were beneficent types in
comparison with the new financier whom Theodore
Dreiser was to describe as a portent of this moment. Dreiser's Frank Cowperwood, who was drawn
from one of the real Titans, believed neither in ·the
rights of the masses nor in their strength: all he believed was that men like himself were sent into the
world to produce and perfect its mechanism and habit-
able order. Meanwhile, New York was becoming the
almshouse of the poor of half the planet, and foreign
countries were deliberately dumping their paupers and
criminals in the United States, their blind, their crippled, their insane. Several of the continental nations
were making the town a penal colony, and its slums were
rapidly approaching the European level. One could welcome, as Whitman and Melville did, all seekers of a
promised land in the spirit of Emma Lazarus's *The New*

Colossus[1] while sharing the feelings of Horace Greeley regarding the menace of this mass-immigration to the still experimental and vulnerable American system. It brought in hordes of peasants a thousand miles removed from the educated freemen who had founded and maintained the republic.

Whitman, who was more and more disturbed by the spread of poverty in the United States, was shocked by something he saw in 1879, two good-looking young Americans carrying bags and iron hooks, plodding along spying for rags and bones. It astonished him as similar sights astonished the novelist Howells in a country where Thomas Jefferson had never seen a pauper, where few had ever thought of a pauper existing, and he felt that if, like the countries of Europe, we grew vast crops of desperate nomads it would mean that our republican experiment had utterly failed. He saw the leading newspapers "getting into the hands of millionaires" and the people "swindled," as he said, "robbed, outraged, despised," and, complaining of the "more and more overshadowing and insidious grip of capital," he felt that economic problems led all the rest.[2] Many writers were alarmed by the growing division of classes and the spread of poverty along with the increase of wealth, Melville, for one, who had been deeply aware of the poverty of England in *Redburn* and was one of the first to be aroused in the United States. In *The Tartarus of Maids* he had attacked the horrors of the industrial system in one of the paper-mills of the Berkshire region, as he had satirized in *The Confidence-*

----

[1] "Give me your tired, your poor,
   Your huddled masses yearning to breathe free,
   The wretched refuse of your teeming shore,
   Send these, the homeless, tempest-tost, to me:
   I lift my lamp beside the golden door."
            —Emma Lazarus, *Inscription on the Statue of Liberty.*
[2] Horace Traubel, *With Walt Whitman in Camden.*

Man the growing greed for money, which made fools or knaves of most of the people in the book. Sidney Lanier who, like Melville and Whitman, would have preferred an agrarian system, was up in arms against the regime of trade, and Mark Twain, capitalist that he was, said that the unionized workman was the greatest of all the births of the greatest of ages. He called himself a sans-culotte, while Howells became a socialist. What Whitman would have liked to see was a world of small owners, a country of homesteads and freeholds without poverty or wealth, and it was difficult to pin him down when it came to political programmes, or, for that matter, creeds of any kind.[3] Sectarians of all sorts claimed Whitman as their own, theosophists, anarchists, socialists thought he was their man, but, "radical of radicals" as he said he was, an old-time Jacksonian democrat, he did not belong to any modern school. He thought all the radical sects were working to produce what he was trying to produce in a way of his own, but, feeling that he might be "convicted of a hundred philosophies," as he said, he could not commit himself to any of them. He found he was more of a socialist, however, than he had ever supposed he was, "not technically . . . but intrinsically in my meanings." Moreover, he thought a "heap" of Henry George. He was always eager to hear more of "this single tax fandangle" and said his poems "threw off sparks that way."

Henry George had returned to New York to stay in 1880, after writing *Progress and Poverty* in San Francisco, the most widely read book that had ever been written on economics which he had partly set up himself in type. By birth a Philadelphian, he had early been impressed on a visit to New York by the contrast

---

[3] "I never had any 'views'—was always free—made no pledges, adopted no creeds, never joined parties or 'bodies.' "—*With Walt Whitman in Camden*.

of poverty and wealth and the slums of the city, a misery that appalled and tormented him, he said, and
would not let him rest for thinking of what caused it
and how it could be cured. A masterful, energetic man,
short, bald, erect, with a reddish beard, he had had an
adventurous life as a sailor and a printer, visiting India
before the mast, then settling in California where he
worked as a compositor and journalist in San Francisco.
On a filibustering expedition in 1865, he had set out to
help Benito Juarez, defending the liberties of the Mexicans against Maximilian, but the ship with ten thousand rifles in the hold on which he was second in command was overhauled and stopped in the harbour by a
revenue-cutter. He had set type in Sacramento, where he
was hired as a ticket-taker when Mark Twain came to
this capital of the state to lecture, and he gambled in
Comstock silver stock, twice tried mining unsuccessfully
and planned to start a newspaper in the mining region.
Desperately poor in San Francisco, with a family to support, he wrote for *The Californian* with Mark Twain
and Bret Harte, studying the art of composition and
the qualities of style for which he was widely known as
an economist later. For, like Thorstein Veblen, Henry
George was one of the few economists who counted as
writers. In editorials signed "Proletarian" he wrote especially for workingmen, urging them to think about
social and political questions and find ways of checking
the further division of classes. With a brooding philosophic mind, serious, devoted and conscientious, given
to long "thinking rides" on his tan-coloured mustang,
sometimes across the bay in the Oakland foothills, he
had been haunted by the thought that, as people came
in and a country grew, the condition of the workers became, not better, but worse. He had written an article
in the *Overland Monthly* on the new transcontinental
railroad predicting that this vast enterprise in private

hands was bound to involve gigantic public evils, for the great increase it brought in trade and population was destined to make the majority poorer still. Why was it that the increase of wealth was invariably accompanied by increase of want? And what was the cause of the recurrent industrial depressions? His answer came to him one day suddenly as he checked his horse on a hill over the water in San Francisco. He had never heard of the physiocrats but had happened by himself, after his own observations, on a theory like theirs, and in 1877–1879 he wrote it out in *Progress and Poverty* in a poor little house with windows overlooking the bay.

It was the Irish land-question that first gave George his world-wide fame, an outstanding question at the moment in the English-speaking countries, for his advocacy of land-nationalization was a stirring reply to landlordism, the sensational bone of contention in the Irish rent-war. But the land-question at that time was a world-question as well, and Henry George soon had followers in every country. Later, however, his tour of England in 1880–1881 was remembered for another reason that was less specific, not because of his special theory, which had all the defects of a panacea, but because he roused public attention to poverty and its causes. The first great popular spread of the socialist-labour cause in England followed the appearance of George and his agitation, accelerating the general movement for a better social system, attained by whatever theory and whatever means. For he wrote with imagination and with passionate feeling, grieving over the human suffering and the tragic waste of human powers that were caused in part by unjust institutions. He pictured a possible social state in which poverty would be unknown and the better qualities of men might develop in freedom, in which government, no longer a repressive force, would be a source of benefits, the administrator of the great coöperative society of the future. In short, he presented a vision of the world that realized Jefferson's ideal and suggested a plausible method of achieving this goal.

In all this Henry George no doubt over-simplified human motives, for he never allowed sufficiently for the will-to-power that had always driven the strong to prey on the weak. But with Tolstoy, Edward Bellamy and others he crystallized in the eighteen-eighties a widespread popular feeling for social reform, a feeling reflected in Howells's novels, in Mark Twain's *The American Claimant* and in books like Albion Tourgee's *Murvale Eastman*. This was a Christian-socialist novel, like Howells's *The Minister's Charge*, by the author of *A Fool's Errand* and other novels of the years of reconstruction in the South, in which a second minister acted the part of a workingman and tried to apply Christianity to industrial problems. Mark Twain, who had been urged to write a novel round Henry George's theory, touched on this at least in *The American Claimant*, in which a young English peer renounced his class and heritage and came to the United States to work with his hands. He went to meetings for the discussion of *Progress and Poverty* and *Looking Backward*. Meanwhile, Lester F. Ward, who never became a socialist, was also obsessed with the problems of the submerged and the poor, attacking monopolistic privilege and dwelling on the need of education as the chief hope of the masses and the under-man. Lester Ward, like Henry George, had something in common with Thorstein Veblen, who was to acknowledge him later as a precursor of his own, and George himself acclaimed a work that Lester Ward's brother, who was also a printer, had written and set up in type with his own hands. Cyrenus Ward's *The Ancient Lowly* was a vast untidy pioneer book on the life of the working classes of the ancient world, presenting an astonishing body of facts, suppressed or ignored by historians and scholars, on the organizations and strikes of the workers of old.

It could almost have been affirmed that American writers as a class and type were instinctively on the left politically and had always been so since Thomas Jefferson formulated his American programme, which was something new under the sun, unlike the plan of Hamilton that was largely a continuation of the English system. It expressed an American experience and feeling that sharply diverged from the European, and Philip Freneau and Charles Brockden Brown, like Robert Fulton and Charles Willson Peale, agreed with Thomas Jefferson and took him as their man. Other Jeffersonian writers and artists were Joel Barlow, Alexander Wilson, William Dunlap, Brackenridge and Parson Weems, and the three outstanding writers of the generation after theirs were also adopters and followers of the Jeffersonian line. Washington Irving, Cooper and Bryant, all of them Hamiltonians born, became partisans of Andrew Jackson, who was Jefferson's successor, and Herman Melville and Walt Whitman were ardent Jacksonians both, as long as the true line of democracy lay with this party. But when the Jacksonians entangled themselves with the Southern slave-holders and the new Republican party appeared with Frémont, the writers bet on the "mustang colt,"—Stephen Foster's phrase for him,—as four years later they flocked round Abraham Lincoln. Emerson, Whittier, Longfellow, Irving, Bryant and Whitman alike were all for the candidate Frémont and the Republican party, when this party's concern was for human, not property, rights; for what marked the American imagination and set it off from others was a natural faith in the capacities of the average man. It constantly dwelt on the "plain" man, who remained in Europe the under-dog, and who had been freed and enlarged by American conditions; and in politics it was democratic because it wished to protect this man from the baleful conditions that stultified him everywhere else. How often the hero in American writing was the plain man seen as a woodsman or a sailor, as Natty Bumppo, for instance, the forester and scout, as Mark Twain's Mississippi pilot, as one of Audubon's pioneers, as Bret Harte's Sierra stage-driver Yuba Bill. He appeared in Melville's Jack Chase, the captain of the top, as in Winslow Homer's fishermen with their seasoned faces, confronting with quiet strength the perils of the deep, in the farmers, the mechanics, the ferrymen of Whitman, even in Lincoln himself, plainest of mortals, idol of the national fancy. This general type in a hundred aspects possessed the American imagination as the type of the gentleman possessed the English mind, as the military martinet possessed the Germans, and it explained the old feeling of Americans that the world was beginning afresh with them, that they were appointed to liberate the masses of mankind.

The American writers understood that this "plain" man was not merely plain, that if he and his kind were commons they were "kingly commons," potentially heroic, at least, if not actually so, and the same American imagination that loved to dwell upon him chose also to show him at his best. To reveal the hero in the ordinary man, the nobility in the least prepossessing, was an object of innumerable writers in both prose and verse, Emerson, for one, who liked to think of the virtues of "porters and sweeps" and of what he called the "gods in low disguises." The fable of the Shepherd of Admetus was a favourite of his. With what pleasure Mark Twain made much of the "lightning" quickness of the river-pilots, as Bret Harte dwelt on the adroitness of Yuba Bill, as Cooper showed Natty Bumppo triumphing over the learned Prussian, the naturalist who knew less than the simple scout. So in *Jim Bludso* and *Little Breeches,* John Hay, like Bret Harte, exhibited heroic traits in the unloved Pikes, as the Georgian Richard Malcolm Johnston revealed in his rude farmers the highest qualities of honour and delicate feeling. So Mark Twain chose Huckleberry Finn, a little ragamuffin, to embody his conception of truthfulness, loyalty and goodness. These writers drew their characters as the diamond-cutter shapes the stone in a way to produce the greatest lustre, feeling that the characters themselves were intrinsically precious, as Whitman felt when he said that the men in the mountains, in the mines, on the plains of the West were equals of the Homeric gods and heroes. They divined, they demanded the heroic in men, and their conception of the democratic was a process of levelling upward with this as a goal. Its aim was to produce "great persons" in widest commonalty spread, persons with the legendary traits of kings, including what Emerson, speaking of kings, called their "grand standard or suggestion of atmosphere and manners."

No doubt there was much in the pioneer life, in the struggle with the wilderness that evoked and developed the heroic in ordinary men, as the ancient life of the soil and the sea, so largely elemental, had begotten simple, spacious, lofty types. So had the labour of building the country, which had bred the great lawyers and soldiers of the past, the national heroes of an earlier day who played a part in the public mind like that of the millionaires, briefly, a generation later. When, about 1845, Judge Thatcher hoped to see Tom Sawyer "a great lawyer or a great soldier some day," he was expressing a standard for the young that ceased to be held as, more and more, money became the conventional basis of esteem. With the spread of urban life and the growth of business interests, the superior types of old were passing away, and the Civil War in retro-

spect seemed what Melville called it, the "sad arch between contrasted eras." The wilderness had been transformed, the farm had ceased to attract young men, and
John Burroughs had shrewdly noted the gradual disappearance of the large and original characters he had
known as a boy. Picturesque, primeval, gnarled, they
had suggested the forest trees that had also vanished
in their millions from the face of the country; and who
looked now for the "pageant creatures formed for noble
tragedies" such as Melville, in Captain Ahab, had borrowed from life? For these characters only appear in
books at moments when they exist in life, or as images
that are vitally present in the general mind, and there
actually existed in the older America, imbued as it was
with the Bible and the classics, "ungodly godlike men"
like this master of whalers. There were khans of the
plank and kings of the sea and worthies on the farms
with a "thousand bold dashes of character" like the
captain of the "Pequod," types that were passing among
writers too, for who was to compare, in the immediate
future, in force and scope and energy, with Melville
and Whitman?

These were no "common shallow beings found on
soundings or near shores" but "ponderous and profound," like the sperm-whale of Melville, types in their
love of space and freedom of the great mid-century
American years, full-blooded, magnanimous, genial,
large and deep. They belonged to the days of hero-wor-
ship when Emerson wrote *Representative Men* and
Carlyle found the essence of history in the lives of
heroes, when Plutarch was universally read, when
"character" was a word in every mouth and the chief
subject of study was moral greatness. This was the era
of the American writers whom after times called classic,
an era that passed with the coming of the new analytical realism, in which heroic feeling gave place to sci-

ence. The new generation distrusted the heroic and saw it as theatrical, precisely as the anti-romantic Howells denied the reality of genius, describing it as a myth kept up to intimidate the modest. In Howells's eyes it was undemocratic to maintain these suggestions of the more-than-human,—he was opposed to all titles in art as in life,—and this was symbolic of a change of feeling that spread through the world with the growth of science and left men without heroes or the memory of them.

Whatever this augured for the future,—a loss of the sense of the heights and depths, the extremes of the human scale and especially the tragic,—it was apparent that literature was firmly established in the United States, in every section of the country, with the new generation. This literature was young still,—there was little of any importance in it that had not been produced within the lifetime of men who were living,—but how much had happened since Joseph Dennie remarked that becoming an author in America was as hopeless as founding an academy of science in Lapland. There was as little promise in it, this critic of Jefferson's time had averred, as in publishing for the Eskimos an essay on delicacy of taste. In the train of Washington Irving and Cooper and the poets of New England, a literature had appeared all over the South and the West, and Emerson's "rank rebel party," destroying the old, building the new, had given birth to continental writers. Mark Twain, for one, writing of Europe, had cut the umbilical cord that united the still infant nation to the mother-culture, and in Melville and Whitman, with two or three others of comparable weight, America as a whole had found its voices.

INDEX